GREAT WESTERN
AND
LONDON AND SOUTH WESTERN RAILWAYS.

AVAILABILITY OF
RETURN TICKETS
BETWEEN
LONDON
AND
WINCHESTER

On and after January 2nd, 1911,

The Return Halves of Ordinary, Tourist, and Ordinary Week-end Tickets issued at Paddington or Westbourne Park to Winchester will be available to return either by the GREAT WESTERN RAILWAY COMPANY'S ROUTE to Paddington or Westbourne Park, or by the LONDON AND SOUTH WESTERN RAILWAY COMPANY'S ROUTE to Waterloo or Vauxhall.

Similar Tickets issued at Waterloo or Vauxhall to Winchester will be available to return either by the LONDON AND SOUTH WESTERN RAILWAY COMPANY'S ROUTE to Waterloo or Vauxhall, or by the GREAT WESTERN RAILWAY COMPANY'S ROUTE to Paddington or Westbourne Park.

In like manner the Return Halves of Ordinary and Cheap Return Friday to Tuesday Tickets issued at Winchester to Westbourne Park or Paddington will be available to return either by the GREAT WESTERN RAILWAY COMPANY'S ROUTE from Westbourne Park or Paddington or by the LONDON AND SOUTH WESTERN RAILWAY COMPANY'S ROUTE from Vauxhall or Waterloo, and similar Tickets issued at Winchester to Vauxhall or Waterloo will be available to return either by the LONDON AND SOUTH WESTERN RAILWAY COMPANY'S ROUTE from Vauxhall or Waterloo, or by the GREAT WESTERN RAILWAY COMPANY'S ROUTE from Westbourne Park or Paddington.

BY ORDER.

(2,000).   WYMAN & SONS, Ltd., Printers, Fetter Lane, London, E.C. and Reading.—18507a.

THE DIDCOT, NEWBURY & SOUTHAMPTON RAILWAY:

a new history

1882 - 1966

Kevin Robertson

Noodle *N.B.* Books

GREAT WESTER
RAILWAY
TAKE NOTICE
ALL PERSONS TRESPASSI
ON THIS RAILWAY OR
INJURING THE FENCE
WILL BE PROSECUTE
BY ORDER OF THE
DIRECTORS

The continuing search for new material on the DNS has thrown up a number of true gems since I started collecting material 'a few years ago'. It would perhaps have been appropriate to have produced this work in 2010 - fifty years since closure to passengers south of Newbury - or 2014 - fifty years since closure to all through traffic, whatever, there will always be an anniversary somewhere. But published in 2010 and the wonderful image left would not have been available, nor for that matter the one below. What the one left shows, is that there is always something new to learn, this being the only image ever seen looking south from the pedestrian bridge to St Giles Hill and recorded at such an angle as to illustrate the hitherto unknown piece of fencing and unusually worded notice that existed at the end of the loading dock - also a salutary lesson as regards complacency. The neatness of the scene is apparent, the grass banks cleanly trimmed with trackwork, ballast and cess in good condition. The signal box has its steps outside (extension will come in 1942/3) whilst the provision of point rodding and signal wires tells us this view was taken after the abolition of the power signalling in 1933 and with it the substitution of electric by conventional mechanical ground disc signals. We are of course looking towards Bar End, along a route now populated not by track and trains but by tarmac and cars. Of the two rail vehicles seen, that nearest the camera would appear to be a horse box, further away a simple open wagon. At the end of the dock siding is the lineman's hut whilst leading off to the right is the access to Chesil Street where a wooden gate and further trespass notice cautioned against unauthorised entry. Below, and the photographer has turned around, possibly on the same occasion, with the peace of the day broken by the arrival, and what appears to be, subsequent departure of a Southampton train. Despite the slight blur as the engine accelerates, the number on the buffer beam may be read as 3282. A 'Duke' class 4-4-0 by now nameless. This engine lasted in service until October 1937 and so may assist in dating the image(s) as between 1933 and that date. (See also pages 89-93.)

Both courtesy David Kitchener.

ISBN 978-1-906419-83-7

First published in 2014 by Kevin Robertson
under the **NOODLE BOOKS** imprint
PO Box 279
Corhampton
SOUTHAMPTON
SO32 3ZX

www.noodlebooks.co.uk

Printed in England by Berforts Information Press

Front cover - *Compton, 30 August 1958. Against the background of a cloudless sky, Didcot based No. 3206 departs south for Newbury and Winchester.* *Norman Simmons.*

Rear cover, top - *No more stopping trains to Newbury. The railway is still open - just - although anything no longer needed is being removed. (By early 1966 the remaining workings were an a twice weekly freight from Eastleigh to Bar End, calling at Otterbourne pumping station to deliver coal en-route.) Winchester Chesil signal box was now open 'as required' for the tablet section from Shawford Junction. Between times it lay dormant, it would not be long before the vandals arrived.* *Bob Winkworth*

Rear cover, bottom - Departure from Kings Worthy, February 1960. In less than three weeks there will be no more passenger trains to Worthy Down, Sutton Scotney and beyond.
The Kellaway collection

Title page - The dreams of the 19th century promoters are over. Their successors, British Railways, have deemed the DNS is no longer required. No more convenience for goods or passengers, no more employment - except that is to the itinerant scrap metal dealer - who followed the 1960s closures like a vulture feeding on the pickings. At Bar End the final three wagons, all former GWR 'Iron Minks' had been labelled as 'Not to Go', all other vehicles being removed. Now these that remain lie pushed aside - it was easier to reduce them to manageable chunks of scrap in this way.
Bob Winkworth

CONTENTS

1. INTRODUCTION - *setting the scene*

Thirty years ago I co-authored what was my first railway book. The subject was my enduring fascination with the Didcot, Newbury & Southampton line. I will admit I was naive enough at the time to believe there really was something rather special about this line, certainly better than its other north-south neighbours the Midland & South Western Junction and Somerset & Dorset routes.

Since that time I have, quite correctly, been put right, not just over what was a subjective (but not in any way intended to be selfish) view but perhaps with a more mature realisation that every line, or indeed railway subject, was special. (It was just that some were more special than others!) No seriously, we will all have our favourites, whether that be a route, branch, secondary or main line, railway company, locomotive type, class etc. Indeed such is the very breadth of the railway subject itself, that it never fails to amaze me the degree of knowledge that exists amongst fellow enthusiasts. I defy any to pronounce themselves as a 'railway expert', expert in a particular field, yes, but the subject really is too vast to have the same degree of knowledge across the spectrum. Perhaps the definition of an expert should be one who knows where to look and also who to ask.

Also back in 1982 I had what was considered a 'proper job'. Being involved in research for a railway book was an enjoyable pastime, my family might have believed it more of an obsession and if so I apologise unreservedly. Whatever, I could not have imagined the path this first book would lead to. Indeed post 1982 I recall discussing with my former research partner, Roger Simmonds, "...now DNS is finished, what do we do now?" The answer at the time was both simple and obvious, 'the Lambourn branch'. Why, beacuse so many of the staff we had spoken to on the DNS had referred to working on the Lambourn line, thus it was the natural follow on. That too of course resulted in a book: and then two others on the same subject since!

But to return to DNS matters proper. In the late 1970s and early 1980s Roger and I had been privileged to locate and speak to numerous railwaymen who had spent all or the greater proportion of their working lives on the DNS line. I hesitate to mention names, but men like Jack Carpenter, Harold Gasson, Jack Green, Graham Hawkins, Harry Hiller, Bill Hiscock, Ernie Penny, Ted Talmage etc. These and others were the ones who told us the true story of

the railway. Not the facts, dates and figures available from dusty archives, but the tales and happenings, the daily life, the ups and downs, the stories that would otherwise have been lost forever. Here then I will romanticize slightly and not just about the DNS. Take any railway, open or closed, any railway location, locomotive type etc and ask who were the persons who made it, worked on it, maintained it, travelled on it? Dates facts and figures will remain, indeed that was how railway books had been portrayed for many years before, I like to think that since then more of the social history has been recounted from those who were actually there at the time. But despite much success in our studies, sadly we missed speaking to many others as well.

Naturally with the publication of any book more information will come about, as was the case with the original book that resulted in the 'DNS Supplement'. Indeed the genus for this was an envelope of photographs that arrived, damaged in the postal system, with the contents barely intact. I recall it was a Saturday, I was asleep having been on night duty. My wife woke me with the words, "I think you might want to see these". She was right of course, as a railwayman's daughter she could recognise important material, whilst also freely admitting the talk of railways in the house was as great as it had ever been. (The images concerned were those of Burghclere which formed the nucleus in the second book.)

There matters might have remained. Certainly any suggestion as to publishing anything further on the DNS was hardly considered viable. But the collecting bug continued, not artefacts and hardware, but paperwork and images. The boxes started to bulge, the files straining at the seams.

Years later and in consequence of a different lifestyle the opportunity for publication presented itself again, 'Burghclere Signalman', 'Winchester Great Western', 'Sutton Scotney - Life at a Country Station' 'DNS' (a colour album) and 'The Railways of Winchester' - the last named dealing with the LSWR main line as well, all allowed for a further release of material into what seemed an almost insatiable appetite for DNS material.

Around this came others books on other subjects, Southern, Great Western, various locomotive types (notably 'Leader') and of course the privilege of being trusted by a number of authors to publish their own works, again in many cases the result of a lifetime's interest in a particular topic.

Running a publishing business has its advantages (I can promise the disadvantages probably outweigh the positive aspects!), but it does permit the outpouring of a whim on occasions. I will not mention the other books that have emerged driven more by the heart than the head (there certainly has been more than one), suffice to say that throughout the past years there has still been one over-riding topic of interest to me, the DNS line, and this time in its final years, the period from 1948 to 1966, the period when most alive today will recall it. This had also been the period omitted, for reasons of space, from the original 1982 book.

Indeed this particular period has received scant attention in the past, photographs and facts to some extent yes, but not, I believe, a more intimate view as is indeed deserved. (Go back before this to the 1960s and published information on the DNS railway was rare.) An article in the 1955 'Railway Magazine' followed almost 20 years later by a book by Oakwood Press, both from the pen of the late T. [Tom] B. Sands. I yearned for the latter as soon as I heard of its forthcoming release. Whilst excellent in its own way, I was perhaps slightly disappointed the emphasis was very much on the history that had caused the railway to be built, important of course, but not what I personally wanted: to learn more about the line in the period in which I recalled it. That then is the genus behind this work.

I am also determined to conclude my own studies into the DNS with this last book. I have no wish to go on seemingly duplicating facts ad-nauseam, so this will indeed be my final book on the subject. Thus having 'sounded the market' beforehand it appears I am not alone in finding the period 1948 - 1966 of interest and for that I thank all those whose kind words have given encouragement over the years.

This final work will then follow on in, I hope, a logical sequence to the earlier books, but also a little in the form of my earlier 'Lambourn - Revisited', where new information is interspersed with photographic breaks, snippets and specific topics rather than a month by month / year by year history.

I had also always promised myself that the time to retire would come when my final book on the DNS appeared. The former is true but I am not sure I am yet quite ready for the pipe and slippers awhile.

From the list of titles above I will truly admit I have been staggered by the interest the DNS has generated amongst others, and privileged too that it has been possible to be one of those charged with recording a history that might otherwise so easily have been forgotten.

Kevin J Robertson

2. New information on the Early Years

It would be very easy in a work such as this to take the option and repeat from the outset the same history as before. This is something that has not been attempted or intended. Instead there is an assumption that the reader is already aware of these basic facts and as such what follows is set out as a supplement to the various published works as well, it is hoped, as a stand-alone volume in its own right. Whether this has been achieved by the time the final page is reached will be judged by the reader.

That said, there is invariably more information, not just on the main period in question 1948 - 1966, but prior to this, and as such it is opportune to include this, for the sake of completeness and it is hoped, interest. So, the last statement is not to be read as an excuse, indeed it is to be hoped nothing of that type is needed.

We start then with a comment on what were the precarious finances of the DNS[1] as existed in 1883. Bear in mind at this time the line between Didcot and Newbury had opened, but was yielding little revenue, whilst parliamentary sanction had been given for the route south of Burghclere/Litchfield to divert to Winchester rather than had been originally proposed, Micheldever.

RAIL1057/783[A] unfortunately undated, but likely to have been sometime after July 1883 is an interesting report setting out the assets of the DNS against expenditure for completion.

'To complete line to Winchester including junction at Whitchurch; £294,500.

'Allowing for available assets, deficiency thereof; £105,168.'

This was broken down to the following issues;

To complete 'Southern Section' - sic (Newbury - Litchfield) £ 25,000.

To complete Litchfield to Winchester £245,000

Junction at Whitchurch £30,000

Winchester to Southampton £350.000'.

The financial assets were put at £189,332 which included funds tied up as the parliamentary deposit which would only be released when the line had been completed to Winchester. To make matters worse the only immediate funds able to be accessed were uncalled share capital and then only at the rate of £34,000 every three months.

It was against this perilous financial position that the DNS reached the decision to secure the services of an outside individual who they hoped would secure their future. What they achieved was the appointment of J Staats Forbes, and who reading between the lines of surviving records, appeared to have the remit of curtailing any ideas of further expansion for the DNS. In this it is reported he arrived just too late to prevent work continuing towards Winchester, which also begs the question, was any work ever undertaken towards Micheldever? This question is not answered by Sands nor seemingly is it referred to in the minutes.

Forbes remit may well have had the backing of the more influential shareholders (we are not told who these were), but with in 1884 earnings for the section between Didcot and Newbury were reported as just £9,187 annually, the realisation that any return on investment was unlikely must have had been a hard lesson for the unfortunate investors.[2]

Whatever, we know that by the issue and call upon debenture stock, the railway was indeed eventually completed to Winchester.

However, at this stage we need to move away from the politics and hard discussions and instead refer to the construction, inspection and opening of the line between Didcot and Newbury.

Away from the politics newly released material on the formative years has also revealed details of certain of the various contracts signed appertaining to the construction. One of these is dated 12 November 1880 between the GWR T.H. Falkiner and Sir Thomas Tancred the last named pair the contractors charged with the construction of the DNS railway. The involvement of the GWR is explained as the document relates to a siding and works near to Newbury so as to facilitate construction of the new line from Didcot. A number of minor contractual niceties appear amidst the usual legal jargon, such as the cost of the facility being put at £5 per annum whilst 'servants and workmen' of the contractors, when upon land owned by the GWR, coming under the control of the Newbury Station Master.

A. References given are as the National Archive at Kew.

Opposite - *Upton as portrayed in the early years of the 20th century. If there was ever a golden age of railway travel then this must surely be it. Labour was cheap, the railway a respected employer, whilst the DNS had little if any competition for the transport of goods and passengers through the countryside which it traversed. Unfortunately for much of this terrain it was a bleak landscape with seemingly inhospitable downland both south of Didcot and then south of Newbury. Possibly because of this visage, at some stage men working across the railway began to call it the 'Gold Coast', a slightly unfair comparison with part of West Africa. (After various wars the Gold Coast became fully a British colony in 1901 - it achieved independence as Ghana in 1957.) The painting is by the artist Sean Bolan, renowned for his superb portrayal of railways in this period.*

The List of Applications WILL BE OPENED on TUESDAY, 25th JULY, and CLOSED on MONDAY, 31st JULY, for London, and TUESDAY, 1st AUGUST, at 12 o'clock, for the Country.

5 PER CENT. PREFERENCE SHARES.

CONSTRUCTION OF A NEW AND INDEPENDENT RAILWAY TO SOUTHAMPTON DIRECT.

A NEW AND DIRECT THROUGH-ROUTE
to and from LONDON (Paddington) and SOUTHAMPTON,
AND
A NEW AND DIRECT THROUGH-ROUTE
TO AND FROM
SOUTHAMPTON and BIRMINGHAM, MANCHESTER, and SCOTLAND.

The Line will be Worked, Stocked, and Maintained in Perpetuity, as part of their system, by the

GREAT WESTERN RAILWAY COMPANY,

Who have agreed to forward by it

THE WHOLE OF THE UNCONSIGNED TRAFFIC
to and from LONDON and SOUTHAMPTON,

AND TWO-THIRDS OF THE UNCONSIGNED TRAFFIC
to and from SOUTHAMPTON and the NORTH *via* DIDCOT.

ISSUE OF £500,000
"Southampton Section" 5 per Cent. Preference Shares
(OF WHICH A CONSIDERABLE PORTION HAS ALREADY BEEN SUBSCRIBED)
OF THE

DIDCOT, NEWBURY & SOUTHAMPTON JUNCTION RAILWAY,

In 50,000 Shares of £10 each at Par, payable as follows:

10s. per Share payable on		Application.	
10s.	"	"	Allotment.
£1	"	"	1st October, 1882.

(handwritten: 1st Call. £800.0.0. left)

The balance in calls not exceeding £2 per Share, at intervals of not less than three months; subscribers being at liberty to pay up their Shares in full, whereupon they will receive interest at 5 per cent. per annum on the Unealled Capital.

THE FIRST SECTION of the Railway, from DIDCOT to NEWBURY, was opened for Public Traffic in April last. The Second or "Southern" Section, is now in course of construction, and a Special Act for the construction of the "Southampton" Section, under which the present Issue of Capital is authorized, has passed the Committees of both Houses of Parliament.

DIRECTORS.

Chairman, LIEUT.-COL. SIR ROBERT JAMES LOYD LINDSAY, K.C.B., V.C. & M.P. (Berks), Lockinge House, near Wantage, Berks.
Deputy-Chairman, JOHN WALTER, Esq., M.P. (Berks), Bearwood, Wokingham, Berks.
VISCOUNT BARING, M.P. (Winchester), Stratton Park, Winchester.
GEORGE PALMER, Esq., M.P. (Reading), The Acacias, Reading.
SIR JULIUS VOGEL, K.C.M.G., 135, Cromwell Road, S.W.
JOHN HENRY COOKSEY, Esq., Ex-Mayor of Southampton, Kingsbridge House, Southampton.
GEORGE THOMAS HARPER, Esq., Portswood, Southampton.
THOMAS EDWARD HOWE, Esq., Rosenau, Datchet, Bucks.
WILLIAM HOWLEY KINGSMILL, Esq., Sydmonton Court, Newbury.
WILLIAM GEORGE MOUNT, Esq., Wasing Place, Reading.

ENGINEER.
JOHN FOWLER, Esq., C.E., 2, Queen Square Place, Westminster.

BANKERS.
THE LONDON AND COU TY BANK, 21, Lombard Street, E.C., and its Branches, including Newbury, Oxford, Wantage, Abingdon, Basingstoke, Reading, Winchester.
MESSRS. SLOCOCK, MATTHEWS AND SOUTHBY, Newbury, Berks.
MESSRS. MADDISON, ATHERLEY, HANKINSON, & DARWIN (TOWN AND COUNTY BANK), Southampton.

SOLICITORS.
MESSRS. LAKE, BEAUMONT & LAKE, 10, New Square, Lincoln's Inn, London.
MESSRS. PEARCE, PARIS & SMITH, Southampton.

STOCK BROKERS.
MESSRS. BRUNTON, BOURKE & Co., 18, Finch Lane, Cornhill, E.C.
MESSRS. PANMURE GORDON & Co., Hatton Court, Threadneedle Street, E.C.

SECRETARY & OFFICES.
CHARLES H. BINGHAM, Esq., 6, Westminster Chambers, Victoria Street, Westminster.

THE DIRECTORS of the DIDCOT, NEWBURY, AND SOUTHAMPTON JUNCTION RAILWAY COMPANY are prepared

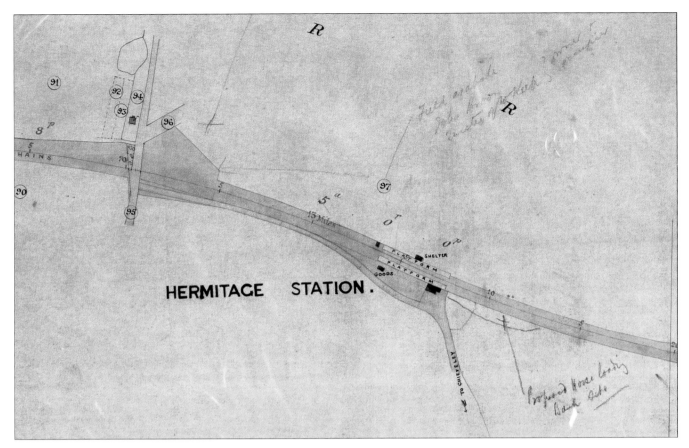

HERMITAGE STATION.

Sample land plan depicting the area that would become Hermitage station. A number of versions were produced for most areas that would become the stations as well as where deviations or additional land was subsequently found to be required. This one is slightly unusual in that it refers to the proposed positioning of various structures.

Presumably the actual siding was incorporated into the railway itself as later built. But this would not have applied to a further siding that appears to have existed between what would later be the 13½ and 13¾ mile-posts from Newbury - between Churn and Upton. Here, in what was known as the deep cutting, there is map evidence of a possible quarry or other working within the chalk to the west side of the line. The map, an official GWR 2-chain survey of the Didcot - Newbury section in 1895, clearly shows three small cuts into the chalk at this point and certainly of sufficient size to accommodate a siding. They are however indicated as having been at the top of the cutting and so may also indicate a base for the contractors work.

Construction of the northern section had commenced on a wet Tuesday, 26 August 1879, in a field north of Newbury, between Woodspeen Terrace and Beaconsfield Terrace. (The ceremonial spade and barrow used now form part of the family collection on display at Highclere Castle south of Newbury the ancestral home to the Earls of Carnarvon.)

Possibly the first report of a passenger carrying train over the part completed route occurred just under two years later on 28 July 1881, when the directors travelled from Newbury to Compton in a train consisting of three vehicles, a first class and a second class carriage together with a brake van, hauled by the contractors engine

appropriately called 'Newbury'.

In the early spring of the following year, the Board of Trade Inspection train traversed the line on 31 March 1882. This commenced at Newbury behind the contractors engine, 'Lady Cornewall' (sic), and of necessity stopped at a number of locations en-route to Didcot. One of these was at Hermitage where a group of local school children watched in silence as the train passed, that is before a shower of pennies from the train turned their serious stance to delight. This train consisted of a first class carriage and a saloon car adapted for the purpose of the inspection.

Another contemporary report from the day concerns an 84 year old woman from Beedon who had never before seen a train. She was wheeled by her daughter in a bath-chair three miles to view the passing train and purportedly exclaimed, '...aye, and if I live I will ride in one when it is opened.'

Of necessity the inspection train traversed the whole route in the course of which it passed the site of the navvy camp at Upton before reaching Didcot. Here the 'Lady Cornewall' was detached and replaced by an 'express' engine for the return to Newbury although this was delayed slightly by a Great Western express running on the main line. The contractors engine later returned to Newbury stopping at several places to drop off workmen and others who had earlier ridden on the inspection train. As reported

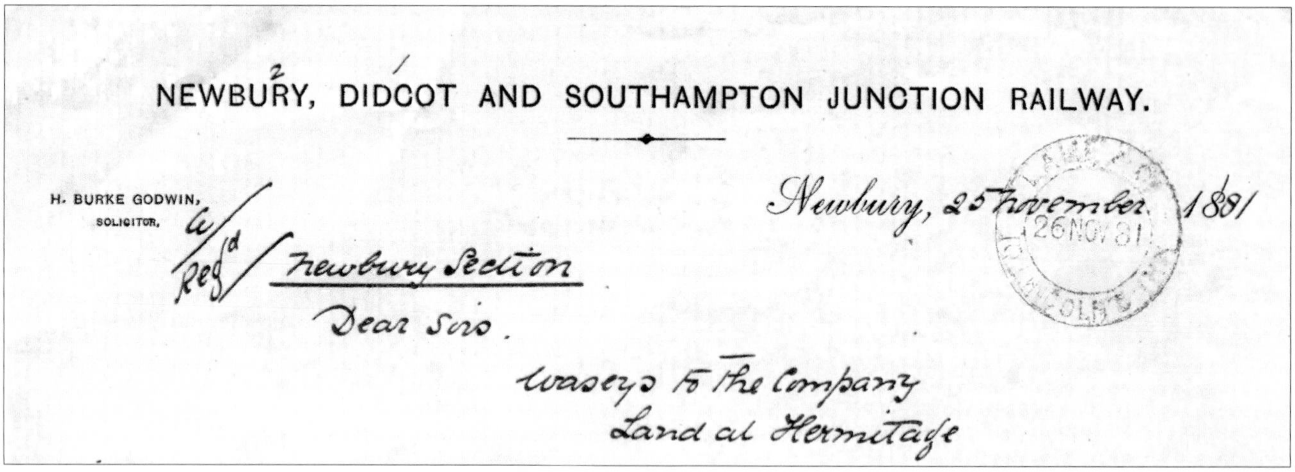

NEWBURY, DIDCOT AND SOUTHAMPTON JUNCTION RAILWAY.

H. BURKE GODWIN,
SOLICITOR.

Newbury, 25 November 1881

26 NOV 81

W/ Regd / Newbury Section

Dear Sirs.

Wasey's to the Company
Land at Hermitage

Above - *1881 letter heading with the title for the railway incorrectly recorded. Clearly this has been identified - as witness the numerical annotation! (The content of the letter is of no consequence.)*

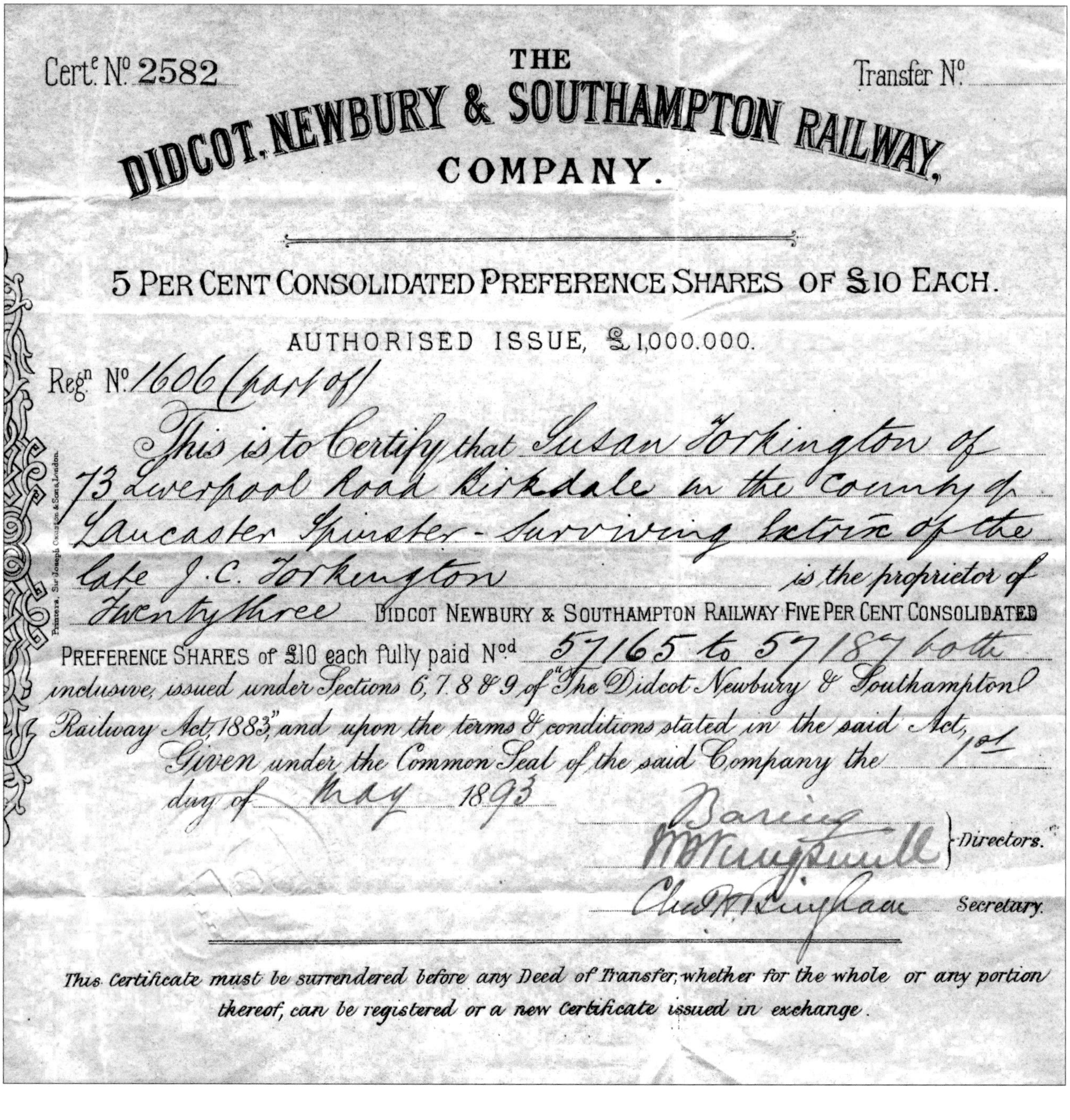

Cert^e N° 2582

Transfer N^o

THE
DIDCOT, NEWBURY & SOUTHAMPTON RAILWAY
COMPANY.

5 PER CENT CONSOLIDATED PREFERENCE SHARES OF £10 EACH.

AUTHORISED ISSUE, £1,000,000.

Reg^n N° 1606 (part of)

This is to Certify that Susan Torkington of 73 Liverpool Road Birkdale in the County of Lancaster Spinster - Surviving Extrix of the late J. C. Torkington is the proprietor of Twenty three Didcot Newbury & Southampton Railway Five Per Cent Consolidated Preference Shares of £10 each fully paid N°s 57165 to 57187 both inclusive, issued under Sections 6, 7, 8 & 9, of "The Didcot Newbury & Southampton Railway Act, 1883," and upon the terms & conditions stated in the said Act.

Given under the Common Seal of the said Company the 1st day of May 1893

Baring
W. Bingham } Directors.

Chas W. Bingham Secretary.

Printers, Sir Joseph Causton & Sons, London.

This Certificate must be surrendered before any Deed of Transfer, whether for the whole or any portion thereof, can be registered or a new Certificate issued in exchange.

elsewhere, Colonel Hutchinson of the Board of Trade was basically satisfied with the state of the new line, his report also including some useful information on the state of the permanent way and which was of, '...flat bottom rail at 68lbs per yard secured to wooden sleepers by means of fang bolts and dog spikes...'.

The formal opening was set for 12 April 1882 for which the GWR provided 30 saloons and ran two special trains between Newbury and Didcot.

Another document this time between the DNS Company and Messrs. Falkiner and Tancred relates to the construction of the Southampton section of line[3] and is dated 25 August 1833. This also refers to previous documents appertaining to the construction of the line between both Didcot and Newbury and Newbury southwards, but includes the specification for the ill fated Aldermaston to Burghclere connection and which, we are informed, would have been double track throughout.

Detail was similar for both the Aldermaston line as well as the route south of Burghclere and included such financial examples as 'Ironwork in bridges at 20/- per ton, timber in bridges (creosoted) at 4/- per cubic foot and earthworks at ½d per cubic yard although an additional 4d would be paid if earth was required to be moved more than 3½ miles.'

Modifying and amending the required work for the 'Southern Section' so far as the actual destination was concerned, was covered in an indenture of 8 September 1884 between the contractor and the DNS This provides a joyous list of specifications. Amongst the paragraphs detailed are sections on such detail as fencing and formation, viz;

'.....Larch post 6'8" long and 6" x 3" or of equal section at the smallest point ....". Cuttings and embankments (except where they exceed 20' deep in solid chalk) shall be 30' wide at formation level. '......those above 20' shall be 36' wide at formation level. The sides of the cuttings may be vertical but the Contractors must, without extra charge, slope the sides of these cuttings should it be required by the engineer.'

This particular comment was destined to be of particular relevance in consequence of the steep cuttings at Tothill and Larksborough. The idea, particularly at the latter location, of a vertical wall of chalk rising 60' above rail level meant that it was hardly any surprise later when chalk falls were frequent.

'......after the cuttings and works of the railway shall have

Despite extensive searching no views of the construction of the northern section have been found. Indeed the only known view of construction south of Newbury is that of the cutting in the station area at Winchester, already reproduced in the Winchester booklet - see bibliography - and consequently not duplicated here not least for reasons of space. Instead the above view shows the course of the earthworks from Woodhay south towards Tothill and Highclere, not in 1884 or thereabouts, but instead more than a century later, at a time when the A34 Newbury by-pass was in the early stages of construction, one of the first tasks to clear the track-bed of the former railway of vegetation so as to form an access route for use by the contractor's plant. As is known, the new road follows the route of the railway almost entirely from Tothill through to Enborne, albeit of course on a much wider formation. One may also smile slightly at the earth slippage that occurred in the southbound road cutting at Tothill not long after the by-pass opened. The 20th century engineers had not bothered to research the instability of the ground at this point - which had caused exactly the same problems to the railway contractor more than a century before.

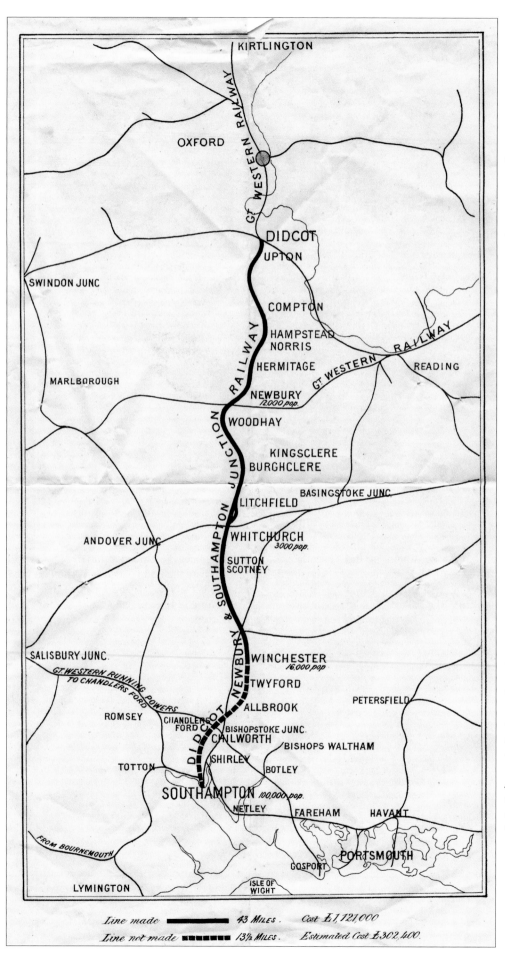

KIRTLINGTON

OXFORD

G^T WESTERN RAILWAY

DIDCOT

UPTON

SWINDON JUNC.

COMPTON

HAMPSTEAD
NORRIS

HERMITAGE

G^T WESTERN RAILWAY

READING

MARLBOROUGH

NEWBURY
12,000 pop.

WOODHAY

KINGSCLERE
BURGHCLERE

BASINGSTOKE JUNC.

LITCHFIELD

ANDOVER JUNC.

WHITCHURCH
3000 pop.

SUTTON
SCOTNEY

SALISBURY JUNC.

G^T WESTERN RUNNING POWERS
TO CHANDLERS FORD

WINCHESTER
16,000 pop.

TWYFORD

ALLBROOK

PETERSFIELD

ROMSEY

CHANDLERS
FORD

BISHOPSTOKE JUNC.

CHILWORTH

BISHOPS WALTHAM

TOTTON

SHIRLEY

BOTLEY

SOUTHAMPTON 100,000 pop.

NETLEY

FAREHAM

HAVANT

FROM BOURNEMOUTH

PORTSMOUTH

GOSPORT

LYMINGTON

ISLE OF
WIGHT

Line made ▬▬▬▬ 43 MILES . Cost £1,121,000

Line not made ▪▪▪▪▪▪▪ 13½ MILES . Estimated Cost £302,400.

An undated plan, but certainly post 1882 - for it was after this year that the decision was made to attempt to proceed to Southampton. BUT, whilst useful from the perspective of indicating a general outline of the course for the DNSJR (sic) railway, either the original draughtsman was careless or there remain further unanswered questions. No proposed lines are shown - nor the East Illsley branch which had been authorised under the original act but was destined never to be built.

From the hatched part of the scheme we may assume the railway was either at, or by now well on the way to completion at Winchester, in which case what is the 'loop' shown above Whitchurch? If this is supposed to be the connection with the LSWR it is incorrectly shown, there can be no logical purpose for any other form of connection at this point.

Then we turn to Highclere, or rather the lack of it. This station (between Woodhay and Burghclere) is simply omitted, but Kingsclere is shown. Again a slip by the draughtsman or was it a suggestion that Highclere might have been called Kingsclere - even if five miles apart!

Finally it may be seen that the populations are shown for Newbury, Whitchurch and Winchester. (The 2012 figures in the same order although without specific boundaries shown are 28,000, 4,500, and 41,000.)

As before, illustrations of the southern section outweigh those between Didcot and Newbury. This commercial card shows Hermitage looking west from the high ground of Cold Ash Common, the railway south to Newbury is identified by the fencing and low embankment.   *Roy Marr*

been completed and the temporary roads removed, the bottoms of the cuttings shall be levelled down to the proper height with the uniform inclinations already described and to the correct levels for receiving the ballast - broken stone or gravel on which the sleepers are to rest. If it should happen that no material fit for ballast be found in the excavations of the line.........or in case of a deficiency of such material whether in quality or quantity, the Contractors shall procure the stone at their own cost. The ballast shall be broken stone flints or gravel, free from clay or other improper substances and shall be spread over the surface of the foundation to the specified thickness from one end of the line of railways to the other but so as not to be less than 2½ cubic yards per linear yard of single line of railway. In all cases where the railway is constructed on viaduct or bridges the space below the rail shall be ....filled up with ballast or approved dry filling and in all cases the ballast shall not be less than 1' in thickness under the sleepers.'

'The permanent way will consist partly of flanged rails already delivered on the ground and the remainder of bull headed steel rails weighing 80 lbs. per yard supported on cross sleepers by cast iron chairs weighing 38 lbs each and fished with deep fish plates weighing about 40 lbs per pair. Detailed drawings of the rails and fastening will be furnished by the Engineer. Each nail to be marked with the name of the maker, the year, and month of manufacture and the letters DNS R.. The Engineer or his assistants shall have full power to test the rails in such manner as the Engineer

shall require and to inspect the rails at all times during their manufacture, and the maker is to afford every facility and to supply any reasonable extra labour and appliances for their so doing, but not withstanding each inspection or testing any rails may be rejected on delivery and which in the judgement of the Engineer are defective in any respect. In laying the permanent way the bull headed rails shall be used in the main lines exclusively and where a part of the line is at present laid with double line of flange rails one of these lines shall be taken up and the rails be re-laid in sidings at the stations......The sleepers to be of sound memel or dantzic timber 9' x 10" x 5" diameter square....'. [4]

The minute books of the DNS company also provide a feast of fascinating material which was disseminated to the shareholders at the half yearly meetings, some of which at least were held at the Westminster Palace Hotel, London. At the summer meeting of 1882 for example, the Directors appeared to deliberately hype up enthusiasm for an extension to Southampton. Examples were given of how it presently took some 4 hours to travel from Southampton to Newbury via Basingstoke and Reading. The comment being made that it was quicker to proceed via London. This was just what those supporting the extension wanted to hear although transferring such opinions into financial support was very different. Moral support for the Southampton extension was also offered from further afield and included the citizens and council at Ventnor, Isle of Wight, although perhaps surprisingly no

Great Western Railway.

No. T. 119.   (For use of Company's Servants only.)

Commencing on Monday, May 5th, 1890—Upton will become a Train Staff Station, and the Train Staff Sections will be Didcot to Upton—Upton to Compton—and Compton to Newbury East Junction, and the following will be the Special Instructions for working the Single Line between Didcot and Newbury East Junction during the time that Compton and Upton Stations are closed.

1.—On and after Monday, May 5th, in order that Compton and Upton Stations may not have to remain open for the exchange of the Train Staffs for the Train leaving Didcot for Winchester at 3.30 a.m., the following regulations must be observed :—

2.—The Signalman at Compton after he has received the Train Staff for the Section between Newbury East Junction and Compton from the Engineman of 7.5 p.m. Mixed train from Winchester, (or the last Up train from Newbury, if one is running later,) must hand it to the head Guard of 7.5 p.m. train, (or the last Up train from Newbury, if one is running later,) and the Booking Porter or person in charge at Upton after he has received the Train Staff for the section between Compton and Upton, from the Engineman of 7.5 p.m. Mixed train from Winchester (or the last Up train, if one is running later,) hand it to the head Guard of 7.5 p.m. train who will take both Train Staffs through to Didcot, and the Guard on arrival at Didcot must deliver them to the Signalman in the East End Cabin.

3.—One of the special through Train Staff Tickets from Didcot to Newbury East Junction, shape half circle, and colour buff, must be given by the Signalman of the East End Cabin at Didcot to the Engineman of the 3.30 a.m. Goods Train from Didcot to Winchester, the Train Staffs for the whole of the sections between Didcot and Newbury East Junction being shown to the Engineman when the through Special Ticket is given to him.

4.—The Engineman of this Train is held responsible for seeing the three Train Staffs before accepting the through special ticket, and he must give up the through special ticket to the Signalman at Newbury East Junction on arrival there, who is responsible for collecting it from him.

5.—The special Train Staff Ticket from Didcot to Newbury East Junction must be cancelled by the Signalman immediately it is received by him and it must then be sent to my office.

6.—The Engineman of 6.25 a.m. Goods Train from Didcot to Bristol, viâ Newbury, must be given at Didcot one of the Ordinary Train Staff Tickets for the section between Didcot and Upton, and he must be shewn the Train Staff for that section.

7.—The Signalman at Didcot must hand to the Guard of the 6.25 a.m. Goods Train from Didcot to Bristol, viâ Newbury, the Train Staff for the section between Upton and Compton, and also for the section between Compton and Newbury East Junction, and the Guard of the 6.25 a.m. train from Didcot will be responsible for handing the Staff for the section between Upton and Compton to the person in charge at Upton, and that for the section between Compton and Newbury East Junction to the person in charge at Compton on arrival at those Stations.

8.—After the Station Master (or person in charge) at Upton and Compton has received the Train-Staff for his section from the Guard the ordinary Staff working will be resumed.

9.—The Train Staffs and Tickets work as under :—

FROM	TO	SHAPE OF STAFF & TICKET.	COLOUR.
Didcot ...	Upton	Round	Red
Upton ...	Compton	Triangular	White
Compton ...	Newbury East Jun.	Staff Annetts Key } Ticket Square }	Blue

Through Train Staff Ticket from Didcot to Newbury East Junction, half circle, colour buff.

10.—This cancels the instructions contained in my circular No. 258, dated June 10th, 1886.

JAS. W. GIBBS,

Superintendent of the Reading Division.

MAY 2nd, 1890.

STARKEY, PRINTER, READING.

Official notice heralding the introduction of Upton (sic) as a Train Staff section in 1890 - previous to this the line between Didcot and Newbury had been so equipped only at Compton, meaning that just two trains might travel on the line at the same time. The new provision at Upton increased the capacity of the line to three - Hermitage was similarly equipped in 1891. Of interest is the hand-written note top right, "Posted in Porter's Room, 'do' in goods van & one given to Guard who signed for it" - does this mean a particular guard's van(s) was allocated to DNS trains? As referred to in the caption on page 23, on 4 July 1918 authorisation was given for the train staff to be superseded by what would become the familiar Electric Token..Why this should have been considered necessary is not clear as the only advantage to be gained was the physical size of the equipment having been reduced. Possibly it was yet another example of the GWR updating facilities at anothers cost. The estimated cost was £600 - although possibly this applied to the whole line as far as Winchester. Certainly south of Newbury the single line instruments were housed within the Booking / Station Masters office and it is reasonable to assume the same applied north of Newbury. ETT working between Didcot and Newbury would continue until the line was doubled in 1942 but it is interesting to note that Hampstead Norris was never given the distinction of a staff / token section.

SECTION		CONFIGURATION / COLOUR	TOKEN MACHINE SERIAL No.
Didcot East Junction	Upton & Blewbury	A - Red	20
Upton & Blewbury	Didcot East Junction	A - Red	78
Upton & Blewbury	Compton	B - Blue	86
Compton	Upton & Blewbury	B - Blue	420
Compton	Hermitage	C - Green	105
Hermitage	Compton	C - Green	81
Hermitage	Newbury East Junction	D - Yellow	84
Newbury East Junction	Hermitage	D - Yellow	66

The colours given are those that applied certainly by 1930. When the colour system was introduced is not completely clear, it is possible also that the colours may have been different in 1918 compared with what later became the standard.

monies were forthcoming from this quarter.

South to Winchester

Somewhat surprisingly no date is given for commencement of work south of Newbury but this could well have been a simple immediate continuation following completion between Didcot and Newbury. What is known is that this construction work was based solely upon the Newbury - Litchfield section and it was not until 22 March 1883 that progress began on the ensuing 15½ miles from the latter point as far as Winchester.

One month earlier on 22 February 1883 the Engineer had reported the exceptionally wet January had held up progress in Penwood (sic) - Tothill, cutting. Later in the same year, the next shareholders meeting of 23 August recorded work was proceeding well in Southampton with some 12,000 cu.yds. of excavation completed together with ¼ mile of track formation. Work was also continuing with the tunnel (sic) under the LSWR at Winchester Junction without any disruption to the latter's traffic.

Seven months later on 17 March 1884, it was made known that a temporary suspension of work had occurred in Southampton from October 1883. Already by this time some £100,000 had been spent there, principally it must be said on land purchase. Much of this was now fenced off and involved a strip stretching from Wyndham Place near the present Southampton Central railway station, northwards along the east side of Hill Lane for about ½ mile and thence north-west for nearly a mile towards St. James Church in the Upper Shirley district. At this time the area was still mainly open country, the unfinished works would remain moribund and melancholy for some years causing annoyance and inconvenience to local inhabitants. The viaduct at Southampton was half finished together with all its remaining piers and abutments. Progress elsewhere reported that Winchester Tunnel was 2/3rd's complete, and Highclere station nearly finished. Whitchurch tunnel (sic) - carrying the line under the LSWR, was also completed.

The final shareholders reference for 1884, that of 16 September, informed those present that aside from a distance of less than 1 mile, the formation was now complete from Newbury as far as Litchfield. Presumably that not finished was at Burghclere where work was recorded as in progress. (Is this taken to mean Burghclere where the station of that name was later built, or where the actual Burghclere village was? In the latter the area would be in the vicinity of what was later Highclere station.) South of Litchfield all excavation work was finished save for the cutting at Worthy Down and unspecified work at Winchester. Interestingly the cutting at Worthy Down, meaning the one north of the later station site, was then referred to as Wallers Ash cutting. In later years it would be

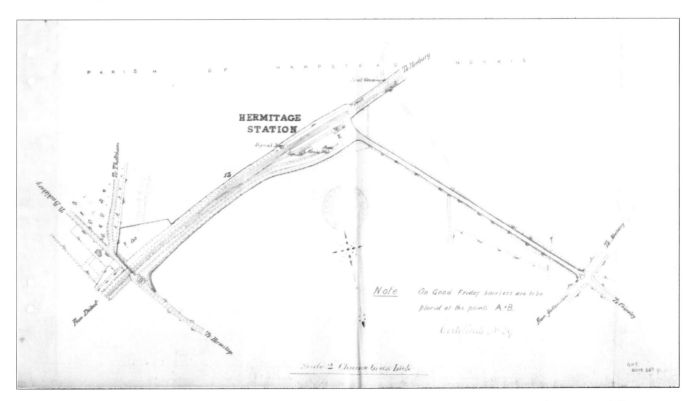

1891 ground plan from Hermitage. Public access to the station site was either from the Yattendon - Newbury road (better known in more recent times as the B4009, or as was less known, from the Bucklebury - Hermitage road. Of interest is the long -forgotten legal necessity of closing the railway access road to public traffic on one day every year. This was usually a bank-holiday (as less traffic would be inconvenienced), although perhaps slightly strange Good Friday is the referred to day on the plan. Such closure was necessary to maintain the integrity of any private road - not just railway - although in the former case, signs indicating 'Private Road' were another requirement and were provided at both access points.

Personalities

Above - Brigadier-General Robert James Loyd-Lindsay, 1832-1901, of Lockinge estate near Wantage. He was chairman of the DNS until 1884 when ill-health forced him to step down. Elevated to the peerage in 1885 his estate encompassed much of what was then the north Berkshire downland. He was also a devotee (and the first chairman of the Council) of the National Rifle Association .

Above - James Staats Forbes, chairman of the DNS from 1884 and possibly until the time of his death in 1904. Under Forbes work was suspended at Southampton (never to resume) whilst he undertook a policy of appeasement with both the GWR and LSWR much to the chagrin of the shareholders who saw in this program little chance of any return upon their investment. Forbes probably saw little option whilst his actions would indeed lead to the consequences the investors feared.

Left - Henry Molyneux Herbert, 4th Earl of Caenarvon 1831-1890 whose seat was at Highclere Castle.

known as Christmas Hill cutting.

Contemporary press reports in local newspapers were to be found accompanying progress on the new railway. One of these was within the 'Andover Advertiser' for 4 May 1883 and appertaining to Whitchurch. "...Rapid progress is being made here with the new railway, one example of which is worthy to record, namely, that of the arch over the road leading from Bell Street. This arch was begun on 2 March and completed on 28 April. It is 80' long and contains upwards of 144,000 cu. ft. of brick and flint work. Although the piers and wings are only faced with 9" brickwork, upwards of 200,000 bricks have been used, of which the arch contains about 70,000. It is said that 250 tons of cement have been used in its construction."

Perhaps one of the most interesting new finds relative to the early history has been the report on the failure of the Tothill covered way which occurred on 5 July 1884 following a period of prolonged heavy rain. Fowler as Engineer produced a report to the directors on the matter. This was presented on 15 July and which more than a century after the event at last affords the answers to a number of previously only guessed at issues.

The 'covered way' itself was in reality a 130' long bridge similar in design to that provided under the LSWR at Whitchurch. Trial shafts sunk before construction had indicated a depth of 26' of gravel overlying a bed of hard clay. In consequence of this construction went ahead but after a period of rain it was found the clay would slip, often running down the nearby cutting side to accumulate at the base and according to Fowler, '...with mud up to rail level.' By July 1884 the covered way had been completed for some 8 months however the result of continual heavy rain was to force the bottom of the cutting upwards by some 3-4' and this time carrying the rails with it. At the same time the skew face - it is not specified which end this was at - was carried away and the actual brickwork cracked through. Fowler reported that a iron bridge of 3 spans was to be substituted, '..one advantage being that it will free the line for the running of ballast trains.'

Other issues were more easily dealt with including an indenture dated 23 January 1855 this time between the GWR and DNS appertaining to the provision of the necessary connection between the two company's lines at what would later be known as Enborne. Here the GWR would for their part, lay in a double junction to the new line having a radius of 1000' which would be continued by the DNS on their own land so as to form a loop on the new single line. A signal box was proposed on the east side of the new railway which would have 22 levers, 12 for signals, 3 for points, 2 F.P.L.'s and 5 spare. The new box was to be provided by the DNS and despite also providing the GWR with a new block post on the Berks. and Hants railway, was situated alongside the minor route rather than the main line. Whilst on the face of it this may appear an unusual concession by the GWR, it did allow for ease of changing the single line staff. Although the full costs are not reported, that work carried out by the GWR and chargeable to the DNS was estimated at £385.

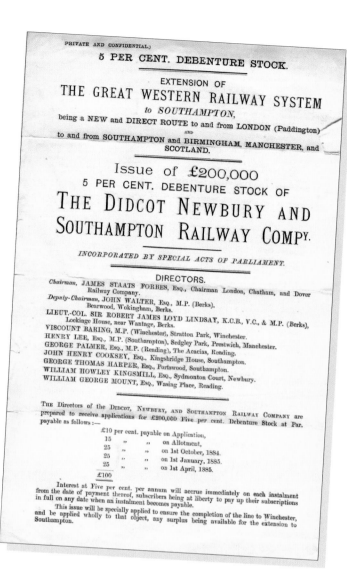

PRIVATE AND CONFIDENTIAL.)

5 PER CENT. DEBENTURE STOCK.

EXTENSION OF
THE GREAT WESTERN RAILWAY SYSTEM
to SOUTHAMPTON,
being a NEW and DIRECT ROUTE to and from LONDON (Paddington)
AND
to and from SOUTHAMPTON and BIRMINGHAM, MANCHESTER, and SCOTLAND.

Issue of £200,000
5 PER CENT. DEBENTURE STOCK OF
THE DIDCOT NEWBURY AND SOUTHAMPTON RAILWAY COMPY.

INCORPORATED BY SPECIAL ACTS OF PARLIAMENT.

DIRECTORS.
Chairman, JAMES STAATS FORBES, Esq., Chairman London, Chatham, and Dover Railway Company.
Deputy-Chairman, JOHN WALTER, Esq., M.P. (Berks), Bearwood, Wokingham, Berks.
LIEUT.-COL. SIR ROBERT JAMES LOYD LINDSAY, K.C.B., V.C., & M.P. (Berks), Lockinge House, near Wantage, Berks.
VISCOUNT BARING, M.P. (Winchester), Stratton Park, Winchester.
HENRY LEE, Esq., M.P. (Southampton), Sedgley Park, Prestwich, Manchester.
GEORGE PALMER, Esq., M.P. (Reading), The Acacias, Reading.
JOHN HENRY COOKSEY, Esq., Kingsbridge House, Southampton.
GEORGE THOMAS HARPER, Esq., Portswood, Southampton.
WILLIAM HOWLEY KINGSMILL, Esq., Sydmonton Court, Newbury.
WILLIAM GEORGE MOUNT, Esq., Wasing Place, Reading.

THE Directors of the DIDCOT, NEWBURY, AND SOUTHAMPTON RAILWAY COMPANY are prepared to receive applications for £200,000 Five per cent. Debenture Stock at Par, payable as follows :—

£10 per cent. payable on Application,
15 " " on Allotment,
25 " " on 1st October, 1884.
25 " " on 1st January, 1885.
25 " " on 1st April, 1885.
£100

Interest at Five per cent. per annum will accrue immediately on each instalment from the date of payment thereof, subscribers being at liberty to pay up their subscriptions in full on any date when an instalment becomes payable.
This issue will be specially applied to ensure the completion of the line to Winchester, and be applied wholly to that object, any surplus being available for the extension to Southampton.

Officially it has always been stated that the GWR would never invest in the DNS so as to create independent access to Southampton for fear of open hostility at the numerous other locations where both the GWR and LSWR connected. Different locations were where either would play the major or subservient roles or even as equal partners. There was also a acknowledgement in the corridors of Paddington and Waterloo that various parts of the country were recognised as 'GWR' or 'LSWR' territory, hence the arrival of an interloper such as the DNS created a situation where the status-quo might well be affected. But this document, dated July 1884, could have changed all that. Why the 'Private & Confidential' and by the wording 'Extension of the GWR system...' does this mean the GWR were the backers? We shall never know. Clearly a risk someone was prepared to take.

Around the same time an inspection of the route was carried out by 'Officers of the Great Western Railway' together with 'The Engineer and Contractor from the Didcot & Newbury Company', and provides for an important snapshot as to the final stages of construction.

"The Junction:- the signals are in a forward state. Woodhay

At long last and after more than quarter of a century of searching, perseverance pays off: the elusive view of the opening to Winchester turns up!

It was always known that photographs had been taken of the opening day but it was not sure if any had survived - witness what appear to be one of possibly two photographer s on the wall on the right hand side.

This lack of success was particularly galling as whilst 1885 was still relatively early for mass photography, other railway openings had seen their initial days recorded. (Now of course all we need are views of the construction and of course the opening of the northern section in 1882, but perhaps that is being greedy.)

But to return to Friday 1 May 1885 and what is immediately apparent is the freshness of the chalk against which the station building appears largely complete although it is yet to receive its decorative ironwork. (Fortunately this decorative embellishment would survive demolition decades later and for some time rested with Winchester Museum service. It has since been passed to the Great Western Society at Didcot and may one day hopefully be on display.)

The bricks for the line and indeed the station building here may have come from Pinewood, not geographically the nearest brickworks as there were several in south east Hampshire, but possibly the easiest from which to transport bricks.

In time for the opening, the necessary furniture was provided by the GWR for Winchester and the other stations south of Newbury at a cost of £372 1s 1d, although just three months later an additional £12 6s 9d was necessary. In the photograph, flags are seen bedecking the canopy, tunnel mouth and signal box, whilst there is a multitude of observers not only on the station approach where a number of horse drawn carriages await, but also on the path above the tunnel. Note, contrary to one particular internet site, Winchester tunnel was <u>never</u> constructed on the 'cut and cover' method, it was far too deep for this. If further proof were needed look at the land above the tunnel - undisturbed. The DNS style cottage will be seen above the tunnel: which would serve until 1948 as the Winchester station master's house.

The special train has arrived at what was later the 'up' side, the down platform complete but not yet in use. At the north end of the of the building, it is just possible to discern the original water tank provided, supported in timber legs and only present for a very short time.

There is also only a single starting signal - that at the north end of the down platform was not provided until at least 1893. The sharp curve of the track inside the tunnel is accounted for by the single line of rails only after that point, although certainly some realignment took place later. The track in the down platform would appear to be of the inside-key type.

The locomotive(s) used at the head of the train are not recorded, whilst contemporary reports indicate the special train consisted of four first-class carriages, twelve second / third class, three brake vans and a saloon, not necessarily in that order.

*Study of the original print reveals the nearest vehicle to be a bogie 3rd to Diagram D4, lot No 431 and almost new at the time. Its running number was in the series 1723-1752. There then follow four 2nd / 3rd class vehicles and what may well be a Brake 3rd, to Diagram 20 and having four compartments - two either side of a central guards compartment. The remainder of the train is indistinguishable. On all the coaches oil lighting is used * and there are footboards commensurate with the period. Those most recently outshopped can be identified by the lighter colour roofs. (On the opening day the first train comprising the vehicles referred to above, left Winchester carrying invited guests and proceeded to Newbury. There it was boarded by further invitees and augmented also by four additional vehicles and a second locomotive. It then returned to Winchester for the formal opening ceremony. What is not certain is at what stage during the day the image was taken.)*

The view was taken from the footbridge which allowed the footpath from Chesil Street to cross the railway and continue to St Giles Hill. A passenger footbridge between the platforms was not needed at the time and was not provided until after the line to Shawford Junction opened in 1891.

One final point of note is to refer to the steepness of the cutting side on the right, this of course would later collapse in late 1891 resulting in much sloping of the hillside being required.

* During the period when oil-lighting was still standard, a junior porter would often walk along the roofs of the carriages at Winchester lifting the lid of the roof covering to exchange the oil lamps. Folklore has it that on occasion the lamp slipped landing on the dress of the lady sat in the compartment underneath and covering her in soot. In the main station building at Winchester there was originally a room specified as a store for carriage foot-warmers.,

Hermitage, probably sometime before 1914 and most likely in the early years of the century. The view shows the original tile-hung platform canopy as had been provided at Upton, Compton and here - these were removed and replaced with a lightweight covering by 1919, whilst it will also be noted the ballast makes a covering over the sleepers.   Roy Marr

- this station is incomplete at present. The goods siding has not been put in. The signals are in a forward state. Highclere - the goods sidings are rather backwards. The signals are in a forward state. Litchfield - the goods sidings are not yet commenced and there is only one signal up at present. Whitchurch - the sidings and signals are incomplete. Sutton Scotney - the sidings are not complete and the signals are backward. Winchester - everything is in a very backward

state, the Goods Shed is not complete, the sidings are not in, the extensive goods yard requires ballasting and the passenger station buildings and yard are very incomplete."

General Remarks - "...the line requires a great deal of ballast between Winchester Station and Sutton Scotney. There is between these stations a cutting in a very incomplete state. The platforms should be paved the length of the buildings. The telegraph posts are all up, but the wires are not yet put up between Whitchurch and Winchester. Clocks are required for all the stations and signal boxes. Cart weigh-bridges have been provided at Winchester and Whitchurch only and are required at the other stations. Platform weighing machines should also be provided in the goods sheds. At Whitchurch a small lock-up in the shed and a Goods Office are required. At Winchester there should be a lock-up in the Goods Shed, and an office for the Checker. W.C. and Urinal for the goods staff should be provided. An unloading bank for furniture vans is required."

A handwritten notes in the margin presumably by a DNS official, refers to the issue of what is probably the requirement for platform weighing machines and states somewhat pointedly that, "...these were not asked for on any other occasion". Unfortunately it has not been possible to confirm the original requirements specified for such

Whitchurch: October 1883

An accident happened on Monday evening in a cutting on the new railway works north of Whitchurch *(Larksbarrow cutting)*, by which two navvies were seriously injured. It appears the two men were engaged in undermining the cutting to admit the wagons , when a large quantity of earth fell on them before they could escape. One was buried completely and the other nearly so. They were rescued from their perilous position as quickly as possible by their mates and being found dreadfully crushed and injured, were conveyed to the workhouse and speedily attended to by Drs Hemstead and Masters. It was feared at first that one would succumb to his injuries, but we are pleased to hear that both are now progressing favourably and hopes are entertained for their recovery.

facilities and which were probably only in the form of notes by the Engineer.

T.B. Sands is of the opinion that the opening south of Newbury had originally been fixed for 24 March 1885, but was delayed due to the inability of the GWR to find sufficient staff. This may well have been the case, as the requisite Board of Trade inspection had taken place on 21 March although in the event it was some 6 weeks before the formal opening and public services began. Details of the Board of Trade inspection have been given elsewhere (- see page 10, column 2, of the DNS book), although what was not recounted was the reference made by Colonel Hutchinson to, '...temporary points leading to ballast pits and contractors sidings and also temporary water tanks which have to be removed'. It would be very interesting to know where these temporary facilities may have been, possibly even altered in location as work progressed. (A 'ballast pit is also believed to have existed near Enborne.)

In the meanwhile the GWR reported to the DNS that on 24 April 1885 they had inspected the facilities at Woodhay and found the goods shed was not yet roofed whilst the platform was also rough. A number of other items were also deemed incomplete including the absence of a loading gauge, no coal bins, a wooden cabin was required for the ground frame and there were no lamps in the toilets.

Shortly after this on May 14 1885, a written notice emanating from the Telegraph Department of the GWR then based at Paddington reveals details of the new circuit arrangements for telegraph connection between the stations and signal boxes on the line. This was detailed as follows;

'A connection has been made between the Didcot, Newbury and Winchester circuits. The station and signal boxes will now be as under.....
Didcot Office
Didcot Centre Box.

A slightly later view of Hermitage: the platform canopy has been altered and the sleepers are visible. It is tempting to suggest the men are holding the tools of their trade: what is the train staff on the extreme left so the man is likely to be the porter / signalman as it is unlikely traffic would warrant a full time signalman: shunters pole, stations master, unknown, and finally amongst the adults, a further porter / signalman again with train staff / carrier. This latter item may be used to assist in dating the image as the trains staff was superseded by the electric train token in 1918/19. The boy appears to have a model bi-plane, in which case it could well be very close to 1918/19, any earlier than that and it might have been expected that the men would have been away in the war. The station master could well be Mr E Wilkins who was in post by April 1917 and who remained until about February 1920.   *Roy Marr*

Bell Street Whitchurch, towards St Mary Bourne recorded around the turn of the 19/20th century. In the distance is Bell Street bridge with the railway embankment running over the top. It was within the cement of the brick arch that a gold sovereign was sunk by a well-wisher - later to be retrieved by the navvies who may well have spent it within the Bell Inn - the landlord at the time being Charles Carpenter. The two ladies present outside the hostelry give the impression they would be well able to deal with any troublesome railway builders!

Collection Ted Moss, courtesy Geoff Kelland

Upton
Compton
Hampstead Norris
Hermitage
Newbury Loop Box
Newbury Top Box
Newbury Station
Enborne Junction
Woodhay
Highclere
Burghclere
Litchfield
Whitchurch
Sutton Scotney
Winchester

Certain of the named references are of themselves of particular interest and especially those appertaining to locations at Didcot and Newbury. The actual equipment installed and through which a communication was made was the single needle disc block telegraph, essential in the regulation of traffic and allied to the wooden staff and ticket arrangements then in use on the single line. The actual telegraph instruments were, at the branch stations, housed within the station buildings and utilised not only for signalling purposes but also to communicate re general traffic and train purposes. (Note there is no reference to any communication being available with the level crossings at Compton and Fishers Lane.)

The period from May 1885 to mid 1891 found the railway almost in a sort of moribund state, as if it were holding its breath and awaiting developments. But behind the scenes it was a very different matter. The company were continually wrangling to secure the necessary funds to reach Southampton although this was eventually given up for lost in 1888 with the passing of the DNS Act of 7 August of that year which authorised the construction of the line to Shawford Junction. Neither was it easy going so far as relations between the DNS and GWR over the actual working south of Newbury. Contemporary reports show the GWR made several inspections of the line, each time finding errors which they would insist the DNS put right. The fact that the little company had not the resources to comply was of little consequence with the result these issues were rectified by the GWR who would then charge the DNS for the work, so adding the cost to an already accumulating debt which also accrued interest.

One such example concerned the signal box at Burghclere as reported on 23 January 1886;

GWR - "...the lock up desk should be fixed to the floor..."

DNS - "The contractors should strictly do this but it appears rather absurd for them to be required to send a carpenter 30 miles to drive a few nails or put in a few screws.......as a rule these (the lock up desks), have been removed to the booking office where the instruments now are."

The comment above is interesting for another reason as by implication it would appear the single line instruments, meaning the telegraph instruments, may well have been first located within the signal cabins but were then quickly

removed to the main buildings. Assuming this interpretation to be correct the obvious question is 'Why', but no answer can be found. Neither is any help forthcoming from the previously quoted memorandum of the GWR Telegraph Department at Paddington of 14 May 1885.

Another issue raised is the distance of 30 miles from Burghclere referred to by the DNS so far as the contractors need to travel were concerned. Assuming this to be Messrs. Falkiner & Tancred, it has never been found where this company had their main depot. Their London office address appears on the signed contracts but by implication they may be assumed to have been based relatively local to the Hampshire / Berkshire area.

Another GWR report listing deficiencies in the DNS is dated 12 June 1886:

Woodhay - station not yet painted.
Highclere - gravel in goods yard to be levelled.
Litchfield - platform wall (not specified.)
Whitchurch - front door of house will not open properly.
Winchester - lamps not yet fixed in goods shed.
General, station master's houses and station offices have not been papered and ceilings whitened.

Further inspections recounting similar alleged shortcomings were recorded on a number of other occasions including one shortly afterwards on 31 July 1886 when much of the report is taken up with the door of the house at Whitchurch. The GWR stating it will still not open properly whilst in response the DNS declare they can find no fault with it!

Interestingly no similar behaviour was reported earlier at the time of the opening of the line from Didcot to Newbury. Was it a possibility then that the antics of Forbes and the DNS directors were antagonising Paddington? Perhaps this may well have been the case for as again reported by Sands, 'At a half-yearly meeting in 1890, a DNS shareholder complained of the "hostile and disparaging attitude" of the Great Western staff towards the railway. "The guards on the trains are openly contemptuous and speak of a journey on the railway as a trip across the wilderness."

Between 1885 and 1887 the inability of the Company to reach Southampton began to manifest itself in frustration and disputes amongst the shareholders as to the best option that should now be taken. Strength of feeling also grew against Forbes with a committee of dissidents formed in London commenting, "...the services of Mr. Forbes, secured at a salary wholly disproportionate to the funds at the disposal of the Company, ought to be dispensed with".

Dissent grew further following a meeting of 100 shareholders held at the Westminster Palace Hotel in June 1886 subsequently reported to the Board by J.E. Le Feuvre (a prominent shareholder) on 19 June 1886. The directors were accordingly advised that a resolution had been passed, "....that all steps be taken to complete the railway to Southampton and to use Preference Stock authorised by Act of Parliament."

Le Feuvre's continued that the shareholders committee proposed the line between Winchester and Southampton have the ruling gradient altered from 1- 106 to

'On to Shawford' - or should it even be 'On to Twyford'. This was the literal end of the line at Bar End from 1885 until 1891, the chalk embankment abruptly ceasing. The earlier Itchen Navigation may be seen alongside with St Catherine's Hill in the background.

1- 100 to save cost and with their own estimate of the finance required as follows;

Earthwork / Excavation	£ 90,000
Bridges	37,000
Permanent Way	30,000
Tunnel	28,760
Fencing	5,200
Metalling	1,000
Telegraph etc.	1,000
Miscellaneous	1,000
	£193,960

- the more usual amount to quote for miscellanea, or contingencies, in a railway contract was 10% of the total and so equivalent to some £19,000. This would have taken the proposed figure to over £210,000.

In addition a separate list of suggested station costs was given;

Twyford	£ 2,500
Allbrook	2,500
Chilworth	2,500
Shirley	5,000
Southampton	10,000
	£22,500

This is the first time actual station costs are quoted for any of the stations on the line - built or proposed, from which it is also clear the first three named stopping places would have been of minimal size, possibly comparable with the intermediate stopping places south of Newbury. Curiously omitted is any reference to the cost of a stopping place at Chandlers Ford.

The land cost was quoted for at £50,000, thus giving a total projected cost of £266,460. A footnote added the cost of Chilworth tunnel could be reduced by a further £15,000 by altering the gradient, presumably to one steeper than even 1 in 100? Taking this last issue into the equation a figure of £251,460 is shown as being required. The shareholders report suggested this could be funded as follows;

Southampton Corporation 4% Debenture Stock	50,000
Landowners 4% Debenture Stock or rent charges	50,000
Shareholders to subscribe	100,000
Contractor to take Debentures	50,000
	Total £250,000

The report concluded that, "The Corporation of Southampton unanimously agreed to recommend the ratepayers to temporarily forgo the construction of all public improvements to be provided for their special agreement with the company.....".

In response the DNS Directors noted quite correctly that no engineers name was given to support the shareholder's suggestion whilst based upon the advice of their own engineer, Sir John Fowler, the previously quoted official figure for the same work of £350,000 should still apply.

There matters seem to have stalled, although on exactly what issue is not clear. Was it the difference in costs or was the suggested investment by Southampton Council?

In reality, probably both. In the event the only concession gained by the shareholders was to get the Board to agree not to proceed with a proposed Bill of Abandonment for the line south of Winchester at this time although as is known, this was eventually incorporated into the DNS Act of 1889.

Extending the railway south from Winchester was to be an issue destined to be aired many times at subsequent shareholders meetings, many of these gatherings turning into what are best described as 'tumultuous' occasions. In just one area was there common ground and that was the need to find an alternative to the dead-end that existed at Winchester. With little option, the idea of a junction on the LSWR main line between that company's stations at Winchester and Shawford was adopted. To those shareholders originating from the Newbury area this was the obvious solution, but not so those who had supported the railway and came from Southampton. From this latter group were alternative suggestions for junctions at Allbrook, Eastleigh, or Chandlers Ford, although each would require more capital than was likely to be accessible. Not surprisingly the LSWR were totally antagonistic to all such proposals and accordingly the first parliamentary attempt in 1887 at securing powers to continue from Winchester to Shawford failed.

The directors then played what was almost their last trump card by announcing they intended to complete the connection at Winchester Junction as had been authorised in 1882. The fact that the time for completion of this spur had almost lapsed was lost to the LSWR who little relished the prospect of DNS trains using their own station at Winchester. It was a case of the lesser of two evils and the LSWR reluctantly agreed to the Shawford connection but now on two conditions, the first that the DNS relinquish any intention of securing an independent route to Southampton, and secondly that the DNS station at Winchester be the interchange point for traffic. No running powers would be granted beyond here, although through workings would still be permitted should DNS traffic traverse the Hurstbourne - Fullerton line, something only possible if the Whitchurch loops were completed. Indeed at this time it almost looked as if there would have to be trans-shipment of passengers at Winchester. Common sense however prevailed, in an agreement between all three parties, for although locomotives would not work through for some years, rolling stock did. The alternative could well have been a return to the inconvenience associated with the type of arrangement as had existed at various locations on the GWR where a break of gauge between the broad and standard (narrow – sic) gauges had occurred.

On to Shawford

The subsequent history so far as completion of the route from Winchester on to Shawford Junction in lieu of Southampton is in part at least recounted elsewhere[6], the contract to build the line from Winchester to Shawford Junction awarded to J.T. Firbank on 22 May 1890. As if to emphasise the precarious financial state of the little company, this was to be paid for in part share / part cash

terms although as the limited resources of the company are now well known this is not really surprising. This contract was against a working agreement for what was known as the 'Winchester and Twyford' line (sic) which was signed by the three relevant parties, the GWR, LSWR, and DNS on 10 October 1889.

Despite extensive searching little new detail has emerged concerning the actual construction of this the final link of the erstwhile DNS. However, from contemporary correspondence dated 21 January 1891 it would appear a successful approach was made to the Board of Trade for part of the originally proposed viaduct at Shawford to be substituted for embankment - possibly as a means of saving costs. The Engineer for the Shawford Junction line was W.S. Galbraith, an LSWR man, who had also been responsible for the Ford viaduct in Devonport. In both cases Galbraith decided to utilise concrete for the main structure facing the exterior only with brick - or in the case of Ford, limestone blocks. At Hockley there is a suggestion that within the centre of the pillars there may even be a chalk infill, however test borings carried out in 1996 do not so far confirm this. As such Hockley is one of the earliest surviving concrete viaducts - Ford was demolished in 1990, whilst it is to be hoped that Hockley will eventually be granted listed status with its future then secured. Some at least of the blue 'engineers' bricks used were obtained from the firm of 'Blanchard' at Bishops Waltham being transported by rail to Winchester - LSWR station. The final two mile journey for the bricks from the station to the site of work contracted to the Winchester firm of Steve and Luke Bull, Bros. This concern had a yard in College Street at Winchester, haulage between Winchester and Hockley undertaken by their own horse and carts. Sadly views of the construction of the Shawford Junction line and in particular the viaduct even though it was as late as 1890/1, have not been found.

Around the same time the minute books report that in connection with the opening of what they record as the 'Shawford Junction' line, "...additional facilities would be desirable at Winchester Goods Station…", meaning Bar End. In consequence enlargement of the goods shed bays took place together with the construction of a road and siding for Messrs. Simmons and Gifford. Several figures are provided as to the costs involved which included additional land at £676. A combined total of £18,668 was apportioned between the GWR and DNS

Clearly completion of the connection to Shawford was seen as a matter of some urgency to the DNS but perhaps not so to the other participants. For in early July 1891 correspondence took place in which the DNS were anxious for work to be accelerated. It would appear at least two parties were involved, the GWR and Messrs. Saxby & Farmer, the latter responsible for installing and modifying the existing signalling. From the tone of the letters, which became more and more acrimonious as time passed, it would seem as if the GWR were in overall control on the ground which would perhaps explain the singular lack of urgency.

One of the major areas of delay was the installation of the new scissors crossover south of the platforms and what would now become the down siding and new single line at this end of the station. Saxby and Farmer were involved in the actual work, the components reportedly on site around 21 July 1891, although it would still be some time before they were installed. Matters degenerated further over the following weeks with a series of letters between the DNS and GWR each blaming the other for the apparent inactivity. Aside from disputes over trackwork - and perhaps although it is not mentioned signalling as well - there was lengthy correspondence over the most desirable site for the waiting room and footbridge at the passenger station. The inference being that even at this late stage an alternative location, although where this was to be is not mentioned, would have been preferred. Bearing in mind the events that took place at Winchester only a few weeks later on 21 November 1891, it is perhaps fortunate that the facilities were built in their actual positions. In the event further correspondence over delays to completion, particularly of the footbridge took place and it was not until the autumn of 1891 that the new works were ready for inspection and opening.

Completion of a line from Winchester - Bar End, to Shawford Junction might have been expected to be the cause of some celebration to the DNS Company, but as is recounted, following inspection by the Board of Trade on 25 September, traffic simply commenced one week later on 1 October 1891. It had been hoped to open earlier but delays had been encountered in consequence of bad weather. (The date was incorrectly referred to on P13 of the original DNS book as 1 January, this was not corrected in the errata that appeared in the second printing or within the subsequent supplement.)

The extension of the route to Shawford was no doubt the reason for the increase in size of the signal box at Winchester although at this point an anomaly does occur, for the Board of Trade report also refers to another signal box at Bar End which was, '...subject to separate report'. Regretfully this report does not exist in the usual system of files at the Public Record Office - 'MT6 series'. It would be reasonable to assume this is in fact a reference to the small Ground Frame hut at Bar End from which access could be obtained from the yard onto the main line. However against this is that the Inspectors' were usually very clear and precise in their designations of signal boxes compared with

ground frames. Had there have been a separate signal box it would be presumed to have been a separate staff section - the Winchester to Shawford Junction single line was at first operated by 'Train Staff' with a change made to Tyer's No. 7 Electric Tablet at a later stage. A final complication in the puzzle is the photograph that is reproduced at the top of page 56 of DNS Supplement. This depicts a train having left Bar End passing Garnier Road bridge on its way to Shawford around 1900. Aside the engine is a 'stop' signal controlling traffic heading the opposite way towards Winchester. Where would this have been controlled from - probably not Winchester Station as the distance would have been too great?

The same photograph also provides proof that LSWR materials were utilised for the two mile extension to Shawford - the signal being to pure LSWR design. (It appears two stop signals were provided on the post - one beneath the other. Although indistinct it certainly appears that the lower arm was also a stop signal. In railway terms the phrase is 'top to bottom - left to right', hence the highest arm would have been for passenger trains journeying from Shawford Junction to Winchester and Newbury, with the lower arm for direct access into Bar End yard. A complication of the latter move would have come in that if a train were thus able to secure direct access into Bar End yard without first travelling to the Station then the section would still be deemed occupied unless the 'train staff' were either taken by hand to the signal box or as hinted at there was indeed a separate signal box and hence possible staff section between Winchester and Bar End.)

Returning to Winchester, in mid August 1891 with

preparations being made for the commencement of services on the new line at least two official notices were issued, most details from which have fortunately survived and which were located within a useful file of contemporary GWR paperwork under the P.R.O. Ref. 'RAIL 253/510.' The first of these papers is dated 15 August 1891 and emanated from the office of the Reading Superintendent, Jas. W. Gibbs, dealing with 'Alterations at Winchester'. Regretfully the right hand side of the notice is missing within the records and as a result it is typed below with gaps or italics to indicate where words are missing or have been assumed by the present writer.

"No. T 312
ALTERATIONS AT WINCHESTER.
Commencing on Wednesday ....
August 19th. 1891, all Down Trains will..*now*......
run to the Down Platform at Winchester...
and unload there, and all Up Trains will. *in future*..
start from the Up Platform.
The Catch Point will be taken out of.....
the Down Line at the tunnel end of .Down Line
Platform.
The following alterations will be made in the ....
Signals:-
The present Down Home Signal ....
North End of Tunnel will be fishe.....
made into an inner Distant Signal, and.....
new tall disc (*) Signal will be erected at the
Facing Points and will act as the Down........
Home Signal. It will work on the same.......
wire as the Down Inner Distant Signal....
end of tunnel.
The Up advanced Starting Disc inside the.......*tunnel will be
removed.*
After this working is brought into use.....no shunting of
vehicles must be done at the .....tunnel end of Station after a
Train has been signalled from Sutton Scotney."

* - the words 'tall disc' are crossed through with a pencil on the original notice.

The earlier reference to Twyford was the intended first stop on the originally proposed route south of Winchester on to Southampton. The new Shawford Junction line resulted in the railway passing no nearer than about one mile from the actual village. Indeed completion of the connection to Shawford Junction was the final nail in the coffin relative to independent access south of Winchester, so far as the DNS were concerned, but not so perhaps should a new company be involved. (Such a method was indeed adopted in Wiltshire by the former MSWJ system in building their link from Marlborough to Savernake under the guise of the nominally independent Marlborough and Grafton Railway.) Enter then into the arena a decade later the 'Southampton and Winchester Great Western Junction Railway' who proposed to complete the line south of Winchester following almost the same route as the 1882 prospectus, except that is at Shirley where a more westerly course would be adopted. This

The fact the DNS company had offices at 11 Oxford Street, Southampton has been reported previously.

What may not be so well known is that the precarious financial situation of the company resulted in the following letter address to Capt. W Gipps on 17 July 1900.

"Sir, As I have let the house 11 Oxford Street to you, will you kindly inform the Didcot & Newbury Company of this fact ....it is my request that the rent of offices should have been received by now."

Signed, Matilda Hill, 60 Belle Vue Road, Southampton.

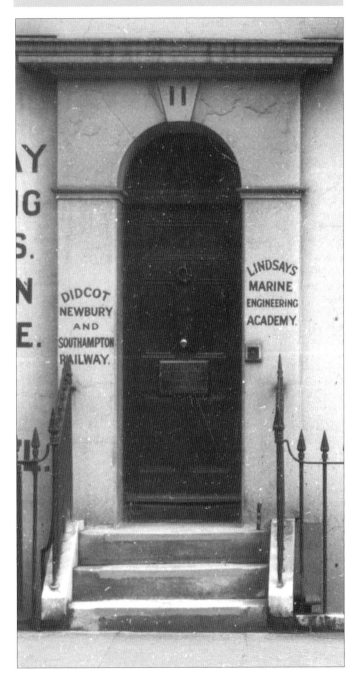

Inscription by the door of the DNS office in Southampton. A London office was also provided.

GREAT WESTERN RAILWAY.

Rifle Contest at Churn,

THURSDAY, JULY 5th.

NOTE.—*Churn is situated between Upton and Compton Stations.*

In connection with this event, the following Railway arrangements will be adopted :—

A Temporary Platform will be erected at Churn where Passengers can leave, and join the under-mentioned trains.

For the convenience of Passengers from London, a Carriage will be detached from the 11.45 a.m. Express train from Paddington at Didcot, at 12.45 p.m. in connection with the 1.0 p.m. train from Didcot to Newbury, which will call at Churn.

In the Evening a Special Train will leave Churn at 6.45 p.m. for Didcot, in connection with the 2.8 p.m. up fast Express from Plymouth to London, which will call at Didcot at 7.9 p.m.

The 10.30 a.m. train from Didcot to Newbury (in connection with the 9.0 a.m. train from Paddington) will call at Churn at 10.45.

The 11.26 a.m. train from Newbury to Didcot, will call at Churn at 12.2 p.m.

A Special Train will leave Churn at 5.55 p.m. for Compton, where Passengers can join the 6.42 p.m. train from that place to Newbury and Stations beyond.

HY. LAMBERT,
General Manager.

PADDINGTON,
July 2nd, 1888.

BURT & SONS, 58, PORCHESTER ROAD, BAYSWATER W.

shown up in the movement of men and materials destined for Southampton en-route to the South African wars. Unfortunately the grandiose sounding S&WGWJR had no more success at securing funds as its earlier counterpart and despite a proposed working agreement between the DNS and GWR for the intended route, signed on 13 January 1902, with no money to allow work to commence the project was stillborn from the outset being finally abandoned in 1905.

The year 1891 had thus witnessed what was destined to be the final extent of the DNS so far as north - south potential were concerned. The various schemes for expansion already referred to coming to nought. One however has deliberately not been mentioned until this point. This was in 1897 (some reports refer to 1899), when a group of DNS shareholders put forward a plan for a 22 mile extension north-east from Didcot which, after crossing the Thames near Wallingford, would follow the Thame valley for several miles to make a connection with the Great Central at Quainton Road near to Aylesbury. Relations between the DNS and GCR had always been cordial and indeed such a link would have afforded considerable advantage to the larger concern so far as access to the south coast were concerned. It is perhaps doubtful that the matter was taken too seriously by the GCR at this time who were then devoting all their energies into the completion of their route to London. Indeed George Dow in his classic trilogy on the history of the GCR fails to refer to the proposal at all. Geographically too the proposed line would not have been a easy task, having to dissect the hills of the Chiltern ridge. Little else is heard of the suggestion although perhaps the GWR, fearful of

company had, the notional at least, backing of the GWR. It was time to fight the battles of 1882 all over again enlivened this time with stories of, '...malicious delays to Didcot line trains at Shawford Junction.....the presence of a light engine on the LSWR would sometimes be sufficient to delay a Didcot train for upwards of an hour....', no doubt the Shawford Junction signalman, an LSWR man, was instructed accordingly!

Whether such obstructive tactics played a part in the success of the 'S & WGWJR' in securing their Act is unlikely. More likely was the point made that the restricted line capacity of the LSWR main line had recently been

such a prospect did enter into an agreement with the GCR to provide a connection from the GWR at Banbury to Woodford Halse on the GCR line. As such trains from the latter could travel south, but on Great Western metals and if the destination was to be Southampton, there was no guarantee the DNS line would be used. Indeed more revenue could be accrued by the GWR as a result of keeping such traffic on its own lines as long as possible, in other words via Reading and Basingstoke. This feature of routing north - south trains via Reading and Basingstoke was an aspect destined to be affect the fortunes of the DNS throughout its independent existence. Nevertheless good relations were

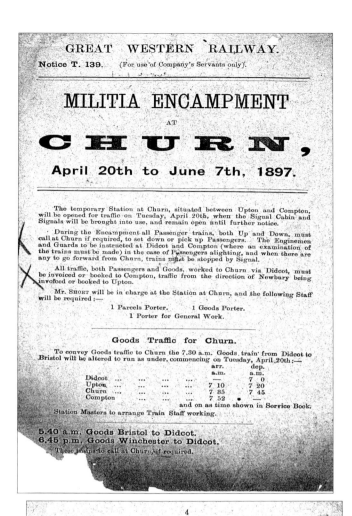

GREAT WESTERN RAILWAY.

Notice T. 139. (For use of Company's Servants only).

MILITIA ENCAMPMENT

AT

CHURN,

April 20th to June 7th, 1897.

The temporary Station at Churn, situated between Upton and Compton, will be opened for traffic on Tuesday, April 20th, when the Signal Cabin and Signals will be brought into use, and remain open until further notice.

During the Encampment all Passenger trains, both Up and Down, must call at Churn if required, to set down or pick up Passengers. The Enginemen and Guards to be instructed at Didcot and Compton (where an examination of the trains must be made) in the case of Passengers alighting, and when there are any to go forward from Churn, trains must be stopped by Signal.

All traffic, both Passengers and Goods, worked to Churn via Didcot, must be invoiced or booked to Compton, traffic from the direction of Newbury being invoiced or booked to Upton.

Mr. SHORT will be in charge at the Station at Churn, and the following Staff will be required :—

1 Parcels Porter.	1 Goods Porter.
1 Porter for General Work.	

Goods Traffic for Churn.

To convey Goods traffic to Churn the 7.30 a.m. Goods train from Didcot to Bristol will be altered to run as under, commencing on Tuesday, April 20th :—

	arr. a.m.	dep. a.m.
Didcot	—	7 0
Upton	7 10	7 20
Churn	7 35	7 45
Compton	7 52	

and on as time shown in Service Book.
Station Masters to arrange Train Staff working.

5.40 a.m. Goods Bristol to Didcot.
6.45 p.m. Goods Winchester to Didcot.
These trains to call at Churn, if required.

MONDAY, APRIL 26th.

Special with 4th Battalion Oxfordshire Light Infantry,
Littlemore to Churn.
(About 170 Officers and Men).

		arr. p.m.	pass	dep. p.m.
Oxford		—		1†15
Kennington Junction			CS	
Wheatley		1†35	X	1†55
Littlemore		2†5		2 25
Kennington Junction	A	2 30		2 36
Didcot (Collect Tickets)		3 0		3 8
Upton			CS	
Churn		3 25		4†0
Compton	B	4†5	X	—
Compton	C		X	5†15
Upton			CS	
Didcot				6†3

† Empty train.
Formation—1 Van, 5 Thirds, 1 Compo, 1 Van, and 1 Milk Truck.
A An engine, accompanied by a Shunter, to be at Kennington Junction to work the train forward.
B Cross 2.46 p.m. from Winchester at Compton.
C Cross 2.45 p.m. Special from Reading at Compton.

Special with Berkshire Light Infantry,
Tilehurst to Churn.
(About 140 Officers and Men).

		arr. p.m.	pass	dep. p.m.
Reading		—		2†45
Tilehurst		2†52		3 30
Cholsey and Moulsford	A	R 3 48 L		
Didcot (Collect Tickets)		4 5		4 17
Upton	B	4 25	X	4 30
Churn		4 40		5†10
Compton	C		CXS	
Hermitage			CS	
Newbury East Junction	D		CXS	
Newbury		5†50		6†0
Reading		6†35		

† Empty train.
Formation—1 Van, 5 Thirds, 1 Compo, 1 Van, and Milk Truck.
A To run to Relief Line at Cholsey and Moulsford, and precede 2.5 p.m. H. & O. train ex Paddington from there.
B Cross 2.46 p.m. from Winchester at Upton.
C Cross 5.15 p.m. Empty train from Compton at Compton.
D Cross 5.30 p.m. R.R. Goods from Newbury at Newbury East ... run.

MONDAY, MAY 10th.

Special with 4th Battalion Oxfordshire Light Infantry,
Littlemore to Churn.
(About 420 Officers and Men).

		arr. p.m.	pass	dep. p.m.
Oxford		—		1†15
Kennington Junction			CS	
Wheatley		1†35	X	1†55
Littlemore		2†5		2 25
Kennington Junction	A	2 30		2 36
Didcot (Collect Tickets)		3 0		3 8
Upton			CS	
Churn		3 25		4†0
Compton	B	4†5	X	—
Compton	C		X	5†15
Upton			CS	
Didcot				6†3

† Empty train.
Formation—1 Van, 11 Thirds, 2 Compos, 1 Van, 2 Horse Boxes, and 1 Milk Truck.
A An Engine, accompanied by a Shunter, to be at Kennington Junction to work the train forward.
B Cross 2.46 p.m. from Winchester at Compton.
C Cross 2.45 p.m. Special from Reading at Compton.

Special with Berkshire Light Infantry,
Tilehurst to Churn.
(About 350 Officers and Men).

		arr. p.m.	pass	dep. p.m.
Reading		—		2†45
Tilehurst		2†52		3 30
Cholsey and Moulsford	A	R 3 48 L		
Didcot (Collect Tickets)		4 5		4 17
Upton	B	4 25	X	4 30
Churn		4 40		5†10
Compton	C		CXS	
Hermitage			CS	
Newbury East Junction	D		CXS	
Newbury		5†50		6†0
Reading		6†35		

† Empty train.
Formation—1 Van, 9 Thirds, 2 Compos, 1 Van, 2 Horse Boxes, and 1 Milk Truck.
A To run to Relief Line at Cholsey and Moulsford, and precede 2.5 p.m. H. & O. train ex Paddington from there.
B Cross 2.46 p.m. from Winchester at Upton.
C Cross 5.15 p.m. Empty train from Compton...
D Cross 5.30 p.m. R.R. Goods from Newbury at Newbury East Junction.

Receipt of this Notice to be acknowledged to the head of Department, on the accompanying form, by First train.

JAS. W. GIBBS,

Superintendent of Reading Division.

READING, April 15th, 1897.

F. W. Starkey, Printer, Oxford Street, Reading.

Opposite and this page - *The area around Churn was part of the estate of Lord Wantage and so it was really no surprise when he suggested the isolated location may be suitable for a rifle contest. As is known, the result would be the stopping place at Churn, renowned later not only for military as well as sporting purposes, but as the only railway stopping place in Berkshire to have no road access - one of only a handful in the UK. (The isolation of Churn would later form the basis for one of the tales in the 1912 volume 'Thrilling Stories of the Railway' by Canon V L Whitechurch entitled 'Sir Gilbert Murrell's Picture.')*

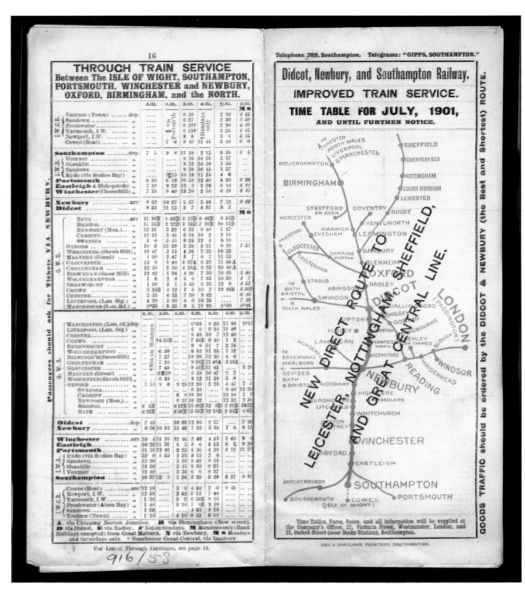

The 1901 DNSR timetable / brochure. Within, pages referred to local services as well as through coaches to Manchester. There were also several pages devoted to the towns and villages along the DNS route proper and their attractions to the visitor. The map viewed on the front cover conveniently ignores all other railways south of Newbury likely to provide an competitive route to the DNS - who could blame them!

maintained between the GCR and DNS, an outward show being the provision of a through coach via the Banbury - Woodford line and which commenced in 1901. (From 1-7-1903 a through restaurant car train was established, leaving Southampton Docks at 7.05 a.m. having connected with the cross channel steamers and thence forming part of the 7.30 a.m. departure from Southampton Terminus via the DNS route. The ultimate destination of this through coaches was Newcastle-on-Tyne where arrival was scheduled for 5.23 p.m.. A return working arrived at Southampton from Didcot late in the evening. Stock for these was provided by the GCR. The service was suspended in 1916 but restored again in 1921 although somewhat altered in that the DNS was only used for the northbound working. The following year 1922, the restaurant car was attached and detached at Oxford but otherwise it continued to run until 1939. At its peak in the years prior to that time there was even the opportunity of a through coach or coaches to Glasgow and Scarborough. See illustrations p84/85.)

The level of train service was one which continued to create animosity between the DNS and Paddington. As an example of this correspondence from 1899 may be quoted in which Paddington were requested to run more trains. The response from the GWR was that already the service provided exceeded that required by the existing traffic levels and that should the DNS insist on more trains then they should also be willing to guarantee a minimum of 1/6d per train mile to cover the requisite costs. In this area the GWR were being no more than reasonable, it was a case of saying, 'put up or shut up'. The DNS apparently decided on the latter option, there being no record of any increase in train service immediately after this time whilst correspondence on the matter abruptly ceased. What is perhaps best described as petty bickering over general costs, facilities, and above all train services and timings would however continue.

By the turn of the century it was 15 years since the line had reached Winchester and despite all the difficulties encountered during this time the DNS had succeeded in continuing to trade independently without the apparent backing or support of the GWR. This would now change, although such change would not become obvious for a few years.

It started on 1 January 1900 when a loan of £16,000 from the LSWR, which had been given to allow the completion of the Shawford Junction extension, was due for repayment. This loan had also accrued interest and due to the inability of the DNS to meet its debts, it is perhaps fortunate the various creditors did not force its liquidation and sale. In an effort to delay repayment, the DNS began negotiating for a further loan of £6,336 7s 6d to cover interest, but then suddenly changed its mind and requested a figure from the LSWR to discharge the debt. As a result £19,160 was agreed which was paid by Lord Wantage - the former Sir Robert Loyd-Lindsay. It was by no means an insignificant sum although in his time as Chairman, Loyd-Lindsay had openly supported the railway in several financial transactions.

It was only after his death in 1914 and in an attempt to settle his estate that the truth was revealed and that the money had in fact been advanced by the GWR. But why such a gesture to the railway after years of ill feeling? Perhaps there was still a fear at Paddington that the precarious financial may even at this late stage result in the route passing out of the control of the DNS and in consequence another company may have ease of access into the Great Western at Newbury and so to Didcot. The only likely player was the LSWR although it must be a matter of conjecture as to whether they would have been interested at this time.

The 1902 working agreement for the ill fated 'Southampton & Winchester Great Western Junction Railway', had been signed on behalf of the DNS by W.H.M. Gipps, the Company's Traffic Manager. He, as is known, had offices at 11 Oxford Street Southampton for which a rental of £30 p.a. was paid to allow use of the first floor at that address. Gipps himself was paid a salary of £500 p.a. an increase from his commencing rate of £300 p.a.. The extra was awarded with effect from 17 June 1897 and no doubt in recognition of his successful efforts at not only securing through traffic for the DNS but in attracting additional local revenue through negotiation with both the GWR and LSWR. (See footnote 8 at this point.) But in this area there were obvious limits, for whilst the GWR were prepared to send an amount of un-consigned north - south traffic via the DNS instead of through Basingstoke clearly it was not in their interest to route all north - south traffic this way as loss of revenue to themselves would understandably occur. Gipps would have realised this and so it is strange to report that in 1896 and again in 1898 he had canvassed the GWR to double the route south of Didcot and send all traffic this way. Not surprisingly such requests were rejected out of hand although perhaps as one of the few senior officers of the DNS who had some practical railway experience he was listened too with some understanding by his Board.

His enthusiasm in such areas could at times create embarrassment, such as when on 10 December 1896 he persuaded the Directors of the DNS to meet with the Directors of the GWR with a view to his proposals for doubling the line. Earl Cawdor for the GWR responded at the meeting in a totally cold manner, to the effect that he knew nothing about any proposal for doubling the line but instead believed the purpose of the gathering was to discuss the purchase of the DNS by the GWR! Any response to or by Gipps is not reported!

Gipps was aware the fortunes of his employers railway were totally dependant upon its market value as a through route to prospective customers. He also acted as General Manager to the little Lambourn Valley Railway Company, a dual role which appeared to have the sanction of the DNS for he was able to persuade his larger masters to permit facilities to the LVR at the Southampton office in return for the little company paying 10% of the property rental costs.

Possibly in consequence of an alarming fall off in receipts reported at the directors meeting of 29 May 1894 a Traffic Committee was inaugurated from 12 June the same year and which in turn had appointed Gipps as Traffic Manager (8). A few years later a further adjunct towards increasing traffic came with the appointment from 6 February 1902 of three 'Traffic Canvassers' to work on an initial 3 months experimental basis at a wage of 25/- weekly (£1.25) plus commission of 3d per ton traffic gained. It is not known if the appointments were continued later.

J.S. Forbes as Chairman of the D.N.& S. was well briefed as to the precarious financial situation of the company. Indeed throughout its 40 odd years of nominal independence it was destined never to pay as much as a penny dividend to the luckless holders of ordinary shares. Forbes though did make efforts to generate extra traffic, one example an undated approach to the GWR over the issue of Sunday trains. This was rejected by Paddington despite Forbes comment that people would wish to visit Winchester Cathedral on a Sunday as much as they would visit Canterbury Cathedral. (Forbes connections with the South Eastern Railway are thus also identified.)

Following his untimely death in 1903, Gipps was succeeded in the post of Traffic Manager by Alfred Price who by 1905 at least was assisted by an Inspector Donohue. It would appear this man had been in post for some time before, as on 20 July 1905 DNS Board Minutes record an increase in his wage from 35/- to 37/6d weekly. A further reference to Donohue occurs in 1911 when Price made a successful application to the Directors for a bicycle to be provided for his Inspector. This was approved subject to the cost not exceeding £5. Although in themselves such oblique references may be of little consequence save perhaps for slight amusement as to costs a century later, what it does suggest is that contrary to the previously supposed theory, the DNS did retain a small number of staff themselves, this number being quoted as four by 1913. (Who the other two staff were is not reported.) It previously being supposed that all staff were provided by the GWR as the operating company.

Rent was also collected from GWR staff who occupied company property, notably the station masters. In

Year Ending	Gross Receipts from Traffic	Passenger Numbers	Goods & Minerals	Earnings mile / week
	£ s d		Tons. cwt.	£ s d
Dec 1882 *	5,806 17 8	43,473	37,058 10	8 18 7
Dec 1883	8,632 15 1	54,850	75,601 12	9 15 3
Dec 1884	9,187 4 5	61,509	69,769 17	10 7 10
Dec 1885 **	13,087 8 11	99,824	81,367 7	9 0 8
Dec 1886	16,101 13 10	130, 130	86,909 19	7 4 0
Dec 1887	16,542 19 5	131,134	89,178 4	7 8 0
Dec 1888	16,751 17 2	131,355	91,228 2	7 9 10
Dec 1889	18,302 19 2	141,443	101,435 4	8 3 8
Dec 1890	19,160 4 4	152,435	101,230 9	8 1 4
Dec 1891	19,515 16 1	137,384	113,229 3	8 14 6
Dec 1892	21,647 0 4	143,513	136,951 16	9 11 2
Dec 1893	20,760 15 10	144,419	124,515 7	9 1 6
Dec 1894	22,739 16 6	162,418	141,154 7	9 15 8
Dec 1895	22,975 2 3	156,903	148,391 12	10 0 10
Dec 1896	24,217 2 7	164,936	153,394 16	10 11 8
Dec 1897	26,243 9 1	184,644	156,741 0	11 9 5
Dec 1898	28,033 6 0	188,263	161,256 10	12 5 0
Dec 1899	29,158 13 6	191,541	174,654 6	12 14 10
Dec 1900	30,886 4 7	199,763	173,980 9	13 10 0
Dec 1901	31,842 0 0	203,744	175,958 14	13 18 4
Dec 1902	34,327 2 2	220,523	192,142 9	15 0 0
Dec 1903	34,613 18 9	225,566	211,280 8	15 2 6
Dec 1904	37,528 18 10	224,177	226,411 17	16 8 1
Dec 1905	36,422 9 10	223,067	214,264 8	15 18 5
Dec 1906	36,478 13 8	222,254	219,718 2	15 18 10
Dec 1907	37,617 14 4	220,922	233,674 10	16 8 10
Dec 1908 *	39,424 16 10	231,489	239,289 8	17 4 7
Dec 1909	40,825 5 9	255,550	248,491 13	17 16 10
Dec 1910	42,222 0 1	257,481	256,764 10	18 9 1
Dec 1911	42,110 6 1	246,401	263,795 8	18 8 1
Dec 1912	42,690 8 3	236.401	252,094 4	18 13 2
Dec 1913	44,692 15 11	251,192	256,568 19	19 10 8
Dec 1914	44,465 14 0	not available		19 8 8
Dec 1915	44,741 18 10	not available		19 11 1
Dec 1916	44,694 17 2	not available		19 10 8
Dec 1917	44,750 4 0	not available		19 11 2
Dec 1918	44,731 10 4	not available		19 11 0
Dec 1919	44,737 14 9	not available		19 11 0
Dec 1920	44.761 19 8	not available		19 11 3
Dec 1921	44,882 15 5	not available		19 12 4
Dec 1922	44,866 16 3	not available		19 12 2

1904 this was quoted as £5 p.a. for cottage rental but the following year had risen from 2/- to 2/6d weekly at most stations, equivalent to £5. 4/- to £5 10/- per annum. The exception was at Winchester, where no doubt due to the importance of the Station Master post an annual rental of £10 was deducted. (It is not certain how many houses, aside from those at or adjoining the stations, were actually owned or rented by the railway. Some suggestion has been made that at Winchester a number of terraced dwellings in Bar End Road may well have been erected for the use of railway staff. Likewise George Behrend has referred to railway cottages at Kings Worthy. It would appear a house was also rented for the Station Master at Hampstead Norris. Aside though from the obvious railway style station / house at or near the various stopping places, the DNS. design structure does not appear elsewhere.)

The subject of rental accrued from the occupancy of the station houses was a matter of some debate between the DNS and GWR which was destined to continue for some years. The first time this occurred was on 2 December 1900 when Gipps reported that the DNS had not been credited with the monies due to them. In approaching the GWR accountant he was met with a blank response, '.....these are GWR men and the money therefore goes to the GWR...'. Gipps however was not prepared to let matters rest and eventually secured a £1,000 credit from Paddington together with adjustments on outstanding finances re various other works carried out and at that time owed to the Great Western. Despite such success, disagreement would continue on the issue until at least 1905 by which time Gipps successor, Alfred Price commented, 'I have nothing definite to report on this matter to the (Board) meeting on Thursday evening. I am still in correspondence with the GW Company'. Any further outcome is not reported.

Traffic Carried.

A detailed breakdown of figures for actual traffic at the individual stations is generally not available for the years prior to 1903. One exception is fortunately found in the minute books of the DNS company which records gross earnings against passenger numbers and goods tons. Dates are also quoted and although not referred to as such may be presumed to refer to the previous 12 months.

Period ended 23-2-1899

Gross receipts;
Didcot - Newbury   £7273 14s 9d
Passenger numbers   41,124

Goods tons.   41,363
Gross receipts;
Newbury - Winchester   £7755 0s 4d
Passenger numbers   65,099
Goods tons.   30,733
Period ended 1-1-1900

Gross receipts;
Didcot - Newbury   £6850 3s 7d
Passenger numbers   39,982
Goods tons.   41,238
Gross receipts;
Newbury Winchester   £7858 18s 2d
Passenger numbers   67,916
Goods tons.   31,802
Gross receipts;
Winchester - Shawford Junction   £ 460 8s 6d

The greater tonnage of goods on the northern section may well be accounted for by through traffic from the Great Western, whilst the increased passenger figures south of Newbury is probably explained in the importance of stations such as Whitchurch and Winchester together with the actual number of stations south of Newbury (8 compared with 5 north of Newbury). Interestingly a footnote appears against the 1900 figures to explain the fall off for the Didcot to Newbury section which refers to less men having been at Churn camp.

Two final entries appear against the years 1899/1900 and relate to revenue generated by traffic to and from the Winchester Agricultural show. These are for the period ending 23-2-1899; £438 3s, and for 1-1-1900; £460 8s 6d.

An associated entry sometime afterwards gives the earnings per mile figure that these and other receipts represent;

Period ended   12/1898   £13.10s 5d
              1/ 1/1900   13. 5. 2d - even so both the figures for year ending 12/1898 and 1/1/1900 are at variance with later published figures for the whole story of the company as released in 1923.
              17/8/1900   12. 14. 8d
               7/3/1901   14. 5. 3d
              16/ 8/1901   12. 4. 7d

Between the years 1895 and 1901 various improvements were made in the passenger service at the instigation of Forbes. The first of these was the introduction

Opposite page -

* Earnings only from 13 April 1882 when the line between Didcot and Newbury was opened.

** The decrease in earnings per mile is explained with the opening of the line between Newbury and Winchester which immediately led to increased operating costs.

Approximately 65% of earnings was taken up with operating costs paid to the GWR and to a lesser degree the LSWR, but in addition to this what revenue remained was taken up either by payment of the guaranteed dividend to holders of Preference shares or by paying off earlier loans taken out when that had been insufficient revenue for this same dividend.

Carrier / outside porter at Winchester.

of a new 'fast' service from Didcot: given this designation as it omitted stops at certain stations. Despite such kudos the sporadic service as existed at that time meant the train would pass by stations where passengers were waiting. Accordingly by 1902 it is shown in the timetables as omitting stops at just Upton and Hampstead Norris, although a footnote in the timetable for the latter location stated, 'Calls to pick up passengers for London on notice being given at the Station not later than 12.30 p.m.'. Shortly afterwards it assumed the role of an all stations service.

Of greater significance was the introduction from 1 July 1897 of a through Southampton to Paddington via Newbury service with one train in each direction daily. As previously a number of stops were omitted, although in the 'up' direction there was some flexibility as the train would stop to collect passengers for London from either Whitchurch and Burghclere as well as at its booked stops of Winchester and Sutton Scotney (the choice of having Sutton Scotney as a regular stopping place in preference to Whitchurch would appear slightly strange). The return journey was theoretically non-stop between Newbury and Winchester although this time it would pause at any of the intermediate stations to set down passengers from London on notice being given to the guard at Newbury.

A further increase in train speeds came with the provision of a coach slipped at Newbury off a morning Paddington - Weymouth train. This was then taken forward calling only at Whitchurch and Winchester and according to Sands, with 19 minutes allowed for the 12½ miles south of Whitchurch afforded the fastest ever booked service on the line - an average speed of 39½ m.p.h.. Certainly speeds higher than that stated were not uncommon in everyday working but except when delays were caused by a late crossing at one of the intermediate passing loops, the timetable was liberal enough to afford a degree of latitude. With slight variance these trains continued to run until the 1914-18 war but were not subsequently restored.

North of Newbury journey times varied from 37 - 49 minutes, figures that would remain little altered for the life of the railway. Possibly the fastest service on this section appeared in the timetable for July - September 1894, shown leaving Didcot at 3.05 p.m. and running non stop to Newbury in just 32 minutes, an average speed of just under 33 m.p.h.. Elsewhere in the timetables a few intermediate stops appear to have been omitted mainly in the years prior to 1914 after which the service was almost always an 'all stations' journey.

Despite this there could still be long gaps between trains, in 1894 for example there was a 4-hour gap between 'up' trains after the departure of the 10.20 a.m.. Attempting to travel south was little better, for in 1902 the gap between services from Didcot for Newbury was from 2.57 p.m. until 7. 20 p.m.! Matters did improve marginally later, although with the limited train service of 5-6 runs each way daily these were not isolated examples.

Mixed trains appeared in the timetables until at least 1906 - and possibly later. Mostly they were the first 'down' service from Didcot through to Winchester, regretfully no photographs of such workings have been located.

Despite the limited success the company achieved in attracting regular traffic, there were occasions when undoubted one-off success did occur. One of these was in 1910 in consequence of the second Royal Counties Agricultural Show at Winchester. This has been mentioned briefly already and together with detail of certain other special events, was referred to in a report of 12 July 1910 prepared by Alfred Price.

"Jas. G. Vokes Esq.
Dear Sir,

The following particulars of Traffic etc, will be of interest to the Directors at the Traffic Committee on Thursday next.

Royal Counties Agricultural Show. Winchester.

"The Agricultural Show at Winchester closed on Friday June 10th. The last day was unfortunately very wet, and the passenger traffic was, in consequence, much smaller than it would otherwise have been.

On the three proceeding days, Tuesday, Wednesday & Thursday we had very heavy passenger traffic to and from

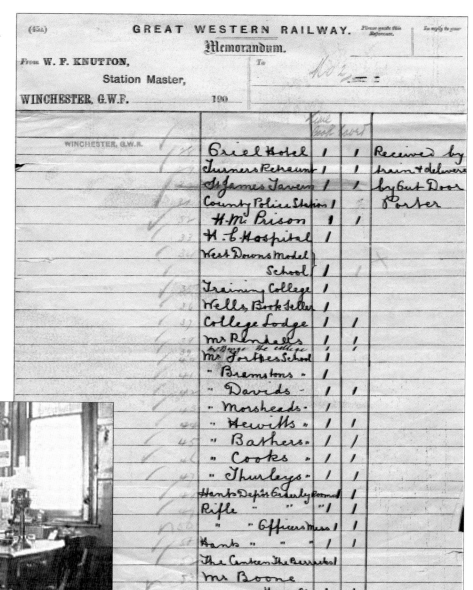

Winchester by ordinary trains and special excursion trains.

Below I give particulars of the number of wagons of exhibits, machinery live stock etc etc, conveyed to and from the show by this company's route:-

Live Stock. Inwards 82 wagons. Outwards 82 wagons.

Machinery etc. Inwards 294 wagons. Outwards 511 wagons. Total - 675 wagons.

We also had 70 consignments of poultry inwards and 186 consignments of poultry outwards.

A large proportion of the timber used in the construction of the show ground was also secured to our route viz;- 39 wagons - 103 tons.

Newbury Races. June 21st & 22nd.

Special Trains were run to Newbury on both dates and were well filled. On the first day we had 33 passengers from Southampton and on the second day 83 passengers from Southampton.

Royal Mail Company's Sale of Old Stores etc. June 16th.

From this sale we secured 13 tons of traffic for London.

Excursion to Anglo Japanese Exhibition.

An excursion train was run from Winchester to Shepherds Bush on June 25th, by which we had about 300 passengers.

Bournemouth Centenery Fetes.

I arranged with the Great Western Railway company for the issue of cheap tickets to Bournemouth by ordinary trains from stations on our line, daily during the continuance of the fetes. I also arranged a day excursion train to Bournemouth

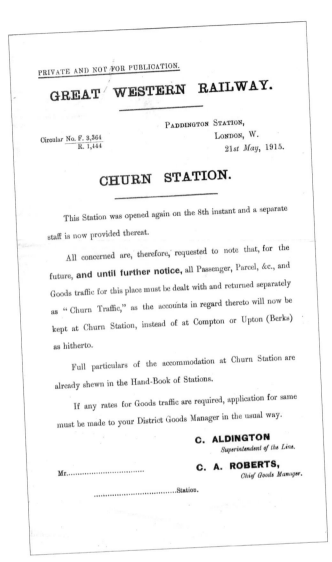

GREAT WESTERN RAILWAY.

PADDINGTON STATION,
LONDON, W.

Circular No. F. 3,364
R. 1,444

21st May, 1915.

CHURN STATION.

This Station was opened again on the 8th instant and a separate staff is now provided thereat.

All concerned are, therefore, requested to note that, for the future, **and until further notice,** all Passenger, Parcel, &c., and Goods traffic for this place must be dealt with and returned separately as "Churn Traffic," as the accounts in regard thereto will now be kept at Churn Station, instead of at Compton or Upton (Berks) as hitherto.

Full particulars of the accommodation at Churn Station are already shewn in the Hand-Book of Stations.

If any rates for Goods traffic are required, application for same must be made to your District Goods Manager in the usual way.

C. ALDINGTON
Superintendent of the Line.

C. A. ROBERTS,
Chief Goods Manager.

Mr..............................

..............................Station.

from Reading and stations to Winchester inclusive on Monday July 11th. This train was well filled.
Excursions to Isle of Wight etc.

I have arranged the usual day excursion trains from London, Birmingham etc to Southampton in connection with the Isle of Wight Steam Packet Company's excursions round the Island during July and August. This year I have arranged an earlier arrival at Southampton which will, I think, be of advantage.

Yours truly,

Alfred W. Price."

Whether such momentum at gaining additional traffic was maintained is unclear. But notwithstanding such increases, it was as if subsequent to 1905 the directors were almost resigned to their fate. The DNS railway would not and could not afford a reasonable return to the shareholders as long as the GWR retained a controlling interest. Aside from the aspirations of an independent route to Southampton, matters may well have been different had the railway not been dependant upon the GWR for the provision of locomotives and rolling stock. On this topic there does not appear to have ever been any suggestion as to an alternative and which could only have been through the LSWR or by DNS owned equipment. Indeed it was as if the GWR were content to afford the little company just enough room for manoeuvre to prevent either bankruptcy or direct involvement by the LSWR, but never enough to allow for any possible expansion.

Why then did the DNS not sell out to the GWR early on? Probably simply because many of the directors were the holders of ordinary shares and which would have been virtually worthless at the time of any takeover. But that is not to say the matter was never discussed - the abortive meeting of December 1896 notwithstanding. Instead in 1903 considerable correspondence was generated between the Directors and Mr. F.P. Robjent, described as an 'Independent Financial Advisor' of Newport, Glamorgan, who was also a shareholder in the DNS. Clearly in this way Robjent could hardly be described as being totally independent, although what his actual financial stake was in the railway is not reported. Robjent reported to the Board the obvious, that under the mantle of control exercised by the GWR the DNS were hardly independent and that their only possible hope for expansion was either to be totally independent or to reach Southampton. In this respect Robjent hoped the Directors could interest the GWR in a rapid take-over. His conclusions were that if the correct options were put forward there would be some recompense for all shareholders. Unfortunately no detail is given as to how this happy state of affairs may have been achieved and especially bearing in mind no dividend had been paid to the holders of ordinary shares since the time the line opened.

Possibly his idea was to encourage expansion whilst powers to build the 1902 'Southampton & Winchester Great Western Junction Railway' were still alive. Certainly this is referred to in his letters, for as such the GWR could have saved a degree of face with the LSWR whilst achieving a direct link to the coast. The GWR would thus not be seen as openly pushing for Southampton themselves. But it was destined not to be and instead the Directors voted to maintain their independence within the constraints imposed by Paddington.

But the straight jacket imposed by the GWR had also been identified elsewhere. For in April 1907 another share-holder, the Rt. Hon. Sir F.R. Falkiner - was this a relation of T.H. Falkiner, one half of the contractors 'Falkiner & Tancred' who had been paid partly in shares when the line was built - sent a memo to the Board initially outlining the unsatisfactory working of the railway by the GWR. Possibly no satisfactory response was forthcoming for this was followed by four pages of neatly and closely typed script covering a multitude of perceived errors and inadequacies over the working agreement and against the GWR.

Such a report would normally have been expected to draw a reasoned response but instead it was almost as if a few home truths had been raised and the response of the DNS was to almost plead with Falkiner to withdraw what was established as the only copy. The document itself,

'Station Road' Kingsclere probably around 1900. Four possible proposals for railways to serve the village were suggested. The most likely the Aldermaston to Burghclere line which would have involved a station near to the present day roundabout on the A339. Station Road has long since been renamed Newbury Road and indeed may have had this name before the short-lived change to Station Road, in the belief the coming of the railway was imminent. At least two of the properties seen remain intact, that on the left is known as 'The Old House', its roof dormers and front door still visible. A surviving low wall also indicates where the railings once stood. To the right is 'Ivy Cottage', its windows too a distinctive feature. At the end of the first set of railings it is possible to discern an opening to what was 'Frogs Hole'.

which survives at Kew under the reference, 'RAIL 1057/813' also carries various hand written responses from an unknown hand clearly attempting to address the issues raised. But Falkiner had researched his subject thoroughly, for instead of the DNS being able to refute the issues raised, only in matters of detail were items found wanting. Just as others had done previously, so Falkiner also suggested negotiations should take place with the GWR over a possible take over. It must then be conjecture as to why the whole issue was not pursued further, Falkiner intimates he would be moving abroad shortly afterwards so perhaps in some way this was a loop-hole for the DNS to escape through. What was needed was perhaps a man with the character of Gipps to negotiate with the GWR. Instead it was almost as if the DNS board now displayed the behavioural patterns of an ostrich.

So why did the GWR never support the DNS openly or otherwise, for to do so would certainly have given them access to Southampton. On this we cannot be certain, perhaps it would have opened up similar requests for

financial assistance from any number of other worked lines, perhaps it was lack of available finance, or perhaps it was simply to avoid open hostility with the LSWR. Probably the latter is the most likely, already the GWR and LSWR came into contact at a number of locations, Basingstoke, Salisbury and Exeter the most obvious. In two out of the three the GWR was the minor player, it was probably not worth the potential difficulties elsewhere to support what was a minor venture. Even so, with hindsight such inaction must be considered regrettable and a lost opportunity.

The whole situation was perhaps best hinted at by the last Chairman of the DNS, Frederick Beresford Turner, who in the presentation of the final Report of Directors and Statement of Accounts to the shareholders AGM at Caxton Hall, London on 23 February 1923, stated;

".....(For the year ended 31 December 1922.). It is with feelings of much regret that your Directors are compelled to sever their long connection with the Railway after their many years of strenuous effort to improve the position of the Company and make it a dividend paying concern. While

The new railway running at the foot of St Catherine's Hill south of Winchester - from the state of the fresh chalk also not long after 1891. Beyond is the Itchen Navigation, at this time still seemingly in reasonable repair. Between the railway and waterway is the original narrow public road. This was superseded by the Winchester by-pass in the 1930s and then the M3 sixty years later.

A few years later and slightly south - it is possible to orientate the two images from the underbridge and navigation. Now foliage has covered the previously bleak embankment side - notice too the increase in crossbars and insulators on the railway telegraph poles - most probably due to improved communication but perhaps with some wires rented out to the GPO.

their hopes in that respect have unfortunately not been allowed sufficient time to meet with actual success, the receipts of the Line had materially increased for many years until the upward movement was arrested by legislation stereotyping the earnings of the Railway under the scheme of Control in conjunction with the Great War...".

As in previous years Debenture Stock holders received their due interest but similarly there was no such good fortune to the holders of the £307,210 of ordinary stock. Their investment was never repaid, a gaunt reminder of their lost capital still existing a century later in the surviving earthworks of the 44 miles of cuttings and embankments between Didcot and Winchester.

The Unfinished and Proposed Lines.

Had of course the various extensions and connections proposed over the years been completed then the story of the DNS railway company may well have been very different. In consequence this may be an appropriate point to briefly recount those proposals for expansion which were destined not to appear and which have not been previously referred to within the text.

Geographically north - south ;
Didcot - Micheldever - this was the first 1873 proposal for a line under the auspices of the then DNSJR company. The later built railway would follow its course almost exactly

from Didcot as far as Newbury but at the latter point there would be no connection with the GWR and instead the line would continue over the Great Western and then almost due south under Greenham Common to a point north of what was Burghclere station. South of Litchfield a deviation from the later built line would see the route pass near to Laverstoke House, the property of Mr. Melville Portal and who under an agreement could require the construction of a 700yd. tunnel together with a station.

Upton (sic) to Lambourn - October 1899 proposal for a 17½ mile light railway to run from Lambourn via Kingston Lisle and Wantage to Upton. This actually got as far as having a prospectus issued in which it was stated the construction costs would be £5,000 per mile and the proposed line would, '...serve a population of some 15,000 at present mainly devoid of rail connection...'. (Clearly it was prudent not to mention the Wantage Tramway which had been in operation since 1875!) Other than references to the proposal in both the DNS and Lambourn Valley Companies minute books of the period, nothing else is heard of the scheme.

Compton - East Ilsley - authorised as part of the original DNS route in 1879 and diverging north of Compton station to run almost due west for some 2½ miles. For reasons that were probably financial, the branch was never built although there is also a distinct lack of information on the route in the

BILL FOSTER'S BURGHCLERE

Bill Foster comes from a GWR family. His father started as a signal box booking boy, his grandfather worked on the track whilst his great-grandfather was reputedly one of Brunel's men.

Fred Foster (Bill's father) clearly had ambitions beyond simply recording train times, for he took and was successful in passing courses in railway signalling and later station accountancy so enabling him to apply for the post of Station Master at Burghclere. The family, Fred, his wife and son Bill, arrived at Burghclere around 1937. Fred destined to be the last holder of the Station Master post at the station.

Bill's mother outside the station.

Why Burghclere is not certain. Bill is of the opinion the prospect of having a house for his family probably appealed, although the Hampshire countryside and limited train service was a far cry from his father's previous railway experience in the London area.

Bill recalls life at Burghclere as being idyllic. As a small boy there was always so much to do and see which included using the railway as an extension of his playground. He would regularly be given a lift on the footplate - 'Duke' class engines are recalled, whilst another pastime was to climb into the guard's van of the up goods and hide in the locker where the Guard kept his flags and shunter's pole. Never was there a thought he might be missed, get lost or be forgotten. The Guard somehow always knowing when to open the locker ready to set him down on the track at the signal beyond the bridge on the way to Highclere. (For reasons not recalled, he never repeated this experience on the way south to Litchfield.) Another occasion saw Bill climb to the top of one of the signals, where he recalls he was photographed.

Bill does not recall the lime-quarry in operation but does remember a water tank wagon arriving and unusually a camping coach parked in the siding. He is certain that is what it was, with a set of wooden steps provided to gain access from the ground and men and women in 'hikers' attire entering and leaving. Possibly a one off event.

Regular family visits came in the form of Uncle Alec and his children who would arrive on Sunday by car. Uncle Alec was a shrewd businessman who enjoyed the lifestyle his business gave him. Bill wonders if the sight of his older female cousins sunbathing on the bank by the station was enough to cause ructions with the local squire?

The family moved on before the war, Fred Foster returning to the signalling grades where he progressed up the promotion ladder in the signal boxes at Greenford West, Greenford East, Park Royal - which had all the windows blown out in WW2, Ladbrook Grove, Portobello Sidings, Paddington No 1 and finally Old Oak Common East.

Bill too joined the railway and spend a few years as a fireman at Old Oak Common. This included some memorably experiences, one when he cleaned one side of an engine, went away for a few moments but when he had returned it had gone out to traffic: half clean / half dirty, also when he covered for an absent colleague on the down 'Red Dragon' express, aged just 17.

Bill's playground: what was probably the down starting signal located on the platform close by the signal box.

Years later Bill and his family returned to Burghclere for a visit. Here he chanced to meet Bill Hiscock, a former Burghclere signalman who was then living in the station house. Bill Foster's opening comment was, "I used to live here as a child". Bill Hiscock remembered instantly, as he had been a young porter / signalman at the station in the late 1930s.

Bill and his young cousin Valerie on the forecourt.

NEWBURY RAILWAY STATION, 1906,

Which will henceforth be an important Junction on the main line express route between the Metropolis and the West of England. The G.W.R. Co. have voted £50,000 on account of a New Station and Works at Newbury.

The original Newbury station complete with overall roof (sometime between 1900 and 1908) which, as the caption comments, was due to be swept away and rebuilt. What the caption does not say was that this was almost entirely at the expense of the DNS! On the extreme left is the bay provided for Lambourn line trains - notice the extended canopy along the platform. To the right the bay here was used by Winchester services although no such canopy extension was provided! Out of sight at the opposite end of the station was another bay used by services to Didcot. On the extreme right the siding contains a motley collection of stock including horse-boxes.

minute books. Until recently it was also understood that no work had ever commenced, however, a new study has revealed a grass covered embankment some 150 yards long within Compton village which would appear to be on the route of the proposed branch. This *may* then be evidence that work did commence, albeit briefly, the embankment a useful dumping ground for spoil excavated perhaps from the deep cutting south of Upton.

Shaw (Hermitage) to Lambourn - the first proposal for a railway from Lambourn to Newbury intended to connect with the fledgling DNS in the parish of Shaw, one mile north of Newbury. The proposed line was rejected by Parliament in 1881. (7).

Newbury - under the terms of the DNSJR. Act of 9 July 1880, a number of variations were made to the original 1873 proposal which included junction connections with the GWR either side of Newbury. Powers however were also contained for the DNSJR. to still build an independent line between these junctions should it later be required. (A graphic example of an almost identical situation would occur at Savernake a few years later.)

Highclere - Kingsclere - Basingstoke - October 1899 proposal for a 13 mile line to be built under the auspices of the 1896 Light Railways Act to run from a junction immediately south of Highclere Station through Echinswell (for Sydmonton), Kingsclere, Wolverton (for Hannington and Baughurst), Ramsdell (for Baughurst and Tadley), Monk Shere, and Sherbourn St. John. to the LSWR near Worting Junction west of Basingstoke. The estimated cost of construction was put at £60,000. Gipps adds the rider that he felt such a scheme would be likely to be opposed by the GWR and perhaps then with a view to not wishing to upset Paddington added, "I scarcely think it would be sufficiently advantageous (referring to the DNS) to make it worthwhile taking an active part in its promotion at the present time and especially having regard to the fact that it would probably be opposed by the GW Company". Some indication as the level of interest from the local populace as to the proposal can be gauged in that just £480 was raised by the promoters.

Highclere to Kingsclere - A line but extending from Highclere just as far as   Kingsclere is referred to again within the minutes of the DNS Traffic Committee for 4

February 1902. This time the response of the DNS is slightly different to the above as approval was given for a connection at Highclere should the railway be constructed. It was also minuted that, '...it was in the company's interest to assist in raising capital should it be necessary.' No detail as to the promoters are given nor as to the actual route to be followed. The DNS themselves were of course hardly in a position to assist financially although it is doubtful if this was the principal factor in the project not going ahead.

Aldermaston to Burghclere - commencing from the GWR near the 45¼ mile post west of Aldermaston this was a 10½ mile line running south and west to join the DNS just north of Burghclere and so provide a direct link to Reading and Paddington avoiding Newbury. Authorised as part of the 1882 DNS Act, no work was ever commenced. Intermediate stations were proposed at Brimpton and also at Kingsclere where in anticipation of the railway what is now Newbury Road was temporarily renamed Station Road. (See illustration page 39.) The actual site for a suggested stopping place within the village is not precisely clear. The most likely location to have been where the proposed railway would have crossed the road just south of the present A339 junction.

Burghclere to Kingsclere - although referred to as a c1902 proposal for a Light Railway between the points mentioned, there is some doubt now as to whether this suggested line was in fact that mentioned above in 1899 between Highclere and Basingstoke via Kingsclere.

Whitchurch to Chilbolton - part of a suggestion made by Mr. Benjamin G. Lake, of Messrs. Lake, Beaumont and Lake, solicitor to the DNS contained in a letter sent to the General Managers of the GWR and LSWR on 5 September 1879.

Whitchurch Loops - connections to and from the LSWR at Whitchurch and which, according to 1880 plans, would have allowed both DNS and eastbound LSWR services at the LSWR Whitchurch station to reach Micheldever. Under the DNS Act of 1882 with the former company authorised to extend southwards, the loop would have taken the form of a connection for southbound DNS trains to reach the LSWR facing towards Andover. Suitable connections between the rails would allow LSWR services direct access north toward Newbury. According to the redoubtable railway historian T. B. Sands, the LSWR also suggested a further loop at

Micheldever allowing trains from Newbury to swing north toward Basingstoke. This would thus have created a triangle at that point. From an operational viewpoint such an additional facility would appear superfluous. (A connection at Micheldever had been the original furthest point south intended for the DNSJ.R. Co. (sic). It was only later that a destination in keeping with the company title was adopted, viz. Southampton, and plans for the Whitchurch - Micheldever line abandoned.)

Winchester Junction - more exactly described as the location where the D.N.& S. dissected the LSWR via a bridge under and at the same point where the Mid Hants

The beginning (and end) of the DNS station at Winchester - now the footway to the multi-storey car park that occupies the site of the passenger station. The buildings either side of the approach may still be identified, indeed the route is officially called 'Old Station Approach'. The name perhaps somewhat ironic as this was the newer of the two stations at Winchester, the original 'old' station, on the former LSWR line still operating. How many will recall the advertising boards, the lamps and the various notices - few perhaps. Fewer still may even have heard of the time from 1885 to around 1891 when Didcot engine drivers and firemen would lodge at Winchester in-between turns of duty. Evidently there was a recognised locoman's lodging house, probably nearer Bar End. Where this was and who might have been the landlady will probably now never be known.

Railway (Winchester Junction to Alton) diverged from the LSWR main line. Here a number of connections were proposed over the years including one authorised in 1882 on the south west side of the intersection. Despite protestations by the LSWR this was never built.

Another suggestion is dated 10 May 1913 for the same location, and was for the LSWR to utilise the DNS as a relief route around Winchester. This could have been achieved with the construction of a ¾ mile spur between the two companies from south of Wallers Ash tunnel to north of Kings Worthy. An alternative route for the spur is also given on an undated plan - but no doubt emanating from the same period - this time for a connection on the north west side, running from the DNS to face north into the LSWR. This same document continues with a recommendation that the DNS would then have to be doubled from Sutton Scotney south to accommodate the

additional traffic which should not be arduous as, '...on this section everything is provided for a double line and the cost of doubling should not therefore be very great.' Shortly afterwards it continues,'...I should also like to see the section between Winchester and Shawford Junction doubled, a distance of 2 miles 16 chains, but on this section there is the question of the viaduct, near Shawford Junction, which was most unfortunately constructed for a single line only. The cost of widening this viaduct would I fear be very heavy.' Having set the proposal, the anonymous compiler goes on to promote the advantages to be gained by both DNS and LSWR companies although naturally this is heavily weighed in favour of the former with tolls able to be charged to the LSWR. Indeed it was almost as if the DNS compiler was desperate for the work to go ahead for towards the end of his narrative he suggests an additional loop running south east to allow southbound LSWR to join the DNS one mile north of Kings Worthy Station. Whether this was to be co-terminus with the previously mentioned proposal or an alternative location is not clear. In this it almost appears as desperation, something the LSWR no doubt realised and nothing more came of the suggestion.

In the 1930's two radically opposing proposals also appeared for connections between the two companies at this point. The first was in connection with the building of the Winchester by-pass which would have meant the use of part of the trackbed south of Bar End for the new road and as a result abandonment of the line south of Winchester Junction - in similar way to that suggested in 1882. Due to the strategic importance of the line this was not acted upon. The second suggestion is only recorded as a red line drawn on a 1930's Ordnance Survey map located in B.R. Archives and shows a connection almost identical to that again previously reported by the anonymous DNS scribe in 1913 but with the footnote that this would allow southbound SR traffic to bypass Winchester SR station.

Winchester to Southampton - an independent route south of Winchester was authorised as part of the 1882 DNS Act but never completed due to financial constraints. From Winchester the proposed line was to the east side of the Itchen Valley past Twyford to Colden Common from whence it turned west to cross the LSWR main line at Allbrook north of Eastleigh. Continuing west the route took in Chandlers Ford before crossing over the Eastleigh to Romsey line before turning south west and passing a little east of Chilworth. Here there would have been a tunnel, 379 yards long under Chilworth Common and then down the valley to Shirley passing under Winchester Road near to its junction with Wilton Road. Stations would have been at Twyford, Allbrook, Chilworth, Shirley, Southampton Town, and Southampton Pier. The last named on a short extension

beyond the main station at the end of Bargate Street. Earthworks were commenced in parts of Southampton and where in 2013 the traces of the proposed course can still be discerned. (Winchester Road at its junction with St. James Road in the form of a sunken playing field which is part of the opened out cutting, also in the area between Hill Lane and The Polygon where part of an embankment may just be discerned. A station was also proposed to serve the Shirley area of Southampton and in consequence 'Didcot Road', 'Newbury Road' and 'Station Road' were christened. The latter had its name changed to 'Stratton Road' in 1905 when it was realised no railway would be provided.)

Winchester to Shirley - this was an actual suggestion by Gipps referred to in undated correspondence. Again it was an effort to break the strangle hold on operations that terminated effectively at Winchester. His suggestion was for a line from Winchester following the course of the previously proposed route but terminating at Shirley. From this it was hoped to gain access into the lucrative football and cricket traffic to the area - both grounds were then within a mile of the Shirley area. Gipps continued that a possible extension could be made later to the centre of the town (Southampton) "as funds permit". It would have been a most expensive extension intended for only occasional traffic. As would be expected the project was destined to exist only as a paper suggestion although somewhere along the way the geography of the area was seriously corrupted as the proposed route from Winchester to Shirley is referred to as via Chandlers Ford and Hamble!

Moving ahead in time slightly, the idea of an extension to Southampton and on basically an identical route to that originally proposed in 1882 was resurrected again in 1900 under the title the 'Southampton & Winchester Great Western Junction Railway'. Promoted by shareholders of the DNS company which in consequence of the LSWR

Left - Commemorative silver platter inscribed, "Presented to W H H M Gipps Esq.. on his marriage by the Directors & Officers of the Didcot, Newbury & Southampton Railway as a mark of their esteem and regard. July 18th 1899." The original is almost 10" in diameter, hallmarked, and produced by Mappin Bros of Regent Street. It appeared at a railwayana auction in 2012 and was fortunately saved by a collector rather than being melted down for scrap or having the inscription removed. Sadly the marriage was destined to be a short one for Gipps died in 1903 (see page 29). We know nothing of his bride, nor how decades later the platter was to eventually end up in an antique shop in the west country before finding its way to auction. There is an indication (the London Gazette 9 November 1897) that Gipps had served in the Royal Artillery, as he is mentioned as having been promoted Captain from 10 November 1897. Assuming this is the same Gipps, it should be mentioned that he had been employed by the DNS since 1894 having previously worked for the LNWR..

Courtesy private collector

To the Directors of

The Great Western Railway Company.

In consideration of your permitting me to walk upon the ~~your~~ Line of Railway between *a point 2" 15* and a point *8 : 14½* *chns* from *Newbury on the Didcot Newbury + Southampton Junction Railway in the Parishes of East Woodhay Highclere and Burghclere in the County of Berks* I do hereby acknowledge and declare that such permission is, and shall at all times be exercised by me, upon the express condition that the Great Western Railway Company are not to be held liable, either to me or to my representatives, for any pecuniary or other responsibility, for loss of life or personal injury, or loss of or damage to property however caused that I may sustain in the exercise of such permission. And I do hereby undertake and agree at all times to keep the Great Western Railway Company well and effectually indemnified against all pecuniary and other responsibility, costs, damages and loss (if any) which may be incurred or sustained by them in respect of the causes aforesaid, or any of them, or in any way incidental to or occasioned by the exercise of the permission hereby granted; and I do also admit and declare that the Great Western Railway Company are at liberty at any time, and from time to time, either temporarily or wholly, to withdraw such permission.

Dated this *Twelfth* — day of *July* One thousand eight hundred and *Ninety two.*

Witness,

W. Y. Hall
Highclere Estate office

George Sexton
July 12th 1892

Below - Highclere station looking south and not Burghclere as indicated by the photographer. (The confusion arising as the location was indeed in the Parish of Burghclere.) The scene is not quite as built, although certainly as it appeared shortly after 1910 when the loop had been extended north at this end of the platform, and for the time with modern bull-head fittings. The original vignoles flat-bottom rail may be seen running through the platforms on both lines. Highclere was where Queen Victoria would have alighted when visiting Highclere castle - hence also the name of the station. (Could this also be why there had been the extension of the loop, to assist in dealing with special workings?) (See also caption to image page 69.)

Left - A walking permit from, 12 July 1892. Such permits were issued as an 'at your own risk' facility to allow gamekeepers and suchlike to access the railway between set points. This one was from 2m 15ch to 8m 14½chs, where the railway adjoined land belonging to the Highclere estate.

Burghclere Station.
8105.

Tothill cutting looking north circa 1919, the infamous bridge carrying what was later the A34: at the time known simply as the Newbury to Winchester road, is in the background. (Road designations, 'A', 'B' etc, were first used from 1923 onwards, using a system originally planned some years earlier but interrupted by WW1. The designation started to appear in road atlas' shortly afterwards. The stop signal is the Highclere down home signal, positioned on the outside of the curve for maximum visibility. In 1942/3 the passing loop was extended from the station as far as Tothill bridge. Tothill was the location where the original 'covered way', (elongated bridge) failed during construction. This failure was due to instability of the soil in the area. Years later the same message had to be learnt all over again with the building of the A34 Newbury by-pass, as slippage of the cutting sides occurred on a regular basis both during construction and subsequent to the road opening. (A cruel enlargement reveals the bridge in its original state prior to the additional support being added.) The gradient post (indicated), is the summit of the second highest point on the line south of Newbury and marks the end of the climb which had begun at Enborne Junction. The railway is now on a falling gradient through Highclere to the approximate mid-way point between Highclere and Burghclere after which it climbs again to the true summit of the route south of Burghclere.

affording part of the finance for the Shawford Junction connection could not be seen to be openly backing it for themselves, here was a final chance for the little company to extricate itself from the stranglehold exerted by the two big players, the GWR and LSWR. Their hoped for bill was indeed obtained, but moneys were not forthcoming and in 1905, the time limit for construction, faded without a single barrow of earth having been moved (9).

Although not backed openly, or apparently even privately by the GWR, the completion of the route to Southampton could not have been ignored by Paddington had it been achieved. It is likely that this would also have

seen a resurrection of the Aldermaston - Burghclere connection, previously the last of the proposed extension lines to be abandoned, as late as June 1891.

Extension to Bournemouth - Following a deputation from residents of this town, plans were drawn up for a 30½ mile line commencing with a triangular junction at Shirley and thence west through Totton, Lyndhurst, and Burley Street before turning south to a terminus in Bournemouth. The actual station in the latter town to have been, ".....in a garden attached to a house or villa in Dean Park and known as 'Broad Hays'". In addition a connection from near the

terminus involving a 220yd. viaduct would have connected the route with the Bournemouth West to Poole line of the LSWR. A further branch would run from Burley street to the LSWR at Ringwood. As far as the DNS were concerned this was a genuine proposal and was embodied in their 'D.N.S. (Bournemouth & Poole) Extension' Bill of 1883. The citizens of Bournemouth however probably had other things on their mind, for with their town then far from ideally served via a branch from Ringwood, their rational was no doubt to spur the LSWR into action. The fact the DNS proposal was quickly thrown out not least because of the destruction of some 110 acres of woodland that would have been involved, was of little consequence. The outcome was an LSWR Act of 1883 which resulted in the construction of the Brockenhurst to Christchurch line via Sway so giving more direct rail access to Bournemouth.

Extension to Portsmouth - Recently found papers amongst a small file of correspondence (P.R.O. Rail 1057/821), report an approach made by the 'Portsmouth Railway Extension Association' of Prudential Buildings, Portsmouth, to the DNS for a line from Winchester via Botley Common to the former location which would have been 24 miles long. The matter was evidently suggested around late 1894 by a DNS shareholder who was also a member of the association. The response of the DNS was understandably bland bearing in mind their own circumstances. No capital

or parliamentary sanction was ever gained and with the DNS no doubt content to let matters take their course as clearly promoting open support could have had resulted in difficulties with the LSWR over the running of trains from Winchester to Shawford Junction. Interestingly, although perhaps slightly out of context in so far as the DNS are concerned, the Portsmouth association were clearly eager to pursue an alternative rail connection from whichever means it was possible and the same papers refer to a suggestion by them for a line linking Portsmouth directly with Basingstoke , '....so as to afford direct access to the GWR....'. Certainly it is true the GWR had themselves always regarded Portsmouth with an eager eye but the possible advantages of open support were clearly offset by greater disadvantages. (T.B. Sands suggests a similar approach was also made by the citizens of Portsmouth to the DNS around 1881-3 but was considered inappropriate at that time.)

The Bourne Valley light Railway - Finally we may refer briefly to a May 1899 proposal for a Light Railway under the terms of the 1896 Act to run from Whitchurch and Hurstbourne to Eastdown. It was referred to in official documents as the Bourne Valley light Railway. Diverging from the DNS just north of the LSWR bridge at Whitchurch, the new line would have run parallel with the South Western main line as far as Hurstbourne before heading north west to serve St. Mary Bourne, Stokee, Hurstbourne Tarrant, Upton, Vernham Dean, and Eastdown. A total length of 11¼ miles - a figure of 12 miles is also quoted. An additional connection facing London would also have been provided with the LSWR at Hurstbourne whilst the connection with the DNS at Whitchurch would have faced towards Winchester. Four references as to proposers are mentioned, Mr. A.F.M. Downie of Alton, W.H.M. Gipps, Mr. Harper - believed to have been a Director of the DNS - and surprisingly perhaps the LSWR themselves. The Earl of Portsmouth is listed as objecting to the scheme. It would appear the 1899 proposal got as far as a Public Enquiry but was afterwards abandoned. The idea was resurrected again in 1901 but with similar lack of success, whilst in 1910 the local press carried a report of a further attempt to breath life into the idea. This however also floundered .(10).

1. At various times during the period 1873 onwards various different

derivatives for the company title were used. For the sake of simplicity the recognised term 'Didcot, Newbury and Southampton' (DNS) is used whenever possible.

2. The attitude of the GWR to the DNS was quite perverse in practically every area in which the two companies handled the management of the line. Any initiatives taken by the DNS to stimulate traffic were usually met with a cold response from Paddington who seemingly took every opportunity to remind the DNS of its own obligations under the Working Agreement. Many of these cases were extremely fussy such as the later naming of stations at Woodhay, Highclere and Burghclere, thereby causing dismay and confusion to the very people who would use the railway. As a final aside it is worth mentioning that assistance on behalf of the DNS in compiling the working agreement was given by none other than Henry Oakley, General Manager of the Great Northern Railway.

3. The contractors, Falkiner & Tancred do not appear well known in the field of railway construction, indeed no record appears of any other railway construction work they may have performed in the south of England up to the turn of the century. Consequently details of the steam engines they may have used on the DNSR contract are scant. Records from the Manning Wardle works list reveal two locomotives used by the firm, the first an 0-6-0ST of the builders 'M' class an inside cylinder machine to standard gauge. Built in July 1870 with works No. 291, it was originally supplied to a company in Wigan and was used by Messrs. J. Aird on their contract at Fleetwood Dock carrying the name 'Fanny'. Its subsequent movements are unclear but it later found its way to Didcot for use on the construction where it was reported to have carried the name 'Lively'. Following completion of the DNS it was afterwards recorded in the hands of yet another contractor, Messrs. Robert T. Relf & Son, and used in the building of the Lydford - Devenport (PD&SWR) line. The second machine was another standard gauge 0-6-0ST again with inside cylinders and to standard gauge. It was to the company's 'K' class, works No. 662 and new in June 1877. This machine was first reported with a contractor in Rutland at which time it bore the name 'Seaton'. It is reported as having passed to Falkiner & Tancred at Newbury at an unknown time. Whether the name was retained is not recorded. This particular engine later went overseas to Turkey. What is known is that at one period whilst in use on construction of the DNSR the name 'Newbury' was carried. The practice of naming contractors engines after relevant locations during a line's construction was not unusual although the names were often removed before a new contract took place. At least two other engines bearing the names 'Mark Tapley', and 'Waverley', are also known to have been used during the construction of the line between Didcot and Newbury. No other details of these machines has come to light. Similarly no record has been located to identify the engine referred to as used for the 1882 Board of Trade inspection, 'Lady Cornewall'. It is not reported which, if any, of these engines may have been

retained for the construction south of Newbury although it is known that four locomotives were used at the start of the work on 3 March 1883.

4. In contemporary reports the Southern Section referred to the line from Newbury to Litchfield and the Southampton section from thence southwards. This was because south of Litchfield the route to Winchester diverged from that originally proposed' namely to Micheldever.

5. No hardware in the form of nails stamped with evidence of the company name or initials appear to have survived - corrosion no doubt took its toll. Cast iron chairs to support inside-keyed bull-head rail and lettered D.N.S.R. do however exist. On the original route these were last in use probably on part of the former down loop at Kings Worthy and possibly also on the loading dock siding at Bar End. In the former location they were still in situ in the late 1950s albeit the loop was out of use by this time. The Bar End siding referred to is suggested as retaining the inside keyed chairs also but this is not confirmed. A number were however located in the late 1970s at Morris Cowley, near Oxford within a siding about to be lifted. The inference then is that at some time the GWR had exercised their usual good house-keeping of cascaded use for its permanent way. Thanks to the assistance of Colin Dawson, then of the CCE Department, BR Western Region, at least three were salvaged from the scrap merchants, one now on view within the small relics museum of the GWS at Didcot.

6. See the 'Didcot, Newbury & Southampton Railway' by Karau, Parsons & Robertson and also 'Didcot Newbury & Southampton Railway Supplement', by Robertson and Simmonds, both published by Wild Swan. Reference is also made within this chapter to the earlier paperback 'The Didcot, Newbury & Southampton Railway' by T.B. Sands, published by Oakwood Press in 1971.

7. The full story of the Lambourn Valley Railway is told in 'The Lambourn Branch' by Robertson and Simmonds published by Wild Swan. See also 'Lambourn Revisited' published by Noodle Books.

8. Details of the fall off in traffic reported in 1894 and as having occurred in 1893 when compared with 1892 can be found in the table on page 34.

9. Although the Southampton & Winchester Great Western Junction Railway was unable to raise its necessary funds that is not to say the idea of railways as an investment was unattractive elsewhere. An example of this may be given, again involving the Great Central, and who in an attempt to support their extension to London offered a share issue of some £2 million in 1901. It was over-subscribed four fold.

10. P.R.O. Ref; Rail 1015/1 & Rail 1057/828.

Early days at Shawford Junction. The train is approaching on the LSWR main line from Winchester with the DNS diverging / joining on the right. Note the glimpse of double track leading off to Winchester DNS on the right. It is not known how long this arrangement persisted although clearly it became a single line before running over the viaduct.

Churn Station.

...calling at Churn, by request, of course! Above is the original stopping place high on the windswept downs and with no metalled road access. The design of the station building was unique for the DNS, whether it was a modified GWR or even military design can only be guessed at, for no plans or close up photographs have been discovered. The single siding was facing Upton & Blewbury and located at the far end of the platform on the right. Left is a grounded coach body - added for an unknown purpose.

Next stop Compton (right), well actually we have just left Compton as the station is in the background. This really is a spectacular image recorded as late as 1940. The former MSWJ 2-4-0, No 1334, is heading south, whether this is another example of the Sunday milk train is possible - see page 87, although on this occasion it will be noted to have three coaches and for the time, of modern construction. The October 1941 public timetable (the closest we can find to 1940) reveals a severely restricted passenger service and with the following rider applicable to all routes, 'Trains are liable to be cancelled at short notice'. Between Didcot and Newbury there were five trains each way on weekdays although in the Down direction the service was hardly likely to retain let alone attract patronage for after the 7.37a.m. down there was a gap of over five hours before the next working at 12.45p.m. After this matters were more evenly spaced out although the final down working, 6.30p.m. off Didcot was slightly unusual in that is was non-stop to Newbury, even so it was also the slowest of all, allowed 50 minutes for the 17 miles, an average speed of just 20mph. The Up service was more regular although all trains called at all stations - Churn of course was a request stop except for the first down train which shows a definite stop and the first up, which by comparison will not call even upon request. One train in each direction is shown on Sundays but which did not venture south of Newbury.

Between Newbury and Winchester there were five trains, four of these were through services from Didcot south the through journey time anything up to two and one half hours. (In the Up direction there were only two through services, passengers having to change and then wait at Newbury.) Again there was a long gap between the 9.05 a.m. departure and the next at 2.00p.m. However on Saturday only there was an additional unusual working in the form of the 12.35p.m. from Newbury which ran only as far as Whitchurch arriving at 1.08p.m. Here there was a 32 minutes wait where any through passengers had to alight. Then at 1.40p.m. it was off again for Winchester but omitting the call at Worthy Down, the only train of the day to do so. The same timetable also fails to show any service beyond Winchester in either direction.

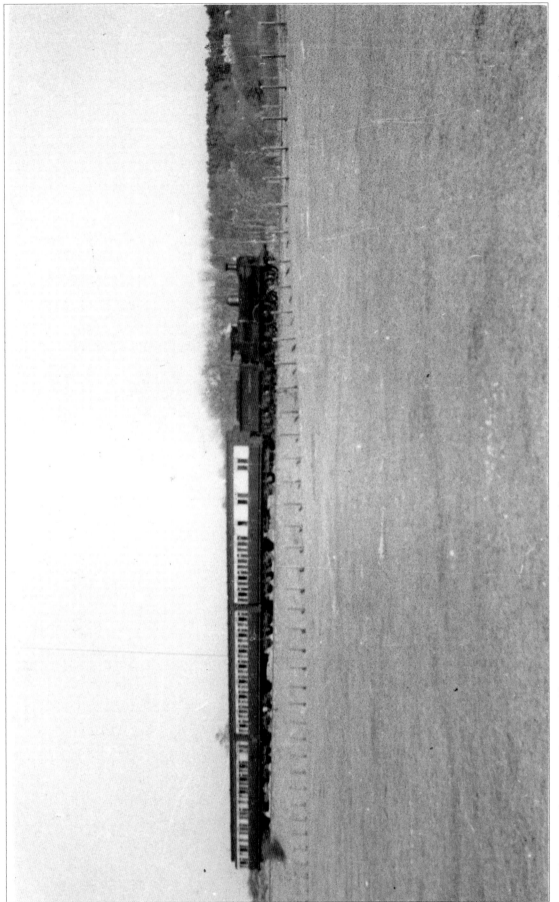

No 1334 reported as 'near Hermitage' but on an unreported date. From the clerestory coaching stock this would appear to be slightly earlier in years and again points to possibly being the Sunday working. (The three MSWJ 2-4-0, engines, two of which were regularly based at Didcot and the third at Reading, were regular performers on the Lambourn line but other than on Sunday were far less common on DNS workings.

Now to Newbury, where (**above**) sometime after 1935, a 'Duke' class 4-4-0 waits in the up bay before departure to Didcot. Trains arriving from Winchester would, if their wait was to be more than a short length of time or if the up platform at Newbury was required for another working, pull forward and then set back into the bay platform. **Below** - What is probably a brand-new 2251 class 0-6-0 having just left Newbury for Woodhay and beyond. The Lambourn branch is the third line of rails on the left. The engine is No 3211, one of three members of the type (Nos 3210-12) allocated new to Didcot in late 1947 specifically for DNS workings. With the signal also off for a departure from Newbury towards Lambourn it is possible to conclude the train is the 4.25p.m. off Newbury (2.56p.m. Oxford to Southampton service.) The Lambourn working will be the 4.35p.m. all stations to Lambourn.

WINCHESTER CAMP RAILWAY.
PLAN & PROFILE.

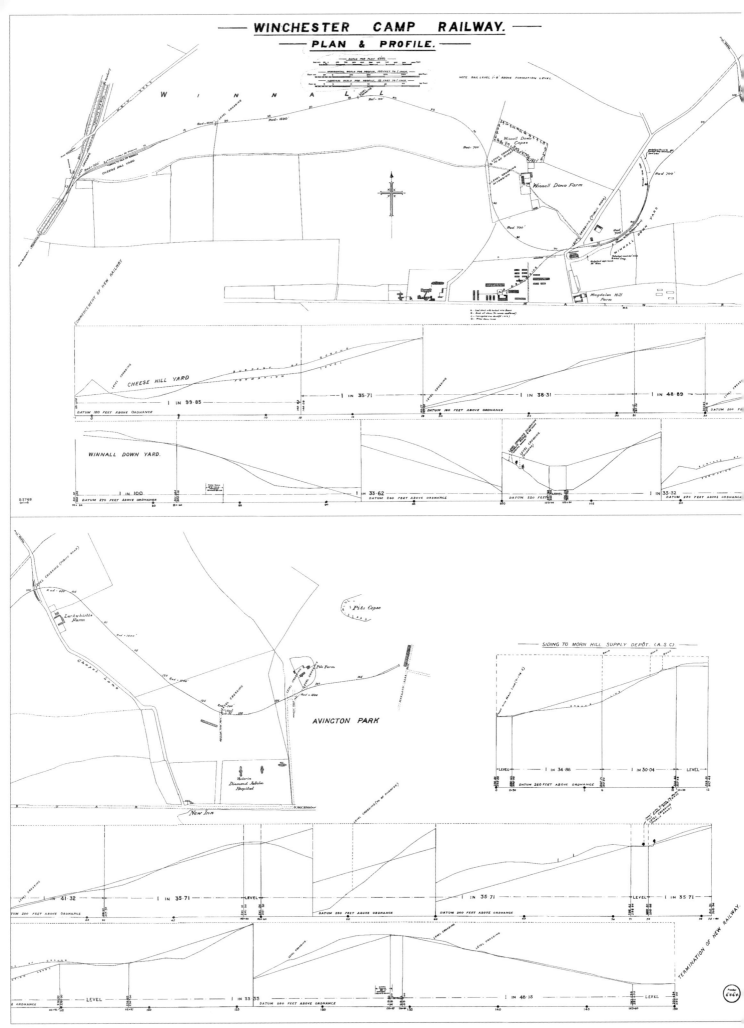

3. By rail to Winnal

The subject of the wartime camp line from just north of Winchester to Winnal is one which has fascinated for many years. Partly this must be because of the sheer lack of information, odd snippets coming to life every so often which only add to the mystery surrounding the facilities.

Hopefully now a more complete story can be disclosed and one which has brought together records from railway, wartime, and personal sources.

We start in 1914, some time before the rail connection was established, with an exert from an account by Herbert Halliday published in the Hampshire Observer of 26 December 1914, entitled 'From Winchester to the Front - Departure of an Army Division'. "Scenes such as no other town, with the exception of Southampton, has witnessed during the present war engaged Wintonians during the week-end, when what the Court Circular described as the 27th Division of the British Expeditionary Force left their canvas town on Morn-Hill and marched to Southampton to embark for an unknown destination. Few were sorry to leave the camp, but most regretted parting with Winchester, where all agreed they had been well looked after and catered for. Their stay on Morn-Hill (sic) was a period during which the British climate proved its versatility. Every sample of weather, with the exception of the heat of the dog days and the snow of mid-winter was displayed for the benefit of the brave men who had returned from the tropics and were therefore unaccustomed to these differences. Our readers will remember that they arrived in Winchester during the bitterest weather we have experienced since the autumn set

A poor quality illustration of the original, tented-camp, at Morn Hill.

in. Clad in the thin khaki drill which they wore in the tropics, the men shivered and turned blue with the cold as the biting north-east wind nipped them with its icy tooth. For the first days they suffered the rigour of this grip of real winter, for adequate stores had not arrived, and they found it impossible to keep warm. They awoke in the morning to find the country all round them white with frost, but this they did not mind, for exercise could make them warm, and there was an abundance of food." (Other British troops stationed at Morn Hill or possibly Winnall Down Camp included the 14th, 15th, 16th Welsh Divisions, 17th London Irish Fusiliers, Welsh Fusiliers, 21st, 22nd 24th London Regiments.)

This brief information alone is of interest, for whilst the remainder of Halliday's account deals with his subsequent postings, the above brief note confirms the existence of a camp at Winnall as early as 1914. However, after this date through to 1918 information is scarce. What is known is that by 1918 a military hospital had been established at what was referred to as 'Magdalen Camp' - there already existed the 'Victoria - Diamond Jubilee' hospital nearly. Accommodation at the Magdalen Camp facility was for 252 beds. (Contemporary with the facilities at Winnall, a second military hospital was established in the Winchester area at Hazeley Down Camp near Twyford, where there was also a hutted army base. This had 105 beds. No rail connection was provided here and it is not known if this was ever considered. Other contemporary army camps in the Winchester area, such as that at Hursley Park, are not relevant to this description.)

But to return to Winnall and more especially its railway connection from the DNS. Records found in a bound volume 'Great Western Railway - War Reports of the General Manager to the Board of Directors - 1914 to 1919', at last provide the background to the provision of the rail accommodation to Winnall. Two entries exist, the first of 10 May 1918, when it was reported, "Some discussion is taking place with regard to the establishment of a big camp for American troops near Winchester. If this becomes an

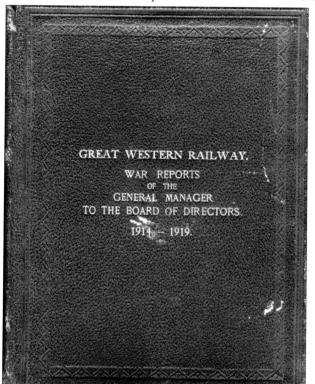

GREAT WESTERN RAILWAY.

WAR REPORTS
OF THE
GENERAL MANAGER
TO THE BOARD OF DIRECTORS
1914 – 1919.

Contemporary postcard - American troops.

out on that line to admit of the heavy trains that would require to pass being dealt with. As the line is a worked line, I have been in communication with the Chairman of the undertaking with regard to it." Subsequently on 11 November 1918 it was reported the cost of the siding connection was £4,543 - presumably just referring to the connection with the DNS route itself north of the tunnel. Not mentioned specifically as regards Winnall but relevant, is an slightly earlier entry in the same GWR volume dealing with the general operation of military railways in the UK. The Government asking that the respective railway company's operate and maintain the various military lines on their system. This was agreed by the GWR and so we may conclude the Winnall Camp line was therefore operated by the Great Western throughout its brief life.

Another fortunate find which has added considerably to the knowledge available, is the plan reproduced opposite which comes from the archive of John Mann. Although undated, this is reported as showing the camp line at its zenith and is worthy of some study. Points

accomplished fact it will mean the utilisation of the Didcot, Newbury and Southampton railway in connection with the transportation of the American troops disembarking at Liverpool, and considerable works will have to be carried

Construction of the camp railway, circa 1918, with African-American troops prominent. This is the first view to indicate the use of an initial narrow-gauge railway, used no doubt to remove spoil prior to the opening out of the cutting - the depth of which may be gauged by the men stood in the trench. Notwithstanding the ready availability of powered excavators (steam shovels/steam navvys) by this period in history, the ready source of servicemen in the vicinity meant they could be usefully employed. Attempting to locate the image exactly is difficult, but studied under a glass, the lack of apparent building in the background tends to indicate the location as close to the junction with the DNS in the cutting that would later be filled in to become Winnall Valley Road.

Imperial War Museum Q31221

to note are the exchange / storage sidings referred to as 'Cheese Hill Yard' but located close to the junction with the DNS proper, and the similar sidings at 'Winnall Down Yard'. Both of these will be seen to be located on gradients, only the last named having a small headshunt. Two other sidings are shown, whilst at the termination of the route, approximately 1 mile 50 chains from the junction, the line is shown ending in a pair of parallel dead end sidings. In general terms the ruling gradient of around 1 in 36 together with the sharp curves and almost total lack of level track even in the sidings, must have made the working of the line challenging. No doubt specific instruction were provided to cover this but these have not survived.

What is also not known is whether any changes to the layout occurred during the time of operation. The GWR reference to the need to upgrade the DNS for heavy trains is not mentioned again so it may be assumed that at that stage such work was not carried out. (Had it have been, the DNS then, and also post 1923 under GWR ownership, would have been a potentially far more useful railway - having been upgraded at the cost of the Government!)

Some years ago Roger Simmonds undertook his own research into the railway which includes the following previously unpublished notes.

"During the course of the first World War as the action intensified, three large military camps were established on the downs north-east of Winchester. The extreme camp, some 3½ miles from the City centre, was virtually in the estate of Avington Park close to Avington Farm. The other two camps were on Winnall Down and Morn Hill.

Troops of various regiments and nationalities were present at different times, including those from America, Australia, Canada, New Zealand and South Africa as well as British servicemen. The greatest presence was felt by the Americans, who occupied much of both Winnall Down and Avington Park camps. The earliest occupation by the servicemen from the USA was on the 7 November 1917 when a batch of artillerymen arrived at Winnall Down Camp.

The first commanding officer of the Americans was Col. Sam G. Jones who stationed himself at the R.A.S.C. H.Q. Office, Morn Hill Camp. He was very quick to organize entertainment for the troops and a large tent was erected at Winnall Down where regular events, including a weekly boxing competition was held, under the auspices of the Ministry of Information. Local volunteer performers also gave shows to the men in the tent and at special Y.M.C.A. huts erected at the other two camps. The camps provided welcome employment for local civilians with numerous women and young boys were employed to work in the canteens and perform general domestic chores.

Independence day celebrations were held at the camps on 4 July 1918, and entertainments held in the tent at Winnall Down. The 7 December 1918 saw a visit by the wife of General Booth, where she was entertained to tea at Winnall Down and later addressed some 3,000 of the servicemen present.

In the region of 360,000 men had been accommodated at camps in the Winchester area, about three-quarters of these at the three camps on Morn Hill. The main period of occupation was during the summer and autumn of 1918. This may have prompted the War Office to provide rail access from the DNS to serve the camps.

Work began on construction of the camp line on 1 October 1918 under the direction of Captain Oscar T. Wood, an assistant engineer to the GWR. Captain Wood served in the British army and was undertaking the work for the War Department. After being demobilised, Mr. Wood became the resident engineer in charge of the camp line.

The new railway was opened on the 20 October 1918 and believed worked as a siding, motive power being provided by an engine stationed at Bar End shed.

As the Americans may have been the prime movers to establish rail access, the U.S. government paid for the construction of the line and supplied a large batch of African labourers to speed the work. Some of these labourers together with sappers from the R.E., worked under the supervision of the GWR Winchester ganger, Sam Harvey. Sam was a hard task-master, on one occasion shortly after the work began at the junction with the DNS, one of the Africans called Sam by a derogatory name, the result was a fearful fight lasting nearly 45 minutes, well remembered and talked about locally for several years. Sam made his point by beating the man and had no more trouble whilst he was involved with the work.

The point of divergence with the main DNS line was just north of Winchester tunnel, approximately one-third of a mile from Cheesehill Station. From here the camp route curved sharply away from the junction in a north-easterly direction and entered a cutting through the Winnall area, at the time open countryside.

A cruel climb ensued up across the downs, the route swinging round to a more easterly direction about a mile from the junction. A siding diverged at this point leading to the former isolation hospital, converted to military use and now equipped with operating theatres. The hospital was put under the control of Senior Medical Officer Capt. H.D. Beasley. This siding was used for delivery of coal and medical supplies. It is not believed any ambulance trains used the line, or if they did these were very few in number. Certainly there is no report of any troop trains, men able to walk generally being marched from the DNS or LSWR station although a contemporary report also indicates road transport may have been provided at times. Consequently with very few exceptions, rolling stock on the line would have been restricted to goods vehicles.

Additional rail traffic included hay and saddlery deliveries, required for the large number of horses kept by the artillery divisions. It is probable that horses were brought into the camps by rail from Bar End Yard as horseboxes are remembered being used.

After the hospital siding, the route turned north-eastwards again, and crossed the service road to Winnall Down Farm at an ungated crossing, close to the farm buildings. A low embankment followed where a second siding was provided close to Larkwhistle Farm. (This last named siding is not shown on the plan and may be taken to have been a later addition. It led to a large hut used by Messrs. Perry & Co. as a cement and timber store. The hut was not a new addition and had been established some time before the railway. The siding had a capacity of ten wagons. On this basis it implies the railway may also have provided some means of transport for the goods of Messrs. Perry - who were responsible for much of the camp construction - see later..)

A second ungated crossing was made with the Easton Road, approached on both sides by a short cutting on a sharp curve to bring the formation to the correct right level.

It is believed at some stage an extension was made taking the railway to Avington Park Camp some three miles from the junction, again this is not shown on the plan. This extension involved an initial steep descent followed by an easing of the gradient until the terminus was reached. Railway facilities at Avington Park consisted of a platform, 780 feet in length, and several sidings including a run-round loop. At one time it was believed a 13 lever signal box may have existed, but this is perhaps now thought unlikely, all turnouts probably operated by hand levers, or at most a ground-frame. (Whilst circumstantially it is believed the railway did reach Avington, it must be stated there is no certain proof of this either in documentary or archeological terms. North of the 'New Inn' Col Bevis's plan – see reference later – indicates a vast layout of huts, but we cannot be certain if this area was what was meant as Avington or if the name Avington was used as being geographically close to the village of that name, but intended to avoid confusion with the other camps in the area. What we do know for certain is that during WW1 facilities did exist at Avington village, but what is not certain if these were linked to Magdalen and Morn Hill by railway.[1])

Construction of the camp buildings was undertaken by the firm referred to above, Perry & Co. of Bow, whose head office was in London. To avoid bad feelings between contractor's employees and the sappers who worked side by side in the work, the private employees were paid the same wages as the servicemen. The labourers used for both the camp buildings and on the railway construction were often unskilled and inexperienced. This probably contributed to a number of injuries. These men, usually demobilised straight out of war duty, were obtained in batches from the Winchester Labour Exchange. In addition to, or possibly prior to the railway being completed, Messrs. John Gale were contracted to transport materials from Bar End Yard during the time the camps were under construction. Numerous steam wagons were hired from many areas including as far afield as Rock Ferry near Liverpool.

The camp buildings were hotch-potch in design with several different materials used in their construction. Many were of a semi-permanent nature being of prefabricated wooden sections having the outside walls covered with chicken wire to which a liberal coating of mortar/plaster was applied. The roofs were covered in pitch. Other buildings consisted of corrugated iron or tin sheet over a basic wooden frame.

Traffic known to have been brought in to the camps by rail included food provisions in addition to timber building supplies, military requirements and coal. In these pre NAAFI days, Messrs. John Dickenson were used for contract catering suppliers. A large bakery was also established at the Winnal camp which supplied bread to all the camps. (Did this even include Hazeley Down?) In these pre NAAFI days Messrs. John Dickenson were used for contract catering suppliers.

There was also a small power station located near the present Farm House. This provided electricity to both Morn Hill and Winnall Down Camps. Near the crossing with the Easton Road behind the New Inn (in more recent times the 'Percy Hobbs' and the 'Neptune'), was a tin shack which formed a cinema providing entertainment for men at both camps. Nearby was a separate fever hospital. This is likely to have found use around 1919 when a number of cases of Spanish Flu were reported amongst the American servicemen. North of both of these, and separated by a number of army huts, was a building shown on a second plan as the 'Camp Prison.' (A second, hand-drawn plan, has surfaced produced by Lt. Col F J Bevis C.R.E. dated 9 April 1919. This only indicates the route of the railway in outline and does not provide any further clues as to its route beyond the approximate area of the New Inn. What this plan does show is the vast number of army huts that existed, a considerable number also positioned on the south side of the Alresford Road opposite the railway and hospitals. A count of the total number of huts at the three camps would indicate in excess of 500, this included those used for all types of military purpose.)

Later in 1920, a large number of American soldiers who had been buried in the adjacent Morn Hill Cemetery were exhumed at the request of relatives for shipment back to the USA. Their coffins were loaded into vans in the hospital siding and taken down to Winchester at the start of their final journey. By the 5 June 1920 a total of 401 coffins had been moved, out of a total of 543 burials.

The regular daily rail working of the line began with an engine and loaded wagons departing Bar End yard at 10 a.m. Following all shunting movements necessary, the engine would return light engine to the yard. At 4 p.m. a return light engine working would be made to pick up the empties and return them to Bar End. The Winchester Bar End yard porter/shunter, Arthur Wellstead, would act as train guard on these trips."

A former GWR ganger recalls that the line was laid using very poor quality rail of both bullhead and flat-bottom type – the latter spiked directly to the sleepers. Much was already badly worn, presenting a difficult top surface which, combined with the severe gradients, caused much slipping

A slightly damaged original of what is reported as the camp at Avington Park. The difficulty comes in attempting to orientate any of the huts to either of the two known plans (that for the railway layout and that by Lt. Col. Bevis. This no doubt made more difficult by changes that occurred as the sites developed. Assuming this to be the location exactly as recorded, then it is possible the railway 'may' have run on the chalk embankment indicated, although it must be admitted any attempt in increasing the size of the image does not make identification any easier!

Imperial War Museum Q30108

by the engines working the line. There are few details, but the story goes that a 'Bulldog' class engine became stuck on one occasion after several attempts to work a train up to Avington Park. A second engine was found and sent up to rescue the unfortunate 4-4-0. Following this, train lengths were restricted to ten wagons maximum – it is not clear if this referred to 'ten loaded wagons' and the equivalent weight for empty vehicles, or vice-versa. (The method of working the line is of interest. With no intermediate signal box provided at the junction, it is likely the points leading to the siding were unlocked by a key on the train staff, which if required to be restored for the passage of an ordinary train between Kings Worthy and Winchester, would have had to be returned to Winchester signal box so effectively 'locking the camp line service in'. The alterative may have been to attempt to operate the camp line workings during a gap in the daily traffic. Certainly 'one engine in steam' operation would have been the norm. Did an incident with the runaway vehicles also lead to the line being operated by propelling movements only from Winchester? See p61.)

Local Winchester resident, Percy Crockford, recorded his memories of that period when, as a boy of 13, he was employed to work on the road leading from the bottom of Magdalen Hill, to the camps alongside the Alresford Road. This came about as ruts had formed due to the passage of gun carriages and these required filling in. (This also indicates that certain traffic had arrived by road rather than rail, although this may also pre-date the construction of the railway.) Normally his father would have been employed but it appears he was indisposed and had advised the Winchester Council that his son, Percy, was capable of driving the steam traction engine. The work was considered urgent and thus for three weeks Percy was employed hauling granite chippings from the City depot, starting work soon after 5.am.

"It would take four men approx 1 hour to load 5-6 ton of chippings into the trailer and we would drive up Wharf Hill, down Chesil Street and at the bottom of Magdelen Hill would start to unload the chippings and the gang of men would start to lay them. This was done all the way up to the Camp (to beyond the old Victoria Hospital), it took nearly 3 weeks. The pay arrangements were that they didn't pay me - but the Council would pay my father his wages, which was £2-3-0 a week, I never got a penny.

"The rest of the war I was employed by Mr Nutter, the butcher in the High Street. I used to make deliveries on one of those big bikes with a basket on the front. Every Friday and Saturday one of my jobs was to deliver sausages up to the camp on the Alresford Road. In total it was well over 1 cwt. It was alright going down the High St but when you came to the bottom of Magdalen Hill it was a case of get off and push. On reaching the camp, there was always a Red Cap on duty and he would give me a pull on the handlebar to get me through the gate, escort me to the cook house, and leave me there.

"I would go inside and the cooks would say "sit

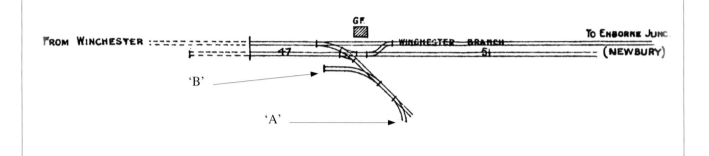

WINCHESTER (CAMP SIDINGS).

24M. 69C.

G.F.

FROM WINCHESTER — WINCHESTER BRANCH — TO ENBORNE JUNC.

(NEWBURY)

17

51

'B'

'A'

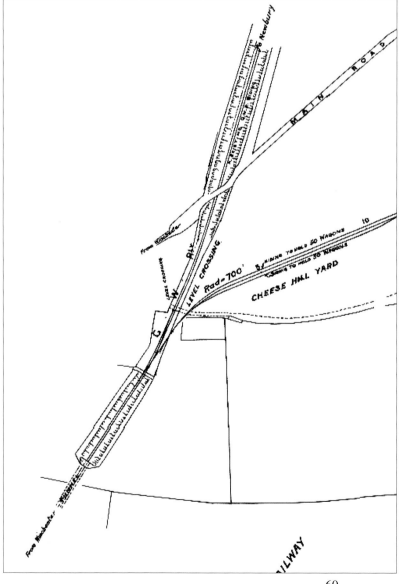

Previously reproduced in 'DNS–Supplement' but deliberately included for a second time as a result of the new information now available. The original schematic drawing appeared in an official book of GWR stations and depots, dated 1922, although the date should not be taken as of particular importance for no doubt the actual survey was a few years earlier. What is interesting is the explanation now available for the siding shown at 'A': the start of the three sidings confusingly referred to on the main plan as 'Cheese Hill Yard'. The trap-points, indicated here as a short siding, which stopped the runaway wagons are also shown at 'B'. As before, notice the headshunt coming to a dead end in the tunnel whilst the layout of pointwork would have allowed a train to arrive at the sidings from either direction and/or run-round using the main line.

One point of particular interest refers back to the main plan (extract left), this concerns the layout at the junction. The top diagram on this page is clear, concise and easy to follow - the figures on the track showing the capacity of each siding in terms of 4-wheel wagons. But refer again to the main plan and it is not completely clear which is double and which is single track at the actual junction. (Unless the running line is indicated with parallel lines and all sidings shown as a single black line. But even then it does not exactly correspond with that above!) Did the junctions arrangements even alter in the light of operational requirements / experience?

down lad" and I got a cup of cocoa - I remember on leaving one day with the bike - we always carried a piece of mutton cloth in the bottom, the cook said, "How's mum off for things son?" I relied, "Well you know what its like…", and he put something in the bottom of the basket under the mutton cloth. I had no idea what was put there, but I said Ta - and left. On reaching the main gate the Red Cap stopped me and asked if he could look in the basket. On pulling the mutton cloth aside he saw the butter. He said, "Where did you get that?" I said, "I didn't pinch it - honest - the cook gave it to me". The Red Cap said, "Is that all the lousy bugger gave you…..". Every time after that he took me to the cook house where he would tell the cook to give me something better than butter to take home.

"I can recall the railway up to the Army Camp, by late 1920 it was out of use and the rails were lifted in 1923/24. We filled in most of the cutting with refuse from the Pumping Station.

"A thing I have always been pleased to help is a horse. When they were waiting to go up to the Camp , they would line up from the bridge at the bottom of town, one gun carriage and six horses (mules). When the Sergeant gave the command for them to start moving, some times those mules just didn't want to go, I've seen them beaten with a whip - sometimes they would even put lighted straw under their stomach to get them to move. There was the time when I was taking the granite chippings to repair the road and one of the sergeants asked if I could pull the lead carriage. Well as soon as the mules realized that I was taking the load they went up as sweet as a nut, no bother."

For the life of the camps, American Military Policemen would be stationed at all exit points into Winchester both for security and to look out for any absconding soldiers. One such M.P. was posted to the junction of the camp line with the DNS and would often stand on the overbridge by Ebden Road - considered a good vantage point. Whilst on duty here, he would be pestered by the local children for flavoured chewing gum, a real treat in those hard times.

Although only in use for two years, the line was not short of incident. The first concerned a string of sixteen coupled open wagons which had been left at Winnall Down Camp on the running line with the brakes pinned down. Unfortunately the severe gradient towards Winchester proved too much, the brakes unable to restrain the vehicles. The impromptu train ran back towards the junction but was derailed at the catch point near the junction and no major damage was caused. Although unrecorded this occurred sometime between 20 November 1918 and 22 May 1919.

The second and far more serious accident, involved a fatality where a labourer lost his life whilst working with a permanent way gang. On the 23 May 1919 major track laying was in progress at Avington Park Camp involving sixty men in two gangs – could this have been when the extension to Avington Park was being undertaken? These men consisted of R.E's. and local labourers under the charge of Cpl. Betteridge R.E.. Work had commenced at 6.30 a.m, a gang of 18 labourers given the task of transporting materials for the work from Winnall Down Camp to Avington Park Camp. Two trolleys capable of carrying 5-tons each were used with nine men traveling on each trolley. (The type of propulsion is not reported, human/gravity, or even horse?)

On one of what were several trips made, the load was of 60 ft rails plus sleepers amounting to 3 tons 6 cwt. The weight of the rails, which were laid across the trolleys, kept them together. When travelling to Avington the men had been warned to slow down but not brake too hard at the level crossing near Larkwhistle, as the sharp bend and quick descent could be dangerous. However, on this occasion the trolley was travelling at about 13 m.p.h. as it approached the crossing. One of the men then appeared to panic and jammed on the brakes too quickly causing the wheels of the rear trolley to lift up and leave the rails going as they were negotiating the curve. The trolley dropped on the near side, the wheels going outside the track and the load shifted. A labourer, William Webb, fell on to the line and one of the fallen rail lengths dropped on his leg and was dragged across his body by the first trolley. Other labourers, Frederick Andrews, Alfred Gosling and Albert Potter sustained only slight injuries. Mr. Webb later died in hospital from the injuries received. He was a local man from Wales Street in Winchester and left a widow and daughter. (The detail provided, weights, speed etc, indicating a formal enquiry was held.)

With many of the American servicemen being repatriated, a steady run-down took place after this time which does tend to cast doubt about expanding the rail system, or even working on it with new rails in May 1919.) Even so, the camps continued their function of repatriating men right through till their final closure in November 1920.

This run down was emphasized by an auction sale, conducted by Messrs. James Harris & Son, held on the 5 May 1920 at Winnall Down Camp which offered various buildings and fitments no longer required by the military. Subsequent sales were held around 3-monthly intervals. Some of the items sold and prices fetched are shown for interest:-

Cook House (£25) Horse Troughs (£12)
Bath Houses (£55 each) Galvanised Iron Tanks (£5)
Timber Huts (£65 the lot) Cooking Ranges (45 sh.)
Horse Shelters for 55 horses (£80)
Timber Rifle Range (£200) 125 Wood/plastered huts (not recorded)
 - and a Men's Dining Room (£50)

Messrs. John Gale, the local carters, were hired to move purchased items and huts following these auctions. Steam Foden lorries were used to move the huts which found new uses, often as private homes, not only throughout Hampshire but to other parts of the U.K. Some of the huts sold individually fetched around the £10 mark. Gale's would charge £10 to knock the building down if required, plus a further £10 to transport it to an agreed location. Re-erection was the responsibility of the purchaser.

A number of the huts were rebuilt as private dwellings on large parcels of land at both Hookpit and Springvale, near Kings Worthy, several surviving into the 1960s. Others were purchased for village community use to became parish halls, scout huts, society meeting halls, salvation army halls, etc.

The camp railway, all or some, remained in use until the military facilities finally closed in November 1920, the track remaining in situ until lifted in 1923. Possibly the last metals being at the two level crossings where the rails could still be seen in the following decade.

Following the route of the line today is difficult, with so much of the formation obliterated. The Winnall Trading Estate and 1930s Winchester by-pass construction necessitated the filling in of the cutting in the Winnall area whilst the later M3 motorway has obliterated more. The site of the junction with the DNS is now surrounded by housing development and used as an unofficial play area by local children. Looking in a north easterly direction a short wide footpath leads to Winnall Valley Road, this marks the course of the line curving away from it's DNS parent. The aforementioned road is laid on top of the former cutting filled in when the estate was under construction. For many years there was a disused occupation bridge under the by-

pass followed by a low embankment showing the route up onto the downs. Why this was kept when the by-pass was built is a mystery, access for the local farmer or consideration that a railway to a future military camp may be needed in the future? The point of divergence of the hospital siding can be distinguished as the low embankment survives more or less intact here.

From this point to Avington Park Camp the route cannot be easily traced as the formation has been levelled and incorporated into an indistinguishable part of land belonging to Larkwhistle and Avington Farms. Similarly the site of the former terminus at Avington has disappeared along with any of the camp buildings.

1. Camp Hospital No. 35 was established 19 January 1918, at the American rest camp, Winchester, England, its personnel being taken from the American Expeditionary Forces casually at that camp. When opened, it was known as the United States hospital, American rest camp, Winchester, England, and on 5 April 1918, received its designation as Camp Hospital No. 35. It occupied two groups of structures, situated about one-eighth of a mile apart, in a portion of the camp known as Avington Park. The capacity was intended to be 250 beds, but later additions were made so that the capacity of the hospital was 500, with an emergency expansion in tents to 679. The majority of the cases admitted were medical, among which were the cases of communicable disease among our troops arriving in England. (A polite term for venereal diseases.) During its existence, 19 January 1918, to 4 February 1919, it cared for 5,226 medical and 177 surgical cases. Camp Hospital No. 35 ceased to function 4 February 1919, and its personnel were reassigned to other stations for further duty. There is another reference to another unit based at Avington, this being No. 4 Motor Transport Training Depot, Avington Park, Winchester.

We are fortunate that the late Medical Officer of Health for Winchester, Dr. J L Farmer, took an interest in the course of the line, recording this one image from the site of the concrete by-pass under bridge, looking up the trackbed towards Morn Hill. To orientate the reader, the back of St Swithen's school is out of camera to the right, whilst the line meanders to the left, passing alongside the corrugated barn indicated in the distance. The view was taken sometime in the 1950s, when the formation was in use as a farm track, but much has changed since, the scene impossible to repeat today not least because of the M3 and levelled land.

Interlude - Harry Hiller's Whitchurch

It is sometimes said that life's journey can swing on little more than a chance. And in so far as Harry Hiller's railway career was concerned, that chance occurred when he was just eleven years of age and living with his parents in Bosham, West Sussex.

The year was 1919, and a gangly young boy of around 10, the son of Arthur Hiller, assisted in moving his father's employer's farm stock the 60 odd miles from the Sussex coast to a new location close by the railway at Old Burghclere.

Harry later recalled to his own children the circumstances of that journey, which involved assisting the farm horses to complete the move by road. It took three days to complete the journey, where and how they were accommodated at night was not mentioned. This was some responsibility for a boy of that age and yet who even then had displayed an ability to cope with the handling of animals – horses in particular - a skill which would indeed be a useful asset in years to come.

Harry was the middle of five children, the others George, Fred, Doris, and Bill. Perhaps surprisingly although some information relative to his early years is known, one thing that is missing is his actual birth date, although it is known he had been baptized in Bosham Church on 4 October 1908. (Both Harry's baptism and his later Marriage Certificates show his full name as Leslie Harry Hiller, although no one amongst his family can ever recall him being other than 'Harry'.)

At Old Burghclere the family settled into one of a group of terraced properties known as 'Weir Cottages', which lay to the west of the railway on what was the road to Kingsclere.

The estate where Harry's father was employed was part of what is now Sydmonton Court, one of two major land-owing areas within this part of North Hampshire. The other estate and which lands bordered that of Sydmonton, belonged to the Earl of Caernarvon, with its ancestral home at Highclere Castle.

These two estates provided the majority of land-based employment for the men of the area, the only alternative work being at the nearby Lime Quarry close by Burghclere Station or alternatively on the railway itself.

At Old Burghclere Harry continued his school education, leaving as was customary at age 14 at which time he commenced work as a carter for the same farmer who employed his father. Here as such he would hone his skills further as a horseman, useful when 'courting' within a year or so..... .

Local families which included daughters had to find them employment as well and invariably this meant 'in service'. Accordingly Harry's sister Doris was placed at a large house on the east side of the railway and where she first met one Caroline Edith Ruttterford, the daughter of a Gamekeeper on the Caerarvon Estate. Caroline lived at Woodcott some seven miles from Old Burghclere.

Harry's work would include driving his horses home at the end of each day and he would often pass the house where Caroline worked. Accordingly it was not

Station gardens certificate for Burghclere dated 1936. (Subsequent prizes were awarded in 1937 and 1946.) The names W E Lewington and L H Hiller appear on the original 1936 award. From this it would appear that Harry returned to Burghclere sometime after 1930 meaning his spell at Lambourn was limited. This was likely to have been post 1933 at which time the station master role had been withdrawn from Burghclere. Mr Lewington was likely to have been of a similar grade to Harry, vis-a-vis porter/signalman.

Courtesy Les Hiller.

GREAT WESTERN RAILWAY
Station Gardens Competition

Third Class Prize Season 1936 £2. Milne General Manager

Third Class Season 19-- £2. Milne

Third Class Prize Season 1946 £2. Milne General Manager

PRIZES

as shown hereon have been awarded to

Mr *W E Lewington & L H Hiller*

Station Master at *Burghclere*

General Manager

uncommon for Harry - and some of the other young men as well - to present a 'show' for the benefit of the girls, who in return revelled at the attention.

Further contact came when there was a local dance, often at the end of harvest, here numerous families would get together to relax after one of the busiest and certainly the most intense time in the farming calendar.

Perhaps with an eye to the future, Harry soon became dissatisfied with the limited life and future potential offered by his carting work and on his own initiative sought out and was successful in obtaining an offer of work as a footman at nearby Sydmonton Court.

But on advising his employer of his pending resignation he was quickly cut down to size with a warning that if he were to leave, then his father would also loose his job and in consequence the family would be turned out of their tied cottage. Such behaviour would never be tolerated nowadays, but employment rights were almost non-existent in the 1920s and Harry had little option but to remain as a carter.

What occurred next appears slightly strange but it seems his employer had a change of heart, for a little while later it was he who approached Harry advising him that if he still wanted to leave there was a job available at the local station and he would 'fix-it' with the Station Master if Harry were interested. Accordingly in 1925 aged 16, Harry Hiller left his job on the farm for good.

At the time Burghclere Station was under the control of Mr Mealings and Harry would have been tasked with a variety of duties all within what was deemed 'Portering'. The term 'porter' should also be seen in its widest sense as it included most things that went on at the station, from collecting and delivering goods, to clerical, yard, and cleaning duties.

At some stage also Harry became interested in signalling, possibly even encouraged by Mr Mealings and which Harry also saw as offering a better financial proposition than remaining as a porter. (There were two station masters at Burgclere with the name Mealings. W.J. Mealings had arrived in the Station Master's post in July 1919 but was replaced by H. Mealings in 1927. It is likely the men were related. Harry would probably have known both during his time at the station. H Mealings later became a District Inspector at Newbury with responsibility for signalling.)

Harry's five years at Burghclere evidently passed without incident and at some stage he studied for and successfully passed the GWR Examinations in Railway Signalling.

More important still was his continued courtship with Caroline with the result that they were married on 22 February 1930, both then aged 21. Naturally this also meant a house move which, was to a council allocated accommodation at Harts Corner, Burghclere, close to the Carpenter's Arms and near to Highclere Railway Station. (As is known, the village names did not correspond with the allotted station names.)

Around the same time, the exact date is uncertain,

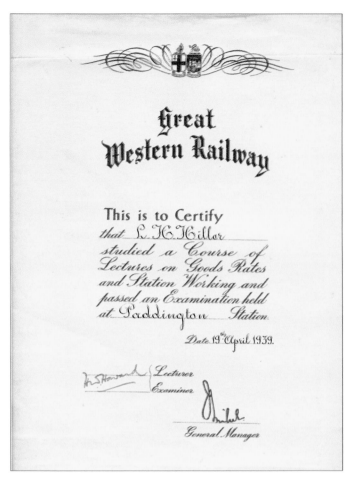

Already qualified as a signalman, Harry's success on the course station working was another rung on the ladder towards becoming a station master.

came the first of Harry's railway promotions, to a s Grade 5 signalman at Lambourn some 17 miles by road from Burghclere. To travel to work he had a motorcycle, although it must have made for a daunting prospect at times during the depths of winter.

Lambourn was the terminus of the 12 mile branch from Newbury an area then, as now, very much steeped in horses and racing. Although posted within the signalling grade, Harry would still also have been involved in general station duties, his experience with horses especially useful with the type of traffic handled.

Again details of his railway life at Lambourn are sketchy, although we do know that it was here that he first met Ken Alexander (another name to be associated with Whitchurch in later years), at the time the lad crossing keeper at Bockhampton just outside Lambourn. Digressing slightly and Ken recalls that at Bockhampton there was a wooden hut which apart from its official use as a shelter for the crossing keeper, was also regularly used by the local policeman as a refuge and means of hiding from his sergeant. Both Ken and the local policeman were less than impressed when an out of control lorry demolished the shelter after it failed to negotiate the double bend in the road either side of the railway crossing.

Coinciding with his posting to Lambourn, Caroline produced the first of what would eventually be their eight children, and an ambitious Harry took the opportunity to better himself by applying for and being accepted for a Grade 3 signalling post at, it is believed, Newbury West signal box.

Aside from the increase in wages there was also now less travelling, although offset against this was a requirement to work around a 24 hour shift seven days a week. (The Lambourn branch had no night trains whilst there was also just one Sunday service.)

The next significant event in Harry's railway career came when he attended a formal course at the Signalling School at Reading in 1936 and successfully passed the necessary examinations. He was now qualified to apply for further promotion which came as a District Relief Signalman based at Newbury, covering 19 signal boxes in an area from Newbury East though to Kintbury, the two signal boxes on the Lambourn branch, as well as all the boxes between Upton & Blewbury through to Winchester. (The term 'Relief Signalman' is used here with caution, and it may well have been that the role was more of a 'rest-day relief man'.)

Unless required elsewhere Harry continued to spend a fair proportion of his time still working the Newbury boxes sometimes accompanied by his eldest son Les and later younger son Peter.

In later years Les Hiller recalled being with his father and brother at the replacement WW2 Highclere box during which time both brothers would learn the rudiments of signalling. Harry would sit in his chair and tap out on the arm various codes, '3 pause 1', '6', or similar. The boys were expected to reply immediately with the correct response. They would also respond to the real bell signals received from neighbouring Woodhay and Burghclere, although it was only ever Harry who would place the single line token outside in the carrier or effect a manual token exchange with the enginemen.

As mentioned, the boys would also accompany their father to Newbury West, a busy box with fast passing trains, here they would watch rather than take part. This was despite Newbury being the home station of the local District Inspector, Joe Gomm. Sons of signalmen often accompanied their fathers in this way, it was a means of encouraging a new generation for the future despite the rule which stated signal boxes were private with unauthorised persons not permitted. Indeed in later years Les Hiller would indeed follow in his father's footsteps as a signalman on the DNS line at Litchfield.

Another recollection from this period was when Les was taken to Newbury to be shown the then new diesel railcar No 18, built especially for the Lambourn line. This would have been around 1938. The machine evidently made a lasting impression on both father and son, for it was recalled by Les more than 60 years later, whilst Harry would later cite the fact that no attempt had been made to save money on the DNS line south of Newbury by running a diesel service in the 1950s.

With a growing family, space was tight at home whilst his daughters Mary, Queenie, and Ann recall the house at Highclere was understandably cramped. Harry also did his best to assist financially working part time on

Harry as Station Master at Whitchurch. Here was a man unfortunate to have been in the wrong place at the wrong time so far as his railway career was concerned. Had Whitchurch remained under WR control he might well have managed to transfer to a similar position elsewhere. As it was on the Southern there was some resentment to outsiders who might arrive and search for roles which could be filled by home grown men. Harry was 'old school', witness his fastidious belief in the standards of the GWR, we can only imagine his thoughts as traffic and standards slipped in the 1950s, some proof of this being from his comments over the lack of trials with diesels prior to closure.

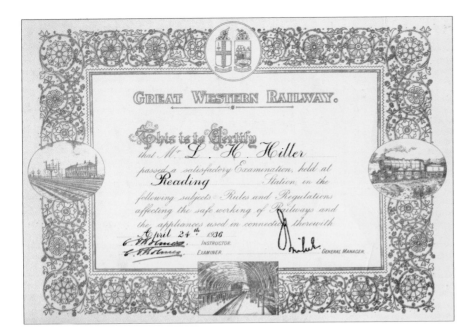

the land as his shifts allowed whilst he also had an area to keep pigs – a side of bacon often hung within the kitchen at their Highclere home.

With an eye to further promotion Harry took and successfully passed the Station Accountancy examinations in 1939. As before he was issued with a certificate which has fortunately survived. This now qualified him to apply for the role of station master although in the event such a position was still some years away. Why there was such a gap is not certain, possibly the circumstances of WW2 and where his role as a signalman was of vital importance, thus meaning any ambitions for a new post had temporarily to be put on hold.

What is known is that he did eventually apply for the Station Master role at Whitchurch in 1945, but at this stage was unsuccessful, the job going instead to a Mr Underhill. Vacancies such as these were advertised on a regular basis with all eligible staff able to apply from anywhere on the GWR network. As such there was often competition for vacancies although sometimes men would prefer to remain within a familiar area but which in turn would restrict the likelihood of finding a suitable vacancy.

Available Station Master posts had also reduced over the years since Harry had joined the railway. The 1930s had witnessed economy with the removal of the SM grade at a number of minor stations. On the DNS this meant that now only Compton, Whitchurch and Winchester retained the grade. Between Woodhay and Litchfield, supervision was under the management of Newbury, although with day to day control of this section in the hands of Foreman Bob Aldridge who had moved from being a neighbour of the Hiller family at Highclere to live in the now vacated station masters accommodation at Highclere. A similar situation existed south of Whitchurch, although for the time being Winchester exercised supervision over Kings Worthy, Worthy Down, and Sutton Scotney.

So far as promotion for Harry was concerned, his failure to be appointed to at Whitchurch role was only temporary, as the same position was re-advertised just two years later in 1947 following the move of Mr R H (Wilf) Underhill to Colnbrook. The result was that Harry was appointed to be Station Master Whitchurch in 1947. (The *GWR Magazine* mentioned the move of Mr Underhill as having taken place in May 1948, although this was simply a somewhat delayed report.)

Unfortunately what should have been a cause for celebration was also tinged with much sadness as Harry's wife of 17 years, Caroline had died in 1947, leaving Harry with a full time job as well as eight children, Mary, Les, Peter, Queenie, Ann, Brenda, Marion, and baby Caroline, all then under the age of 16. At the time there was little if anything in the way of state support for a widower placed in such a role although some family help was provided with Harry's sister coming to live with the family at Harts Corner for two years until the family moved on.

By 1949 though a house move was on the cards and the railway lorry was called for to move the family's possessions the few miles south from Highclere to Whitchurch. It was thus only Harry and the children who made the journey, the actual house move recalled by Les as seeing everything literally thrown into the lorry.

Mary, Queenie, and Ann recall the station house at Whitchurch as being akin to a palace compared with their previous house, and with the luxury of an inside toilet compared with an earth closet. There were also hot water heaters in the bathroom and kitchen, both of these of the gas 'Ascot'. Years later Les recalled the fumes which emanated and which were more noticeable when he returned for a family visit - a smell he had clearly grown used to and ignored whilst living at Whitchurch. There was also a gas ring on the floor of the bathroom used for heating, the actual bathroom being a modification from the original building and converted from what had once been a bedroom. At Whitchurch the two boys shared a bedroom with their father.

At the time Harry's Whitchurch consisted of two

lady porters, Edna Sutton, and Miss Peters – later Mrs Burden, both of whom later left and were replaced by porter Tom Owen, and a lad porter, Ray Wells. There were also three signalmen two being Ken Alexander and Harry Ullett, Harry Hiller had of course worked with Ken previously at Lambourn.

Harry quickly settled into his role, the family recalling that it seemed he was rarely out of uniform as his working day was for an average of 12 hours from 7.40 am to 7.40 pm. He was a strict disciplinarian as far as standards were concerned, one of his regular comments being directed to Ray Wells, "Get y'er hair cut!".

Despite British Railways having taken over from the old Great Western Railway there was no excuse for letting standards slip and consequently the office floor was highly polished – cloths were provided to allow shoes to slide across the surface - it was perhaps a wonder that no accidents occurred as a result.

Another area where high standards were maintained was in the appearance of the station gardens although Harry was the only one who tended to the bushes on the platform. Like a lot of railwayman he was a keen and competent gardener and supplemented the station garden with an allotment nearby on which he kept pigs and also grew what were his favourite flowers – asters. The pigs and the flowers not of course on the same plot! Flower growing was in common with another member of the Whitchurch staff, Ganger Ted Talmage, who had a number of prize dahlia blooms on show in his own garden in Micheldever Road.

The year 1950 saw a revision of regional boundaries, Whitchurch and the DNS line south of Newbury now coming under the control of the Southern Region. Harry like many of his colleagues on the route felt this change to their routine far more than they had nationalisation two years earlier although it would be some

time before major change was noticed.

From now on Whitchurch, instead of being under the control of the Newbury District Inspector, came under Eastleigh, although Harry quickly established an excellent relationship with the District Inspector from the Southern, Fred Capon. Indeed both men shared a common interest in visiting the local pub, not to excess, but certainly when the opportunity presented itself after the official work was done. Harry would also occasionally take the opportunity in arranging later 'refreshment' breaks with some of the regular passengers he would see at the station.

Despite the influence of the southern, Harry's belief in continuing standards was manifest in the award of a 3rd prize in the station gardens awards every year from 1951 through to 1958 inclusive. Even after passenger closure in 1960, Harry's dedication to older standards persisted and 1st class prizes were issued to 'Whitchurch Goods' in 1960, 1961, and finally 1962. Probably after this time it was clear the end was inevitable and both Harry and his remaining staff could be excused for perhaps maybe loosing interest slightly. (Prize classes were determined by the number of points a station achieved. In 1958 for example, Whitchurch managed 115 points and which thus warranted a 'Third Prize'. As a further example, in the same year Stockbridge received the same score and was given a similar award.)

But dealing with the 1960s at this stage is a move too far ahead and instead we will retrace our steps some years back to 1952 during which year Harry is known to have attended and passed two further courses in 'Station Accountancy', these were courses enabling him to coach others in the subject, first at elementary and then at an advanced level. It may be that these skills were achieved in connection with what also by now becoming and expanding role. The retirement of Mr Parsons from Sutton Scotney also meant that Harry's was now the last remaining Station Master between Woodhay and Winchester, for whilst at the

One of Harry's favourite haunts, the King's Arms in Church Street at Whitchurch.

Delivery / collection of goods at Whitchurch by a Foden steam wagon belonging to J Long Jam manufacturer. As mentioned in the text, this company had a factory in nearby Bell Street. Years later there was also a coal merchant operating under the same name at Whitchurch. It is not known if there was any connection between the two.

latter location 'Chesil was now overseen from Winchester City, the remaining eight stations on the line south of Newbury came under Harry's domain. Possibly he took on an expanded role in training the clerks as necessary. (Training of new signalman was undertaken by Whitchurch Signalman Ken Alexander when necessary.)

Away from the railway, the following year 1953, saw a family accident occur but only as a result what was a well intentioned situation. This involved his daughters, Ann and Queenie. At the time the two girls were alone at home together with their youngest sister Caroline, their father being absent on railway business elsewhere. (Harry's role would have required him to make regular visits to the stations and signal boxes under his supervision.)

The two older girls decided it would be appropriate to decorate the station house above the canopy with bunting - in similar fashion to many others buildings similarly bedecked for the coronation.But they also knew that if they had asked their father's permission the result would have been a definite 'No'. That is not to say Harry's views on the monarchy were other than those of a traditionalist, but as Ann and Queenie recounted fifty years later, "…we knew what the response would have been had we asked."

With their father absent Queenie went first, and climbed out of the bedroom window walking across the canopy to drape the bunting, she then successfully made it to the flat roof above the Gents toilet at the north end of the building. Ann followed over the same route, but made the mistake of walking on what both girls had believed to have been slates and which was in fact just smoke blackened glass. She fell through, not just once but a second time whilst attempting to extricate herself. The cut was deep with the scarring still present decades later.

Both girls also knew that regardless of Ann's injury the likely reaction of their father when he returned would be less than sympathetic, and consequently whilst there was no way of covering up either the damage or the injury, they quickly decided that if they smeared 'Windowlene' on the outside of the upstairs window, they could instead explain that the accident had occurred whilst attempting to clean the outside of the bedroom windows. The explanation proved sufficient to mollify Harry although Caroline did evidently proclaim that she had seen her sister Ann - 'Flying'.

From the above it may seem to appear as if the children had a hard life at this time. In reality they will admit they were secretly proud of their local nickname of the 'Railway Children', some years before E Nesbit's book of the same name became so popular. Indeed as in the famous book, the girls would regularly wave at the engine crews they saw passing their station. At the time they might at times have considered they had a difficult life with a father who they regarded as very strict at the time, but now realise it cannot have been easy for their father and like all children they would sometimes deliberately play up.

Harry though was also very occupied in his railway duties and as such perhaps also expected his children to sometimes take on a role for which they were not qualified. An example being when Queenie was unable to advise a passenger of the train times which resulted in a rebuke from her father. On another occasion Queenie sustained a cut to her ankle whilst playing ball against the office wall, Harry ignored the injury and continued to his intended destination – the pub.

Inside the house the kitchen boasted a range for cooking. This was fed on a variety of fuel, sometimes railway sleepers, although these were not the best as the heavy tar content resulted in the complete range once becoming enveloped in flames. One food cooked weekly was fish, Harry of necessity visiting Newbury every Thursday to collect staff wages whilst using the opportunity

to purchase smoked haddock at the town market.

So far as the railway was concerned, Les was by now working as a signalman at Litchfield, the next 'box north of Whitchurch, and indeed it was Les who signalled the fateful freight train south towards Whitchurch in 1954 hauled by No 76017. Les recalled the train passing him in good order, after which and before it had reached Whitchurch, he had been relieved at what was the end of his shift and returned home to Whitchurch on his motorcycle. It was only back at Whitchurch that he saw the results of the spectacular pile-up involving this train. Harry was not present to witness the event, as he had been visiting the stations southwards that morning and was in fact returning to Whitchurch on the northbound passenger service which

Whitchurch as it appeared in late Victorian times. During the 1890s several special trains were run between Paddington and Highclere carrying both royalty and also for guests staying at nearby Highclere Castle. (Two examples were on 26 June 1895 with a 6.30pm arrival from Paddington and on an unconfirmed date in the same month when Queen Victoria arrived and departed from the station.) These workings would then continue south, seemingly as far as Whitchurch - although Winchester was the only place where the engine(s) might be turned. How exactly Whitchurch was involved is not certain, although on every occasion it was noted the Countess of Caernarvon would write to a number of GWR officers thanking them for their assistance, which list included the station masters at Highclere and Whitchurch.

In his book *"Signalman's Reflections"*, - published by Silver Link, Adrian Vaughan provides an interesting story concerning the activities at Whitchurch during the 1940s.

"On the morning of 22 September 1944, Signal woman Alice Hutchinson was on duty in the new signal box at Whitchurch (Hants) - or 'Whitchurch Aunts' as the porter used to call out when trains stopped there, in case anyone should think they were at Whitchurch in Shropshire.

Alice had the 5.a.m. Eastleigh - Alexandra Dock Government Stores train, 54 wagons and a brake van, on the up loop, and as the 7.5.a.m. Winchester to Reading passenger train was following she told the driver and guard of the freight to draw forward clear of No. 7 points - at the north end of the loop, and then set back on to the down loop. This they did, the Winchester passenger passed by and the freight then had to be replaced on the up loop - its previous position, in order to make way for the 7.45 a.m. Newbury to Winchester passenger.

The goods drew ahead until the brake van was clear of No. 7 points whereupon Alice set them normal - and which was a curved path, they were worked by electric motor through a short lever in the box. She then reversed points 11 - the catch point, also worked by motor. Unfortunately she forgot to pull short lever 10 to complete the setting of the route and as a result she could not lower ground disc No. 8 because its lever was held by mechanical locking. (No. 10 was an additional catch point designed to protect the up loop from runaways from the Litchfield direction when No. 7 points were set normal. Disc 8 when cleared would allow a train to set back 'wrong road' into the up platform.)

The down 'stopper' was waiting to come from Litchfield, and time was short. Alice saw nothing wrong, no indicators were 'dangling', all was in order, so as she could not work No. 8 she waved a nearby signal up and down as an indication to the guard to bring his train back. Eager to be of assistance, Guard Rouse, a Didcot man, waved his train back without checking to make sure the road was set. Of course it was not, and with much clattering, banging and crashing his brake-van and four wagons were derailed at No. 10 points - although the brake-van, a gentlemanly Great Western 'Toad' No. 17428, most obligingly re-railed itself at once - but four LMS vans were sullen and refused to co-operate.

The line was completely blocked and buses were at once laid on to take the passengers off the 7.45 a.m. Newbury, waiting at Litchfield, and to cover other disrupted train services. The front part of the goods train, 48 wagons, was meanwhile, hauled through to Litchfield, the guard riding on the last wagon where another brake-van was waiting. This was attached and the train left at 11.40. The breakdown vans, ordered from Reading at 9.40 am, arrived at the lonely spot at 11.25 am. One wagon was re-railed by noon, clearing the down line, and the up line was clear by 2.15 pm."

was stopped prior to the event and eventually propelled back to Sutton Scotney.

Harry alighted from the stopped train and made his way on foot back to the station. Les recalls that an incident such as this enabled his father to put into place his experience of the various rules and procedures for dealing with emergencies, although to be fair others involved were equally qualified and as with any such major incident there would be a veritable plethora of Inspectors, Superintendents and the like quickly on the scene.

Under normal working, Les remembered the various signalmen always maintained a good relationship with the gangers and who were themselves very good at always returning with the occupation key when it was required to restore the section of single line for normal train working, If the gang were working 'mid-section' then restoration was easy, simply by ensuring the trolley was clear of the track and then replacing the occupation key in the key box. However there were also several occasions when the gang would return to their home station but one man might have left the key at the site of work. There was then a frantic dash back to the site of work. The 'JAP' engines with which many of the trolleys were fitted, certainly had a good turn of speed although their riding and stability qualities when used in this way were perhaps open to question.

Away from the unusual and to return to the mundane, and in the 1950s Whitchurch was at the time still busy with freight. Several coal merchants operated from the yard, Messrs, Long, Arthur Wakefield, and Woods, just three of the recalled names. Later Crosby took over from Long, whilst Wood was amalgamated into Corel's. The Sutton Scotney merchant, Messrs Didhams, would also receive supplies at Whitchurch on occasions, arranged to coincide with domestic deliveries scheduled for the area.

For a time a railway lorry was also based at Whitchurch although this would undertake work in an area ranging from Micheldever in the east to Stockbridge and Andover in the west. Bulk rail traffic at Whitchurch consisted of sugar beet and oil, whilst quantities - sometimes vanloads - of water cress were sent to London, Leeds, Manchester, and Liverpool. The watercress traffic alone afforded income worth £2,000- £3,000 per month to the station in the 1950s.

Another volume traffic was fruit for the jam factory of Messrs Long in Bell Street, the railway staff able to earn extra overtime – or was it payment from the consignee?, to assist in the unloading of this traffic. Finally there were

Opposite - Two examples from Harry's time: the first commenced in 1946 and was also the last issue of the old GWR type - Harry being responsible for the years 1947/48. Post 1950 the Southern Region produced a simpler version but even so Whitchurch received an award most years (1954 was the only 'Second' reported, all the others being 'Third'). After 1960 the style was even more plain, 'Whitchurch Goods' being recognised on a simple green and white card.

With the station in the background, a view of the commodious goods shed (similar in size and style to that at Compton), plus the cattle pens and of course the water column. Throughout the 1950s there was one down and one up pick-up freight each way between Didcot and Winchester. The service terminated at each end, any vehicles collected en-route and destined for stations south of Winchester would be left at Bar End and collected daily by a freight which worked from and to Eastleigh.

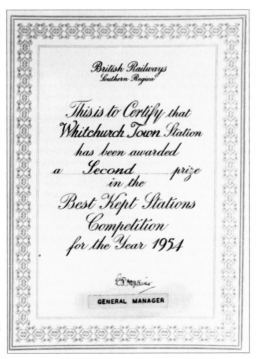

BR Class 3 No 82012 arriving at the station for Newbury / Didcot. The use of tank engines south of Newbury was unusual although certainly not unique. This particular engine was based at Eastleigh from around May 1953 onwards and has probably taking over the non-availability of either a BR Class 4 2-6-0 or T9.   *Mike Esau*

regular deliveries of boxes of meat pies to the Whitchurch butcher, Billy Small. Milk was not handled at Whitchurch.

Such then was the situation in the 1950s although it was already clear passenger traffic was slowly diminishing.

When the end for passenger workings came in March 1960 it was with a sad inevitability. Interviewed at the time by the press, Harry was perhaps understandably vehement in his assertion that services might have been saved by the use of a diesel – and that none had ever been tried. (A diesel car had passed through Whitchurch on test in 1947, but nothing more had happened since.)

It was around this time that Harry acquired his first motor car, a beige Morris 1000, which he kept for a number of years. He was also now alone in the station house, the children having left to start their own lives.

Despite the loss of passenger trains, Harry was still responsible for the payment of wages to Traffic Department staff on Thursday every week and in an area stretching from Woodhay as far as Kings Worthy. Previously this had been accomplished by travelling by service train, but without a passenger service in existence BR instead opted for a weekly taxi service, the cost of which was considerable.

Harry's remaining time at Whitchurch was now drawing to an end, a fact that could hardly have escaped him. The years through from 1960 to 1964 witnessed the inevitable run down of local goods services from the

intermediate stations leaving instead just through goods traffic as the last trains seen at Whitchurch. Indeed Whitchurch itself ceased to handle any traffic in the yard from 1963 after which the sidings were lifted with almost indecent haste, almost as if there was a management decision to ensure that there was no chance of a reinstatement.

Closure finally came in August 1964 although Harry remained in the employ of the railway but with a role much reduced in status. He was now a relief clerk, working from the Station Master's office at Winchester. He would though continue to reside in the station house, taking on the role of official care-taker for the station. Such was his devotion even to this melancholy task that Whitchurch was one of the few locations not to suffer from vandalism.

This was not a happy time for Harry, he is known to have been deeply unhappy at Winchester, partly because of his now lack of freedom, but according to former Winchester Porter Graham Hawkins, due to a strained relationship with the then Winchester Station Master who it appeared had a dislike for former 'Western' men.

Around this time also the present writer, having cultivated an interest in railways, and the DNS line in particular, found himself visiting Whitchurch, and as it happened shortly before the demolition contractors arrived. How I had perhaps found myself at Whitchurch is a slight

INCIDENTS and OCCURANCES Over the years a number of incidents associated with Whitchurch and area are reported both in official and other sources.

The earliest of these was on 15 November 1897 when '517' class 0-4-2T No. 1471 was delayed by 14 minutes at Whitchurch 'due to leaking tubes' whilst working the 7.38 a.m. Winchester - Didcot service.

Two incidents caused by weather conditions during the 1920s have also been documented. The first was during the winter blizzard of 1926 when the 8.16 a.m. Winchester to Newbury became stuck in a drift near Lodge Farm. A local member of the permanent way gang, Charlie Hawkins, set off to locate the missing train, which he found stuck fast in a snowdrift. Two engines were despatched from Didcot to move the now 'cold' (meaning the fire had been thrown out) engine and carriages but they only succeeded in pulling the 'dead' engine off the rails. Yet another engine was then summoned from Didcot and the combined power of the three was successful in both rerailing and moving the stranded train. One slight irony is that some time later, bridge deflection tests were carried out using two engines in steam, somewhat less than the four which had been coupled together on the above occasion.

Two years later on 28 January 1928, the weather was again blamed when the 4.40 a.m. Didcot to Winchester goods ran through the points at the south end of the station loop resulting in 30 wagons being derailed. Approaching from the opposite direction was the 7.13 a.m. ex Winchester passenger service, but this was halted by the actions of staff

from the engineering department working nearby. Mention of their actions was given in the GWR Magazine with gratuities paid to H.E. Talmage - Underman, £1. 1s., Sub Ganger, R. Clark, and Underman N. Wakefield, who each received 10/6d. (Official records for the period refer to two incidents around this time in close succession. The first was on 18 January when it was reported the 4.40 a.m. Didcot goods had passed a signal at danger and then on 28 January when an engine was derailed.)

Other incidents from the period are recorded from the regular reports received by the General Manager although unfortunately without further detail. The first was on 21 January 1925 and related to 'Stones on the line'. A number of derailments are then spoken of, on 6 February 1926 and then on 9 May 1927: so far as the latter was concerned there is mention of 'wagons derailed.' Also on 9 December 1927 with a 'tender derailed' On 19 June 1928 there was a further reference to 'wagons derailed'. We now move to 8 November 1929 when a Mr. Thomas was 'badly bruised'. After this comes 5 September 1934 when some sleepers were reported as on fire. Next a staff issue for on 19 October 1936 'Head Porter' Switzer is mentioned with a septic hand. Finally on 7 March 1937 was a reported collision between an engine and some milk tanks. Reference this last incident, the records are not clear if the Whitchurch referred to was the one on the DNS - there were several 'Whitchurch' locations on the GWR! As an aside the staff recall they could earn 3/- for duty dealing with the one Sunday train.

No 3206 awaiting departure south. The two vans on the right would be used for watercress traffic.   R Blencowe

'Ted' as he was known, provided the catalyst for much of the information gathered by the present author on the DNS line both at Whitchurch and indeed elsewhere. Diminutive in stature, he had joined the railway at Whitchurch as a Lineman's Lad before the First World War. (On an early visit he recounted the story of travelling to Didcot to change the batteries on the engine used for the ATC working on the Lambourn branch.) His recollections were never embellished just purely factual, whilst subsequent visits to official sources invariably corroborated his memories. Ted later transferred to the Engineering Department lodging first with a man whose own ancestry went back to the opening of the railway in 1885, as such there were a new raft of stories to told. (Later on his death-bed this man later insisted on

telling Ted of a crime he had committed many years earlier and for which he had never been caught.)

Ted's recollections were crystal clear over 50 years of railway work, he recalled the prize won by the Sutton Scotney gang for the 'best kept length' in 1931 and stated this was only possible because of the assistance other gangs gave, the derailments at Whitchurch and the upheaval all felt when the SR took over - far more a change than nationalisations to years earlier. Nothing though was said in malice about any event. Many of his recollections having appeared in this and previous books on the railway. A private man, he lived for many years at No. 1 Micheldever Road, Whitchurch tending a superb garden where prize dahlias might be seen. One major regret is that there appear to be no photographs of Ted at work on the railway .

mystery, as I was at the time living in Winchester without private transport. Wandering around the station site it was not surprising that I was quickly challenged by a tall man who having then satisfied himself that I was not in fact a vandal, offered to unlock the signal box and platelayers huts

to show me the scene. The result especially in the signal box was, to youthful eyes, to have a permanent effect, and the start of a love and fascination for railway signalling. Here as a youth I was to experience the kindness of a railwaymen keen to talk of the past – of course I wish I had asked more -

Unusual working. Here a northbound passenger service has / or is in the process of collecting a vehicle from the yard being attached as 'tail traffic' - it could well be a horsebox or might equally be a van load of watercress. The move involving a passenger train would require the trailing point into the yard to be clipped, likewise the facing point forming the exit from the yard on to the up main. Harry's skills in topiary with the neat box hedging may be admired, whilst just visible on the down platform are the edges to one of his flower beds.

Busy times at Whitchurch. Just departed and paused waiting the token for the section to Sutton Scotney is the 10.50 am from Didcot - the 12.57 pm departure south from Whitchurch. Meanwhile a fair (for DNS standards) numbers of passengers await the arrival in the platform of the T9 hauled 11 48 am ex Southampton Terminus - 12 55 pm at Whitchurch. This was scheduled to spend four minutes at the station although the down train had already left and was waiting on the single train indicates the up service had been delayed. The smoke darkened glass canopy which Ann fell through in June 1953 covers the down plat-form. In 1954 there were three booked crossings at Whitchurch although this was the only one involving two passenger trains.

R Blencowe

but the culmination of this talk were several more visits to Whitchurch and the official purchase of the contents of the block-shelf together with other ancillary signal box items for the princely sum of £2.

Harry even managed to circumvent some of the BR 'Red' or should it be Southern Region 'Green' tape, with the result that one Saturday morning the contents of the box were removed, literally just as the contractors were starting to cut up the track into sections a few yards down the line.

Even so some items could not be saved, the token instruments had already been removed, whilst one of the occupation keys was missing. Additionally I was not allowed to purchase the signal box nameplate, likewise what was a glorious row of handlamps within the former gangers trolley hut was left to the mercy of the contractors. No doubt unceremoniously bulldozed over.

For all of this Harry would accept no thanks, he even delivered the purchased items to Winchester for me and where for some years it formed the nucleus of a small collection of DNS items. In later years all were dispersed .

Harry eventually took retirement in 1973, receiving a certificate commemorating his total of 48 years railway service. By now the station house at Whitchurch together with the railway land was owned by Hampshire County Council, although Harry's occupancy as a sitting tenant was unaffected.

Little is known of Harry's retired years, although it is likely he continued to indulge in his various hobbies and interests as before. He had been a member of what was referred to as the Whitchurch Wednesday cricket team. Les comments that his father was no good at playing cricket, but he did regularly cut the grass for them. He would also sometime venture to Southampton to watch the county side in action. His indoor interests included playing cribbage, whilst at some time also he had been involved with the Red Cross.

Harry died in Winchester Hospital in February 1981 and at the relatively early age of 72. He was buried alongside his beloved wife Caroline in Burghclere Churchyard having been a widower for 34 years.

Apart from his supervision of the signal box registers, Harry was responsible for maintaining the station accounts, a task performed with equal gusto. This was recognised in a letter he received from Mr W H Scutt, District Traffic Superintendent, Southampton, on 16 May 1952.

"Mr H Hiller: Station Master, Whitchurch Town.

Examination of Accounts.

I think you will be interested to read the report I have received from the Auditor following his recent visit to your station and I append an extract from a letter I have received from the Audit Accountant."

'Mr Hiller, the Station Master, performs all the clerical duties at Whitchurch Town. Originally Western Region staff, he elected to stay with his station when the transfer was made to the Southern. To make effective the change he has attended Commercial Classes at Salisbury and with the knowledge gained has brought into use Southern books and methods of book-keeping. His efforts are highly commendable....'

Mr Scutt continued, "Needless to say, I am very pleased indeed to receive such a communication and should like to take the opportunity of thanking you for the interest you have taken in the work."

No 7327 entering Whitchurch sometime in the 1950s with a typical stopping train of the period. Whitchurch was unique amongst DNS stations in having a subway linking the two platforms. It is possible Harry may just be glimpsed in his uniform cap on the station. It may be truthfully said that throughout the life of the station from the advent of British Railways in 1948 through to the final closure of the line in August 1964, it was Harry who was in charge at Whitchurch. Harry was one of number of men who held the Station Master post from 1885 to 1960. In date order the others were. Messrs, Crook and I Jones, both within the first ten years of opening. Then in 1895 it was Thomas Sorrell to be replaced by John Taylor in 1897. By March 1903 William J. Foster is mentioned (a Mr Foster had also been in charge at Sutton Scotney some years earlier). Mr Foster had left by 1907 replaced by Ernest Crockford and who in 1915 - it may even have been 1911, had been superseeded by Thomas Burden Chesterton, previously at Chinnor. (Mr. Chesterton was recalled as somewhat dictotorial, an example being that he instructed his wife to undertake all the necessary weeding of the station area.) After this in 1923 comes George Jones and then at an unknown date, possibly around 1931, J.H. Evans, who remained until the post was abolished in November 1934. With reinstatement of the grade, E C Frampton arrived from Acton upon promotion but was replaced by Edward Franklin from Hungerford in June 1938, again arrived on promotion. In 1941 it was George Lomer from Winchester, again a promotional move and then by 1945 by R.H. (Wilf) Underhill until that is Harry took charge.

Top left - Highclere sometime in the 1930s after the Tilley lamp posts had replaced the earlier oil lamps, Tilley lamps were of the paraffin pressure type and were separate from the post. Once lit they were attached to a windlass and wound to the top of the post. Relaying has been taking place through the platforms compared with the view on p56. In the December 1928 issue of the 'Great Western Magazine', Highclere was reported as having won a £5 prize in the annual station gardens competition. Special trains for Highclere were referred to on p69, but once additional special is reported in 1923 when the body of the Fifth Earl of Carnarvon was transported by special train from Plymouth to Highclere for burial.

Top right - Porters at Highclere c1911. the names given are, left: J Badger , and right; H Evans, the latter reported as 'Signal –Porter'. George Behrend in 'Gone With Regret' , when recalling the station in the 1920s, refers to LSWR/SR engines working race-trains to Newbury and with the signals at the station not always being restored between trains if one was following another in the same direction.

Centre and bottom - Two views of Burghclere, none of those seen are named, although in the centre view it is likely some may well be members of the station master's family.

BURGHCLERE STATION

NEWBURY WEEKLY NEWS: 1 September 1887. "We understand that arrangements have been made with the Great Western Railway for the construction of a set of Lime Kilns near Burghclere station by Messrs Forder, and laying down a line of rails from the works to the station. If the proposed junction can be effected in the South Western Railway at Winchester, the lime will be able to be conveyed to all stations on the South Western Railway system,, and along other railways connected with it.

*Top - The true Burghclere and the nearest yet found to any images of the lime quarry at the south east end of the station. The top view is looking from the Kingsclere road bridge south, with part of a goods train stationary on the up line extending back on to the line in the direction of Litchfield. **Middle** - In what is a cruel enlargement, we see the engine of the train setting off from the lime quarry siding having either collected or deposited some wagons. It would appear there are other vehicles remaining in the siding on the extreme left. The products from the lime quarry were taken out by rail although there is no evidence to believe private owner wagons belonging to the quarry were involved. What is also very interesting is the length of what is the up-pick up goods: the number of vehicles left on the main line and the number of wagons being taken out of the quarry. Operations at the lime quarry ceased in 1938 with eight men losing their jobs. The lime workers cottages, on the west side of the line just south of the station remain today, whilst the quarry itself is a nature reserve although accessible at certain times of the year. **Right** - Enlarged from an unrelated image, a distant view of the quarry buildings, c1935, may be seen.*

Right - Sutton Scotney looking south, depicted in a scene from a contemporary postcard dated April 1906. This is the earliest view so far located of the station which probably appears very much as when first opened 21 years before. The same scene would have been very similar to that recalled by Ernie Penny and Mr Parsons years later although by that time a number of trees had grown up on the down (east) side of the line behind what was the original signal box. The small wooden building on the left was a ground frame hut used for controlling the trailing connection to the goods yard as seen in the foreground. Both this connection and the ground frame were removed around 1922 - probably as they were due for replacement and traffic levels did not warrant further expense. The structure of the ground frame then found a new use as a parcels hut at the far end of the station building. In the background the goods shed will be seen complete with sliding end doors, these had been removed by 1934. Possibly the result of damage by a rail vehicle. Both security and ease of working inside were then compromised. Notice also the oil hut at the base of the up starting signal. In the view *below* the scene is looking north from the Wonston road bridge at the south end of the station. The crossover referred to above will be seen to be removed, It was later reinstated post 1943 and remained until closure. (Unloading parcels was obviously quicker from the offside of the train!) The platform lamps at Sutton Scotney were oil lit.

A SHORT HISTORY OF WORTHY DOWN

Army occupation at Worthy Down dates from 2 August 1917. The word Worthy means 'enclosure', and was normally related to a plot of land given to Roman legionnaires by a grateful Emperor when they retired from active service. The first inhabitants, in the fourth century BC, were Iron Age folk called the Belgae. Essentially farmers and stock rearers, their settlement there was by no means a small one, and there may even have been a fort or walled stockade on the Down. Pilots flying over Worthy Down in the hot dry summers of the 1920's and 1930's often reported seeing vaguely discernable traces of the old village at certain times of the year, due to changes in colour of grass growing where the half underground huts had stood.

The earliest maps show the area as being owned by the Pyle family, and it was probably used as a staging post for sheep being driven up to Smithfield market from the West Country. They grazed and fattened on the Down before going on their way.

William Corbett in his 18th century book 'Rural Rides' said of Worthy Down 'There are not many fairer spots in England'.

The Winchester races were held at Worthy Down, and the first recorded race was on 11 September 1753. The annual Hampshire Hunt Cup was held at Worthy Down until 1805, when it began to alternate with Abbotstone Down. In 1887 the Master of the Horse decreed that the valuable Queen's Plate should be shared with Salisbury. This was the beginning of the end, as soon after this, falling attendances meant that racing finally ceased. The last recorded race being on 14 May 1896. A large wooden grandstand stood about where the Soldiers' Married Quarters are now, and one can still see most of the area of the race track from that vantage point.

Of course, the Down looked a little different from its present day appearance. There were no trees to be seen. Most around the camp today date from 1939 when some 8,000 were planted, mainly as camouflage. Until that time the only vegetation was clumps of thick shrubs like elderberry, blackthorn and bramble. The area to the North, next to South Wonston, was known as Gypsy Bushes and was probably an occasional home for a band of travelling people.

On August 2 1917 the disused course was visited by Lt Col J. A. Chamier RFC, who was looking for a site to house the Wireless and Observers School, then being re-located from Brooklands. His report, which one can only assume was made at the end of an otherwise fruitless search, reads that the surrounding area was quite ideal for forced landings, and that the Down itself was fine for flying.

Although it did slope towards the North West, the undulation was not enough to prejudice its use as a landing ground. A further point of consideration could well have been the proximity of the railway although in 1917 the nearest station was of course at Sutton Scotney.

A roughly rectangular site of about 480 acres was requisitioned for an airfield and by the end of the year, the RFC had established the School of Artillery and Infantry Co-operation. First a canvas camp, the Canadian Pioneer Corps aided by German POWs soon erected more permanent wooden / brick buildings also aircraft hangars where the Training Centre is now sited.

In October 1917 two railway sidings were laid on the west side of the railway track, together with a platform to which special trains were run from Winchester for the

Worthy Down in May 1943. The railway runs north - south on the right hand side of the image. It would appear that the DNS was used to transport aero engines as a purpose built crane was constructed next to the line to aid lifting and loading. During the war a leave train ran most nights at the request of the Royal Navy. It became well known due to the antics of drunken sailors returning from a 'beer-up' in Winchester. In the end the RN had to put Officers on board the train to keep order. If the sailors left a mess in the train then they had to clear it up. This often meant them returning back to Winchester as the train returned empty stock. A four mile walk then ensued back to Worthy Down which may well also have acted as a future deterrent not to cause trouble.

A narrow gauge railway existed at Worthy Down although probably only for use in transporting construction materials within the site. Research by Tony Dowland indicates this had been laid along the approach road, maybe to both east and west of the railway. Its purpose was almost certainly in the transport of materials for use in the construction of the aerodrome, much of this coming in by railway. There is no indication so far as to how long the railway survived, its extent, or what motive power might have been used. The view above was taken to show a crashed 'RE8' which had landed on an Aveling & Porter steam roller, whilst fortunately also showing the railway alongside. Tony Dowland collection.

benefit of workmen engaged in the construction of the airfield. During the period October 1917 to October 1918 some 6,000 loaded wagons were handled at the sidings, a more substantial platform later erected for public use. Worthy Down became a recognised halt on 1 April 1918.

This coincided with the formation of the RAF, and Worthy Down was renamed the RAF/ Army Co- operation School, acting as a finishing school for Corps recce pilots. They were given advanced instruction in map reading, artillery/infantry co-operation and contact patrolling, while observers were trained up to wings standard.

There were up to 1,450 personnel on the Camp, training 300 students at a time on 80 aircraft of the Bristol Fighter, RE8 and AW FK8 types.

Nearby Flowerdown housed the Electrical and Wireless School, and Worthy Down provided their flying facilities, effectively a separate aerodrome being set up on the West of the site by the A34 (then called the Whitchurch Road).

In 1924 the RAF emerged from near extinction and two Squadrons of heavy Vickers Vimy (later Virginia) bombers were formed up at Worthy Down. Numbers 7 and 58 Squadrons were part of the Wessex Bomber Area, with its Headquarters at Andover. Later famous officers such as Portal and Harris served on the Station, and the Squadrons were very successful; one or the other of them held the RAF bombing Trophy until 1935.

Accidents were not infrequent. In 1931 a Virginia crashed into the Station Orderly Room, killing three of the four crew. On a lighter note, a similar aircraft was stolen by an 'erk' doing a ground run up. Having never flown before, he nevertheless managed to take off and fly successfully around the area before returning and landing in front of a large and interested audience which included the Commanding Officer and Provost Sergeant! On one occasion an 8lb smoke bomb was dropped on to the Winchester to Newbury road - with no damage (apart from the bomb), and once 10,000 gallons of petrol drained from an underground storage tank into the ditches in the valley below the Officers' Mess. The then Commanding Officer, (Sir) Arthur Harris, was asked by the RAF to pay for the loss, but declined!

The squadrons were re-equipped with the Heyford bomber in 1935, about the time that some new squadrons arrived with smaller aircraft such as Hinds, Gordons and Wellesleys. Their stay was short. The RAF had found that the contours and size of the airfield made it unsuitable for the more modern aircraft then coming into service, and from 1938 the Fleet Air Arm (used to smaller landing areas) began to take interest. First the airfield was transferred to the Coastal Command of the RAF, with Avro Ansons arriving to exercise with HMS Centurion (a ship in those days). On 24 May 1939 the Station was transferred to the Navy, and given the title HMS Kestrel. Telegraphist Air Gunners (TAG's) were trained here on Nimrods(!), and Ospreys.

The German radio claimed to have torpedoed and sunk HMS Kestrel on at least one occasion. In connection with Dunkirk During Dunkirk in 1940, flights of bombers flew offensive sorties over the beaches; the only time that Worthy Down ever fired a shot In anger! In August 1940 it was hit by a force of Junker 88 bombers, though little damage was caused, just one hangar losing its roof.

Worthy Down was actually a very valuable airfield in the 1940-42 period. A decoy site was laid out at Micheldever to attract enemy bombers, and some extraordinarily strong ground defences were erected. Worthy Down was nowhere near any of the planned stop lines designed to halt the (then supposed) imminent German invasion, but a ring of some 31 pill boxes of various designs was erected, most of which still exist. These were thickened by a multitude of fire trenches, the lot being manned by nearly a full battalion of regular infantry, commanded at one time by Major the Lord Tennyson.

Most of the fixed defences were of the Royal Engineer Type 22 octagonal box, either concrete or brick built and crewed by one NCO and five men, with at least one LMG. There were at least two of the rare Pickett-Hamilton 'disappearing' forts, designed to be built actually on an airfield. These could be lowered to ground level when aircraft were using the runways, then made to pop up to engage the enemy when they appeared! The trainee TAGs were known as 'Goons', and lived in ranks of wooden huts in the valley below the Officers' Mess, still sometimes referred to as Goon Valley. Sir Ralph Richardson and Sir Laurence Olivier were two of the famous personalities who served at Worthy Down with the Fleet Air Arm during this period. In 1943 the TAG School moved to Canada, and HMS Kestrel became a resting place for various odd units. Blind approach development went on there, and the USAAF lodged for a while. Two Liberator bombers forced landed in bad weather once, probably the largest aircraft ever to use the airfield. They had full and armed bomb loads on board and had to be unloaded before they could take off again. HMS Kestrel was 'paid off' in November 1947.

In 1952, the Naval Air Electrical School moved from Warrington to Worthy Down, the station being re-opened as HMS Ariel II (Ariel I had been at Warrington). The extra brick huts required to house the school were built in 1952, and are still used today by the Computer Centre. This educational task lasted for eight years, until more economies made the School move to Lee-on-Solent.

At this time, the Corps were looking for a new home, particularly somewhere to house the new Electronic Accounting Development Unit, and the Fleet Air Arm agreed to hand the airfield over to the Army. Its flying swansong was for a few weeks in late 1959, when it played host to Whirlwind helicopters of No 848 Squadron working up to join the commando carrier, HMS Bulwark. In December 1960, control passed, and some would say Worthy Down's most interesting period began.

A major re-build took place around this time and when complete the then Secretary of State for War, John Profumo, officially opened the new camp on 20 June 1961. By this time the railway had ceased passenger service although there is some suggestion that occasion special trains for servicemen may have continued for a short while after March 1960. Certainly post 1960, there was for some time a fixed notice at Winchester City station giving instructions to arriving servicemen as to how to reach the camp.

(Abridged with minor amendments / additions from 'Worthy Down 70 Years On' by Maj. R G Howard, other unaccredited websites were consulted. With grateful thanks also to Tony Dowland.)

On 13 July 1918, a handwritten note in the GWR archives refers to "...the water supply at the Aerodrome at Worthy Down near Kings Worthy has failed. Application has been made (at the request of the Officer in Charge at Worthy Down) to supply 15,000 gallons daily commencing tomorrow from Winchester. Can we arrange for five of our tanks to be sent to Winchester or Newbury tonight or tomorrow to work to the sidings at Worthy and work back for refilling." The matter was swiftly referred to some well known names on the GWR, including Messrs. Aldington, Churchward, Collett, Wright and Williams with the result that the line was to be specially opened for the working if needed and the train accompanied by a locomotive inspector. Four (filled) wagons left Swindon at 5.00 a.m. the following day with two other empties collected en-route: one at Challow the other at Didcot. At the last named location arrangements for these two vehicles to be filled were left in the hands of the appropriately named, Foreman Drinkwater. The vehicles despatched from Swindon were Nos. 31, 35, 36 and 42.) Locomotive power to work the tanks between Winchester and Worthy Down was provided from Winchester without the need for an extra engine. The tanks were refilled at Winchester as needed. A record exists for the first four days of operation which may also have been the limit of use, as the file concludes with a note of 2 August 1918 referring only to the period 14-17 July.

Date	No of tanks supplied	Special mileage Incurred		Total mileage	Remarks
		Loaded	Light Engine		
July 14	8	83m 41ch	83m 41ch	167m 2 ch	Special Swindon to Winchester and back.
July 15	10	4m 0 ch			Special Winchester to Worthy Down
		4m 0 ch			Special Worthy Down to Winchester
		4m 0 ch		12m 0 ch	Special Winchester to Worthy Down
July 16	5	4m 0 ch			Special Winchester to Worthy Down.
			4m 0ch		Light engine Winchester to Worthy Down
		4m 0 ch		12m 0 ch	Special Worthy Down to Winchester
July 17	5	4m 0 ch			Special Winchester to Worthy Down
			4m 0 ch		Light engine Worthy Down to Winchester
			4m 0 ch		Light engine Winchester to Worthy Down
	5	4m 0 ch			Special Worthy Down to Winchester
		4m 0 ch		20m 0 ch	Special Winchester to Worthy Down

This page and next page top - Early days at Kings Worthy. The views bottom left and next page top are similar and so may well have been taken on the same occasion. Both are looking south with what appears to be just a locomotive and brake-van, the engine carrying an 'F' headcode: one lamp centrally on the buffer beam and one immediately below the chimney. This indicated a 'through freight'. Could it then perhaps be a special working?

Centre - Down Winchester (Southampton) working. In this and the others views of the station shown here, mention may be made of the inside-key bull-head rail running through the down platform. Much of this was supported on rail-chairs stamped DNSR and dated 1882 or afterwards. This indicates the down line was the original set of rails and the up line was added when the station was opened.

Bottom - Looking north towards Sutton Scotney, probably not long after opening. (Worthy down was not added until 1918.) The platform trolley on the down side hardly seems to have moved between most of the images. One change reported here fairly early on was the provision of Electric Train Staff catching apparatus provided sometime year ending 31 December 1913 at a cost of £36 0s 2d.

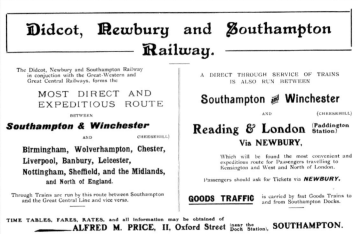

With good relations established between the DNS and Great Central companies very early on, the natural progression was the provision of a through service between Southampton and the north from 1901. As a means also of affording a direct rail service to passengers arriving via cross-channel ferry at Southampton, through coaches were added to the first northbound departure from Southampton, each day alternating between GWR and GCR (later LNER) stock. Until 1916 when the service was suspended but again upon reinstatement in 1921, there was even a restaurant car for these workings although from 1922, this did not venture further south than Oxford. The service continued to run until 1939, with at its peak years even the

opportunity for a through coach(es) between Southampton, York and even Scarborough. In the final years it was only in the up direction that LNER stock was seen, the down coach(es) being worked on the route via Reading and Basingstoke. (See timetable map on p32 and referred text on p33.)

(See timetable map on p32 and referred text on p33.)

In the top view opposite, we see a DNS train supplemented with two through coaches. The locations is rounding the curve to joint the main line at Enborne meaning this is an up direction working. In the lower view a train, with what appears to be the same two GWR vehicles, is seen approaching Winchester tunnel from the direction of Kings Worthy and Winnall. (In the down direction the LNER vehicles were detached at Didcot and worked to Southampton via Reading and Basingstoke.)

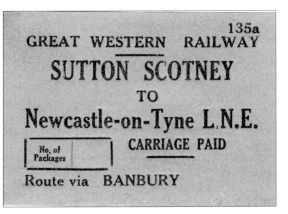

26 June 1933 and trouble at Winchester Junction. The DNS train is passing sweetly underneath the LSWR heading for Newbury, unaffected by and possibly blissfully unaware of the circumstances unfolding above. Earlier that day on the SR main line, a derailment had occurred right on the junction of the Alton line with the main route between Winchester and Southampton. The situation made more difficult as King George V was due at Southampton later the same day to open the new graving dock named in his honour. Here the SR breakdown crane is working to restore the line….which they succeeded in doing although the 'Royal' was subsequently reported as having been delayed.

W H C Blake

No excuses for this one deliberate repetition with the earlier 'Winchester Great Western' book. This image is a favourite, not just because of its quality but especially because of information it conveys. For 15 years from 1925 to 1940 there was a single solitary train south from Didcot to Winchester every Sunday. Here it would terminate, any passengers desirous of travelling further south were compelled to walk the one mile to Winchester (Southern Railway) station to continue their journey.

Departure from Didcot was at 12.55 pm, calling all stations to Newbury arriving at 1.38pm. After just 12 minutes the train was off again - all stations to Winchester arriving at 2.57pm. Here the engine would detach and run the short distance to Bar End and turn before coupling to the opposite end of the train ready to return north. Leaving Winchester at 3.30pm arrival at Newbury was 4.37pm. During the 33 minute lay over at Winchester, the photographer has captured one of the rare occasions when a scheduled passenger service departed north from the down platform. Was this the practice every time, or did the crew not have time to shunt into the up platform? Indeed, why did the train not arrive in the up platform?

Leaving Winchester it was all stations to Newbury where just 13 minutes were allowed for the service to be shunted into the Lambourn bay and the engine run-round. Now it was tender first to Lambourn, arriving at the Berkshire terminus at 5.33pm. Run round again and the final leg was depart for Newbury at 6.15pm, Newbury at 6.58pm with a final departure for Didcot at 7.45pm arriving at 8.37pm. 112 miles and a maximum of 50 stops (dependent upon Churn and a few of the halts on the Lambourn line). From 6 November 1932 operation south if Newbury may also have been rather interesting as following that date Enborne and Winchester was worked on Sundays by pilotman using tokens withdrawn at each station the previous evening and left in locked boxes. (This in itself raises questions, for with a passenger train working, points would have to be clipped for either way working - or was the pilotman a relief signalman who operated each box as the train arrived? No photographs have been found to show where these 'locked boxes' might have been located, as with the exception of Winchester, up to 1942 all the token instruments were located in the booking office at the stations.)

The engine, not that matters too much, is one of the three former MSWJ 2-4-0s which saw regular use on the DNS and Lambourn lines during the period.

What an idyllic way to spend a Sunday…..

Above - *Having discussed engine changing at the north end of the station, it is only correct we should describe the procedure as applied to down trains. Here an unidentified 'Duke' class 4-4-0 has arrived with the signal cleared for the engine to run straight to Bar End. Meanwhile the Southern engine will be in one of several locations - dependent upon the timetable. Thus it could well be waiting on the single line south of the signal box, or if a conflicting move were likely, within the loading dock opposite the signal box. Ironically the loading dock is where in later years BR would hold engines even as large as a 9F when waiting to take over a tank car train.*

A less than perfect image of a train about to depart north* sometime in the inter-war era. The guard may be seen waving his flag whilst a porter busies himself and another man, a clerk perhaps, observes from the platform. Five passenger trains per day, six days a week, over 75 years between 1885 and 1960 and this procedure could well have been re-enacted 117,000 times.

*There is some suggestion this may have been an excursion working but this cannot be confirmed.

Inspection train at Winchester. This is the companion view to that seen in the original volume and depicts a '517' class 0-4-2T on a special working. The occasion is not formally identified but is very likely to have been when the great and the good visited Winchester to inspect the new power signalling installed in 1922. Why Winchester was chosen for this installation is easily explained. Firstly the GWR could offset some of the charge against the DNS - on the basis the signalling here needed renewal and they could get another company to pay for it. (Paddington were nothing but shrewd.) Secondly, the installation was of untried and untested technology, if difficulties had occurred then any delays to traffic would be limited - unlike if the equipment had been installed in a main line location. Finally Winchester was within daily travelling from the signal works at Reading. Specialist assistance was thus available within a few hours - compared with perhaps overnight if the location chosen had been hundreds of miles further. So with those comments in mind please continue over the page... .

On a grey Monday 21 December 1925, Southern Railway signal lineman Edward Wallis visited Winchester. Aside from being a professional railwayman, Edward was also an enthusiastic photographer and avid collector of railway tickets - in the case of the latter what he may have purloined from the station is not recorded. Edward would doubtless of been aware of the power-signalling system then in use at Winchester - installed in 1922 and removed in 1933 - whilst what he recorded at the time of his visit history may well count as unique, for the accompanying five views are the clearest record yet of the signalling system in existence for that short time.

Above - The 1922 signal box built to contain the 16 lever Siemens frame. Size wise the frame was small, only about 4-5 feet in length so leaving plenty of room for the tablet instrument to Shawford Junction and token instrument to Kings Worthy - the domed tops of which can be seen through the windows. (Winchester was thus the first DNS location to have these vital instruments removed from the booking office into the signal box.) Noticeable is the complete absence of point rodding and signal wires, the whole operation worked by electricity, hence the ventilation bricks in lower part of the structure which contained the batteries. The signalman will be noted as will the drunken telegraph pole. In 1942 the box was extended at the north end taking the steps inside. Whilst this was taking place trains were still running and the duty signalman was required to enter and exit by ladder from the window every time a tablet / token exchange was required.

Right - The up main starting signal, No 2 in the power frame, with No 3, 'Shunt ahead on up main' beneath. Operation of either lever would first verify the position of the points in the tunnel, No 22, after which the signal would respond to the respective motor on the signal post - again hence the absence of any obvious operating wires. Until 1942 the loop at Winchester ended where the two lines converge, just within the tunnel. With several up passenger trains still changing engines at Winchester, a procedure that would continue into BR days, the working was under careful control. Firstly a GWR engine would wait close to the tunnel on the down line. Next the passenger train would arrive with the Southern engine and come to a halt at the signal seen. When confirmed as stationary, the signalman would allow the GWR engine on to the single line within the tunnel, the driver allowing room for the Southern engine to approach behind. The Southern engine would then uncouple and run forward until clear of the crossover. When the signalman changed this the Southern engine would run back into the down platform. The points would then again be reversed and the GWR would back on to the waiting train ready to depart. Despite what might appear to be a fraught procedure carried out in darkness, there is no record of any untoward incident in over 60 years of working.

It was unfortunate that on the day of Edward's visit the weather was a typical damp and dismal December day, even so the scarcity of views showing Winchester in detail at this time warrant their inclusion. In reality the station changed very little throughout its existence , the track layout remained constant from 1922 until 1966 and the only obvious changes were certain signal replacements and the disappearance of the Pears's Soap advert.

Today the only true railway items that remain are the bridge in the distance as seen in the top view, which carries East Hill above the railway, and in the view opposite page bottom, the tunnel mouth and station master's house.

The enlargement right, is included to give some detail of the solenoid operated Siemens ground signals of the period.

Top left - *Located deep in a cutting, Winchester was never an easy place for photography, especially at the north end. Here perseverance has paid off with a view of what is probably a new 22xx awaiting departure yet coupled to old stock.*

Centre left - *'Yet another view of the tunnel mouth?': well yes, but then look carefully and see how foliage has encroached behind the Up main starting signal, rather surprising it was allowed to gain such a hold. In later years, probably around 1942, white paint was added to the brickwork behind the signals to aid sighting. Despite the paucity of resources affecting the DNS at the time of building, the neatly patterned brickwork at the top of the tunnel will be noted. Out of view to the left was a corrugated metal hut used as an oils store. Its final use was somewhere to keep salt used to prevent freezing of the pointwork.*

Below - *The classic view of the station during the inter-war years. Nearest the camera on the down platform was the 'Gents', the similar facility on the up platform was at the south end of the main building. The gas lamps were changed to electric in later years, believed to have when under the tenure of the Southern Region. (Repainting of the stations at Winchester and Whitchurch by Messrs Albert Dibb, was approved on 1 May 1930 at a cost of £336 6s 10d, to include cleaning. Why just two stations were dealt with when all were the same age, and presumably therefore in the same condition, is not reported.)*

Top - Winchester from St Giles Hill with Garnier Road just visible in the background, clearly also before the days of the Winchester by-pass and modern day M3. This is certainly not a conventional DNS train but must be a special excursion. Such workings would probably have commenced almost as soon as the connection to Shawford Junction was available from 1891, although GWR and LSWR engines did not broach each others metals via the DNS until after 1910.

Down DNS train at Eastleigh. Tank engines were invariably used by the LSWR / SR on passenger services which changed engines at Winchester. No 367 was one of ten class T1 class 0-4-4T built in 1888. All had been withdrawn by 1951.

Above - *The development of private motoring in the 1930s had three direct effects on the infrastructure of the DNS. The first was at Tothill where the bridge carrying the A34 over the railway was given an additional support located directly in what would have been the formation of a second track should one ever have - or wished to be laid. It is very likely this was one of the reasons doubling was not extended beyond Woodhay in 1942, as there was also the need to maintain the integrity of the road bridge to carry as much road traffic as possible. Next was here at Sutton Scotney, where the brick arch taking the railway over the A30/A34 was replaced with a single span girder bridge. The view is looking east, with the A30 twisting left and then right towards Basingstoke and the A34 branching off to the left shortly after the bridge. Recall the DNS when originally built, had been provided with earthworks, including bridges, suitable to take a second line of rails. Here the replacement bridge was suitable for just a single line and as can be seen, was also placed on the west side of the abutments. This meant that when the loop was extended at Sutton Scotney (the station is just off camera to the right), the entry into the loop for southbound trains was via a curved path - the only station where this applied post 1942. The bridge provided was of sufficient span to take major road widening although this was never carried out. It was removed after closure.*

Left - *T B Sands in his pioneering book on the DNS deals primarily with the early years of the company although when speaking of the 1930s he comments, "One or two weak bridges north of Newbury were strengthened and by 1939 Great Western engines in the 'blue' route classification could work anywhere on the line, as also could some 'red' route engines in an 'emergency - a term capable of very wide interpretation." It has often been wondered where exactly these upgrades took place as no reference has been located in the minute books of the period. But after much investigation, here is proof. Between Hermitage and Hampstead Norris at least one bridge was involved, ditto one north of Upton & Blewbury. But Sands fails to mention there was also one south of Newbury close to Litchfield station. It is depicted here, just north of the stopping place and hard by the modern day 1934. A former girder bridge over a farm track has been replaced with this concrete bridge, albeit single track - the abutments may be seen to have been built for two tracks. Bearing in mind the line north of Newbury was later doubled, a second decking was later provided alongside those previously mentioned.*

The third change was when part of the formation between Bar End and Hockley was shifted westwards to accommodate the construction of the Winchester by-pass. In the arial view right, the course of the new road may be seen and plotted against the railway running alongside. An impression of the amount of work involved in realigning the railway is better gained from the lower view. The old - right - and new - left alignments apparent. In connection with the road, this was the time the suggestion was made to abandon the railway south of Winchester Junction and provide a connection similar to that later built in 1942. In the light of history it was indeed fortunate this was not acted upon. Decades later both railway and road are but history although Hockley viaduct still survives and is now part of a valuable cycleway. Ironically the land once scarred by the road construction has been returned to nature although in its place there is the visibly worse cutting through Twyford Down. The view below was recorded on 11 February 1937. (The Winchester by-pass came into its own very much in WW2 when in the preparations for D-day one carriageway was completely closed off and used for the storage of equipment destined to be sent across to France.)

The completed work - road and rail in harmony. The new Winchester by-pass almost complete and ready for traffic. Work had originally started on the project in 1931 but just as a single carriageway road. Due to financial difficulties construction stalled shortly afterwards but the scheme was revised in 1934 this time as a dual-carriageway with work starting in 1935. The original estimated cost at the time was put at £360,000 although the final cost was subsequently given as £450,000. Opening was in stages from 1938 with the road fully complete from 1 February 1940. In this view taken prior to opening, orientation may be gained from the distant view of Winchester Cathedral. The railway runs on the extreme left - to the left hand side of the roadway. The rear of the down distant signal applicable to Shawford Junction may also be seen. To the right of the road the depression in the ground was known as 'plague valley' so called as this was where Winchester's victims of plague were buried. To the right on top of the hill is the distinctive clump of trees that was such a feature of St Catherine's Hill. Notice the dog on the path heading towards the photographer.

Miss K M Kenyon

Above - *As referred to on the page 96, the 1930s had seen a upgrading of the line to take heavier engines but even before this much relaying had been carried out by the replacement of the original flange rail with standard bull-head track. Here a group of men comprising the Kings Worthy gang plus others drafted in pose during a break in their relaying labours. Clearly this was being done between trains as witness the Look-Out man on the extreme right complete with his arm-band. The photograph was taken immediately south of where the DNS passes under the SR main line with the bridge for the latter in the background. Behind the group the railway continues on to Worthy Down.* Graham Hawkins

Above and opposite - *Relaying immediately north of the DNS station at Whitchurch in 1926. (One other view in this series appeared on p38 of the original DNS book.) The track recovered is of the original flange rail type and as seen in the image on this page, had a flat foot. It is being replaced with standard bull-head rail and sleepers, both having previously been unloaded alongside. Small wonder it was said manual permanent-way work was the hardest job on the railway. In the background the SR West of England main line crosses over the DNS.* British Railways

Interlude - Motor Economic System of Maintenance

In 1904, the GWR instigated what was called the Economic System of Maintenance on the Golden Valley Branch in West Wales. As the name implies, the idea was to effect savings in the cost of men employed on track work by providing for a scheme whereby a more flexible method of operation would effect economy. Part of this included the use of a hand operated velocipede - basically a bicycle which ran on one rail with a skeletal side-car frame to one side at the end of which was a single wheel running on the other rail. Movement was achieved by a fore and aft movement on the handlebars. This was associated with the introduction of a method of working whereby the ganger or men working on the line could safely take possession of a stretch of railway as long as they had with them a brass 'occupation key', which as the name implies allowed them to safely work on the line confident in the knowledge no train could arrive. As such the need to provide flagmen either side of the site of work was negated.

The removal of the occupation key meant a staff / token could not be withdrawn from the signal box so a train could not proceed. Occupation 'Key Boxes' were provided at intervals along the line, the ganger able to restore his key into any one of them. Once he had also removed his trolley from the line, the railway was again clear for a train to proceed. In this way he did not have to return to the signal box to 'give up' the possession. Communication with the signalman, to advise the key had been restored into the instrument, was by means of a portable telephone carried on the back of the velocipede but which added considerably to the weight of the vehicle. (This portable telephone was a massive affair the size of several bricks. Carried on the rear of the velocipede, it could be plugged into the signal box telephone circuit at any of the key boxes. Later, fixed telephones were provided within the key boxes.) In this way greater flexibility in working was achieved and with it manpower savings.

Having proved itself, a large number of single track branch lines were equipped in like fashion up to about 1930, although not at this stage the DNS. Instead in 1912 an investigation as to its suitability recounted, "Certainly could not recommend the new system be adopted on the Didcot to Winchester line. We have all our work cut out to keep lines in good order now that fast trains are running thereon and because considerable part of the road is of flange rail secured by clips to sleepers." (Hence the comment on the previous two pages on the replacement of the flange rails.)

Move forward in time and by the late 1920s technology had advanced, for now instead of hand operated trolleys a petrol driven variant was available. Now the ganger and his men could cover a far greater distance, with time being saved in travelling to the point of work. The motorised trolley could also be physically manhandled off the running rails by four men and with the key restored into a key box, the line was free for the passage of trains. The ganger was also provided with a smaller motorised inspection trolley of his own.

The system was approved for the DNS line south of Enborne on 8 October 1931 at an estimated cost of £5,930 and brought into use around November 1932. Why it was never installed on what was then the single line north of Newbury is not reported. It remained in use until the demise of the railway in 1964 although alterations in consequence

POSSESSION OF THIS KEY AUTHORISES GANGER TO OCCUPY THE LINE BETWEEN WHITCHURCH AND 10 ML 59½ CH

of the doubling to Woodhay in 1942, and then with the closure of various signal boxes south of Newbury from 1950 onwards (starting with Lodge Bridge in 1950 and then Highclere, Litchfield, and Kings Worthy in 1955), saw changes to gang lengths and therefore alterations to areas of responsibility. It should be borne in mind that the length of line the permanent way gang was responsible for did not always correspond to the token section, meaning the consent of neighbouring signalmen through a key control instrument in the signal box would be required before the occupation key could be withdrawn. Unlike the token system where there might be up to 36 tokens per single line section, there was only ever one occupation key per gangers section. This was inscribed on the face as to the piece of line it related to. Similar to the tokens, there was also a different configuration at the end of the actual occupation key to its neighbour. In this way a key could not be replaced in an incorrect key box.

If operated correctly the system worked well. The equipment being simple but robust and reliable. The biggest problem would be a lost or forgotten key. The actual key was made of brass, 6" long and weighing half a pound. It was hoped its size would mean if placed in a pocket it would not be forgotten. But human nature meant there were times when the key was misplaced or the gang returned to the signal box with their trolley only to discover the key had been left, 'for safe keeping', in the nearest permanent way hut to where they had been working. A quick dash back with the trolley was then required, although still safe in the knowledge no train could use the line until the key was restored. But if time was short and a train was due care had to be taken. With their small wheels and little if any springing, excess speed could easily result in the trolley becoming derailed: they were notoriously unstable at speed especially when driven over facing points, or certain types of catchpoints. It was also recognised that a trolley could not be guaranteed to operate track circuits.

Accordingly to reduce the risk of forgetfulness, some men attached lengths of chain to the key, at the end of which was a clip which would be put through a waistcoat or coat button. Others would attached the key to a chain which in turn would be linked to a piece of wood, the latter often of the type used to hold the rail in its chair.

The system was continued in use by the Southern Region following their takeover of the line south of Enborne in 1950, working instructions as to its use appearing in the 1960 Sectional Appendix which are reproduced overleaf. With the closure of the DNS we cannot be certain how many keys actually survived. We know that at the end of operations there were eight in use, a figure that had probably remained fairly consistent since 1942 when the system was modified as a result of the doubling between Enborne and Woodhay. (Double line occupation key was only ever used in one location on the GWR and not the DNS.)

One occupation key, applicable to the line between Whitchurch and Sutton Scotney, was purchased upon closure of the line by a private collector from its key box inside Whitchurch signal box literally just as the contractors

were in the process of dismantling the line in the summer of 1966. Three others were saved by different individuals and now also reside in private collections. It would be interesting to know where these had originally been salvaged from. We may never know if the remaining four are still in existence.

The wording on each is similar and simply states, 'Possession of this key authorises the ganger to occupy the line between……..', the length in question being given.

Of the four that have been located, the distances involved (in north-south order) are:
'10ml 59½ch and Litchfield' [1]
'Whitchurch and 10ml 59½ch'
'Whitchurch Town and Sutton Scotney' [2]
'Sutton Scotney and 19ml 30ch'

1. This key has had its starting point altered at some stage with the '10ml 59½ch' engraved on a piece of brass cut out and then set into the original key.

2. This key has been ground down and the locations added. It may therefore not be original, but the change is certainly post 1950 when the suffix 'Town' was added.

October 1960 SOUTHERN REGION Western Section Sectional Appendix

ENBORNE JUNCTION to SHAWFORD JUNCTION

POWER WORKED TROLLEYS - A system of engineering inspection and maintenance involving use of power-worked trolleys is in force between Woodhay and Winchester Chesil in connection with which telephones are provided affording communication with nearby signal boxes. These telephones are available for use of train crews and guards must always carry a key of the telephone boxes.

1. Three Engineering Gangs are employed and the home station and the sections of line for which they are responsible are shown below.

2. In order to avoid sending out handsignalmen in accordance with Rules 215 217, when it is necessary to run trolleys along the line, or to carry out operations which would render the running of trains unsafe, telephones and occupation key boxes have been fixed at places named below.

Places where telephones and key boxes are fixed, giving the mileage

	m	ch		m	ch
Group No. 1			Group No. 5		
Woodhay Station	2	20	Whitchurch Town Station	12	57
Key Box No. 1	3	29½	Key Box No. 8	13	53
Key Box No 1A	4	40	Key Box No. 9	14	49
(Highclere Station)			Key Box No. 10	15	45
			Key Box No. 10A	15	75
Group No. 2	4	40	Key Box No. 11	16	41
Key Box No. 1A	5	40	Key Box No. 12	17	37
(Highclere Station)			Sutton Scotney Station	18	33
Key Box No.2	6	40			
Burghclere Station			Group No. 6		
			Sutton Scotney Station	18	33
Group No.3			Key Box No. 13	19	30
Burghclere Station	6	40			
Key Box No. 3	7	27	Group No. 7		
Key Box No. 4	8	14	Key Box No. 13	19	30
Key Box No. 4A	9	2	Key Box No. 14	20	28
(Litchfield Station)			Worthy Down Station	21	19
Key Box No. 5	9	76			
Key Box No. 6	10	59½	Group No. 8		
			Worthy Down Station	21	19
Group No. 4			Key Bo No. 15	22	24
Key Box No. 6	10	59½	Key Box No. 15A	23	21
Key Box No. 7	11	63	(Kings Worthy Station)		
Whitchurch Town Station	12	57			
			Group No. 9		
			Key Box No. 15A	23	21
			(Kings Worthy Station)	24	23
			Key Box No. 16	25	26
			(Winnall Siding)		
			Winchester Chesil	25	73

Note - One Key is provided for each group.

The Telephones in:	Communicate with Signalman at:
Group No. 1	Woodhay
Group No. 2	Burghclere
Groups 3, 4 and 5	Whitchurch Town
Groups 6 and 7	Sutton Scotney
Group No. 8	Worthy Down
Group No 9	Winchester Chesil

Extension bells are provided in connection with the Control Instruments at:
Woodhay, Burghclere, Whitchurch Town, Sutton Scotney, Worthy Down and Winchester Chesil.

Home Station	Section
Burghclere	3m 29½chs. to 10m 59½chs. between Woodhay and Whitchurch Town.
Whitchurch Town	10m 59½chs to 19m 30chs. Between Litchfield and Worthy Down.
Kings Worthy	19m 30chs. to 25m 73chs. Between Sutton Scotney and Winchester Chesil.

3. Should it be necessary for a throughout movement to be made between groups No. 1 and No. 2 or between No. 8 and No. 9 the trolley must be removed from the single line before the occupation key which is in the ganger's possession is placed in the key box, and the occupation key for the next group must be withdrawn before the trolley is replaced on the single line to continue the movement.

4. The section of permanent way between 2m 20chs. (Woodhay station and 3m. 29½chs. is worked under ordinary maintenance but a motor trolley may be worked over this portion of line.
The ganger or man in charge of a motor trolley when operating the trolley between 3m 29½chs. and Woodhay station is responsible for assuring himself that no engineering work is in progress that will affect the safe working of the trolley and that his speed is such that he can stop short of any obstruction or men working on the line.
If any ganger or man in charge, other than the ganger or man in charge of the power-worked trolley is working a trolley or doing any work likely to cause an obstruction between 3m 29½chs. and Woodhay station, handsignalmen must be sent out in accordance with Rules 215 and 217.

5. During working hours the motor trolley or Inspection car may be stabled in the dead-end sidings at Sutton Scotney and Woodhay stations under the care of the signalman, provided the occupation key is given up by the ganger, who will be responsible for seeing that the motor trolley or inspection car is protected by a red flag being placed upon it.

6. On Sundays, or at any other time when the line is closed, the ganger may occupy the line for inspection purposes provided he is in possession of the electric train token for the section of line to be occupied and when he requires this arrangement to operate he must give prior advice to this effect to the signalman at the signal box at which he will require to collect the electric train token for the section concerned.
The signalman at the signal box, so advised by the ganger, must immediately before closing the signal box, withdraw an electric train token and place it in the token box outside the signal box, and ensure that the token box is securely locked.
The ganger must obtain the electric train token before occupying the single line and upon completion of the occupation, place it in the token box at whichever end of the section he finds most convenient before the signal box is opened. The ganger must ensure the token box is securely locked.
When opening the signal box at the end of the section where the electric train token has been deposited, the signalman must obtain the token from the token box, advise the signalman at the other end of the section and after replacing the electric train token in the instrument, carry out the tests required by Regulation 26 (testing Block Indicators and Bells) of the electric token block regulations.
An entry must be made in the train register book of the circumstances, also the time the electric train token is withdrawn and restored under these arrangements.

POSSESSION
OF THIS KEY
AUTHORISES
GANGER TO
OCCUPY THE LINE
BETWEEN
SUTTON SCOTNEY
AND
19 ML 30 CH

POSSESSION
OF THIS KEY
AUTHORISES
GANGER TO
OCCUPY THE LINE
BETWEEN
19 ML 59 CH
AND
LITCHFIELD

Above are the other two keys referred to in the text known to have survived. The various knocks and marks in the brass have been caused by years of use

Left - *Worthy Down post 1953. The point of the image is to illustrate the run-of set of rails at right angles to the end of the headshunt - indicated. Kings Worthy was the home station of the local gang although a trolley from either the Whitchurch or Kings Worthy gangs could well arrive here. Permanent–way huts, eith made of brick or sleepers were provided at intervals throughout the gang lengths.*

Again, timewise out of context for this section of the book, but included to show a gangers p/way trolley and trailer parked in the siding: the vehicles were captured by chance at Highclere in May 1960 on the occasion of a railtour - see pages 214/215 for details.

Similar 'occupation' key type working for permanent way maintenance was in use principally on the SR and LNER. The original yard crane and also the loading gauge were authorised for removal on 5 February 1930, however a replacement crane was subsequently provided as seen.

The GWR official photographer visited a number of locations on the DNS in 1942/43, the records showing the various images recorded under, 'Didcot - Newbury progress'. Although immensely grateful for the views that were recorded, the best of which have already previously been seen, there were still some locations that were not visited. One of these was Highclere, where at the end of the extended loop we see the down home signal, up advanced starter, motor points and auxiliary token hut.
Westinghouse Brake & Signal Co.

The years 1939 to 1945 have been spoken of in the original work. Footplate and operational memories are also contained within the various Harold Gasson books and also 'Didcot Engineman' published by Wild Swan.

Some new factual information has also come to light including a reference to the date of 30 September 1939 as to when Barton Stacey Halt is first referred to in records of the GWR Engineering Department. It must though be advised that at this time work 'on the ground' was often taking place prior to a reference appearing in official records. Suffice to say Barton Stacey Halt (the 'Halt' designation is exactly how it was referred to) would have come into use around this time.

The need for the stopping place may well have been to facilitate the transport of workmen engaged in building the nearby army camp of the same name. Certainly there were never any goods or siding facilities. Little else is known of the stopping place for on 1 March 1941 the below notice appears in the working timetable, itself a retrospective notice. No record of the referred to Workmen's notice has been found.

WEEK DAYS.
STATIONS, HALTS, ETC., CLOSED.

Barton Stacey Halt.   From December 2, 1940.

BARTON STACEY WORKMEN.

The arrangements shewn on page 2 of Workmen's Notice No. 72 are cancelled.
                                              From December 2, 1940.

Viewed from the opposite side looking north and we have the end of the up loop, the catch-point and sand-drag and also a view of Tothill bridge in the background. The black band on the signal post was nothing to do with camouflage but was intended to highlight the track-circuit diamond against the post. We also see the interior of one of the auxiliary token huts with the actual instrument stood on top of a wooden cabinet. A number of token carriers are also piled in a heap on the left. In the background is Tothill bridge with its additional support in the formation that might otherwise have been used for a second line of rails. On 24 November 1938 piling tests on the subsoil had been authorised for the Ministry of Transport at a cost of £241. The cost being recoverable from the government.
Westinghouse Brake & Signal Co.

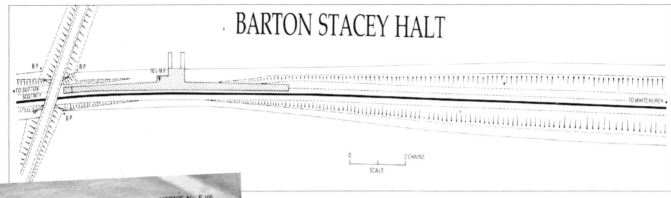

0   2 CHAINS

SCALE

GREAT WESTERN RAILWAY.
(FOR THE USE OF THE COMPANY'S SERVANTS ONLY.)

Notice to Enginemen, Guards, etc.

SUNDAY and MONDAY, DECEMBER 20th & 21st, 1942.

BRINGING INTO USE NEW SIGNAL BOX AT

KING'S WORTHY

Between the hours of 7.0 a.m. Sunday, December 20th, and 5.0 p.m. Monday, December 21st, the Signal Engineers will be engaged in bringing into use a New Signal Box approximately 395 yards North of, and on the opposite side of the line to the existing Signal Box, which will be taken out of use.

The following New Signals will be brought into use :—

	FORM.	DESCRIPTION.	POSITION.	DISTANCE FROM SIGNAL BOX.
A		Down Main Distant.	Up Side of Line.	1,389 yards.
B		Down Main Home.	Down Side of Line.	107 yards.
C		Down Main Starting.	Ditto.	564 yards.
D		Up Main Distant.	Ditto.	2,048 yards.
E		Up Main Home.	Up Side of Line.	671 yards.
F		Up Main Inner Home.	Ditto.	15 yards.

Top - *Barton Stacey Halt, hard by the A303 overbridge.*

Notice - *Standard notices to advise staff of new works would have been issued for all the locations on the DNS. Only one has survived for Kings Worthy.*

Bottom - *Taken from what is believed to have been the summer 1946 working time table showing the cancellation of some of the numerous additional services that had been provided during WW2. It is believed there was also a regular Winchester to Whitchurch service for staff at the Portal's bank note factory at nearby Overton.*

During the time it was open, Barton Stacey was served by two trains each way daily. The first was the 7.05 departure from Winchester, and shortly afterwards came the unadvertised 6.40 a.m. workmans trains from Southampton Terminus calling at all stations. This was hauled by an SR engine with three coaches. Most of the passengers were itinerant workers employed at Worthy Down and Barton Stacey billeted in temporary accommodation at Winchester and on Southampton Common. Many would do all they could to avoid purchasing a ticket, such as climbing in and alighting from the wrong side and deliberately overwhelming a ticket collector by sheer force of numbers. Matters became so bad railway staff were compelled to ride on the trains to attempt to check tickets en-route.

After departure from Barton Stacey, the service would continue to Whitchurch returning south as an empty coaching stock working (ecs).

In the reverse direction there were again two stopping services. The first of these was the 3.25 pm. ex Didcot at about 4.53 p.m., followed 15 minutes later by another unadvertised working which had run ecs to Whitchurch earlier. Both trains operated six days a week. With the closure of Barton Stacey the workmens service was eventually cut back to Worthy

PASSENGER TRAINS.

...men's Trains between Winchester and Worthy Down.

5 45 a.m.	Workmen's Train Winchester to Worthy Down.	
7 15 a.m.	Workmen's Train Winchester to Worthy Down.	
10†30 a.m.	Empty Train Winchester to Worthy Down.	(S.O.)
11†25 a.m.	Empty Train Winchester to Worthy Down.	(S.O.)
12†40 p.m.	Empty Train Winchester to Worthy Down.	(S.O.)
4†30 p.m.	Empty Train Winchester to Worthy Down.	(S.X.)
6†10 p.m.	Empty Train Winchester to Worthy Down.	(S X.)
6†10 a.m.	Empty Train Worthy Down to Winchester.	
7†40 a.m.	Empty Train Worthy Down to Winchester.	
11 0 a.m.	Workmen's Train Worthy Down to Winchester.	(S.O.)
11 50 a.m.	Workmen's Train Worthy Down to Winchester.	(S.O.)
1 15 p.m.	Workmen's Train Worthy Down to Winchester.	(S.O.)
5 0 p.m.	Workmen's Train Worthy Down to Winchester.	(S.X.)
6 30 p.m.	Workmen's Train Worthy Down to Winchester.	(S.X.)

Discontinued.

The following Workmen's Trains will be run between Winchester and Worthy Down in lieu of the above :—

	EACH WEEK-DAY. arr. a.m.	EACH WEEK-DAY. dep. a.m.	S.X. arr. p.m.	S.X. dep. p.m.	S.O. arr. p.m.	S.O. dep. p.m.
Winchester	—	6 45		4†25	—	3†45
King's Worthy	C|S	6 50	C|S		C|S	
Worthy Down	6 55	—	4†35		3 55	
Worthy Down	—	7† 5	—	4 45	—	4 15
King's Worthy	C|S	—	C|S	4 50	C|S	4 20
Winchester	7†15	—	4 55		4 25	

6.50 a.m. Workmen's Train Newbury to Didcot.
6.10 p.m. Workmen's Train Didcot to Newbury (SX).
1.50 p.m. Workmen's Train Didcot to Newbury (SO).

To call at Upton and Compton.

Down and finally discontinued in 1946 - as per the reproduced notice.

North of Newbury at Hampstead Norris, a wartime facility had been set up at what was known as Burnt Hill. Personnel destined for the location would arrive here whilst petrol would also be delivered by rail in 5 gallon jerry-cans.

Sometimes wagons loads of these would remain in the siding awaiting collection, much to the trepidation of railway staff should an air-raid be sounded.

Elsewhere, pit props were despatched from Highclere and at Burghclere the Rank organisation took over a nearby country house for the preparation and storage

Costs of New Works DNS Line 1940 - 1946

1. Doubling of line and lengthening of loops. The following expenditure on works for the Ministry of War Transport to facilitate the working of war time traffic was noted, the cost in each case to be borne by H M Government.

		£	
Didcot to Newbury	Chief Engineer	215,000	
	Signal Engineer	38,600	
	Chief Mechanical Engineer	4,250	Refers to the provision of watering facilities at Newbury East Junction
	Land	450	2 acres, 1 rod, 27 perches of land purchased by the Company
	Total Didcot to Newbury	**£248,300**	
Enborne Junction to Winchester			
Enborne - Woodhay (doubling)	Chief Engineer	24,467	
	Signal Engineer	7,760	
	Land	450	3 acres, 0 rod, 20 perches of land purchased by the Company
Highclere extension of loop	Chief Engineer	3,978	
	Signal Engineer	5,100	
Burghclere extension of loop	Chief Engineer	2,843	
	Signal Engineer	5,400	
	Land	30	32 perches of land purchased by the Company
Litchfield restoration of crossing facilities	Chief Engineer	4,961	
	Signal Engineer	5,670	
	Land	40	1 rod, 3 perches of land purchased by the Company
	C/Forward	**£299,921**	

of wartime propaganda films. These would be delivered and despatched from the station under conditions of some secrecy. Also at Burghclere, the now abandoned lime quarry saw quantities of waste previous created as part of the production process, removed for agricultural use. This traffic continued for much of WW2 and explains why the siding and connection to the quarry were retained during the 1942/43 improvements when the quarry itself had already closed. This traffic eventually ceased post WW2 and the quarry siding together with its associated track and signalling were out of use in 1946. This was also the first cut-back in the infrastructure facilities of the DNS. It should also be mentioned that many of the goods sheds on the DNS were used to store fodder previously held at the main GWR provender store at Didcot, a simple case of not keeping all assets in one place. (Speaking of horses, it is worth mentioning at this point that on 27 October 1932 the GWR had taken over the cartage agency at Winchester formerly operated by Messrs White and Co. The price paid was £200, which included £24.5s for each of four horses, plus equipment. The total being £154.10s. The balance was an ex-gratia, or 'good-will' payment. In connection with this transfer a stable was now provided at Bar End for an additional £280.)

Whilst the DNS may not have seen major infrastructure changes until almost three years after the start of war, that is not to say there were not some less obvious changes. One of these was the signal-boxes remaining open for 24 hours, the men now working a 12 hour shift with changeover affected on Sunday. Staff from the locomotive department at Winchester could also earn overtime acting as firewatchers at the passenger station. At some stage an end-loading ramp was also provided at Bar End. There was also a late evening, 11.30 pm Saturday only, train on a Saturday from Winchester calling at all stations to Sutton Scotney (now the railhead for Barton Stacey). This was very popular with servicemen and continued to run throughout the war, even during the improvement works, although it was stated to 'Be liable to cancellation at short notice'.

There was an amusing incident at Worthy Down at some stage and from the detail, probably after the improvements. An up goods arrived at Worthy Down and the guard's van was detached, the brake being screwed on whilst shunting was taking place. A second guard was also present 'learning the road'. Upon completion of the work the train was reassembled ready to depart, each man walking down the opposite side of the train. The signal was given for the engine to continue and with both men on board they set off - but not in the direction they believed. Neither had checked to see the van was re-coupled to the rest of the train, each assuming the other had undertaken this basic task. In the black-out they commented the driver was, 'getting a move on', only to have a severe awakening as they derailed at the catch-point two miles down the line at Kings Worthy.

Kings Worthy also features in a report of an incident that occurred at 5.00 p.m. on 21 February 1940. Taken from the official report, "The signalman at Kings

Worthy reported to the Length Ganger that the telephone was not in working order and on making an inspection the Ganger discovered a steel cable, approximately 400 yards in length hanging over the telephone wires. The cable was removed and the telephone restored to working order. I understand that the steel cable fell from an aeroplane which was towing same during target practice. The cable has since been taken over by Insp. Allen, Signal department, Reading."

By the spring of 1942 staff began to notice the appearance of surveyors and inspectors at the various stations, no reasons being given. Clearly though behind the scenes matters were moving fast, for in August engineers vehicles began to be seen at various locations and of both the mobile and static type. These included mobile workshops as well as messing vehicles. At Whitchurch they were housed in the siding alongside the down platform whilst as accommodation a camping coach was also noted. (Some of these 'camping coaches' were hastily converted four or six-wheeled passenger vehicles and when used by men for long periods were reported as becoming 'less than sanitary', indeed vehicles in such use on the GWR were on occasions necessarily returned to Swindon for fumigation purposes. It is likely there were two or three bases for accommodation whilst work was in progress on the DNS, the workshop and coach locations changing as work progressed.)

Once work commenced and services were suspended the replacement bus service began. Two single deck vehicles were used, but to the same schedule with one following immediately behind the other. The bus service represented a 50% increase in journey times compared with the train: a situation that would also replicate itself years later when the trains were permanently withdrawn. Initially both buses operated on the same route but it was not long before there was a modification whereby 'Bus 1' left Newbury and called at Woodhay, Litchfield and Whitchurch. 'Bus 2' would run from Newbury calling at Highclere, Burghclere meeting up with the first vehicle at Whitchurch. South of Whitchurch, 'Bus 1' called at Sutton Scotney and then direct to the Southern Railway station at Winchester. 'Bus 2' called 'all stations' to Winchester Chesil although the route here was somewhat convoluted as after Worthy Down it had to retrace its route back through Wonston not being permitted to run the whole way through Worthy Down. Despite the obvious restrictions, it appears there were few cases where passengers travelling solely between intermediate stations south of Newbury were inconvenienced. In the reverse direction operation was to an similar schedule.

The new works saw the line under total engineers possession between 6 a.m. and 6 p.m. daily. Outside this time there was a pick up goods in either direction although of necessity shunting was carried out in conditions of total blackout. The blackout was also the cause of an incident which when read now sounds comical but could so easily have had far more serious consequences. This took place on 28 August 1942 and involved the 8.28 p.m. Winchester to

Schedule of new Works - Didcot - Winchester, 1942/43.

Rail services suspended	4 August 1942
Didcot East Junction to Upton doubling complete and into use	14-17 February 1943
Churn alteration completed	11-14 April 1943
Upton to Compton doubled and into use	11-14 April 1943
Ilsley signals into use	11 - 14 April 1943
Compton to Hampstead Norris doubled and into use	28 February to 7 March 1943
Hampstead Norris new signal box into use	18 April 1943
Pinewood Halt new Ground Frame into use	17 February 1943
Hampstead Norris to Hermitage doubling into use	14 to 17 February 1943
Hermitage to Newbury East Junction doubling into use *	10 to 17 January 1943
Enborne Goods Loop into use	11 to 13 July 1943
Enborne Junction signal box changes into use (new lever frame)	6 December 1942
Enborne Junction to Woodhay doubling into use	6 December 1942
Woodhay new signal box into use	9 October 1942
Highclere loop extensions into use	25 to 28 October 1942
Highclere new signal box into use	28 October 1942
Burghclere loop extensions into use	8 to 13 November 1942
Burghclere new signal box into use	13 November 1942
Litchfield new loop into use	28 February to 3 March 1943
Litchfield new signal box into use	3 March 1943
Whitchurch loop extensions into use *	28 February to 3 March 1943
Whitchurch new signal box into use	3 March 1943
Lodge Bridge new loop and signal box into use	28 March 1943
Sutton Scotney loop extensions into use	1 to 6 November 1942
Sutton Scotney new signal box into use	6 November 1942
Worthy Down, new signal box, track alterations into use	14 February to 5 March 1943
Worthy Down, new platform and buildings into use	8 March 1943
Worthy Down, connection from SR at Winchester Junction into use	EITHER 5 March or 5 May 1943
Kings Worthy loop extensions into use	20 to 21 December 1942
Kings Worthy resited signal box opened	21 December 1942
Winchester loop extensions opened **	11 to 14 October 1942
Shawford Junction, down relief line to Shawford station into use	14 March 1943

* No date is given for bringing into use engine watering facilities at Newbury East Junction and Whitchurch.

** No date is given for the completed extension to Winchester signal box but was probably at the same time.

Various examples of Progress Meetings at which the ongoing work on the DNS line was discussed are shown on pages 312/313.

		£	
	B/Forward	**299,921**	
Whitchurch extension of loop	Chief Engineer	3,472	
	Signal Engineer	7,000	
	Chief Mechanical Engineer	2,700	Refers to the provision of watering facilities at Whitchruch
	Land	20	10 perches of land purchased by the Company
Lodge Bridge provision of crossing facilities between Whitchurch and Sutton Scotney	Chief Engineer	4,838	
	Signal Engineer	5,450	
	Land	20	14 perches of land purchased by the Company
Sutton Scotney extension of loop	Chief Engineer	4,343	
	Signal Engineer	6,900	
	Land	50	13 perches of land purchased by the Company
Worthy Down provision of crossing loop and connection to the Southern Railway	Chief Engineer	35,799	
	Signal Engineer	7,500	
	Land	65	31 perches of land purchased by the Company
Winchester provision of an additional loop*	Chief Engineer	4,649	* 'additional;' may be taken to be the extension of the loop
	Signal Engineer	4,050	
	Land	40	1 rod, 3 perches of land purchased by the Company
	Total	**£384,117**	

Summary (taken from official figures which do not always correspond).		
Total	Chief Engineer	£306,725
	Signal Engineer	89,000
	Land	1,875
	C.M.E.	6.950
	Cost of Chief Engineers Work Didcot to Newbury	215,000
	Cost of Chief Engineers Work Newbury to Winchester	91,725
	Average cost per location (10) Newbury to Winchester	9,172. 10s

Other work during the period:			£
2	Improved telephone facilities		9,500
3	30 January 1942. Tothill Bridge, Highclere to be strengthened by the Ministry of War Transport, work to be carried out by the Chief Engineer		2,240
4	It was agreed that the following applications for private siding facilities be acceded to on the terms specified and subject to agreements being entered into in each case		
	Hermitage: for the Ministry of Works and Buildings	Chief Engineer	8,063
	(see note at the end of this section)	Signal Engineer	60
5	1 October 1943. Provision of a new enginemen's cabin at Winchester	Chief Engineer	240
		C.M.E.	25
	26 November 1943. Contract let to Messrs W F Woolford for the above work. Estimate £170, actual cost £124.		
6	26 March 1943. £130 to be spent by the Hampshire County Council on the road over a bridge at Highclere.		
7	6 October 1944 Reconditioning of Messrs W W Halls Pinewood Siding of the Air Ministry		161
8	27 October 1944 Contract let with the Home Counties Tarmacadam Co. Ltd. For tar spraying roads at Highclere, Whitchurch and Sutton Scotney. Estimated at £190. Actual cost of		194 4s
9	24 March 1944. With Messrs Caffin & Co., a contract for the maintenance of the new permanent way between Didcot and Winchester on a prime cost basis (Cost fixed on 6 October 1944)		1,050
10	27 March 1942. Contract let to Messrs Caffin & Co., for the laying of new permanent way for the cold storage depot at Hermitage. (Above figure includes work carried out by this Company at other locations on the Great Western system)		7,671 1s 3d
11	Sir Robert McAlpine for the line between Didcot and Winchester. 1st payment estimated at £94,000		
		27 January 1942	94,231 7s 4d
	Additional payment	23 November 1945	44,151 4 s 8d
		Total	£138,382 12s

Summary (taken from official figures which do not always correspond).	
Cost of Signal Engineers Work Didcot to Newbury	28,600
Cost of Chief Engineers Work Newbury to Winchester	60,400
Average cost per location (9) Newbury to Winchester excluding Woodhay	5,848.88899
(Cost of each hand-generator £459.16667)	
Cost of construction Sir R McAlpine contract	138,382 12s
Other work paid for by H M Government & Departments	19,524
Other work paid for by Great Western Railway	11,133 4s
Other work (unspecified)	130
Totals	
Work by HM Government	551,581 12
Work by GWR	13,008 4s
Other work during the period	130
Total	**£564,719 12s**

Southampton passenger train As the engine was a Southern M7, we may assume Southern men were involved. It appears that for whatever reason, the signalman at Winchester was also in a hurry to see the train away, having just previously seen the GWR engine uncoupled and run on to the shed at Bar End. With the GWR engine clear he passed the single line tablet to the crew of the M7 which promptly set off. Unfortunately said signalman had omitted to change the route to the single line, whilst the Southern crew also failed to notice which line they were on. Now good fortune took its part, for running on the down siding the spring loaded facing point leading to loco shed had returned to its normal position but even so the crew continued in blissful ignorance past the goods shed before coming to a less than graceful end in the sand drag at the end of the yard headshunt. For once there were no vehicles either in the goods shed or on the goods shed road. The incident appears in official records on 4 September 1942, whilst the whole episode is all the more surprising considering it was certainly still daylight at the time. (See p143 for illustration of the layout at Bar End.)

With services restored another incident is reported although this time undated. The engine hauling the 7.45 a.m. Newbury to Winchester train failed completely at Lodge Bridge when the inside motion became detached with bits digging itself into the ballast. Again it was lucky the train was only travelling slowly at the time. The points at either end were clipped and traffic continued to pass in both directions on the 'up' line.

With the improvement work now complete, the longest point-to-point timing was the nine minute allowance for trains between Whitchurch and Litchfield. Tom Sands reports in the lead up to D-day, the DNS was carrying a peak service of 120 trains per day, or an average of one working every 12 minutes. More trains also ran south, hence the need for almost continual token-transfers. In the midst of this maelstrom personal supplies had to be catered for and the gangers trolley's were used to take water to the signal boxes at Lodge Bridge and Worthy Down although on occasions at the latter, the railwayman was able to make use of the NAAFI canteen. After D-Day there were any number of workings with POWs from Southampton to locations in the Midlands. Possibly this amount of traffic was also the reason all the DNS signal boxes were subsequently regarded as Class 4 from their original Class 5 status.

At this stage it may be interesting to consider briefly the options open to the railway had the DNS been put out of action south of Winchester. Certainly the Worthy Down spur might well have been converted to either way operation whilst another option could have been the provision of a loop facing west at Whitchurch to allow trains to pass via Hurstbourne and a reinstated Hurstbourne - Longparish link.

One final amusement relative to the wartime era may be reported. At Hermitage there was for some time a 'lady signalman'. Hampstead Norris had a train which wished to proceed south but was unable to obtain any response form Hermitage and so instructed the driver of the waiting train to proceed south 'with caution' and report back. This the driver did, stopping outside the signal box at Hermitage where the female was found cowered in one corner and a mouse making an intermittent appearance around the lever frame. She would not emerge until the creature had been removed, a relatively easy task for the fireman to deal with using his shovel. There matters should have ended, with 'normal service resumed', but no, now her wrath was directed at the crew for their cruelty at dealing with a 'poor defenceless creature'. The loco crew made a swift departure.

Apart from the major works completed in 1942/43 other improvements to facilities were also proposed during the period, including:

28-2-1940 - Kings Worthy: Coal wharf for Bryer Ask Ltd.
16 June 1943 - Churn: Siding for Messrs Bosley.
19 April 1945 - Worthy Down: proposed platform screen.
It is not known which may have been completed although it can be said for definite the Churn siding was never built.
On an unknown date there is also reference to a contract for 'painting and cleaning the signal boxes and stations'. This was awarded to Messrs Walden from Henley on a 'prime cost' basis.

It should also be mentioned that in connection with the doubling of the DNS, the original plan had been for a 'West Ilsley Signal Box' with 14 levers and measuring 24' 2" x 12' 8" x 8', in the event IBS signals were installed instead.

It is reported the DNS saw much Ambulance Traffic during WW2, limited information on this coming from a 1944 copy of WW2 booklet supplied via the late Arthur Wellstead.

Actual Ambulance Trains were stationed at a number of locations, one of these being Newbury racecourse. Winchester Chesil was one of a number of stations (but the only one on the DNS proper) considered a loading point. Ambulance Trains using the DNS line were given a point to point timing between Winchester and Newbury of 55 minutes, later increased to 65 minutes, and a time for traversing the northern section of 36 minutes.

A USA military hospital is shown at Hermitage although patients for here were dealt with at Newbury Racecourse. Winchester Chesil would serve the following hospital area: Eastleigh, Southampton, Lyndhurst, Lymington and Basingstoke, and also the following specific venues: Royal Hampshire County, St Swithun's School - at the time a USA hospital, No 4 Casualty (military) clearing station. Should 'Chesil not be available then an alternative loading and unloading point was designated in Basingstoke Down Goods Yard although this was noted to be from ground level. Motive power for these Ambulance trains was often provided by LNER ex GE 4-4-0 and 4-6-0 types. (Ambulance trains, or more accurately the turning of engines of ambulance trains was the reason the turntable at Winchester was considered for replacement. Clearly this must have been approved prior to 1945 although for whatever reason the work was not even commenced and indeed completed until later. Necessary earthworks were undertaken under contract to Messrs Leonard Fairclough Ltd for £3,111 1s 6d against an estimate of £3,260 The continuation of the work would imply it had been sanctioned by and approved prior to 1945, no doubt charged to the Government, and the GWR would ensure they would also benefit from the facility. When complete - see page 144 - the new turntable was vacuum operated and made by Cowen Sheldon and of 65' diameter, this compared with the 42' original.

In connection with the new works there were variations in the positioning of certain of the key boxes for the Motor Economic System of maintenance as well as some other general changes.. The 1960 (post 1955 signalling alterations) list was shown on p104, with below the changes to working shown applicable to the route immediately after the improvements. (Only the actual changes are shown.)

Places where telephones and key boxes are fixed, giving the mileage						
	m	ch			m	ch
Group No.3				Group No. 8		
Burghclere Station				Sutton Scotney Station		
Key Box No. 3	6	40		Key Box No. 13	18	33
Key Box No. 4	7	27			19	30
Litchfield Station	8	14		Group No. 9		
	9	2		Key Box No. 13		
Group No. 4				Key Box No. 14	19	30
Litchfield Station				Worthy Down Station	20	28
Key Box No. 5	9	2			21	19
Key Box No. 6	9	75		Group No. 10		
	10	59½		Worthy Down Station		
Group No. 5				Key Box No. 15	21	19
Key Box No 7	10	59½		Kings Worthy Station	22	24
Whitchurch Station	11	63			23	21
	12	57		Group No. 11		
Group No. 6				Kings Worthy Station		
Whitchurch Station				Winnall Siding GF	23	21
Key Box No. 8	12	57		Winchester Signal Box	24	23
Key Box No. 9	13	53			25	26
Key Box No. 10	14	49				
Lodge Bridge	15	45		Telephone Communication		
	15	76				
Group No. 7				Group 1	Highclere Signal Box	
Lodge Bridge				Groups 2 & 3	Burgchlere Signal Box	
Key Box No. 11	15	76		Groups 4, 5 & 6	Whitchurch Signal box	
Key Box No. 12	16	41		Groups 7, 8 & 9	Sutton Scotney Signal box	
Sutton Scotney Station	17	37		Groups 10 & 11	Kings Worthy Signal Box	
	18	33				

Note - One Key is provided for each group.

Extension bells are provided in connection with the control instruments at Highlcre, Burghclere, Whitchurch, Sutton Scotney and Kings Worthy.

The occupation key for Group 1 (see page 102) is labelled as between Woodhay and Highclere stations.

Gangers trolleys are too light to operate the spring catch points at Burghclere, Lodge Bridge, Worthy Down, and Kings Worthy. Wrong line working is authorised for gangers trolleys at these points. All other catch points are 'Type F'.

Northern section note: Compton Crossing to be closed 3 minutes before a train is due. Fishers Lane Crossing to be closed 2 minutes before a train is due. (Compton Crossing now provided with crossing indicators and bells, also home signals in each direction in lieu of only distant signals. It is presumed, although not mentioned, that Fishers Lane Crossing was similarly equipped.)

Porter Alfred Sacree outside the public entrance to Winchester Chesil booking office in Southern Region days. The throwback to the days of the WW2 blackout with white paint to the edge of the brickwork will be noted.

Since publication of the original book on the DNS in 1982, interviews with two further members of staff, Tom 'Tim' Timpson and Ron 'Plumb' Warner have enabled new information to be gathered both first hand and on their recollections of colleagues from various times.

Tom started work at Winchester in 1942 as a van boy under the direction of the station master Mr Arch, known as 'Grandad'. Mr Arch was recalled as a very pleasant man who wore a 'Homberg'. Despite his title, the role would include attending to the signal lamps every Thursday. Officially the route to reach the signals north of the tunnel was via Easton Lane, but Tom would walk through the tunnel as this was of course much easier. The practice of taking this short cut was later banned.

The next year, Tom was advised of a signalling vacancy at Worthy Down in what was a Class 5 box - all DNS boxes were the same grade in 1943. He applied for this and was successful, being first tested by the Newbury District Inspector Bob Sullivan. Here was another man recalled as being very pleasant who always wore a bow-tie. Before taking up the post he had to visit Paddington where he was interviewed and successfully approved for the position by Ch. Insp Honeybun.

Tom recalls that at the time Worthy Down station was run by single porter who had been promoted to Foreman in Charge even though he was the only member of staff! (Probably because of the volume of traffic.)

Tom would cycle to Worthy Down where traffic was very busy at this time, the connection from Winchester Junction regularly used by empty stores trains of 60 vehicles including brake van. One evening a train arrived from Winchester Junction and the driver requested to put 10 vehicles off as he considered the load was too heavy. Ten vehicles were thus uncoupled ready to be shunted into the

yard but the crew omitted to pin down sufficient brakes on the remainder of the train with the result it ran back on spur line as far as the catch point and was partly derailed. The engine types used on military trains included GWR 28xx / 38xx, and for a time USA 2-8-0, LMS 2-8-0 and WD austerity types.

The military would regularly set up a Bofors gun facing the signal box. This was used for practice on a regular basis. Unfortunately one day the gun crew aimed too low and hit the brickwork above the front of the box windows.

Worthy Down was tasked with counting the number of wagons on up trains which were recorded in a special book.

After five years at Worthy Down, Tom transferred to Winchester where he remained for a further two years. At Winchester he worked opposite 'Knobby' Bryant although he admitted their relationship was not particularly good. The signal box at Winchester box was recalled as always damp due to its location on the side of the cutting. In the locking room on plates under the frame was stencilled the word 'Montgomery' – was the frame originally intended for that location?

Other staff at Winchester included Arthur Wellstood and Bert Tyrell. Both had been at Winchester for many years. Arthur recalling the time a train ran back out of control down the camp line. Bert spoke of when he was a lad having the duty of walking along the top of the carriages in the platform to drop the oil lamps into place in the carriages. One day whilst doing so a lamp fell through on to the lap of a lady passenger. Bert Tyrell also recalled a nightly mail train from Winchester in earlier years.

For engine changing at Winchester the Southern engine would often wait over in the loading bay opposite the box. Sometimes there was also a coach to attach or detach from the passenger workings. On one occasion a Southern crew who were evidently in a bit of a hurry ran back with this extra coach on to the waiting GWR stock in the down platform but forgot to couple up the complete train. On receiving the signal from the Guard (who for that matter had also omitted to test the brake!) they left with only part of the train.

During WW2 Winchester yard was recalled as being busy as a collecting point for wagon sheets, there was also large quantities of margarine, butter and soap, all of which would be distributed to various government stores in the area.

Annually a diesel railcar would come travelling light to Winchester to inspect the tunnel. It was used so steam from an engine loco would not obscure the view for the engineers.

Moving on in time, after closure one signal from Whitchurch (DNS) was 'borrowed' by the S & T department as a temporary replacement for use at Waltham near Micheldever.

With takeover by the Southern, Tom applied for and was successful in gaining promotion to the higher grade Shawford Junction signal box, where he also recalled Dr J L Farmer, the then medical officer of health for Winchester, as a regular visitor.

Ron Plumb worked at Kings Worthy from 9 October 1946 to 1 February 1947. He recalls walking from the station southwards on one occasion in company with the signalman from Worthy Down, searching for the Winchester - Kings Worthy token which had fallen off an engine sometime after leaving Winchester Tunnel - he could not recall if it was found.

After Kings Worthy, Ron went to Hampstead Norris until September 1948. He also recalls a period of snow when he was stranded at the station and had to sleep in a platelayers hut for five nights. There were no trains over the northern section of the DNS line for two weeks that winter.

Ron's most poignant memory is how by 1946 the railway had changed from a major feeder route to the south coast to that of a branch line whose facilities greatly exceeded the needs of the traffic.

It has been suggested that metal sleepers may have been used in places on the running line in places, this is not confirmed and there is no photographic evidence to support the allegation. On a more sinister side was the the later revelation that the bridge carrying the railway over the River

Hermitage with the bulk of the buffer-depot in the background. Rail access was via a trailing connection at the south end of the up platform which also fed the loading dock. To afford as little information to any outside party, the locations was officially referred to as 'Long Lane Receiving Depot.'

Test near Whitchurch had been 'chambered' ready to receive explosives on 25 November 1940 as a means of delaying the progress of an invading army. Little other information on this point has been found aside from the fact that this had only also been sanctioned at one other (unknown) site on the GWR.

George Behrend in *GONE WITH REGRET* again gives a delightful anecdote of life on the DNS during the early years of conflict;

'The engine finished its pumping and left Lambourn just before seven in the evening so as to arrive at Newbury, and reverse out again under Blackboys Bridge while two trains, one unadvertised, came in for Paddington. Then with a pause of only eight minutes, in which to sneak a little water, it would depart for all stations to Didcot except Churn, changing the staff at Hermitage, Hampstead Norris, Compton and Upton & Blewbury. For Churn had no road to it, only a track, and apart from its use by one farm and a cottage, existed solely upon the wartime needs of the Army. In the second war it came once more to life, for here we took the Army examination. The cavalry officer who had been so contemptuous ("You cannot go motoring all across here" and how he sneered at the word "motoring") unbent a little on being told that the distance between the telegraph poles was not the standard one. "You seem to know a lot about it; whose gallops are these?" came the next question, and giving the correct reply: "Steve Donoghue's," I passed the examination with colours flying. The following year the cadets came by railway. We sent them back to Oxford by giving notice to the stationmaster at Newbury, though some doubt arose as to whether we had done this soon enough, the train's departure having been advanced four minutes. So there was an anxious moment on Churn's forgotten cinder platform, both arms stretched heavenward until the 22xx pulled up with a grinding of brakes and the cadets swung aboard. Evidently Army officers not in the Engineers could not start a train for a polite "Aren't you coming with us, Sir?" was the only response to a right away signal. Great Western railwaymen were the most courteous in the world; even high officers of the Southern would privately admit that their rival's entire line functioned on the loyalty of the outside staff. On Sunday nights Churn was ghostly, deserted in the moonlight. The 2-4-0s driver, anxious to get home to Didcot, would draw up smartly at Upton & Blewbury, with its lengthy siding full of stabled vans in the days before Moreton Sidings had been built. The porter in charge, the same late Bob Aldridge, who later returned to Highclere as foreman, had a retired porter to help him deal with the increased traffic, whose principal task was to inspect the vans for the rolling-stock return. When he burst into the office one morning with the news that one of the vans had a bomb inside, Bob thought he must be joking, and not in the best of taste either. Bombs did not lie about in vans, they went off! Still, he humoured the old man by going to have a look, and sure enough, beautifully padded in its cradle, reposed a large, unexploded German bomb! From his artillery service in the first war, Bob Aldridge was security minded. Superiors they might be at the other end of the

wire, but he would give Didcot Goods every opportunity. "Have you lost anything?" "We do not lose things here," came the rather haughty reply. "You are quite sure you haven't lost anything?" "Positive." "Not even a bomb?" Bob told me he thought the telephone would explode even if the bomb itself did not go off before they took it away. The need to find a special engine in a hurry, which he took pains to emphasise, added to Didcot's discomfiture. While those in high places received the full blast of the military experts to whom the non-arrival of the bomb had been reported, its loss was so secret that the usual search and consignment note procedure could not be followed in the usual way. Meanwhile there was the constant fear that the bomb might choose to go off in some really damaging location, such as the centre of the Severn Tunnel. For the bomb was destined for Upton-on-Severn, but even this could not be put on a circular, since it was the secret location of a research laboratory. In any case to admit that there was a stray bomb somewhere on the system was not good from any point of view. Transits took longer during the National Emergency of course, but that was all. So no one thought of looking for it among those peaceful thatched cottages under the downs."

Further information concerning the early days of conflict and traffic on the railway has been sourced from Paul Lacey in his book *A HISTORY OF NEWBURY & DISTRICT MOTOR SERVICES Ltd. 1932-1952*. In this he refers to the role of public transport in dealing with evacuees from London and Southampton during the first days of September 1939, ".....In addition there were some 500 mothers and children brought into the area from Southampton who were billeted at Woodhay, Burghclere and Highclere, together with a group of 30 who were placed at Highclere Castle. Whenever necessary they were met at the nearest station on the 'Didcot, Newbury & Southampton' line by Newbury and District buses." Presumably Mr. Lacey was aware in his comment of the confusion of names and villages in referring to the stations.

A final point over Lodge Bridge signal box in the more technical sense, is that with the establishment of the the crossing place here and the other new crossing point at Worthy Down, the token configurations were amended out of necessity south of Whitchurch. They now read;

Whitchurch - Lodge Bridge	'B'
Lodge Bridge - Sutton Scotney	'C'
Sutton Scotney - Worthy Down	'A'
Worthy Down - Kings Worthy	'D'

Instrument numbers are not reported. This table though should be read in conjunction with the original installations for token instruments which is reproduced on page 314. From the earlier reference it will be seen that Kings Worthy - Winchester was already a 'D' and so clearly this was altered at this time to either 'B' or 'C'. As with all the revised signalling arrangements for the crossing loops a total of 26 tokens per section were provided.

Note: Hermitage Cold Store

'Buffer Depots' to give them their more accurate name, were established from around 1940 onwards as a means of storing food mainly due to the fear of interruption of supplies in consequence of U-boats. At least 42 storage sites are referred to on the internet although this comes from personal observation rather than an official list. Whilst the facility at Hermitage was clearly of WW2 build, other locations for storing food involved requisitioning empty warehouses and mills. Hermitage was the only site on the DNS and together with the other depots was intended to hold sufficient basic foodstuffs to supply the population for three months. There appear to have been a common theme to most, with space for dry goods, a cold-store and on occasions a grain store. (A grain store was later established at Membury near Lambourn.) Most of the buffer depots were also near a railway - as at Hermitage - and also as at Hermitage, had siding facilities extended to the site.

There is no record of traffic in or out of the depot although clearly some foods would have had to be used on a rotational basis and replaced with new stock.

Two sidings, one either side of the main store were provided, the actual rails set into concrete. (See illustration page 250.) These were fed from a headshunt and loop enabling trains to deliver goods having arrived from either direction. The sites were still in use after WW2 and possibly until the end of rationing. It is believed they may have continued in use even longer for fear of further conflict during the 1950s and possibly even beyond although by now coming under the control of Civil Defence

The site at Hermitage was declared redundant after the railway closed and for a time was used as storage by a commercial organisation. After this it lay moribund and not unexpectedly became vandalised. It was later cleared for housing.

No 6134 setting back into the 'refuge' siding at Hermitage which also afforded access to the Cold Store - the latter may be glimpsed behind the engine. It is unlikely the train seen would have served the store as most goods were transported in closed wagons. It has been suggested in the Pryor signalling diagrams series that a single lever open air ground frame was provided to operate detonators for the up distant signal some little distance behind the last wagon of the train. (The last vehicle of the train seen is positioned almost parallel to the turnout serving the Cold Store.) The use of this access siding as a refuge was probably limited as services between Newbury and Didcot were hardly intensive. Consequently it would be rare for a train to need to use the facility and avoid delaying a following service. . The view was taken on 24 March 1953.

T B Sands

An truly evocative scene at Winchester captured by the camera of Henry Meyer. The engine, a member of the ubiquitous 22xx breed awaits departure south: the signal for which is already clear. In the order of a dozen passengers have alighted and are making their way across the footbridge and down the steps to the exit on the up side. The boards forming the walkway across the footbridge were already badly worn with gaps through which it was possible to glimpse and see the roof of the coaches and even on to the locomotive footplate. There was no exit from the down side, certainly post 1891 that is, when the ensuing chalk fall rendered the pathway that had once led to and from St Giles Hill impassable. The date is not given but would probably be in the late 1950s, and certainly from the shadows an afternoon train. This was a fair number of passengers for any DNS train, but hardly sufficient to dispel the legend 'BR's Rural Crumb-Catcher'.

6. From Summit to Decline

From early 1943 through to about 1946 the former DNS was at its peak so far as both traffic and infrastructure were concerned. At last the dreams of the early pioneers had been realised, although it is doubtful if any of those worthies would have been alive to witness the fact.

In Britain's darkest times, from Didcot through Newbury to Southampton had been one of the main arterial routes to the docks at Southampton and yet this rebirth would now turn into something of an Achilles heel, for what now existed now a line that was both expensive to operate and equally expensive to maintain.

With the inevitable but, it must be said, welcome, reduction in military and 'Government stores trains' the railway reverted to its peacetime position, a rural cross-country branch although also now deserted by many who had of necessity had to find alternative means of transport in consequence of the restrictions of the past few years. Passenger levels would tumble further after petrol rationing finally ended in May 1950.

This decline was also obvious to the staff, small wonder the DNS - probably along with other routes – was referred to as 'The Lingering Die, 'The Line that Refused to Die' (although it did in the end – more accurately it was killed off), and of course 'BR's Rural crumb-catcher'.

A scan of the public timetables for the period reveals little change between services as applied in the summer of 1937 and the summer of 1947, with the same basic five through trains between Didcot and Southampton each way on weekdays. The first up morning passenger service also started from Winchester, indicating the shed was still in use at the time. On Saturday evening there was a late evening train south from Newbury, locally referred to as the 'boozer' and often used to convey people back from an evening out in Newbury. Between Didcot and Newbury there was an extra service each way on Saturday, whilst it was only on this, the northern section, that there was any Sunday service and then only one train each way. Incidentally several symbols from earlier times still appeared in the timetable, indicating 'motors, carriages and horses' may be dealt with at various stations whilst additionally there was reference to more modern times in that parking was also available.

One signal box register for the pre-war days has survived from Sutton Scotney and covers the period 13 April to 11 November 1947. This is a valued reference to the traffic then running confirming the number of passenger trains as well as an average of two local freight workings per day. At this time it was only the Didcot to Newbury section that witnessed the passage of through freight workings, a regular Birmingham Oxley to Westbury freight running via the DNS and so avoiding Reading.

The Sutton Scotney register also shows that in addition to the trains, the line was occupied usually for an average of 20 minutes three times a day either side of Sutton Scotney by the ganger and his men under the 'Occupation Key System', (this type of track occupancy would be replicated elsewhere.) In addition a typical day would include at least one additional train working, referred to as a 'box-to-box' special advised from Newbury, the information having been received there from Control at Reading. If the special was to commence on the Southern, then the Control Office at Southampton would notify their counterpart at Reading, who would tell Newbury and so on. As examples, on 13 April there was a special light engine working from Winchester for Newbury: on 18 June it was a special goods bound for Southampton Docks; and on 10 September an Inspection Train to Winchester – unfortunately no details of this are given. Perhaps the most intriguing working was on 30 April 1947 when at 11.30 am the '5-1-3' bell signal was sent from Lodge Bridge to Sutton Scotney requesting 'Line Clear' for a Diesel Rail Car. The vehicle travelled as far as Winchester and returned later in the day. No other information has been found to explain its purpose, although the obvious conclusion was this was a trial to ascertain suitability[1]. Unfortunately at the time the Southern were not disposed to allow regular workings of GWR diesel railcars over their lines for fear such vehicles would not activate track circuits. As such any use of a diesel railcar on the DNS would have to end at Winchester, in effect a reversion to the disruptive engine changing procedure and a throwback to earlier days.

South of Newbury the line was only open on a Sunday for the passage of a special working or more usually, engineering work. The frequency of both of these diminished as the years passed.

In comparative terms, at its peak a few years earlier, the railway is said to have handled perhaps 50 - 60 trains daily each way. Whilst this was over a 24-hour period, it still equated to an average of 35 - 40 between 6a.m. and 10p..m., a far cry then from the average of 10 workings each way in 1947. 'Box to Box'[2] specials could thus be fitted into numerous 'spare' pathways whilst for the signalmen there was time on their hands.

As such at the various signal boxes along the line,

---

1. Surviving paperwork suggests that limited traffic receipts had caused Paddington to consider the use of a diesel railcar service throughout from Didcot and in similar fashion to the then recently introduced Lambourn diesel service. With the SR unwilling to trust the vehicles to operate on a regular basis over their lines, due to reliability in activating track-circuits, this would have resulted in either a steam service only south of Newbury or a steam shuttle south from Winchester. Both would have had a negative effect on the savings that might otherwise have been achieved, consequently the plan was dropped.

2. The term 'box to box' special was a GWR term but which persisted on the DNS post nationalisation. Spare pathways, into which an extra working might slot so as not to disrupt other traffic, were known, on the Southern at least, as 'Q' paths. Digressing slightly, the working timetable for the line north of Southampton to Shawford Junction and beyond, indicated several 'Q' paths, and were often used by boat trains departing later than anticipated due to the vagaries of weather and tide affecting incoming ships.

there was plenty of time for cleaning and polishing of the signal box equipment whilst other men turned their hand to more profitable activities such as a barber service or selling home grown produce. At Lodge Bridge one signalman was known to make his way to the nearest pub between trains - this was the Bullington Cross Inn two miles distant - whilst other staff have hinted at more clandestine activities having taken place at Lodge Bridge. Lodge Bridge was the break-section signal box provided in 1942/43 between Whitchurch and Sutton Scotney. Perched high on an embankment it was a desolate and windswept place and not surprisingly quickly gained the reputation of 'Howls Lodge'. Access was along the lane leading to Lodge Farm off the main Winchester to Newbury road, now the A34. Having passed the farm, the lane continued westwards until eventually passing under the railway by means of a brick occupation bridge. It was here that Lodge Bridge signal box had been erected, controlling a passing loop, the latter provided so as to increase line occupancy. Apart from the lights from the farm some way behind, and those from Barton Stacey army camp in the distance, it was isolated. Small wonder also it was both difficult to recruit and retain staff here and as a result the working was in the hands of relief signalmen for long periods.

Sticking with the signalling south of Newbury and probably because of the additional trains which ran, there was often an imbalance of tokens for the single line sections with an excess accumulating as a result of more down trains than up workings. As a standard rule there were 36 tokens per section, 10 of these held in the auxiliary token instruments. When numbers became reduced the lineman from Newbury would visit the location where there were too many held and effect a token transfer. This was of course recorded in the signal box register at each end of the section whilst it was always an even number of tokens that were withdrawn and replaced in order to keep the instruments 'in phase'.

The implementation of the Transport Act of 1947 with effect from midnight on 31 December 1947/1 January 1948 saw the end of the Great Western and also the Southern Railways. They were now respectively the Western Region and Southern Region although still, for the present at least, operating exactly as they had before. The status quo would generally continue for a further two years, for whilst externally the old names and liveries might appear to change operationally little would alter. Indeed staff interviewed in the course of research all recalled that it was the boundary revisions of 1950 that made the change.

However, before venturing on to 1950 we still have to deal with 1948 and 1949 and already economy was in the air at Paddington. Remember, at this stage Paddington, with

the exception of the two miles from Bar End to Shawford Junction, was still responsible for the whole route. Based on the limited daily traffic it would hardly have come as a surprise that on 14 June 1948 a report appeared indicating the crossing loop at Lodge Bridge was no longer required and should be closed, the track to revert to a single line over the five miles from Whitchurch to Sutton Scotney. Even before this, in 1946 a plan was produced at Reading Signal Works showing Lodge Bridge resignalled and able to be retained but switched out of circuit when not required. The work also involved some track realignment at Lodge Bridge to remove the speed restriction on leaving the passing loop in either direction. 'Long section' token instruments would have been needed at Whitchurch and Sutton Scotney. The lengthened and realigned passing loops south of Woodhay which had been provided in WW2, had, with one exception, been designed so as to allow a train a straight run in but a slower, curved, exit. The exception was the north end of the loop at Sutton Scotney where the alignment of the single span road bridge over A34 meant southbound trains had to curve in and curve out.

This 1946 proposal was not acted upon, although there appeared to be no urgency for economy either, as it would be 1950 before rationalisation came to Lodge Bridge. In the meanwhile the newly formed British Railways was preparing a revision of the regional boundaries that then applied, historic tentacles that had encroached into the recognised area of another were to be removed. The result was that from 2 April 1950 the line south of Enborne Junction would be transferred to the Southern Region. It was this change that was to have a far more reaching effect on the infrastructure, operation and staff than nationalisation did two years earlier.

Prior to 1950, two conflicting rumours emerged in 1949 reference the southern section. The first, and to be honest, the more unlikely, was that the complete line south of Woodhay was to be doubled. In view of the traffic being carried, this must be questionable unless some far sighted individual was already looking into diverting the north-south freight workings away from the Basingstoke route. The conflicting and perhaps more likely rumour was in a document from Paddington dated 20 June 1949, which involved the removal of double track between Enborne and Woodhay. Remember, at the time the complete route was under the control of the Western Region and this could be legitimately seen as an obvious means of economy – in the same way as the removal of facilities at Lodge Bridge. In the event singling north of Woodhay would never take place, the plan obviously shelved following the boundary transfer and the SR unwilling, for whatever reason, to pursue this particular aspect of economy further.

Despite genuine glee at locating the view of the first train at Winchester, Lodge Bridge has continued to prove illusive as a photograph. Consequently recourse has been made a specially commissioned painting from Mike Turner and who has responded with a view which is as near 100% accurate as is possible to achieve using as reference the track and signal plans of the location. We know the design and position of the platelayers hut and signal box, whilst the bridge carrying the footpath from Lodge Farm west towards Barton Stacey is seen under the railway. In the distance the railways continues north towards Whitchurch.

Another rarity. The layout immediately south of Worthy Down captured during the single ten-year period between 1943 and 1953 when the signalling remained as per the connection from Winchester Junction. The engine, No 3212, has just departed south for Kings Worthy and is passing the two bracket signals which (l-to-r) allowed trains into the up siding or up platform at Worthy Down - the actual station is just beyond the overbridge. Note - the bracket was not to permit trains to run either side of the island platform. The white diamonds on the signal posts advise the line is track circuited at this point. Also of interest is the cover for the facing point lock on the exit from the line from Winchester Junction - right - indicating this connection might also be used for trains carrying passengers. A second catch point may also be seen on the right just prior to the overbridge. Finally notice the first vehicle, a Hawkesworth design brake certainly no more than seven years old and yet already cascaded away from frontline duty due to the influx of new BR standard Mk1 coaches. The view was taken on 13 June 1953, and which confirms the signals from the former SR connection at Worthy Down remained in-situ regardless of the fact the actual connection had been severed at Winchester Junction from 25 November 1951. (See also image on p140.)

Lodge Bridge ceased to be a crossing point on 7 March 1950, ironically ten years to the day before passenger services would cease. The work involved substituting the various turnouts at either end of the loop with plain track, removing the signals and extending the token section so it was now Whitchurch to Sutton Scotney. The occupation key section was similarly extended, so this particular change also now corresponded with the token section (the occupation key section did not always correspond in the same way as the token section). The redundant equipment was rapidly removed and the wartime ARP signal box demolished with indecent haste. It was almost as if, with the boundary transfer imminent, Paddington was determined to salvage as much as possible!

The boundary changes were officially sanctioned on 27 March 1950 and took effect six days later from Sunday 2 April. On the same day there were some official renamings, Winchester became 'Winchester Chesil' (the same day the Southern station was renamed 'City', whilst Whitchurch DNS and SR became 'Town' and 'North' respectively. Later, certain aspects of SR operating practice would start to apply whilst Winchester signal box was repainted in the then standard SR colours of green and cream. Fortunately, compared with other former WR routes now taken under Southern control, one thing that did not occur was the replacement of any lower quadrant signalling with upper quadrant arms, much of the DNS equipment only dating from 1942/43 and therefore considered good for a few years yet. One thing that did not change was the issue of tickets, GWR stamped tickets continuing to be issued up to the time of closure.

But even under the Southern economy was quickly the order of the day, for on 25 November 1951 the facing connection for up trains to leave the SR at Winchester Junction and reach Worthy Down was secured out of use. The relevant instruments were removed from the two signal boxes and the signal arms taken down. What had once been a loop between the two lines was now retained as a long siding back from Worthy Down and in later years used to store surplus carriage stock, of which more anon. In many ways the removal of this provision was hardly surprising. It had seen little use in recent years, traffic being restricted to the occasional light engine returning to Didcot after an unbalanced train south, often having worked to Southampton Docks.

Certain grades of staff were given the opportunity to transfer back to the Western Region especially if their role was not to continue under the new owners. Other vacancies as they occurred were left fallow and indeed would never be filled. As an example Winchester's last station master, Mr Livingstone left on transfer to Henley in 1949 – he would never be replaced, supervision now coming under the incumbent at Winchester City. Mr Parsons from Sutton Scotney had also left in 1946 and this was another post that the WR had decided not to replace. As has been recounted earlier, it was Harry Hiller who now maintained tradition, the signal boxes for example having two train registers, one removed at a time by Harry for inspection and returned on his next visit.

The situation regarding the station master role north of Newbury is not so clear. Although it is known that at Compton and Hermitage the station master position was retained until the very end.

Neither was economy restricted to the line south of Newbury, for in the same way that Lodge Bridge had been installed as a break-section over the five miles between Whitchurch and Sutton Scotney, so between Upton & Blewbury and Compton, a set of intermediate block signals officially referred to as 'Ilsley signals' (the name taken from the nearby village of the same name) were provided to increase line capacity on this double track section. (These IBS signals were installed in place of the originally intended six-lever signal box planned for here in 1942.) They and the associated ATC ramps were taken out of use on 5 July 1949, although a note attached to the official entry in the minutes records, "the equipment is to remain on site". In consequence of the abolition, minor alterations were undertaken to the locking and signals at the two signal boxes on either side. This reference to the equipment remaining on site is interesting, almost as if the WR were unsure if the existing service could be operated without them or should traffic increase, they might be required again. The timing of this is also of interest, being around the same period as reference to the doubling proposal south of Woodhay. In the event they were never reinstated and the various items were salvaged at a later date.

It appears as if the respective managements at Paddington and Waterloo were now coming to grips with

Mr Livingstone, the last station master at Winchester.

The 10.15 a.m. Southampton Terminus to Alton service being propelled over the DNS line at Winchester Junction on 14 May 1953 by M7, No 30481. The view is looking north towards Worthy Down with beyond the occupation bridge giving access to Woodham's Farm. It was land belonging to Woodham's Farm that was taken in WW2 for the connection from Winchester Junction to Worthy Down. beyond. Recollections of the time are that men were suddenly seen marking out the route without having made any previous reference to the farm itself. The suitability of the bridges on the line for double-track will be noted. According to Tom Sands, there were in the order of 120 bridges on the route between Didcot and Winchester. This is the same location as the view on p100.

their various losses and acquisitions – not just affecting the DNS of course.

One glitch though was the fuel crisis, which gripped the nation in early 1951. Coal was in short supply and as a result one passenger train between Didcot and Southampton and its associate return working was cancelled. With additional output promised from the mines, normal service was resumed a few weeks later. More ominous was the 1953 curtailment of the Sunday-only Didcot – Newbury – Lambourn working (the same train which pre-war had operated the single Sunday Newbury – Winchester service). This was not reinstated although the replacement bus which had been put on during the train's curtailment was retained and on which rail tickets could be used.

For maintenance purposes, two separate regions were now responsible for the railway although for operating at least Western Region engines and stock continued to predominate. Engine changing also continued until Winchester shed, by then a sub-depot of Eastleigh, was closed on 8 June 1953. The shed itself was demolished soon afterwards although in the interim it was used as a temporary coal store by the local merchant A E Early.

With the exception of driver Tom Keon (whose fate is not reported), all the other footplate crews, driver, Harry Blake, and firemen Alack Osman, John Burgess, Cyril Sacree along with shed labourer Walt Travers transferred to Eastleigh. (At Winchester the shed labourer had worked a permanent midnight to 8 a.m. duty and was also responsible for security on site.) A nominal amount of stores was also collected and transferred to Eastleigh, these were listed as; 2 steel bins, 1 bench with vice, 1 enclosed brazier, 3 open braziers, 1 desk in mess room, and 2 glass fronted notice cases. The third Winchester man, driver Tom Hester is reported to have retired at the time of the transfer.

A surviving file of correspondence, between Winchester shed and its new parent depot at Eastleigh covering the period 1952/3, reveals understandable concern by the Winchester men over their potential duty changes as well as details of the final turns carried out from

North and south. **Above,** *No 2221 still with GWR on the tender yet with a BR smokebox numberplate heads north between Hampstead Norris and Compton on 29 July 1950.* **Below** *- Sister engine, No 2226 southbound between Highclere and Burghclere having just entered the cutting at Hackley: the down (fixed) distant signal for Bughclere is on the left. This is the cutting where the goods and tank-car train came to grief in 1963. See page 211.* *Both: J F Russell-Smith*

The brick kilns recorded on 29 March 1967 and reported as. "still in use - but probably for the last time".

The views show the kilns sealed (above) and left: open for extraction subsequent to firing.

A quarry was established on part of what was originally the Pinewood Estate around the 1870s. At an unknown date this turned into a brickworks proper, possibly around the time of the coming of the railway in 1882. The business was acquired by W Brain[1] of Lambourn c1907 with rail facilities provided to what at first was known as Brain's siding. By 1909 the facility was known as the Pinewood Brick and Tile Works. The land was said to yield sand, chalk, gravel and clay, although commercial excavation of the first three were limited and for most of its life clay for brick-making was the principal product. At its peak the works employed 70 people, whilst one of the three sidings was also used by a local coal merchant / carrier in the 1920s/30s. The brickworks were later taken over by Messrs W W Hall and continued in use until 1967 when redevelopment of the site for housing commenced.

1. There was a Mr W Brain employed at Lambourn as the first station master on the independent Lambourn Valley railway from 1898 and probably until that line was taken over by the GWR in 1905. His subsequent fate is not reported although at the time it was reported he was also a local property entrepreneur. It would appear highly likely he was the same person subsequently involved with the brickworks here.

Top right - *The 'engine' used for the producing gas for firing the kilns. (Coal was therefore brought in for the process.)*

Bottom right - *A hand-trolley still extant in 1967.*
                    (Pinewood brickworks images, all J Irving)

Bottom - *No 3210 on the 1050 Didcot to Newbury working passing the entrance to the siding and about to enter Pinewood Halt. A ground-frame was provided to access the siding. After doubling the siding was electrically released by the Hampstead Norris signalman using 'interlocking lever' No 8. No access being available to the up line. Local supposition has it that nearby Pinewood Halt, opened in 1933 at a cost of £127, was provided for the benefit of workers at the brickworks. This is unlikely, as most staff would have come from the local area. Pinewood Halt was a useful facility to serve the expanding area around Hermitage, much residential development having taken place on nearby land once part of the Pinewood Estate. In the same year as Pinewood Halt opened, another new halt, this time at Shaw between Hermitage and Newbury was proposed. Reference to this appears in the records for 28 July 1933 but for whatever reason it was not acted upon.*

R F Roberts

No 2289 leaving the down siding and heading north through the station with coal on 16 August 1948, probably destined for Winnall. On the left is the 'Down Main Inner home and Down Main to Down Siding Inner Home' signal in the wooden post and arm form it appeared probably from 1891 onwards. This signal was replaced in the spring of 1949 with a metal bracket signal which then remained in use until closure. At the same time as this signal was replaced, the wooden posts and arms of the two signals on the station side of the tunnel, the 'Up Main Starting' and 'Down to Up Main Starting' and also the 'Up Main Home' signals (the last named obscured by steam from the engine) were also replaced with metal posts and arms. This also explains the reason for the new signal arm in the background ready to replace the 'Down to Up main Starting' in the view on p127. F E Box

Winchester. These had changed little over the years and saw a Winchester crew taking a train north to effect a changeover with the southbound train, not always at the station referred to in the official notice. The reason for this was timings. If the changeover train was late for any reason, then the relieving crew would be expected to work on until they met the service at the next crossing point. When things did go wrong it was understandable that accusations were made citing laziness on the part of the delayed train.

Meanwhile away from the DNS, there was a name change in direct consequence of the SR takeover. Litchfield signal box on the SR main line near Micheldever was renamed 'Roundwood' from 14 August 1953 to avoid confusion with the DNS station.

The Southern Region was also now finding out how little in the way of passenger revenue the railway was generating notwithstanding the gradual increase in freight revenue accrued from bulk tank-car trains from Fawley northwards which were routed over the DNS. Understandably Waterloo thus looked at ways in which infrastructure economies could be affected. With the abolition of Lodge Bridge there still remained the facility to

cross trains at each of the nine stations south of Newbury. This was considered excessive and plans drawn up to rationalise matters with the removal of the passing loops and signalling at Highclere, Litchfield and Kings Worthy.

In order to achieve this, there was first a slight reorganisation of train times to remove the need for scheduled services to cross at any of the three stations. On the ground Litchfield was dealt with first, on 23 January 1955, a week later than originally intended. It was deliberately the first to be affected as the north end points were badly worn. Kings Worthy was dealt with next on 30 January, followed by Highclere on 6 February. At the same time as the signal boxes were also closed the token sections extended accordingly. Goods facilities at the station yards were retained, access now being from new outside ground frames released by the single line key token. At Kings Worthy the timber signal box was demolished almost simultaneously, although at Litchfield and Highclere the brick shells of the buildings remained, the interiors stripped of all equipment. In all cases plain track was substituted, although the redundant assets were not necessarily removed immediately. The former down line at Kings Worthy was

Top - *Newbury (and Southampton) train in the bay at Didcot. No 3212, a regular performer on the line is in charge.*

Middle - *A deserted Upton & Blewbury station looking south. What would later be a major issue relative to road improvements is in the background - the A417 overbridge. Notice the down starting signal in the off position. By 1957 block-switches, to enable the signal box here and also those at Compton, Hampstead Norris and Hermitage had been installed. This allowed any (or all) to be switched out of circuit, the relevant signals being placed in the 'off' position. A saving on staffing was thus achieved but at the expense of extending the section: the maximum being just one block from Didcot East Junction all the way to Newbury East Junction. On an unreported date in the 1920s, new 'horse landing' facilities had been provided here for £150.*

Bottom - *On 18 April 1960, No 3622 enters Upton with the 3.28 p.m. from Didcot to Newbury due at the station at 3.35 p.m. Passenger services south of Newbury had been withdrawn some six weeks earlier and the Western Region had yet to come to terms with the realisation that three coaches were more than sufficient for the truncated passenger trains. The WR sectional appendix allowed 'heavy engines' of the 49xx, 69xx, 83xx and 93xx type to work south to Newbury subject to a blanket 20 mph speed limit and a further reduction to 10 mph over A4 road bridge near Newbury. R F Roberts*

A travel stained 38xx, No 3839 heading south near Churn with a train consisting at least in part of cattle wagons, 26 May 1961. Notwithstanding their size these engines were in the 'blue category' and consequently were regular performers on heavy freight work both north and south of Newbury.
Michael Hale

No 3211 heads north near Compton. Local engine restrictions at the stations from Didcot to Newbury meant that all engines, apart from 0-6-0 tender and tank types were prohibited from entering the yards and using the yard crossovers.
J F Russell Smith

Local services at Compton - there was hardly anything else!

In the top view No 3206 enters the station from the Didcot direction. Although there is no confirmation, the neat edging to platform garden is indicative of the station having entered the annual station gardens competitions. One certificate only has been found for the stations north of Newbury and relates to Hermitage, this resides in a private collection.

Middle - No 2240 waiting to leave Compton station. This particular loco was much associated with the DNS in later years and seems to have gained a reputation as the 'cuckoo' engine on account of the sound that could be made from the two whistles.

Bottom - Probably a Saturday 'short' working (meaning a service from Didcot terminating at Newbury), a 61xx 2-6-2T waits departure southbound sometime in 1958. The board crossing was in regular use by passengers with prams.

During the 1950s, BR(W) began to experiment with the use of mobile road vehicles for permanent way use. One such test involved such a vehicle unloading concrete sleepers for which purpose trials were undertaken in the loading dock at Compton. The crane and rail vehicles are seen in use, presumably successfully as this type of operation subsequently became commonplace on BR. Whether the sleepers were intended for use in relaying on the DNS is not reported although certainly concrete sleepers were in use on parts of the line south of Newbury in later years.

Top and middle - *Quiet times at Hampstead Norris, seen in 1960 and 1958 respectively. Tanks engines were seen far more north of Newbury but this was probably habit rather than necessity as Whitchurch had a water supply and the distance to here from either Newbury or Winchester was 12 miles: compared with 17 miles between Newbury and Didcot. The trains are respectively north and southbound, the signal-box likely to be switched out of circuit as indeed it was for long period.*

Rod Belcowe and Hugh Davies

Bottom *- A deserted Newbury c1948 and a Winchester train awaiting departure.*

Roger Carpenter

slowly buried under debris from the former down platform, although for some time a kink remained in the single line compelling trains to abide by a cruel and unnecessary speed restriction at what was the north end of the former loop. At Highclere the former loop was still extant five years later, and despite being isolated at either end the local permanent way gang was determined to maintain appearances and still weeded the abandoned section. (The fact foreman Bob Aldridge occupied the station house may have had something to do with it! Following the removal of the station master posts in the 1930 foreman had been provided at most stations although there was a further reduction in status to Grade 1 Porter posts later.) All trains were thus now compelled to use a single platform at each of the three stations.

Despite the lack of local passenger traffic, Waterloo, or to be more accurate Southampton control, did attempt to make the line south of Newbury more useful. The 1950s saw several excursions including a working from Winchester to Weston-Super-Mare for the very attractive fare of 6/- from Winchester. Through excursion traffic was also routed via the line, although in this case it was probably more convenient for the operator. One such train was a Cleethorpes and Grimsby to Portsmouth & Southsea service, a long way and a long time to be cooped up in a railway carriage.

Locally the limited patronage was augmented on Thursdays and Saturdays when the stations from Litchfield to Woodhay and Compton to Hermitage were busier with those visiting Newbury market. To the south Winchester did not have a regular market at this time, although it is recalled Friday was generally the busiest day at Kings Worthy and was known locally as 'pram day'. The 6d train fare to Winchester was compatible with the local bus service but the train was preferred by mothers with prams.

The decline in local passenger traffic was hardly assisted by the public timetable seeming to show fewer through trains running the complete line from Didcot to Southampton. In practice little had changed from earlier years and in consequence a wait of 45 minutes at Newbury in either direction was commonplace. For operating convenience certain of the services now commenced and terminated at Eastleigh although there was one extreme example in the winter 1955/56 public timetable where the first up service in the morning commenced from Shawford at 7.5am having run as empty stock from Eastleigh. As if to compensate in some small way, the 1957 timetable showed a through service from Oxford to Southampton in the afternoon whilst the 2pm Newbury departure was a through train to Bournemouth arriving at 5.2pm. It is not known if a Western or Southern engine was allocated to this service. Around the same time, certain Newbury trains were also diverted away from Southampton Terminus and used either Southampton Central or even Totton as their destination or starting point.

Even so there was little impact of these through workings on the continuing decline in passenger numbers and a traffic census (always a bad omen) carried out in 1958 indicated an average of 143 passengers daily south of Newbury with a corresponding 104 north of Winchester. Not all of these would have travelled the complete route, whilst these numbers were also divided between six trains each way.

With fears already rife about the future, interest in the line reached the eyes of the local newspaper for Winchester, the 'Hampshire Chronicle'. Their contributor 'T.J.' penned a delightful contemporary piece on Kings Worthy as follows: "....The down rails at Kings Worthy,

Trains of the 1950s. **Above** *- No 2221 is seen near the summit of the line south of Burghclere and with mixed stock: a study of photographs reveals a marked inconsistency of coaches used on the line The small tender, still lettered GWR will be noted.* **Below** *- No 3212 passing the '9¾' mile post just south of Litchfield this time heading north. Again the tender is lettered GWR. This is a part of the line where no trace now remains having been buried under the A34.   J F Russell-Smith*

No 2240 slowing for the stop at Worthy Down, as seen from the overbridge looking south. The connection from the Southern at Winchester Junction is on the left, but its weed covered track will be noted. Just visible is a train of stored wagons on the spur: of necessity these would have to have been added and removed from the Worthy Down end. The view is post 1957 as the bracket on the right can be seen now have just signal arm - meaning the up goods siding has been removed. (See p167.) The proliferation of motor cars in the field on the right is not explained.

Opposite bottom - Images of Kings Worthy in the period up to 1955 are for some reason uncommon but on 14 May 1951, No 6329 was recorded on a down service. The tilley lamp-posts will be noted, as will the lengths of rail bolted across the sleeper supporting the front of the down platform.

T C Cole

This page, top - A post mid-1949 view of the tunnel mouth and up main starting signal at Winchester. The view can be dated due the presence of the 'new' tubular metal signal posts and arms. (See note on p132 which also refers back to p127.) At this period engine changing was still occasionally taking place, hence there was still a crossover at the start of the tunnel. Surprisingly there was no fixed signal to authorise its use from the down platform, movement instead being authorised by verbal instruction with the consent of the signalman from telephones on the signal posts.

Centre - Three coaches and a van depart south on to the single line as seen from the St Giles Hill footbridge. The small lineman's hut that once stood at the end of the loading dock will be noted to have been removed.

Bottom - Busy times at Winchester in 1953. The 22xx is arriving with a northbound passenger whilst the presence of the stationary ex LSWR 0-4-2 No 30566, is explained as having been on a special working to Winnall and was awaiting for the single line to clear to return towards Eastleigh.   R Blencowe

No 2200 is of little interest to the man walking on the up platform. This may well be the down pick-up freight (through workings would not use an engine of this type). The dominance of mineral and open wagons immediately behind the tender tell their own story in how general goods traffic was falling away from the railway leaving coal and its associates as the mainstay for wayside stations - not of course just on the DNS.

An unidentified Southern Q1 on an up through goods (possibly sugar beet destined for Kidderminster) about to surrender the Shawford Junction-Winchester Chesil tablet to the signalman. The fact the signalman does not appear to have a token for the section north to exchange, indicates this may well be a crossing move with the freight likely to continue through the tunnel and stop by the Up Main Advanced Starting signal where the fireman could draw a token from the auxiliary instrument as soon as the line was clear. This would also then free the single line towards Shawford for another working. No date is given, although the lack of foliage would point towards winter - but not a particularly cold day for the end windows of the box are open. (The asbestos hut by the signal box is the 'privy': some larger boxes, such as Newbury East Junction had an inside toilet but with only limited privacy provided by cardboard walls. Not surprisingly these were known as 'thunder boxes'.)

Top - Bar End yard from the public footpath footbridge that conveniently crossed the line at the yard throat. On the extreme left is the Simmons & Gifford siding on which stands a single wagon, road access for unloading was also provided to this siding from Domum Road. The passenger train is running on the single line and will shortly pass under East Hill bridge on the way to 'Chesil station. Immediately to the right of this the rails continue as the down siding. The image was taken in March 1950 just about the time the railway passed into the hands of the Southern yet even for this time the yard is quiet. Of particular interest is the engine shed on the right hand side just past the goods shed: the tender seen likely to be from a WR 22xx. The vacant line (the down siding) between the passenger train and van is the likely route taken by the M7 in the incident described on p116.   S C Townroe

Above - Winchester shed in 1948. No 2252 awaits its next duty. The photograph may well have taken on a Sunday as the engine appears out of steam and there is a set of coaches on the left also awaiting use. Notice the telephone cabinet on the end of the shed wall for speaking to the signalman. Although the engine shed was demolished some 60+ years ago, the low retaining wall on the right was still present in 2013.   W A Camwell
Inset - Fireman Cecil 'Mac' Sacree on the footplate of a 22xx at Bar End loco, c1952.   Richard Sacree

Top - *Another gap filled! At last a view of the replacement, yet short-lived turntable at Bar End, in use from c1947 to perhaps only 1953. Prior to this, the turntable was of limited use being only able to take 'modern' engines with the aid of extension bars. Apart from clearly being a member of the 43xx/53xx/ 63xx type, the actual number is not determined. (The 'Petrol' facility was for the use of the various railway goods delivery lorries that would start and finish their delivery round at the yard.*

Richard Sacree

Centre - *Probably taken at the same time as the view 'top' on the previous page, this is likely to be No 2289 coasting with light steam past the yard Ground Frame hut on the way to the station. (No 2289 was the only member of the class paired with a large ex ROD tender and which, according to Harold Gasson, made it less than popular.) The unmistakable vista of St Catherine's Hill dominates the background. S C Townroe*

Bottom - *Alongside the A33 Winchester by-pass, the road still seemingly with its original concrete surface, the train is steaming hard towards Shawford Junction and has just past the down fixed distant for the junction - perhaps the crew are having a race with the lorry? Just three road vehicles are present, whilst the wooden picket fence was a feature separating road and rail for almost the whole length from Garnier Road to the Hockley crossroads.*

Larks Barrow cutting in 1953. Whilst appearing stable here, two years earlier a combination of rain and then frost saw 1,000 tons of chalk removed. So bad was the situation that in was felt necessary to have daily patrols to safeguard against chalk falls blocking the line. (Much of the chalk removed was sold to a cosmetics manufacturer to turn into talcum powder.) The west side of the cutting remains today, although the east has been completely excavated to make way for the dual-carriageway A34.
T B Sands

never used, are rusted and weed-covered, in places they are practically invisible under grass. The station buildings themselves are compact and tidy and in the style of the Great Western Railway of that time. The notice warning against trespassing is of GWR type. The combined 'Booking Office and Waiting Room' can even sport a ticket barrier, and for passengers approaching the ticket window there is an 'In' and 'Out' direction! The 'Ladies Room' can serve other purposes; the provision for 'Gentlemen' is generous. A tap on the platform is labelled 'Drinking Water' - how many respond to this invitation? Two seats adorn the platform, both bearing the GWR monogram in their metal supports.

"Present Day Traffic; - Though Kings Worthy is described on a station hoarding as coming under the jurisdiction of the Station Master of Whitchurch Town, Mr. Masters is the man on the spot, who deals with everything: carries luggage, issues tickets, collects tickets, answers enquiries, deals with telephone calls and is in charge of the activities in the goods yard. Perhaps he would be the first to agree his labours, though varied, are not too onerous. On recent days, with 12 trains a day, he has had to deal with about a score of passengers. Traffic was down at the time of my recent visit; on that day he had had but two, but before my departure, the score was three. Of course, the service does not do much to encourage people to travel. Cheap day

return tickets are of limited use as the last train from Winchester arrives at Kings Worthy at 5.39 p.m. Thus, in the evening, it is impossible to travel by train to Winchester and return. Passengers often buy single tickets and come back by bus...".

This lack of passengers led the Southern to curtail services further in June 1958 to just four trains each way daily. Those four now remained were not retimed and the inevitable long gaps were cold comfort for the luckless few forced to resort to the King Alfred '11' service and Thames Valley '135', buses complete with the cold and unsheltered wait at Whitchurch. A journey having once taken one hour was on occasions double that by road.

Meanwhile the growing strength of the motor vehicle showed itself in a marked increase in tank car traffic from Fawley to Bromford Bridge in the Midlands. In additional there were heavy trains of sugar beet destined eventually for the refiners at Kidderminster. To cater for this traffic some 36 sets of men from the Eastleigh spare gang 'learnt the road'. Even so, many were surprised by the length and severity of the gradients on the DNS and had one Eastleigh crew insistent on putting off some wagons at Kings Worthy before t hey were prepared to continue. Motive power for these trains varied between BR Standard 75xxx, Southern Moguls and Q1s, with

The engine shed at Winchester (Bar End) closed from 8 June 1953 - see p128. From this day Eastleigh took over the workings previously covered by the depot, initially using Winchester men who were of course familiar with the line. The immediate change however, was that Southern T9s now appeared on the former Winchester duties. At the other end of the route Didcot retained its duties, hence through to the end of local services, WR engines from Didcot would still be seen south of Newbury. On the same day 8 June, locomotive changing also ceased at Winchester, a totally logical move although one which had taken more than five years of nationalised ownership to achieve! (The crossover at Winchester immediately inside the tunnel and used to facilitate this move was retained until the end.) Some Winchester turns had seen the crews exchange footplates with men from a southbound train and it is believed this may still have continued for a time. The situation as regards the two passenger guards at Winchester is that it is believed they too transferred to Eastleigh at the same time. As regards coaching stock, one set of coaches had always been stabled at Winchester overnight and at the weekend: interesting to note there was never any report of vandalism to these vehicles. From illustrations of trains covering the period from 1955 through to 1960, WR stock continued to be seen on services. It seems likely then that either the stock continued to be stabled at Winchester and light-engine working took place between Eastleigh and Winchester as necessary, or, and is perhaps more likely, the last train south now had its stock stabled at Eastleigh. There does not appear to have been much if any obvious alteration to the timetable reference these moves so it could well have been some empty coaching stock working was involved. Southern coaching was rarely seen making up the formation of DNS trains. Post 1953 at Eastleigh, it was necessary to assimilate the former Winchester men into the appropriate Southern link and thereby involve them in route-learning of various Southern lines, similarly Eastleigh men were also required to route-learn the DNS. This route learning of Eastleigh men over the DNS would continue at intervals into the 1960s. The Southern T9s would appear on trains until 1960, indeed the last down passenger service was hauled by an Eastleigh T9.

Opposite top - No 30117 at Compton on the first day of regular SR engine use to and from Didcot. The word 'regular' is used deliberately as it is possible there may have been the occasional incursion beforehand. Pre WW2, the class may also have appeared on Newbury race-specials.
Opposite bottom - No 30313 waits at Hampstead Norris whilst an interesting shaped load reposes on the platform.
This page - Still at Hampstead Norris but this time seemingly devoid of custom. What a opportunity to travel in a rake of WR Hawksworth stock.

THE ARRIVAL OF THE SOUTHERN

Right - *No 30313 at Hermitage. The use of the standard 'stopping passenger service' BR headcode for DNS line trains will be noted. SR 'route' codes were not used for trains travelling to Newbury or Didcot.*

Mike Esau

Opposite page - Southern engine, WR stock. No 30285 leaves Compton for Newbury, Winchester and eventually Southampton Terminus on 9 April 1956. (A similar pre-doubling view appears on p51.)   *D Beaver*

Above - *No 30313 alongside the Up main platform at Newbury. The later, post 1956, logo appears on the tender. Despite being on WR main route to the west and a junction for three radiating branch lines (to Winchester, Didcot and Lambourn), Newbury station would see bursts of activity followed by periods of calm. The calm hardly shattered by the arrival and departure of most DNS line trains!*

*Highclere station. This time it is No 30283 which arrives in the forlorn hope of any likely patronage. By this time VIPs destined for Highclere Castle would travel by car to Newbury and thence use a main line service. The date is not reported but with the old BR symbol on the tender means is it likely to be around 1955-57, the loop at Highclere no longer in use and all trains using the one platform. The station was occupied by foreman Bob Aldridge, whilst also being the home base of one of the three p/w gangs. Almost the final irony would come when in February 1960 when painters arrived to attend to the station, to be fair the railway was only closing to passengers that year, goods were expected to continue and buildings need maintenance on a rotational basis, but it was still a point not lost on the few remaining passengers. (The ceremonial wheelbarrow and spade used by Elizabeth Catherine, Countess of Caernarvon for cutting the 'first sod' on 26 August 1879, is on occasional display at Highclere Castle.) **Inset** - the station sign and seat may well have dated from the earliest days.*

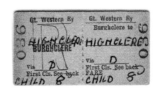
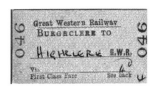

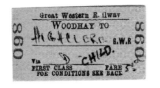

Assorted Highclere destination tickets. There seems to have been little consistency in ticket use / supply on the DNS, with GWR era cards being issued right through to 1960.

Interlude - Passenger revenue

Money received from ticket sales, parcels traffic and the occasional payment for goods despatched (plus 'P.O.D.', demurrage charges collected etc.), had to be dealt with securely and promptly. Each station had allocated to it a leather cash bag, affixed to which was a brass identification plate the bag able to be secured by a lather strap and padlock. The day's takings plus ticket-stubs collected (the latter forwarded to the audit office at Paddington) were placed in these leather bags and in turn placed in a wooden safe within the guards van carried on a set train each day. In BR days the safe was taken to Newbury, after 1953 that for the stations south of Newbury went to Winchester. The safe was returned, along with the cash bags - the view shows the safe at Winchester Chesil plus (top left) a cruel enlargement which unfortunately does not show the name of the line to which it applied. (Centre right - travelling safe recorded on the platform at Litchfield.)

No complete cash bags for the DNS are known to have survived, although several of the brass plaques have. Those for Woodhay and Burghclere are photographed on a typical cash-bag of the period: note the separate Litchfield plaque is to an older design, and also shows much wear. Possibly the others were replaced at some stage but Litchfield with its limited receipts did not need replacement. At least one other brass plaque, for Kings Worthy, was reported to have appeared at auction in recent times. Some of the stations north of Newbury also had their brass plates replaced by engraved ivorine.

151

LITCHFIELD STATION
To be carried out on Sunday, 16th January, commencing at 7.0 a.m.

The points (facing for Down trains) leading from Single line to Down and Up lines, 65 yards Burghclere side of signal box, together with the connection leading from Down line to Single line 697 yards Whitchurch Town side of signal box, will be clipped and padlocked in the reverse position. **The Down line between these points will then be used as a SINGLE LINE for Down and Up trains,** the existing Up line being put out of use.

Litchfield Station Signal Box and all signals operated therefrom, together with the key token 'setting down' and 'picking up' posts, will be put out of use.

The Single line Key Token Section will then be between Burghclere and Whitchurch Town.

The facing points in the Down (new Single) line, 32 yards Burghclere side of signal box, leading to the Down Siding, and the trailing points in the Down (new Single) line, 73 yards station side of signal box, leading from the Down Siding, will, in future, be operated from a new 3-lever ground frame situated on up side of former Up line. This new ground frame will be controlled by the key token for the Burghclere–Whitchurch Town Section. All other points except these referred to above will be abolished.

To enable Drivers of trains to locate their position when approaching Litchfield Station, **a white marker light will be provided on each of the posts which carried the former Down and Up Distant signals.**

The auxiliary key token instrument and telephone, situated approximately 600 yards Whitchurch Town side of signal box, will be abolished.

The existing Engineer's Occupation Key Box at present situated in the signal box, will, in future, be housed in a cupboard adjacent to the former signal box. This cupboard will also contain the telephone.

(P/EW 3, W.S. 1955)   (1) (C.O.S. R.83550)
                                                      (S.D.T.S. R.45227)

The notices relative to work carried out, reproduced above and also on pages 154 and 156 are from contemporary BR publications.

1955 was the year of obvious rationalisation. The earlier removal of the Ilsley signals, Lodge Bridge signal box, and the connection from Winchester Junction to Worthy Down plus the later severance of the sidings at the former stopping place might not perhaps have been immediately obvious to the travelling public, but they could hardly fail to notice when all trains now arrived and departed from the same platform at three of the stations.. Rationalisation at the three chosen for economy was perhaps obvious, but what is not so clear is why Sutton Scotney was perhaps not similarly dealt with? Was it because of the amount of goods traffic still handled or a simpler desire to retain some flexibility in working?

Opposite - *No 2240 pauses, whilst a goodly number (for Litchfield that is) number of passengers alight. The loop has been severed but for the present the redundant track has yet to be recovered.*

This page, top *- Sister engine, No 2234 pauses southbound, the loop now physically removed. The brickwork on the up platform dated from 1942/3 and was especially constructed to allow for the cylinder width of modern engines.*

This page, bottom *- Conversation time, one railwayman and two visitors - plus of course the photographer. In the distance the yard is devoid of any vehicles.*

1955: not a good year (2)

KINGS WORTHY

To be carried out commencing at 10.0 p.m. on Saturday, 29th January until completed on Sunday, 30th January.

The existing crossing loop facilities at Kings Worthy will be abolished. The Down line will be slewed into the Up line at a point approximately 120 yards on the station side of the signal box thus forming **a Single line throughout between Worthy Down and Winchester Chesil.** The existing Up Platform will, in future, serve both Down and Up trains.

Kings Worthy Signal Box and all signals operated therefrom, together with the key token 'setting down' and 'picking up' posts, will be put out of use.

The Single line key token section will then be between Worthy Down and Winchester Chesil.

All points at Kings Worthy, except the following, will be abolished.:—

The points (facing for Down trains) in the existing Single line leading to Down and Up lines, 88 yards Worthy Down side of signal box, will be clipped and padlocked in the reverse position to lead to the Down (New Single) line.

The connection leading from Down Siding to Up line, 218 yards station side of signal box, will be clipped and padlocked in the normal position.

The trap points in the existing Down line and the points in the existing Single line leading from the Down line, 589 yards and 652 yards respectively Winchester Chesil side of signal box will be clipped and padlocked in the normal position.

The facing points in the Down (New Single) line, 54 yards station side of signal box, leading to the Down Sidings, will, in future, be operated from a new 2-lever ground frame to be known as Ground Frame 'A,' situated on Up side of the line, adjacent to the points.

The connection between the Down Siding and the existing Down line, 295 yards station side of signal box, will be re-aligned to lead to the Up (New Single) line and will, in future, be operated from a new 2-lever ground frame, to be known as Ground Frame 'B,' situated on Up side of the line adjacent to the points.

The two new ground frames will be controlled by the key token for the Worthy Down–Winchester Chesil section.

The spring catch points in the existing Up (New Single) line, approximately 600 yards Winchester Chesil side of signal box, together with the 'Limit of Shunt' indicator, auxiliary key token instrument and telephone, will be abolished.

To enable Drivers of trains to locate their position when approaching Kings Worthy, **a white marker light will be provided on each of the posts which carried the former Down and Up Distant signals.**

The Engineer's occupation key boxes, at present situated in the signal box, will, in future, be housed in a cupboard adjacent to the former signal box. This cupboard will also contain the telephone.

(P/EW 5, W.S. 1955)

(1) C.O.S. R.83550)
(S.D.T.S. R.45227)

The immediate after effects of rationalisation at Kings Worthy in 1955. The down line has been taken out of use, the signals removed and the signal box - which may just be seen standing at the end of the loop on the left - is now redundant. It would be demolished shortly afterwards. Meanwhile the former down platform is also being taken apart, what would be left was a mound of earth on which the station running-in board would still stand. Ironically something of this scene still survives today: one solitary telegraph pole complete with a few insulators may still be seen amongst much other greenery that has grown up since 1966. It now looks down over road traffic and not trains.

T B Sands

Top - *On the same day, 18 June 1955, Tom Sands recorded the scene slightly further north and also provides us (inset) with the only view ever seen of the goods shed at Kings Worthy, revealed to have been of corrugated construction. As has been mentioned, with one exception the entry into the extended passing was, post 1943, on a straight run and with a curved exit. Unfortunately this curved exit was retained at Kings Worthy when the down side was taken out of use, and meaning that now both south and northbound trains had a dog-leg at the north end of the station. The severed track of the down loop is obvious with on the right the connection to the yard.*

Middle - *No 6340 with GWR on the tender leaves the station and passes a deserted goods loading platform. Even in the 1950s there were times when horse boxes might be seen loading from this platform.*
Mike Esau

Bottom *- Pre rationalisation at Kings Worthy. No 2289 has just left the station and gained the single line. Views of this end of the station are rare whilst the presence of the timber signal box, which was moved bodily in 1942, will also be noted. At this stage No 2289 is attached to a conventional rather than R.O.D. type tender.* *J L Farmer*

HIGHCLERE

To be carried out on Sunday, 6th February, commencing at 8.0 a.m.

The existing crossing loop facilities at Highclere will be abolished. **The existing Down line will be used as a SINGLE LINE for Down and Up trains,** the existing Up line being put out of use.

Highclere Signal Box and all signals operated therefrom, together with the key token 'setting down' and 'picking up' posts, will be put out of use.

The new Single line key token section will then be between Woodhay and Burghclere.

The points (facing for Down trains) leading from Single line to Down or Up line, 746 yards Woodhay side of signal box, together with the connection between Down siding and Up line, 156 yards Woodhay side of signal box, will be clipped and padlocked in the normal position.

The facing connection leading from Down line to Single line situated opposite the signal box will be clipped and padlocked in the reverse position.

The trailing points in the existing Down (new Single) line, 47 yards Woodhay side of signal box, leading from Down Siding, will, in future, be operated from a new 2-lever ground frame, situated between existing Down and Up lines adjacent to the points. The new ground frame will be controlled by the key token for the Woodhay—Burghclere section.

To enable Drivers of trains to locate their position when approaching Highclere Station, **a yellow marker light will be provided on the posts which carried the former Up and Down Distant signals.**

The Auxiliary Token Instrument and telephone situated approximately 685 yards Woodhay side of signal box will be abolished.

The existing Engineer's Occupation Key Control Instrument at present in the signal box for the Woodhay—Highclere section will be moved to Woodhay. Two new Engineer's Occupation Key Boxes, one for Highclere—Woodhay portion of the section and the other for the Highclere—Burghclere portion of the section, will be provided in a cupboard adjacent to the former signal box. This cupboard will also contain the telephone.

(P/EW 6, W.S. 1955)   (1)   (C.O.S. R.83550)
                                                               (S.D.T.S. R.45227)

Note: The reference to 'yellow' marker lights is in place of the former distant signals. This makes absolute sense, but why in the similar instructions for the three stations, are they 'white' at Litchfield and yet Kings Worthy was 'yellow'? Whatever, they were of course oil lamps - of whatever lens colour - and probably the responsibility of the station porter to clean and refill on a regular basis.

Single line working at Highclere. **Opposite top left** - *On an obviously windy day, the view is from the triple arch brick bridge that passed over the north end of the station. It was from here that former rail passengers would look down on to a deserted railway when forced to use the replacement Thames Valley bus service. The train seen is departing for Newbury.*

Opposite top right - *As at Kings Worthy, there was a definite 'dog-leg' left at the south end of Highclere where the now single track remained to follow its original course. It would not have taken much to allow a clear run without the necessity to reduce speed.*

This page, top - *No 2240 with what is probably a late passenger working, the aforementioned bridge in the background. The severed loop was not removed until after passenger services had ceased.* R Blencowe

This page, bottom - *With steam perhaps escaping from where it should not, No 3210 leaves Highclere with an Newbury working train but on the former down line. As at Litchfield the former WW2 ARP type brick signal boxes were retained although stripped out their contents.* R Blencowe

double heading between the first two types not unknown. The Eastleigh men and machines would take the trains as far as Didcot, and where at least once company rivalry still persisted on Didcot shed. The occasion was a passenger train arrived from Eastleigh T9 the engine from which had gone to the shed for turning before working back. On this occasion the T9 had been left in what was a less than ideal position resulting in the Didcot shed foreman urgently seeking out the Eastleigh crew to, "...move that b*.......engine, none of my men will touch it!" Rivalry with perhaps a little piece of deliberate dislike also showed itself with the comment, "Turn right at Shawford Junction off the timetable and on to the calendar." To be fair, Eastleigh men were also quick to praise the WR main line when working between Reading and Didcot, referring to it as "Brunel's billiard table".

With less opportunities for crossing trains consequent upon the economies of 1955, allied to the slow progress of several made by heavy northbound workings, it was not surprising that these freight services would lose their booked pathways. When this occurred, it was a question of shunting on to the wrong line in order to allow a booked passenger service to pass. At Worthy Down recourse could also be made to the former loop back towards Winchester Junction, although both here and at the stations, care had to be taken because of the presence of catch points installed to prevent runaways at the end of the loops.

There were a number of minor derailments in the 1950s, one in 1953 just before the shed at Winchester closed when the engine which was being prepared for the 6.15 p.m. Reading Goods (a service which had existed for some years) ventured off the turntable without this being correctly aligned. It would appear only a partial derailment occurred

But it might not all be total doom and gloom, as there was the occasional flashback to happier and more lucrative times. One can perhaps only imagine the confusion caused at Woodhay when after having arrived at the station on a Newbury train, the passengers felt their service instead of heading north, being pushed back in the direction they had just come. The reason was literally 'tail' traffic: three horse boxes to be shunted back and deposited in the yard. With the ground signal cleared, the train is now pulling away again with what could be Bert Gardner making his way back to the signal box: on the left and out of camera. Whether the vehicles were full or empty is not reported, but however they were, they would have to moved on from their deposited place as the loading point was at the opposite end of the yard. (Possibly this was done one at a time by pinch-bar and expletive.) At some period Woodhay had a semi-regular special working for horse box traffic, an average of 5-6 boxes per day being delivered empty from Newbury and collected later in the day - staff recall by a 63xx locomotive. How the loaded vehicles were returned, by special train or ordinary service, is not reported. The presence of the bogie vehicle of the far end of the yard is also intriguing with no explanation given, unless perhaps dropped-off due to a hot-box. On the left is the sand-drag where No 76016 came to grief in 1959 - see page 165. Finally, note the height of the up main home signal in the background, reputed as being the tallest signal post on the DNS.

Transport Treasury

as it was righted under the guidance of the District Inspector, even if in complete darkness and without recourse to a crane. Two incidents involving passenger trains are also reported. The first at Sutton Scotney around 1952 when the 7.32 a.m passenger service from Southampton, due at the former station at 8.33 a.m. over-ran the loop upon leaving the station and continued through the sand-drag and partly down the embankment No injuries are reported. According to local railwaymen, the original cause was a trainee signalman 'learning the box' and who, as the train was leaving for Whitchurch, suddenly thought the road was not correctly set and reversed the points from their previously correct position. But this explanation does raise questions, not least that the starting signal could not be cleared to 'off' with the points incorrectly set. The explanation given then does not hold true unless the signal was also replaced and then the points changed – but to do this it would mean changing the points,

The DNS line both north and south of Newbury features in a number of cine films both colour and black/white covering the period around 1959 to about 1962. Some are of several minutes duration, other little more than a few frames although both steam and diesel feature. Quality is 'of the period' but together they form a unique record that can never be recaptured. There are also some brief overhead colour shots of the line when closed yet still intact taken in the vicinity of Compton Crossing, these appear in the firm 'Those Magnificent Men in their Flying Machines'.

One other film should also be mentioned. This was produced as a compilation under the title 'Hops and Downs' and affords several minutes of life at Highclere set amidst a delightfully contemporary backdrop of the immediate post-war years but with later references to the railway's closure.

No 2240 in the down platform at Woodhay in March 1960. Harry Hiller had made the comment the DNS (southern half) could be serviced a two-hourly circular diesel working running Southampton - Basingstoke-Reading (reverse) - Newbury - Winchester - Southampton, with the same in reverse direction so as to give an hourly service. He comments that Waterloo declined his idea. (A straight replacement diesel service was of course referred to when BR produced their report on possible closure.) Bear in mind that issues such as regional variations regarding motive power then applied, SR diesel units were of the DEMU type whilst the WR were using diesel-mechanical sets. In other areas out-dated practice applied simply out of necessity. At Woodhay churns of water were delivered for both the station and station house by passenger train. With the cessation of passenger working the pick-up freight took on the role. When this too ceased, a BR lorry from Andover was involved - note not Newbury, for although geographically far closer it was a different region. Integration did not seem to apply in the 1960s. The other trouble was that even a declining railway needs maintenance and this could be costly, witness three miles of fencing that was replaced between Woodhay and Highclere after 1960.

The Railway Correspondence & Travel Society have produced a monthly magazine for members for many decades. Most issues include a section on member's observations and notes, initially split between the various pre-nationalisation railway companies, and post 1948 into the regions. The same style of entries continue to the present day but are obviously out of reference to this work. A study of the issues from 1947 through to 1967 reveal a feast of information on the DNS line, some factual, some trivia, some assumptions which may or may not have come to pass, but all useful as a snapshot from observers 'on the ground'. Often too this was the only place where an event was ever recorded. Not every incident and occasion known to have affected the DNS is mentioned (possibly the fault of the present author who simply failed to find them!), but what they do provide is invaluable. They are shown below in the form they appeared and against the issue month, although due allowance for time-lapse must be made in observing, sending, and finally printing. At times DNS workings were clearly a favourite of at least one observer - we are never told their names - whilst the gaps may indicate said persons were occupied elsewhere.

1947	January	Due to repairs carried out on the turntable at Winchester Chesil (GW), from 25 November 1946 to 5 December 1946, all GW engines normally turning there were sent to Eastleigh. Six engines were seen each day off the following trains which were always worked each day by SR 0-4-4Ts from Winchester GW on to Southern metals: 7.45 a.m. Newbury to Southampton Terminus, 10.50 a.m. Didcot to Eastleigh, 3.35 p.m. Didcot to Southampton Terminus, and 5.54 p.m. Didcot to Southampton Terminus. The sixth engine was off the goods working. The 10.50 a.m. Didcot is worked by a GW engine throughout normally and is usually a 2-6-0 duty. During the ten days the special working was in force, there being no Sunday trains, the following GW engines visited Eastleigh: 2202/8/21/2/7/9/40/5/89/99, 3396, 4303, 5381/97, 6329.59. Another failure of the turntable on 10 December 1946 brought No 2299 down off the 7.45 a.m. ex Newbury. No 5970 was on the 12.42 p.m. Didcot to Southampton Terminus on 30 November 1946 and is only the second 'Hall' to appear on a Didcot train. The 7.37 a.m. and 12.42 p.m. are the only through GW workings from this line to Southampton.
	July	DN&S line. 63xx class now appear to monopolise the passenger services and 22xx the goods. On 19 May 1947, No 4318 worked the 10.42 a.m. Didcot through to Eastleigh, and No 6329 took the 12.45 p.m. Didcot through to Southampton returning on the 4.55 p.m. Southampton Terminus. 'Bulldogs' and 'Dukes' which not so very long ago shared most of the working on this section are now very rare visitors.
1948	April	Newbury. Passenger traffic on the Didcot – Winchester line is almost entirely in the hands of new 0-6-0's, Nos 3210-2 (DID) with No 3419 (DID) assisting. Goods traffic is worked by Nos 2202/21/2/40 (DID).
1949		No entries
1950		No entries
1951		No entries
1952	May	'700' class 0-6-0 No 30306 was used on the duties of WR 0-6-0 No 2240 over the Winchester, Newbury, Didcot line on 21 March 1952 when the WR engine failed. On Sunday 23 March 1952 the SR engine was on Didcot shed and the WR engine on Eastleigh shed where it received the necessary light repairs. A light three-coach AEC diesel unit ran trials between Didcot and Newbury during the week commencing 28 April. The coaches were 4-wheeled.
1953	July	Commencing with the summer service a number of alterations in the locomotive workings of this section took place. The early morning (approx 2.45 a.m.) Southampton to Didcot passenger duty is now taken by 76xxx class 2-6-0's from Eastleigh shed. This is the first time that this class has worked to Didcot on passenger trains although they have worked the through goods for some time. Instead of the M7 0-4-4T working through from Winchester on the corresponding down journey, a WR engine works to Southampton, it then runs light to Eastleigh, returning later in the day on the approx. 2.0 p.m. passenger train ex Southampton. An additional working to Eastleigh is the engine off the all stations goods train to Winchester (Cheeshill). The 10.30 a.m. (at Eastleigh) and the 12.42 p.m. Didcot to Southampton duties and the corresponding return journeys are still worked by GW engines. The 2.56 p.m. Oxford to Southampton is also 76xxx hauled. Another alteration is that the 7.40 p.m. Southampton Terminus to Winchester (Cheeshill) now terminates at Winchester (City).

1953	August	Further to the notes from the previous month, in addition to the Southern Region 76xxx passenger workings mentioned, one roster calls for a T9 to work the 10.22 a.m. Eastleigh to Newbury and the 12.25 p.m. Newbury to Eastleigh daily, the engine turning via Newbury racecourse. This was worked by No 30285 on 4 July. The revised workings involve a 'circular tour' – Eastleigh, Basingstoke, Reading, Didcot, Newbury, Eastleigh. On 3 July 1953, Nos 76011/12/15/17 were all noted through Newbury.
	October	An additional train for Naval leave personnel left Worthy Down Halt for Paddington at 12.15 p.m. on 14 August and was loaded to 12 coaches. The corresponding down train ran on Saturday 30 August and was made up of 10 coaches which left Paddington at 9.40 p.m. and arrived at Worthy Down at 11.30 p.m. The engine then ran forward to Winchester Chesil and returned for the empty stock which it took to Didcot. The Newbury and Winchester line is normally closed on Sundays but on 30 August it also carried an excursion train from Didcot to Portsmouth Harbour.
1953	December	On the DNS line to Southampton a WR Pannier Tank is reported to have worked the 11.45 a.m. Southampton Terminus to Didcot on 22 October and also the corresponding down train. It is presumed that an engine failure must have made this unusual motive power necessary.
1954	January	Freight trains on the Winchester to Didcot line which are now worked by BR Cl 4 2-6-0's are the 5.35 a.m. Bevois Park (Southampton) to Didcot and the 2.45 p.m. Eastleigh to Didcot. In the reverse direction the 9.50 a.m. Didcot to Eastleigh and the 7.00 p.m. Didcot to Eastleigh are so worked. These trains are restricted to a load equal to 45 wagons inclusive of brake van.
	March	On 2 February 1954 the Hampshire Fire Brigade was called to Whitchurch Town station to supply 1,400 gallons of water to the engine of a freight train. This was because the water column had frozen.
	July	Two unusual special trains were run from Southampton to Winchester (Chesil) recently in connection with the King Edward's School Thanksgiving Service at Winchester Cathedral. The trains were hauled by 2-6-0's Nos 76007 and 76027 respectively, and each consisted of twelve corridor coaches. One train was double headed up the DNS line to Whitchurch for berthing until required for the return journey

One of two 12-coach special workings of 4 June 1954. This was the southbound return working for King Edward's school from Winchester, recorded at 9.00 p.m. destined for Millbrook. Booked departure time was 9.15 pm., the length meant it was overhanging the platform. Both trains had arrived within 12 minutes of each other at 'Chesil, the first train seeing the engine take its now 12 coach ecs stock to Whitchurch just seven minutes later. At 5.52 p.m. the second train arrived, the stock presumably shunted into the yard after which the engine ran light to Whitchurch. It was due to arrive here at 7.02 p.m. At 7.15 p.m. both engines left coupled together on the single 12 coach-ecs working back to Winchester. Here the engines were uncoupled. After the first train had left the stock was collected from the yard ready for the second working seen here. (The up train would have been tender-first as there was no provision to turn.) The engines were Nos 76007/27.

1954	August	A new service, 12.10 p.m. Winchester Chesil to Southampton Central has been introduced for the summer service. Although an M7 0-4-4T was used for the first three weeks, a WR 22xx 0-6-0 was introduced on 10 July with No 2289 and on 17 July No 3212 was used. The WR 0-6-0 runs light to Southampton Terminus after working this train, and then works the 1.56 p.m. to Didcot. The 12.10 p.m. train is the only WR hauled train on the Northam Junction to Tunnel Junction curve excepting special trains and excursions.
1955	April	Since 7 March T9 4-4-0s have replaced Standard 2-6-0's on Eastleigh's two passenger workings to Didcot. Details of these are as follows: Duty 277- 7.32 a.m. Southampton Terminus to Didcot 3.35 p.m. Didcot to Southampton Terminus. Duty 278 7.05 a.m. Shawford – Reading General via Newbury and Theale. 3.45 p.m. Reading General – Didcot. 5.52 p.m. Didcot - Newbury 7.25 p.m. Newbury – Southampton Terminus Duty 279 (10.22 a.m. Eastleigh – Newbury and 12.25 p.m. return) which was a T9 job in the summer of 1953, now remains a BR 2-6-0 duty. On 12 March, No 30117 was on the 3.35 p.m. from Didcot with a three-coach load. In the hands of unaccustomed WR men it gave a most lively run over the hills to Newbury. With Eastleigh men thereafter progress was somewhat more restrained. But a late start was more than recovered and arrival at Winchester was early.
	June	On 10 May WR Diesel railcar No. W21W was noted at Eastleigh on a tour from Oxford University Railway Society via Reading. It returned from Eastleigh via Newbury and Didcot.
1956	March	Occasionally a WR 0-6-0 has appeared on the evening passenger trains from Didcot to Southampton on Saturday evenings. It spends the night and all day Sunday on Eastleigh shed. Locomotives noted are as follows, No 2221 (15 January), No 2240 (29 January), and No 3212 (5 February).
	June	On 1 May 0-6-0 No 2252 working the 7.40 a.m. Didcot to Southampton Terminus, was found to have defective brake gear. T9 4-4-0 No 30285 returned on the 11.45 a.m. passenger to Didcot, the 0-6-0 being sent to Eastleigh for repairs and returned to the WR the following day.
	November	The Newbury – Winchester line is to continue in use for the time being with traffic as sparse as ever.
	December	A WR engine, No 2221 failed with a big-end melted out when working the 4.56 p.m. Southampton Terminus to Didcot at Shawford on 5 November. The train was shunted into the infrequently used up goods yard to allow other traffic to pass, and No 75070 was sent from Eastleigh as substitute engine.
1957	December	'City of Truro' is permitted between Enborne Junction and Southampton Terminus but is not allowed over curves of radius less than six chains.
1958	September	Since the withdrawal of certain passenger services at the end of June, what passenger traffic there was seems to have dwindled further still. On 9 August, the 2.56 p.n. Oxford to Southampton Terminus was noted passing Shawford double-headed by Nos 31613 and 82014 hauling three coaches with few people on board. The Mogul had worked a relief from Portsmouth to the Midlands via Winchester Chesil, Newbury and Didcot and was returning to Eastleigh.
	October	Contrary to expectations this line will still remain open to passenger traffic during the Winter service. The service will remain the same as at the end of the Summer service.
1959	August	Notices are now posted concerning the proposed withdrawal of passenger services between Winchester and Newbury. It is not yet clear whether Winchester Chesil will be retained for passenger purposes and it is believed possible that the Winchester – Newbury section will be closed to all traffic in spite of its improvement during the war years to take modern locomotives and full-length freight trains.

1959	October	A visit to this line on 3 September found traffic to be light. T9 30729 was working the 12.8 p.m. Eastleigh to Didcot formed of three WR coaches, which contained about 12 passengers (mostly returning home from shopping). A 22xx 0-6-0 was on a freight consisting one empty wagon and a brake van. The 10.50 a.m. from Didcot to Eastleigh hauled by No 2252 had only a handful of passengers. The only station which seems to do any business is Worthy Down Halt which is alongside a naval establishment. It is understood that the closing of the DN&S line between Enborne Junction and Shawford Junction will take place in November. The T.U.C.C. will then have heard objections; the Hampshire County Council is not opposing closure.
1960	April	No 76026 which ran away at Whitchurch Town recently was re-railed on 21 February by the Eastleigh and Salisbury cranes. The last day of passenger services was on Saturday 5 March. The last up train, the 5.12 p.m. Eastleigh to Didcot was formed of a three WR corridor set and set LMR open seconds, hauled by No 2240 (81E). The train was well filled, as were most trains on the branch that day. A party from the Society travelled on the last down train, the 5.55 p.m. from Didcot to Eastleigh. From Didcot to Newbury the train was formed of a WR 3-COR set, hauled by T9 No 30120 (71A), which had been specially steamed and cleaned by Eastleigh. On arrival at Newbury everybody had to change, and the five coaches which had worked to Newbury were duly shunted into the down bay by No 30120. No 2240 had attached itself to the 3-COR set and continued to Didcot. The T9 performed well with five coaches. Departure from Newbury was some seven minutes late, connecting with the 6.0 p.m. Paddington –Weymouth. At some stations a few local inhabitants had gathered to cheer the departure of the train, and the engine duly responded on its whistle! At other stations, notably Litchfield, the platform was deserted and the guard duly extinguished the solitary oil lamp. No detonators were let off neither was the engine garlanded Arrival at Eastleigh was 15 minutes late. The line remains open for freight traffic, and Eastleigh hopes to receive some Stanier 2-8-0s from the WR to alleviate the double-heading of some trains. The section between Newbury and Didcot remains open for all traffic.
	June	With regard to previous statements regarding the future of this line, there is at present no question of complete closure. Local freight services will probably disappear before long, but the line will be retained for through freight trains to and from Fawley and the Southampton areas, and proposals are in hand for further development of this traffic.
	September	This line saw a passenger train on 6 August when a 12.02 p.m. Portsmouth Harbour to Birmingham relief traversed the line to relieve congestion on the main line via Basingstoke and Reading West.
1961	January	It is believed three 9F 2-10-0s are to be loaned to Eastleigh by the WR to work the Fawley –Bromford Bridge tank trains. These trains are worked from Fawley to Millbrook Yard double headed by an H16 4-6-2T and a CL 2 or CL 3 2-6-2T. The 2-10-0s would work from Millbrook Yard so avoiding a change of engine at Westbury. No 92205 was noted at Eastleigh shed on the Society's visit on 10 December . A 2-10-0 (believed to have been No 92226) worked a special freight from Eastleigh to Newbury or Didcot via the DN&S line on 14 December. CL 9F 2-10-0s are now permitted between Enborne Junction and Shawford Junction.
	February	With reference to the note in the January issue, three CL 9F 2-10-0s, Nos 92205/6/31, have arrived at Eastleigh to work the tank wagon trains between Fawley and Bromford Bridge via the DN&S line. The 2-10-0s (excepting 92079) have been specially sanctioned to work over the DN&S section. This traffic formerly went via Bristol and the Midland main line to Birmingham, but owing to heavy delays encountered in the Bristol area, the above revised route was agreed, together with the transfer to the SR of the three 9Fs to work throughout. The new working commenced on 2 January.
	March	With reference to the earlier mote, the re-routing of the Fawley-Bromford Bridge tank trains via the DN&S line has not yet taken place. At the time of writing (20 February), these trains are still running via Salisbury, Westbury and Bristol.
	September	The withdrawal of freight and parcels traffic from four stations on the Didcot, Newbury & Southampton line is under consideration. They are, Woodhay, Highclere, Burghclere and Litchfield. Users of these stations are invited to consign goods to Newbury.
	November	A wagon in the 9.53 a.m. Didcot – Eastleigh freight became derailed whilst running through the loop at Worthy Down on 14 October, causing considerable damage to point work. No further trains were able to run over the line that day, which meant two freight trains being cancelled; the 12.15 p.m. Washwood Heath – Eastleigh presumably cancelled at Didcot, and the 7.35 p.m. Southampton Docks – Birmingham was cancelled. The 3.31 p.m. Bevois Park – Spondon tank train was diverted via Basingstoke and Reading being worked by a CL 9F 2-10-0. Normal freight services were resumed over the line on 16 October.

1962		No entries
1963	May	A derailment occurred on 23 March between Highclere and Burghclere when 22 wagons were derailed on the 8.30 a.m. Didcot – Eastleigh freight. The train engine, D6520, was not derailed. Luckily none of the crew was injured, but the line was not cleared until late afternoon on 25 March. It was cleared by the Eastleigh and Old Oak Common breakdown cranes. Whilst the line was blocked, freight traffic was either cancelled or diverted via Reading and Basingstoke.
	August	Freight Workings. A number of interesting alterations to freight workings have taken place in the Southampton and Eastleigh area recently upon the introduction of a new 'Import Express' service from Southampton Docks. The 'Import Express' departs from Southampton Docks at 7.00 p.m. (SX) and at 7.25 p.m. on Sundays, and runs to Crewe via Winchester Chesil, Newbury, Didcot and Oxford. The Sunday services reaches Oxford via Basingstoke and Reading as the DN&S is closed. The train is diesel hauled.
1964	March	With the re-routing of the Fawley – Bromford Bridge tank car trains via Basingstoke and Reading, the future for this line must be bleak to say the least., especially for the Enborne Junction – Shawford Junction section. Only a handful of freight trains now traverse this section, yet it is open 24 hours a day on weekdays. In the down direction the trains are; 9.50 p.m. (SX) Northampton – Fawley tanks (diesel hauled), 1.10 a.m. Washwood Heath – Eastleigh (steam hauled), 10.20 a.m. Didcot – Eastleigh (diesel hauled), 3.52 p.m. (T,Th.O) Sutton Scotney – Eastleigh (steam hauled), 12.15 p.m. Washwood Heath – Eastleigh (steam hauled), and the 8.23 p.m. Didcot – Eastleigh (diesel hauled). Trains in the up direction are: 5.47 a.m. Bevois Park – Didcot (diesel hauled), 5.58 a.m. Chichester – Didcot (diesel hauled), 12.12 p.m. (T,Th.O.) Eastleigh – Sutton Scotney (steam hauled), 3.55 p.m. (SX) Fawley – Leicester tanks (diesel hauled), 6.35 p.m. (SX) 'Import Express' Southampton Docks – Liverpool Edge Hill (diesel hauled), 9.20 p.m. Eastleigh –Birmingham Lawley Street (steam hauled), and the 9.35 p.m. (SX) Fawley – Northampton (diesel hauled). Only two intermediate stations remain open for freight traffic, Sutton Scotney and Winchester Chesil. Of these, Sutton Scotney is expected to close shortly.
1964	July	On 22 May a Matisa ballast machine became derailed at Southcote Junction, blocking the Basingstoke – Reading line. This meant that the up 'Pines Express' had to be diverted by Winchester Chesil, Newbury and Thatcham. To convey Winchester City passengers, a bus was provided to take them to Winchester Chesil, where the 'Pines' called especially. It must be many years, if ever, that a named train has travelled over this line, let alone called at Winchester Chesil, and the local residents residing along the line must have wondered why on earth a passenger train of this nature was traversing the line so long after closure. *(See illustration pages 218/219.)*
	October	Closure of the Didcot, Newbury and Southampton line duly took place on 10 August. The line is now closed completely between Enborne Junction and Winnall sidings just north of Winchester. The reason that the short section between Shawford Junction and Winnall remains open is that a fair amount of steel traffic is still carried to the sidings. To convey this traffic, the 12.12 p.m. (freight) Eastleigh to Winchester Chesil is still retained. The return working is the 2.00 p.m. (freight) Winchester Chesil to Eastleigh. The final freight trains to run over the remainder of the line to Enborne Junction ran on 8 August, but owing to the few freight trains running on summer Saturdays, they ran during the early hours of the morning. The last down train would have been the 1.10 a.m. (freight) Washwood Heath – Eastleigh, and the last up train the 9.35 p.m. (freight) Fawley – Northampton tank cars on the Friday night. All freight trains have now been re-routed via Basingstoke and Reading.
1965		No entries
1966	May	All freight train facilities were withdrawn from Winchester Chesil on 4 April which means closure is now complete of the erstwhile Didcot, Newbury and Southampton Railway. Work has commenced on removing the track on this line, north of Winchester Chesil.
	December	New name plates were put into position at Winchester City during October showing simply 'Winchester'.
1967	April	Although track has been lifted, the fixed distant adjacent to Winchester gas works remains.
	August	From 10 July, Winchester City station was renamed Winchester.

No 76016 'in the dirt' at the end of the sand-drag at Woodhay following its 'coming to grief'. The train had been the 12.32 p.m. passenger working from Newbury to Winchester. An indication of the limited passenger revenue at the time can be gauged from the fact that no complaints were received from passengers on the train. Here the Eastleigh breakdown gang are in attendance with the tender already separated from the engine - the latter also stabilised against falling further.

W Bishop

including releasing the facing-point-lock in the face of the approaching train. Not least the engine crew and guard should also have been observing the signal and points.

A not dissimilar situation occurred at Woodhay in 1959 but this time the fault was certainly that of the footplate crew. The signalman had accepted an 'up' sugar beet train (Southern 'Q1' hauled), whilst the 12.25 p.m. passenger service from Newbury was anticipated around the same time. Both were perfectly legitimate moves, the passenger train due to wait in the platform as the single line section to Burghclere was currently occupied. But as the signalman left his box to collect the token from the approaching goods he noticed the passenger train was arriving faster than usual. He recalled later both crews were exchanging greetings between each other, not a warning but friendly banter. In doing this the crew of the passenger train failed to identify how far down the platform they were with the result that No 76016 ran through the sand drag at the end of the down platform to end up at a drunken angle completely derailed. At the enquiry it was noted that there had been four men on the footplate of No 76016, two learning the road, which was suggested led to the distraction. Despite the 'rough shunt', as at Sutton Scotney there were no injuries and the passengers on the service continued their journey on the next down train, the latter especially routed 'wrong line' through Woodhay. Meanwhile the engine was quickly sheeted over and recovered by the Eastleigh breakdown gang after 3-4 days.

The major derailments of the period, both at Whitchurch, on 23 September 1954 and in February 1960, involved Nos 76017 and 76026 respectively. Both were of similar type and involved down freight trains coming to grief at the catch points at the south end of the loop, caused by the weight of the train on the down gradient pushing it on. The engine unable to halt the progress of what was a partly unbraked train.

The 1954 incident had the potential for a far worse incident had the approaching passenger train from Sutton Scotney been unable to stop. Simply put, signalman Ken Alexander at Whitchurch witnessed the down goods derail, having been unable to do anything about it as the route was legitimately set for an up passenger train en-route from Sutton Scotney. The piling up of wagons behind the tender also caused the up line to be obstructed. The commotion was heard by ganger Ted Talmage but at that precise moment he was occupied 'on a personal matter' at the foot of the embankment some way south and by the time be had regained track level the passenger working had passed. Much now depended upon Ken Alexander although it is likely the driver of the passenger train may have seen his way ahead obstructed. Whatever, the passenger service was indeed halted – having then to reverse the five miles to Sutton Scotney where it met the next up passenger train which had arrived and was waiting. Control dictated both be joined together with the engines working back south coupled together, and of course running tender first. Buses replaced trains for the remainder of the day although such was the speedy work of the Eastleigh breakdown gang that the line was cleared and reopened to traffic by 5.45pm the same day.

Recovery of No 76017 was left until the following weekend, when two 35- ton steam cranes made the lift under the direction of the Eastleigh Motive Power Superintendent, S C Townroe.

Other minor occurrences in the 1950s include a down empty train which became divided in Larksbarrow cutting between Whitchurch and Litchfield, and a derailed tank car on the up line alongside the goods shed at Bar End. The official reference to this incident recorded the cause as "...liquid movement within the tank...", although according to railwaymen, the more likely reason was buffer lock. Finally, and again at Winchester, 9 August 1958, the tender wheels of an unidentified engine derailed at Bar End. This was dealt with by the Eastleigh crane in 2½ hours. (See p220.)

As will be gathered, south of Newbury all calls for repair, maintenance and assistance were directed to Eastleigh with the signalling Inspector based at that

WORTHY DOWN JUNCTION

To be carried out on Sunday, 24th February, commencing at 8.0 a.m.

The facing connection in the Up Main line leading to the Up siding, 24 yards Sutton Scotney side of signal box, will be put out of use, the points being clipped and padlocked in the normal position.

The trailing connection in the Up Main line leading from the Up siding, 244 yards Sutton Scotney side of signal box, together with the Up siding will be put out of use, the points being clipped and padlocked in the normal position.

The existing Up Main to Up siding Home and Up Main Starting signals, 157 yards Winchester Chesil side and 208 yards Sutton Scotney side of signal box respectively, will be abolished.

The undermentioned Shunting signals will be abolished:—

Shunting signal controlling movements from				Distance from signal box
Up siding to Up Main line	..	..	..	50 yards Sutton Scotney side
Up Main line to Up siding	..	..	..	270 yards Sutton Scotney side
Up siding to Up Main line	..	..	..	218 yards Sutton Scotney side

(P/EW 8, W.S. 1957)   (1)   (C.O.S.—R.87314)

This page - Changes at Worthy Down. Above is a pre 24 February 1957 view showing a somewhat unusual move at the station. The engine would appear to be pulling the coaches back out of the station, but the lack of any headcode discs on the tender might well imply this was a shunt move. There would also appear to be passengers in the first vehicle: the latter certainly of LSWR origin whilst the remaining three vehicles are clearly GWR type. Finally we may observe the signalman making his way briskly back to the signal box. There could be several conclusions although the most likely would appear to have been a special 'short' service to Worthy Down, the engine having just run round and will now return to Winchester. Notice the presence of the siding on the left, abolished in 1957. This siding extended for some length parallel with the up line and apart from unloading coal also had bowsers into which liquid fuel could be dispensed. Here at Worthy Down the signalman was also responsible for the issuing of tickets. Notice the brickwork above window level, and which was later rendered as per the image opposite bottom. (The brickwork for the signal boxes was not always of the best quality having been provided partly by POWs in WW2. Even so Worthy Down was the only box so altered. (See also text 169.)

J L Farmer and Michael Hale

Eastleigh based No 76013 waiting in the down loop at Highclere on a crossing move in 1953. Interesting is the use of just a single 'barrier' wagon between the steam engine and the tank cars - usually there were two at the front and rear of any tank car trains carrying flammable liquids. Notice mid way in the train the trailing connection from the up platform which led to the goods yard. This was taken out of use post 1955 but was not physically removed until the former loop was lifted in 1960.
T B Sands

BR Passenger survey Newbury - Winchester. Undated, but conducted prior to June 1958. (Note states, 'census relate to average number of passengers carried daily'.) Services shown italics were withdrawn in 1958.

Down

Down	a.m.	Joining	Alighting	a.m.	Joining	Alighting	p.m.	Joining	Alighting	p.m.	Joining	Alighting	p.m.	Joining	Alighting
Newbury dep.	7.45	3		9.07	12		12.25	7		2.00	8		4.32	16	
Woodhay dep.	7.52			9.15	1		12.32			2.07			4.39		1
Highclere dep.	7.58	1		9.21	1		12.38	1	1	2.13	5	1	4.45		2
Burghclere dep.	8.03	1		9.26	3		12.43		2	2.18		8	4.49		2
Litchfield dep.	8.10	4		9.32	1	1	12.49			2.24	2	1	4.55		1
Whitchurch Town dep.	8.18	3	5	9.40	5	2	12.56	1		2.32	2		5.03	1	1
Sutton Scotney dep.	8.29			9.51	3		1.07	1		2.43			5.14	2	1
Worthy Down Halt dep.	8.39			9.58			1.14	8		2.57	8		5.21	24	
Kings Worthy dep.	8.44		1	10.03	1		1.19	1		3.02	2		5.25		
Winchester Chesil arr.	8.49		5	10.08		8	1.24		8	3.06		12	5.30		25
Passengers remaining in train			1			16			8			5			10
		12	12		27	27		19	19		27	27		43	43
Destination	*Southampton Terminus*			Eastleigh			*Bournemouth*			Eastleigh			Eastleigh		

Up

From	6.28 a.m. Totton			*7.55 a.m. Eastleigh*			*10.18 a.m. Eastleigh*			12.08 p.m. Eastleigh			2.12 p.m. Eastleigh			4.53 p.m. (SX0) 5.12 p.m. (SO) Southampton Terminus		
Up	a.m.	Joining	Alighting	a.m.	Joining	Alighting	a.m.	Joining	Alighting	p.m.	Joining	Alighting	p.m.	Joining	Alighting	p.m.	Joining	Alighting
Passengers already in train		8			2			5			8			5			12	
Winchester Chesil dep.	7.14	9		8.11		1	10.37	2		12.25	4		2.28	5		5.32	12	
Kings Worthy dep.	7.20	1	1	8.16			10.44			12.31			2.34		1	5.39		1
Worthy Down Halt dep.	7.26		15	8.22			10.50		1	12.37	1		2.40		1	5.45		3
Sutton Scotney dep.	7.33			8.3			10.56			12.44		1	2.48			5.54		1
Whitchurch Town dep.	7.45	3		8.41			11.07	1	1	12.55	1		3.02	2	1	6.07	2	4
Litchfield dep.	7.54	2		8.5			11.16			1.07			3.12			6.16		1
Burghclere dep.	8.04	4		8.56	2	2	11.22	3		1.13	2		3.18	1		6.23	1	2
Highclere dep.	8.11			9.01	1	1	11.26			1.17		1	3.23		1	6.28		1
Woodhay dep.	8.17	1		9.07	3		11.32	1		1.23	1	1	3.29	1		6.33	1	2
Newbury arr.	8.25		8	9.15		8	11.40		10	1.30		14	3.36		9	6.41		13
		25	25		9	9		12	12		17	17		14	14		27	27

Sutton Scotney in 1958/59. A tired looking station and a train generating little obvious revenue. (Look very carefully and there may be a single member of the public coming through the gate alongside the main building. Otherwise there are three men on the down platform and one on the up, railwaymen perhaps?) The whole scene was hardly one that could be said to appeal, especially to a generation now freed from the constraints of rationing and instead embracing consumerism and everything that went with it, especially the motor car. This was also a period in time when one of the most famous quotes by a politician comes to mind, "...most of our people have never had it so good...", by Harold MacMillan in 1957. The train is probably awaiting departure, the oft quoted phrase, "lack of passengers invariably leads to good timekeeping" also to the fore. Such a scene was not restricted to just Sutton Scotney either, it was reflected throughout the DNS, and which in itself was a microcosm for so many secondary and branch line railways.

Hampshire Chronicle

location. An Eastleigh lineman was also allocated to the railway, although his tasks were made easy as the equipment was still relatively new and he seemed to spend most of his work on the transfer of tokens, as referred to previously.

Unfortunately this same integrity could not be said to apply to the structure of some of the wartime built signal boxes, where damp and water ingress began to become an increasing problem. As an example, at Worthy Down rendering had to be applied all around the external brickwork above the operating floor windows to the roof. At Burghclere, water was trickling on to the block shelf close to the electrical equipment, regular reports and requests for repairs by both the signalman and Harry Hiller seemingly ignored. It was as if no one department would take responsibility for the necessary roof repairs, one official suggestion being to provide a temporary wooden trough to carry the water away until the necessary remedial action was

taken! Fortunately at the eleventh hour common sense prevailed and the roof was waterproofed as required.

Towards the end of the 1950s road competition for both local and medium distance haulage was starting to have an effect on goods traffic at the stations, while the establishing of a national grid for gas supplies saw the closure of the Winnall Gas Works siding north of Winchester from 29 November 1957. To the loco drivers at least, this was something a relief, for track maintenance within the sidings had always been the responsibility of the owners and in the last years little had been done in the way of the upkeep. With the closure of the gas works so too did the sight disappear of some local residents arriving to collect supplies of coke direct for home use.

Notwithstanding the publicity for the railway consequent upon the article in the 'Hampshire Chronicle', there were still those in Winchester who knew nothing of

Above - No 76028 traversing the single line at Litchfield, northbound. Mike Esau

Left - The traffic that was increasing in the 1960s was freight - but this was through freight and so not locally generated. No 76019 seen entering the loop at Sutton Scotney.

A deserted Winchester Chesil. A visitor to here, or indeed any of the stations would more likely find a scene such as this, seemingly devoid of life and certainly movement. *Brian Connell*

the station tucked away at the bottom of the town. Traffic levels had, if anything decreased, still further and so it came as no surprise when in June 1959 Waterloo produced an internal report on the savings that might be achieved if passenger services south of Newbury were to be withdrawn. This eight-page document concluded that the cost of maintaining four trains each way was £32,219 annually, against revenue of just £9,195. Taking into account additional costs associated with closure there was a case for an estimated net saving of £22,824 per year. The same

Estimated cost of Operation of Newbury - Winchester line by diesel traction		
A	4 trains each way on weekdays (i.e. present service)	£18,000
B	6 trains each way on weekdays (i.e. service prior to reduction in the June 1958 'economy cuts')	£24,000
C	10 trains each way on weekdays (at approximately 90 minute intervals)	£31,000
D	Improved service of 14 trains each way on weekdays (at approximately hourly intervals)	£39,000

report considered the introduction of a replacement diesel service, several options being given:

No mention is made of the Newbury to Didcot section, true, this by now well under the control of Paddington but it is interesting to note how Newbury to Winchester was seen as a separate line with no mention anywhere in the report relative to the potential for through passenger workings.

Even allowing for the reduction in cost of providing a diesel service, the report concluded with the comment, "…there (is) little likelihood of the potential for an increase in traffic as no major residential developments are planned in the area served by the railway."

Curtailment of passenger train, it was recognised, would result in the loss of some parcels traffic currently carried by passenger train although this could be dealt with under the 'zonal motor' scheme. Watercress traffic presently carried by passenger train and despatched from Sutton Scotney and Whitchurch could in future be sent from Micheldever or Whitchurch North, 'on adjoining rail routes.' Evidence of the alternative bus service provided by King Alfred Motor Services and Thames Valley Traction was also given, although it was noted that neither worked through and a connection was necessary at Whitchurch. These connections were often poor and the current 65 minute train journey would in future be replaced by a road

In a example of independent spirit by the Western Region in 1957, 'City of Truro' was rescued from York Museum and returned to Swindon for restoration to working order. Once complete the engine was employed on corporate advertising specials as well as enthusiast specials. More relevant to these pages it had regular work on the DNS, based at Didcot shed and tasked with the 12.42 Didcot to Southampton and 4.57 p.m. return Southampton to Didcot. The actual turn likely to have been a deliberate WR ploy as this service would pick up men from the Southern works at Eastleigh taking them home to Winchester behind the pride of Swindon.

Opposite top - Late afternoon at Winchester. Mike Esau

Opposite bottom - Northbound at Burghclere - and still drawing an admiring glance. Hugh Davies

This page top - Southbound, close to the site of the former Barton Stacey Halt. E W Fry

This page, centre - Leaving Sutton Scotney, southbound. The 1 in 106 climb on leaving the station commenced immediate on leaving the platforms. 'City of Truro' was active on the DNS from 1957 through to 1958. Mike Esau

This page, bottom - At rest at Newbury. Steam engines had their uses, as witness the bucket being filled with hot water! (Meanwhile the tender of the engine is also being refilled from the water column.) The late Harold Gasson recalled that on Mondays at several of the DNS stations, the station master's wife would await the arrival of the train ready to fill buckets with hot water ready for the weeks' washing.

service taking 90 minutes at best and over two hours at worst.

Paragraphs 10 and 11 of the report sounded a warning for the future:

"10. Possibility of use as an alternative route. - The line is to be retained for local * and through freight traffic and will therefore be available for use as a diversionary route should circumstances require this." (* against the asterisk was pencilled in '...for the time being'.)

"11. Retention of Stations for dealing with Local Freight Traffic. - No proposals for closing the stations to freight traffic have been included in this submission, but freight traffic at stations along the line is very light and detailed investigations are in hand to see where else it could be handled to enable the local freight train services to be withdrawn. These enquiries are not yet complete but the probable outcome is that the line would eventually be closed to all passenger and local freight traffic."

Against the background of such damming financial evidence there could be no real opposition to the move and closure notices appeared forecasting the cessation of passenger services between Newbury and Winchester from Monday 7 March 1960. With no Sunday service this meant the final day of operation would be on Saturday 5 March.

With an eye towards the future, 'T.J.' in the 'Hampshire Chronicle' wrote another, more detailed report of the railway, including a complete trip over the route. At 60 column inches of text it is too long to be included in full, although some of his descriptions are so delightful they could not be left out: *"The Newbury-Winchester line offers a calm little journey through pleasantly peaceful country. The great thing to be said for it was that hardly anyone ever travelled by it, and its little three-coach trains never seemed to be carrying more than six passengers so that a man who wanted to use it for a spell of undisturbed peace could always be certain of finding it When the 2.12pm from Eastleigh drew into Chesil Station Winchester, there were four people on board. Two alighted, six joined - total eight, a fair average for that train. Three coaches were hauled by No 2246....no one could complain of overcrowding or lack of comfort. Indeed the cushions and furnishings were of a standard as high as on many main line trains Round the curve we swept to Kings Worthy - right on time. Dead or possibly moribund would be appropriate epitaphs with which Kings Worthy could be described these days. No one joined, no one alighted; I think the porter on the platform would have been astonished if either event had occurred There is an air of damp decay about the whole place which makes one feel it is convinced that its days are over and so under the SR mainline and to Worthy Down. Here the signalmen handle the passenger traffic and, as no one joined or alighted they were not overburdened on this particular day. Steeply uphill, No 2246 climbed away, the sharp bark from the engine echoing in the deep cutting. Over the top she continued downhill to Sutton Scotney,* where no passengers awaited our arrival; no one alighted but two parcels where handed out. Sutton Scotney for many a year had its own Station Master and used to be rather famous for its platform topiary. Some have made efforts to preserve the work but they lose heart with change and threats of closure and so the trim, neat and delightful bushes of yesteryear have become rather straggling unkempt growths. Our halt was brief and on we ran due north to Whitchurch. Evidence lies on the east side of the line of the one time Lodge Bridge signal box and which, having served its purpose, was dismantled and knocked down. Its foundations and numerous fragments of cement and brickwork will for many years serve as its tombstone... So to Whitchurch. Painting has been going on there recently and the place looks spick and span. It is difficult to reconcile this refurbishment with closure but the ways of some are difficult to understand, so one must not be critical of any effort made to ensure a station building or platform becoming a more attractive place! Chesil station please note. Here, on this day, one passenger alighted, reducing our complement to seven. In her place we took aboard one empty pigeon basket and two envelopes; fair exchange? On we climbed, still due north, beautiful views in both directions. Over the main road twice and into Litchfield station, called in case of confusion, Litchfield, Hants. Here the acting station master, despite his stentorian call to everyone, failed to evoke any response; no one joined, no one got off. Litchfield's traffic is very small, some days it is counted in pence. Sometimes I gather, there is no counting to do; occasionally someone may book a through ticket to somewhere, a transaction which increases the takings many hundred fold and may bring in more than all the rest of the week's takings added together. And, it reminds one, that branch lines do help to feed main lines The platform plots and flower beds have lost their attractiveness. Here it was that a lady factotum functioned for a time and credit goes to her for her enterprise in tending the flower beds and making the place generally tidy. Since her departure, Litchfield has been in the hands of a succession of BR officials, some young, some not so young and, as the duties are scarcely onerous previous experience in station mastering is not considered an essential. But it is a lonely job at Litchfield and hours can pass when all one hears is the passing traffic on the road at the foot of the hill. On from Litchfield and over the Hampshire Downs to Burghclere. It is a wonderful part of the run this, past the seven barrows and under Beacon Hill. Burghclere is a fine substantial station, in recent years it has been in charge of a lady who greets every train - though I do not suppose she may know it she is known far and wide to that band of railway enthusiasts who have a love of the unusual; and I use the term in the kindliest way. No one joined, no one alighted. The guard and our friend exchanged pleasantries while awaiting the time of departure, for lack of passengers can certainly lead to good time keeping.....And we were off and still due north to*

Opposite *- Special train of eight coaches leaving Worthy Down northwards and entering Christmas Hill cutting. We may speculate on a short / special working to Worthy Down or a general excursion. The date is not recorded.*

Three stunning portrayals of the railway near the end. **Opposite:** *the north end of Winchester Tunnel,* **above:** *Highclere, and* **below** *Burghclere. Henry Meyer and Richard Perry*

Highclere. Highclere station's transport facilities are few and far between, once more no one joined and no one alighted, we just paused sufficiently long to claim we had stopped. Ornamental bushes adorn the platform - an air of decay prevails So on through the deep cutting and to the Berkshire border, a pleasant part of the route and beautiful in spring time. Woodhay station looks as if it had been erected in a hurry, the station was deserted. As we stopped the porter came out of his office and looked hopefully along as he called out "Woodhay". But obviously he had experienced many other previous unfulfilled hopes and we were scarcely on the move before he was back in his office. Even the 'D' has departed from the Woodhay sign on the platform - there would be little point in replacing it at this late date in the station's history. Timetables like others on the line showed a correct impartiality to GWR and SR loyalties. The Waterloo - Weymouth services of the SR stand cheek by jowl with the Paddington - Taunton and Weymouth services of the GWR.. Last station on the branch, and as

close as can be to the Hampshire-Berkshire border.

And so from one county to another, and on to Enborne Junction where, as at Shawford Junction, one may well have to rest awhile till the main line is clear. Round the curve and on to the main line past the junction signal box and so the end of the branch. Newbury station was unusually quiet, the few passengers leaving the arrival from the south made little difference to its stillness. The timetable and destination board in the booking hall showed another recent change, for the Lambourn Valley line is no more, although the name still features on the board, but, in the space, no times appear. Under the heading 'Winchester and Southampton' the four insertions of train departures will likewise soon disappear and another blank will exist on the station board

The evening train from Newbury southwards consisted of the same three carriages, hauled this time by No 76028. These coaches, had, in the meantime, travelled north as far as Didcot. Passengers totalled three, a figure

Saturday 5 March 1960: the last day.
Opposite top - In sombre attire, the Eastleigh District Motive Power Superintendent Stephen Townroe looks out from the cab of No 2240 waiting departure from Winchester . The train was the 5.32 p.m., the last regular northbound service from 'Chesil.
Opposite bottom - Later in the day, No 75005 had charge of the mid-day departure and was recorded at Sutton Scotney. A E Bennett
Above - Finally, the same engine on its way back south at Burghclere.

Top - Last rites. Highclere on 5 March and with more passengers than it had seen for a long time. The man in the beret leaning out taking the photograph could well be John Smith of the Lens of Sutton firm. The train is likely to have been the penultimate southbound departure.
E T Gill

Middle - Worthy Down on 5 March. Here the station would close to all traffic after the day's service - to be fair it looks like it already has! (Whether it was ever used for camp special workings after this time is not certain.) The train was the 3.38 p.m. from Didcot behind No 75005. *H B Priestley*

Bottom - The same service and this time at Kings Worthy, again hardly an advert for the latest the railway could offer passengers. Just four people stand in watch, seemingly more in curiosity than regret. *H B Priestley*

Last day tickets: dated 5 March 1960, probably purchased as souvenirs and not used for travel.

Left - Newbury on the evening of 5 March 1960. "Under the heading 'Winchester and Southampton' the four insertions of train departures will soon disappear and another blank will exist on the station board". The last regular passenger service awaits departure.

Right - Well wishers at Winchester late on March evening. "Will yer no come back again?" read an inscription on a carriage window..

which remained unchanged all the way to Winchester. On the way south at some stations we just halted and were quickly away, at others, we had to wait for the proper departure time. At some of the stations no life whatsoever was seen on the platforms except, that is, at Whitchurch which by comparison was busy with one man in charge...".

Saturday 5 March 1960 witnessed the trains with far more passengers than usual. The final up train from Winchester, the 5.32p.m. departure, consisted of five coaches hauled by No. 2240 under the control of Eastleigh men. Driver J. Wilmore and Fireman R. Ralph who would also be in charge for the final down service. Accompanying them on the footplate was Mr S C Townroe, the Eastleigh Motive Power Superintendent.

The return working was the 7.25p.m. from Newbury, this time with T9 No 30120 at its head and which had a compliment of over 250 passengers. The train was seven minutes late leaving Newbury caused it was stated, by a passenger, who determined not to left behind, leapt into the train at the last moment causing a door to slam and the drop light to smash. At each of the stations en route crowds of local people were there to witness the occasion whilst upon arrival at Winchester two phrases were found scrawled on the windows, "Will yer no come back again", and "That's yer lot". With no facilities to handle freight, Worthy Down closed completely on the same day, although the signal box and passing loop would remain open until final closure.

A few weeks later a little noticed change was the removal of the turntable at Bar End on 27 June 1960, officially to store at Nine Elms, but it is not known if it was ever used subsequently. Whether it was ever used post-1953 is not reported. (A contradictory report refers to removal having taken place some time earlier on 19 April 1953, involving No 76067 and a crane.)

Meanwhile north of Newbury the Western Region

too were considering plans for economy on their section of line. Records showed that on 25 November 1959 plans were prepared to cover the reversion of the railway to a single line, Those for Hampstead Norris and Pinewood Halt have survived and indicate the facilities to remain would have been similar to those that had existing prior to 1943. The work was scheduled to commence on 25 May 1961, with Stage 1 singling from Newbury East Junction to Hermitage. For reasons not discovered, it was not proceeded with. Probably the cost of the work mitigated against the savings that might be achieved.

The passenger service between Didcot and Newbury now consisted of four trains each way daily, re-timed from the commencement of the summer timetable on 13 June 1960 to save one set of train men. The limited service was augmented with an extra working in each direction running on Saturdays only. Passenger loadings, however, were limited and, as if partly in response to this, the regular service was given over to diesel haulage using just a single vehicle from 12 September 1960. The Saturday-only service remained steam hauled in both directions.

Waterloo meanwhile were starting to realise their redundant assets as trackwork from the severed loop at Litchfield was collected on 13 December 1959, Kings Worthy on 26 March 1960 and finally Highclere on 17 June 1960.

Between Didcot and Newbury there was a maximum of ten through freight workings daily, six of which ran via Enborne Junction and on down to Eastleigh or beyond. Not all these ten were daily services. In addition there was one light engine movement between Didcot and Newbury together with a thrice weekly pick up goods which ran from Didcot to Newbury and on to Hungerford. This working would also serve Pinewood Siding as required. One anomaly from years gone by which still persisted on 'TThSo' (Tuesday/Thursday/Saturday only) was a horse box

Above *- No 6302 restarting from a signal stop after Didcot East Junction, 3.58 p.m. 22 September 1961. Michael Mensing*

Left - *No 3665 approaching Didcot East Junction with empty coke hoppers, 3.42 p.m. 22 September 1961. Michael Mensing*

Above - On Monday 3 September 1962, 9F No 92150 had charge of the 12.40 p.m. Bromford Bridge to Fawley empty tanks, recorded just south of Didcot, soon to start the 3½ mile climb towards Upton and Churn. For a time there was problem with the LMR sending the empty cars back behind an engine of less power than a 9F. This was not a problem on the down journey but the power of a 9F was required for the up (full) working.

R F Roberts

Right - On the same day No 76069 had been summonsed to assist a failed D6530 with the 1.0 p.m. ex Fawley, again approaching Didcot.

R F Roberts

Bottom - Steam power in the landscape. Q1 No. 33021 heads north at Churn on 26 May 1961. The expanse of the Berkshire Downs is apparent, as is the isolated position of the stopping place.

Michael Hale

Left - No 92206 passing Churn with tanks from Fawley, 23 May 1961.

Centre - A few weeks later the same engine was recorded at Compton on a similar working. 3 July 1961.

Both R F Roberts

Bottom - No 76015 disturbs the peace at Compton as it rattles through bound for Eastleigh. David Lawrence

Above - *We now move south towards Hermitage where approaching the station, Q1 No 33037 heads south back towards its home territory. These were the largest true Southern freight engines which worked over the line, the S15 variant never known to have been used. 3 July 1961.*

R F Roberts

Centre - *A grimy and work stained D65xx comes off the WR main line at Newbury East Junction and starts to head north. The view was taken from the conveniently placed Hambridge Road overbridge. In the background the tall industrial building was once the grain store that stood in Newbury goods yard.*

Bottom - *No doubt amidst much shuffling, grunting and squealing, 28xx No 2813 restarts its train from the DNS ready to join the main line at Newbury East - straight ahead the route passes Newbury Racecourse and continues on to Reading. The railwayman will probably have some time to wait before he can cross the rails! This could well be a WR working using the northern section DNS to head west towards Westbury and so avoiding Reading.*

Andrew C Ingram

Enborne Junction, Four images of the two types of freight working seen on the DNS post 1960. The first was the bulk tanker train and the second the mixed inter-regional freight. Bulk workings were invariably the province of the 9F, WR 28xx/38xx type or D65xx - but of course there were exceptions usually when the booked engine was not available. Through freights might well be a 43xx/53xx/63xx or 'Standard'. Loadings were also set down for the weight of train the engine might take, the 9F not surprisingly able to take the most.

Opposite top - A D65xx, possibly No D6520, rounding the curve from Enborne ready to start the 27 miles south to Shawford Junction.

Opposite bottom - Having just gained the DNS, 2-6-0 No 6337 sets forth on the climb towards Woodhay on 21 July 1964 with the 12.15 a.m. Washward Heath to Eastleigh. John Coles

This page - The same working. Having just rounded the curve from Enborne, the train sets out for Woodhay and beyond. . John Coles

Maximum loadings for DNS trains.						
Class of Locomotive	9	8	5	4	3	D65xx
	9F	28xx/38xx LMS 8F	'WC/BB' 'N'	43xx/53xx/63xx75xxx / 76xxx 'Q1' 'Q'	22xx/32xx 'U'	
Max Basic Wagon Units	80	76	55	45	39	68
Notes:	A single 'Basic Wagon Unit' was calculated on one where the weight did not exceed that of a 13 ton capacity wagon 'lightly loaded'. Conversely an individual wagon that was loaded and in so doing now weighted between 28 and 43 tons was calculated as being equivalent to 4½basic wagon units. Allowance also to be made for the brake van and if, as in the case of many types of tank car, roller-bearings were fitted. The 'barrier wagons' at the head and tail of each tank car train were also included.					

This page, top - The uneconomic railway: not just the DNS. Locomotive and brake-van between Woodhay and Enborne. It may well be this is to collect an unbalanced working, possibly the scheduled train in the up having been cancelled. D6521, 24 July 1964. John Coles

This page, middle - On a very wet 23 January 1960, the fireman of 'U' No 31803 leans out ready for a handover of the 'Burghclere - Woodhay' to the signalman. This train could not exceed 39 'basic wagon units' including the brake-van. The wagons would appear to be empties, but no doubt hard work for men and machine on a 'wet rail'. E Wilmshurst

This page bottom - For some time in the 1960s, the Bulleid 'Light Pacific' which hauled an inter-regional passenger working from Bournemouth to Oxford would return south from Didcot on freight via the DNS. An example is seen approaching Tothill bridge southbound.

Opposite top - No 31794 with what appears to be a 25 wagon load, two barrier wagons, 20 tank-cars (probably empty), a further two barrier wagons and a brake-van. The location is between Highclere and Burghclere. A E Bennett

Opposite bottom - A clean, and probably brand-new D65xx heads north through Burghclere with mixed freight. On the extreme left the embankment for the lime-kilns siding may be seen.

Above - The DNS in the 1960s. A unidentified 9F very close to the summit of the railway northbound between Litchfield and Burghclere. (The side of the line on which the telegraph poles stand is always a good clue as to the direction of travel - although they do jump about on occasions!) The photograph was taken from the A34 main road, then a single carriageway which included a 1 in 7 climb northbound for the road to reach its own summit nearby. Many is the time a lorry would stick half-way on the climb. In this windswept landscape with Beacon Hill behind the photographer, a train might be seen against a bleak background, the landscape undulating east towards Hannington. On the extreme right the edge of a mound will be noted, one of several tumuli in the area this one being partly built over when the railway came. This, and others on the opposite side of the dual-carriageway are still present. Fifty years later the track bed still exists at this point although trees and scrub have grown on the embankment side. Indeed most travelling on the A34 today - like the DNS the 1 in 7 climb also consigned to history - would be unaware either had existed.

Above - The same train as was depicted in the rain at Woodhay earlier. (Even allowing for the motor cars of the period and roads of the time - Woodhay station being somewhat distant from the A34 - the photographer has done well to be able to drive from Whitchurch to Woodhay faster then the freight service.) This is Whitchurch on 23 January 1960 but with the freight travelling 'up' on the 'down' line due a failure of the motor-points at the far end of the loop. No doubt a lineman would have been called out but in the interim freight could operate as seen although for passenger working the points would need to be clipped and padlocked or wound over by hand, both time-consuming and difficult. Harry Hiller would have been informed with the priority to restore normal operating as soon as possible. The cut-away edge to the down platform will be noted.

E Wilmshurst

Opposite bottom - The summit breasted, and downhill for a while now regardless of the direction! No 92231 between Burghclere and Litchfield, 26 June 1962. P H Swift.

Right - Another member of the 'U' class but with just two brake-vans passing Whitchurch northbound on Saturday 6 February 1960. With nothing shown in the Special Traffic Notice for the day this is another example of a likely unbalanced working.

Left - *Recorded from the end window of the signal box, the fireman of No 2221 collects the token for the section to Kings Worthy. We may accurately report the date as being pre 1957 as the up siding is still in use - coal apparently being unloaded. The train will be the down morning pick-up goods, which had left Didcot before 5.00 a.m. and would meander its way towards Winchester crossing at least three up workings on the way.*

Above - *Double heading immediately south of Worthy Down, possibly due to the non availability of a 9F. (The engines are Nos 76011 and 31795.) Of interest is the signal in the background, which has lost part of its bracket consequent upon the closure of the up siding at Worthy Down. (See comparative illustration on p126.)*

Above - No 92221 enters the loop at Winchester with empty tank-cars for Fawley, 18 July 1962. In the background is part of what has become Winnall Industrial Estate. The divergence of the camp line from 1918-20 was through the wooden gate on the right, although of course long before the passing loop had been extended in the form seen here.

Right - Unusually a 'Hall' class 4-6-0 on an up tanker train, No 4925 'Eynsham Hall' at Winchester on 5 April 1961. Classified as 'Red' so far as route availability was concerned, engines, the class were permitted over the line subject to specific speed limits at particular locations.

P J Swift

Left - *Photographs of former GW 2-8-0s on oil trains to and from Fawley are rare by comparison with other types. Here though No 3835 was recorded heading north through Winchester Chesil on an unreported date. Possibly their rarity was no more than a desire by the WR to retain control of their own machines, the trains working through WR territory rather than starting or terminating on the region. The photographer reported this as being the; 'second part of an oil train', on 31 March 1961.*

P H Swift

Bottom - *No 76061 heading south with a mixed through working. From this angle notice the reason for the disparity in height between the two starting signals at the end of the platform. The station canopy meaning the Up platform starter needed to be placed lower on the post in order to be seen from under the canopy on the approach.*

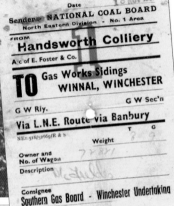

Date 18 NOV 195..

Sender NATIONAL COAL BOARD
North Eastern Division - No. 1 Area

FROM
Handsworth Colliery
A·c of E. Foster & Co.

TO Gas Works Sidings
WINNAL, WINCHESTER

G W Rly.   G W Sec'n

Via L.N.E. Route via Banbury

NEt: 518/52969/R & S

Owner and
No. of Wagon
Description

Consignee
Southern Gas Board - Winchester Undertaking

Inset - *Wagon label for Winnal Gas Works (the spelling 'Winnall' is equally used). Written on the reverse is the somewhat puzzling comment, "Mr Hillary, Worthy Down Halt." Also the details of the actual wagon, No 243494 and tare weight 8T 7cwt.*

Above - A dieselised DNS - not quite. In the years leading up to 1964 so Southern Region D65xx locomotives began to appear ever more on through freight workings. In the top view the second-man is just receiving the Winchester Chesil - Worthy Down token from the signalman. Notice in the background the Up home signal is also placed low down on the post for similar sighting purposes as referred to opposite. In the loading dock a gangers trolley and what are various items of p/way equipment are stored. Some renewals took place in the area of the signal box around this time and it is likely the items seen plus the van were involved.

Right - Another D65xx but this time with a ballast brake and ballast hoppers.
Both Chris Finch

Busy times at Winchester Chesil. In the early 1960s Tim Stubbs was an apprentice at Eastleigh Works. During the evening he would sometimes venture to Winchester Chesil where he was fortunate to record this series of three views showing a down freight arrive and then waiting for the single line section to clear with the arrival of the up diesel hauled freight. After this has cleared the steam freight is again able to proceed south towards Eastleigh.

The slightly unusual sight of a 9F on what is clearly not a tank-car train. (The type were normally restricted to the latter as being the heaviest trains.) By now the footbridge will have seen its last passengers. It was taken down sometime around 1962, having nearly been demolished by the jib of the Eastleigh breakdown crane on a previous occasion - the circumstances of this incident are not reported. As recounted in the text, after August 1964 the tanker trains from Fawley were re-routed by Basingstoke and Reading. This was destined to be short lived as by the end of the decade a new underground pipe-line was being used for considerable quantities of spirit traffic. Tanker trains still leave Fawley
50 years later although these are now mainly containing liquefied petroleum gas.

Chris Finch

Left - Northbound freight between Bar End and Shawford Junction. The looped and wooden fencing was typical of that south of Bar End.

Opposite top - reported as being the northbound 'Solent Freighter' alongside the Winchester by-pass on 17 May 1964. Was this the same as the 'Import Express'? - see page 164. The Winchester by-pass now carried more traffic than before, with the northbound train just about to pass over the bridge we saw being rebuilt on page 97. The down fixed distant signal for Shawford Junction is also visible.
P H Swift

Opposite bottom - End of the line at Shawford Junction. No 76010 is routed over the WW2 extension past Shawford station with freight on Thursday 21 March 1963. This may well be an example of the T/ThO Sutton Scotney to Eastleigh working, see p164.

special, later modified to convey ordinary freight as required. This operated solely between Didcot and Upton & Blewbury and return. Official records show it was little used and in the 12 months ended 31 December 1960 only seven horses were dealt with. South of Newbury the daily pick up goods continued operating in each direction. With heavy through freight workings also now the mainstay of the railway, a number of lengths were relaid with bull-head rail of varying lengths on concrete sleepers. This was not always appreciated by the goods guards, who complained of the

In the early 1960s, Eastleigh Locomotive Inspector Mark Abbott took the opportunity to take his camera with him when assessing the performance of engines on the through freight turns over the DNS. The locations were not always recorded, although opposite top is possibly just south of Hermitage (where the crew, this page bottom, were also recorded. The third man was 'learning the road'.) Opposite bottom may well be south of Enborne although we can be 100% certain the main view on this page is on the climb from Sutton Scotney towards Worthy Down with Christmas Hill bridge in the distance. The relaying of much of the line with concrete sleepers will be noted, as will in the view above, the position of the track to the left of what was a double-track formation.

Mark Abbott

rougher ride they were now subjected to.

The curtailment of services south of Newbury had understandably reduced still further the compliment of passengers travelling on the northern section. Indeed to even the casual observer, the sight of a poorly patronised single coach unit slowly trundling between Didcot and Newbury could hardly bode well for the future. The 17-mile journey took an average of 40 minutes inclusive of the six intermediate stops.

At the time, and on the surface at least it appeared as if Paddington was making genuine efforts to attract patronage by reducing the cost of cheap day tickets to the stations north of Newbury and, whilst this did have a positive effect on passenger numbers, the limited train service was not always convenient to maximise any potential benefit. A single diesel car was still more than sufficient, consequently any increase in revenue was negligible.

Therefore it was no real surprise when, on 20 September 1961, an internal WR report revealed that savings of £4,632 per annum would be possible if the line from Didcot to Newbury were closed to passengers.

Paddington's report was prepared in similar fashion to that of Waterloo two years earlier and commenced with a geographical description of the route followed by the conclusions of a survey on passenger loadings. Investigation revealed the principal traffic flow was south of Compton involving just two trains, the 7.40a.m. ex Didcot and the 4.25p.m. from Newbury. Both these carried an average of 21 passengers, and considering the time, it was not surprising when it was stated 18 of these were school children attending the grammar school at Newbury.

Including the above, a breakdown of the full loading of passengers using the railway for the week ending

	Joined	Alighted
Didcot	24	18
Upton & Blewbury.	10	10
Churn.	nil	nil
Compton.	47	48
Hampstead Norris.	4	2
Pinewood Halt.	2	1
Hermitage.	6	3
Newbury.	62	73

6 May 1961 was as follows:

Not included in these was an average of eight journeys by railway staff.

Operating costs were also given for the 12 months ended 31 December 1960 (not perhaps a totally realistic period as up to 5 March 1960 some through traffic from passengers south of Newbury might be expected to be included.) Whatever, there were 43,577 local journeys, i.e. 'branch to branch' for which receipts were just £2,916 - an average ticket value of just under l/4d. Through forwarded tickets were 5,519 and netted a further £3,033 whilst through received tickets totalled at 7,200, were £2,567. The respective total was 56,296 journeys for £8,516. Parcels traffic amounted to 5,055 forwarded at a value of £2,112, also 8,012 received for £2,303, a total for parcels of £4,4,15. A grand total of £12,931. What is interesting from this is

A dieselised DNS - too little and too late. Four types of diesel unit ran over the line at various stages. The first were the GWR railcars at odd intervals in the 1940s and 1950s. Then in April 1952 (see p160), there were trial trips of an early 4-wheeled AEC set. From Winchester south Southern Region Hampshire DEMUs sets were used for a time in 1960-61 and finally between Newbury and Didcot, WR diesel mechanical vehicles took over all except one passenger working after through trains to Southampton had been withdrawn in March 1960. From photographic evidence it would appear only a single car was ever used - ever needed. Indeed divide the number of passengers carried by the number of services and it was unlikely any of the sets carried more than a handful of passengers at any time.

Opposite bottom - The 3.28 pm Didcot to Newbury working at Compton on 3 July 1961. The uniformed member of staff could well be the Station Master.
R F Roberts

This page, top - On 3 September 1962 we have the unusual sight of W55035 with tail traffic in the form a milk tank. This was the 4.30 p.m. Newbury to Didcot working recorded at Hampstead Norris. It is believed this was a less than common occurrence.
R F Roberts

This page, middle - Again on 3 July 1961, the same working as seen opposite but now leaving Compton for Hampstead Norris, Pinewood Halt, Hermitage and Newbury.
R F Roberts

This page, bottom - Finally on an unreported date in 1960, a single car, again at Compton but this time with a evening northbound working.
R Blencowe

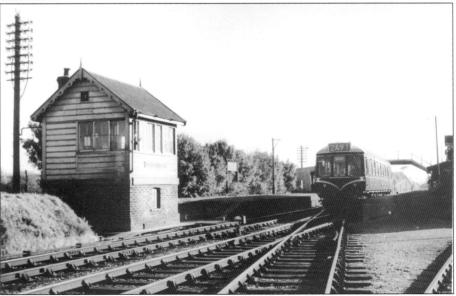

The 7.18 p.m. from Newbury complete with wreath on the smokebox, leaving Compton on the last day of passenger workings between Newbury and Didcot, Saturday 8 September 1962. Notwithstanding the occasion, this is the only image found of the last train - and the engine number was not recorded! The train consisted of seven coaches, but was reported as carrying just 24 passengers when it left Newbury.

that parcels revenue exceeded that of local traffic! No figure is given for goods traffic either local or commencing / terminating on the line.

Total operating costs were recorded as £9,668, which included £1,592 for the wages of the traffic department staff, i.e. station staff and signalmen but did not included any provision for 'civil engineering repairs to trackwork or buildings'. We are left to ponder on whether the £9,668 included engineering department staff and general day to day maintenance of buildings and trackwork.

Paddington's report estimated that the wages of three staff, the station master at Compton, a porter at Hermitage and a leading porter at Upton & Blewbury, could be saved if the line were closed. Further savings would be made on two drivers and two guards.

There was a noted concession that the existing competing bus service was 'so infrequent' and that Compton was poorly served. Indeed anyone wishing to travel from Compton to Newbury were currently faced with a two mile walk to either East Ilsley or Hampstead Norris from where the bus service would be accessible.

Even though revenue was roughly in line with operating costs, the conclusions drawn were that closure to passengers was to be recommended and accordingly the relevant notices were posted. Compared with the earlier closure of the line south of Newbury, a number of objections were received including a petition from 115 villagers at Upton as well as a letter from an engineering company at Compton, whose staff travelled on the railway.

Consequently on 13 December 1961 a Transport Users Consultative Committee hearing was held at Newbury at which those who objected to closure could give evidence. Aside from the objections by passengers, a BR representative was present to answer questions and who, when asked if economy could not be achieved by the removal of the Station Master at Compton with supervision exercised from Newbury, responded that the Newbury man was too busy. Clearly the railway suffered from 'short term memory' as it was only a few years earlier that the

postholder at Newbury was indeed supervising the station as far south as Litchfield! A further suggestion from the floor was to achieve economy by the conversion to single line. Interestingly the reply from BR made no reference to the 1959/61 plan for singling as had indeed been proposed and instead spoke of the need to retain both lines as the freight service was still heavy. The final outcome was approval by the TUCC for closure, based on a vote of 11 to 2.

With the way now clear, formal closure was announced from Paddington on 4 July 1962 to take effect from Monday 10 September 1962. With no Sunday service the last regular trains ran on Saturday 8 September, again mostly diesel-hauled apart from the normal Saturday extra steam service which carried a wreath on the smokebox. The last train of all was the 7.18p.m. from Newbury, specially strengthened to seven coaches, which departed seven minutes late, due according to the 'Newbury Weekly News', "...as a result of a small political demonstration on the platform," though whether this related to the closure was not stated. Even allowing for the poignancy of the occasion, there were just 24 passengers, a poor comparison with the 250 who had travelled south from Newbury in March 1960.

Closure to passengers also meant complete closure of both Churn and Pinewood Halt as neither handled freight. Elsewhere, Upton & Blewbury, Compton and Hermitage remained open for freight and would do so until final closure although whether any actual freight was dealt with was another matter. The situation as regards the Pinewood Brickworks siding and the Cold Store at Hermitage is not certain. Track access was certainly available until the very end although it is doubtful if traffic continued much into the 1960s.

South of Newbury dwindling local receipts had already seen local freight withdrawal from Litchfield from 13 August 1962. Before the year end Woodhay, Highclere and Kings Worthy would also cease to handle freight, the first two mentioned officially from 31 December and Kings Worthy from 1 October 1962. The official date did not always coincide with the actual date and it may well have

Above - To reduce congestion at Winchester City station, Winchester Chesil was reopened as the terminal point for the then Southampton Terminus to Winchester diesel shuttle on busy summer Saturdays in 1960 and 1961. The dates reported as having been from 18 June 1960 to 10 September 1960 and again from 17 June 1961 to 9 September 1961. With staff having been withdrawn from 'Chesil by this time, a clerk was sent to walk to the station when required complete with a cash float and tickets, here he would also act as porter if required.

Bottom - Steam and diesel at Winchester Chesil - but this poses a question. If passenger services ceased in March 1960 and diesel services did not commence until June 1960, how can it be the two are seen side by side? We have no definite answer to this one although there are a number of possibilities. Was the diesel standing in for a failed steam train - probably unlikely: a driver-training / trail run - a possibility: an extra working between Winchester and Southampton for which a diesel was available - again a possibility: or did the diesel service actually start in 1959 rather than 1960? Proof if ever it were needed that there will always be unanswered questions! In the top view the platform safe will again be noted, which presence again raises questions….. . (See also further illustration p221.)

Left - Amidst the demolition of the down-side waiting shelter, footbridge and platform canopy, signalman 'Knobby' Bryant watches a down through goods passing his station.

Bottom - The Winchester Station Master's house seen from its approach path looking down on to Alresford Road.

Probably at the same time as recording the goods trains crossing at Winchester (double page spread pages 194/197), Tim Stubbs also took what is the only known interior view of the signal box in its operational condition post 1942/43. Prominent is the 'hurdy-gurdy' - real name the hand-generator for the motor points and closer to the camera the tablet machine to Shawford Junction. (The token machine to Worthy Down was behind the camera.) The frame is of 27 levers including two spaces. Levers No 23 (the north end loop points) and No 10 are reversed. On the block shelf are lamp and signal repeaters, a gong to Worthy Down and a bell to Shawford Junction, above is the illuminated diagram. Home comforts are not forgotten with a stove, various pans, dish cloths and spare glass globes for the lamp. There are also carriage cushions on the locker, certainly a comfortable place to work. Post 1964 and with the cessation of through workings, a relief signalman would be sent from Winchester City to Chesil to 'open up' as necessary for the freight service to Bar End. Within a few short years the place would be deserted and the vandals would move in with almost everything seen here destroyed.

Tim also recorded these two final views. **Above** is looking towards the station with the 'down siding to up main' signal in the off position. Possibly this was done with the co-operation of the signalman rather than for operational purposes. Notice in the distance one of the arms is missing from the bracket - a temporary situation probably for maintenance, it was restored and survived until the end.

Right - South towards Shawford. On the left is the down siding leading to Bar End, the rails on the right the only ones to Shawford Junction. This latter track is now on concrete sleepers, rumour has it that these lengths were subsequently recovered and used elsewhere - a refinery in Middleborough was mentioned. The signal is the down main advanced starting signal, applicable to the right hand set of rails but placed on the left. There still exist traces of the white paint on the bridge behind today.

HIGHCLERE

(Between Woodhay and Burghclere Signal Boxes)

To be carried out on Tuesday, 18th October, commencing at 9.0 am

The down and up marker lights, situated 1,632 yards Woodhay side and 1,273 yards Burghclere side of the centre of the platform respectively, will be removed.

(P/EW 39, W.S. 1960) (1) (O.O.—R.83350)

LITCHFIELD

(Between Burghclere and Whitchurch Town Signal Boxes)

To be carried out on Tuesday, 18th October, commencing at 11.0 am

The down and up marker lights, situated 1,380 yards Burghclere side and 1,890 yards Whitchurch Town side of the centre of the Platform respectively, will be removed.

(P/EW 39, W.S. 1960) (1) (O.O.—R.83350)

KINGSWORTHY

(Between Worthy Down and Winchester Chesil Signal Boxes)

To be carried out on Tuesday, 18th October, commencing at 2.0 pm

The down and up marker lights, situated 2,123 yards Worthy Down side and 1,598 yards Winchester Chesil side of the centre of the Platform respectively, will be removed.

(P/EW 39, W.S. 1960) (1) (O.O.—R.83350)

This page, top - With the need removed to identify exactly the position of the intermediate stations and which had been provided with marker lights since 1955, the Southern Region realised some small economy might be achieved by their removal, even so it was seven months since passenger closure. To be fair drivers, and guards, were expected to know the route over which they travelled, whilst for the future goods trains that might call would do so in daylight hours.

This page bottom - Engineers coaches in the yard at Compton on an unreported date. Of equal interest is the purpose for which they were present. The temptation might be say in WW2, for this was certainly the type of mobile messing / workshop train that would have been seen. The presence of the ariel adds an air of the latest technology to an ancient six-wheeler. We can be certain they were not camping-coaches!

T B Sands

Above - The February 1960 derailment at Whitchurch. Colour views of the 1954 accident, involving No. 76017, and this incident have appeared elsewhere and need not be repeated. Suffice to say No 76026 has come to rest against one of the lengths of stout packing left behind from the earlier incident. The engine has been secured around the dome with a wire hawser passing under the rails: this is to prevent it slipping any further until the breakdown cranes can deal with the situation. What may not be so well know is there was also a near miss involving a similar situation in 1956. Again a down goods was involved due to stop at Whitchurch as a passenger train had been accepted from Sutton Scotney. Seeing the goods approaching and clearly unable to stop in time, the signalman reversed the road sending it south on to the single line - this was on the premise he had not yet received 'train entering section' for the up passenger working. The goods finally came to a stop some little distance further on. At the subsequent enquiry the signalman was criticised as it might well have led to a head-on incident. One former Winchester (GW) fireman, by then 'passed' as a driver at Eastleigh recalls he would often have to tell the Southern men when going over the hump at Litchfield, "Sorry driver you are out of control." A lot of whistling from the engine to request the guard to give as much assistance as possible was then needed.

Right - The aftermath of the 1963 derailment between Highclere and Burghclere, looking south towards Burghclere station. Again, numerous colour views of this have appeared elsewhere. As an indication of the speed at which this incident was dealt with, Burghclere made the call to Southampton Control over the accident which was received by the motive power at Eastleigh at 9.40 a.m. The crane and crew were summonsed and ready to leave at 10.15 a.m. (Actual time of departure was 10.45 a.m.) They arrived on site at 12.20 p.m.

been that no goods had been dealt with for some little while prior.

Overall the railway was now in its final stages of decline, peeling paint work, grass infested sidings and derelict buildings all contributing towards an air of dereliction. Surprisingly then in 1963 there was potential expansion when Messrs. Conder's, steel fabricators, reinstated the former Winnall Gas Works siding north of Winchester for use in the movement by rail of their steel products. A single set of rails now led back at an angle from the running line into a store shed, accessed from near the site of the former north ground frame. One wagon was brought in and reportedly photographed, but after that – nothing. Despite the cost involved no other trains ever visited. It is suggested due a disagreement between Conder and BR over demurrage costs. For the DNS this was a major blow as traffic to and from the site could have been considerable. Indeed for some years bolster wagons loaded with steel girders were dealt with at Bar End and then in the goods yard at Winchester City, each adding to Winchester's already congested roads with the movement of lorries through narrow streets. This should have been unnecessary for special instructions were printed in the sectional appendix about working to Winnal and propelling back from the site to Bar End with brake van leading. Sometime after 1964 the site at Winnal was tarmaced for use as a car park, with, it is believed, the rails still in situ!

Any contact between Paddington and Waterloo over the future of the DNS as a through-route is not reported, although the later Beeching report would indicate there was no future for it as a freight line. Already on 31 October 1963 a memorandum from the Divisional Manager at Paddington quoted, "There is a very definite possibility that the line between Didcot and Newbury...(will be) closed for all purposes and the trains that are running via this route will be routed via Reading and Basingstoke. In view of this I would suggest that expenditure for maintenance etc is kept to a minimum, and only the most essential repairs etc. are carried out".

At this stage Waterloo must have either reached the same conclusion or likely been informed, as the run-down of the remaining local services continued from that office. Burghclere and Whitchurch ceased to handle freight from 6 May 1963, although towards the end the only wagons were coal for a local merchant conveniently delivered when working the area. This left just Sutton Scotney and Winchester open. Elsewhere the former bay platform at Didcot once used by Newbury and Winchester trains was also foreshortened by 160' and a temporary stop block erected.

But whilst this was occurring, through-freight was still running and brought with it a continuing crop of incidents. Three are recorded in 1962, the first at Burghclere on 17 March when the leading wheels of No 7324 came off the track. Re-railing was accomplished by the Eastleigh steam crane in 15 minutes. Then on 30 April one set of wheels of a tank car came off at Woodhay. Again the steam crane was used. Next at 1.53a.m. on 22 August two tank cars derailed, 'all wheels' at Sutton Scotney. The official report records the incident notified to Southampton Control just two minutes later, the breakdown gang called out from Eastleigh who left the shed at 3.42am. Arrival at Sutton Scotney was one hour later, the gang taking 65 minutes to effect rerailing using the steam crane. We are not told if this was an up or down working, nor if the tank cars were loaded or empty – indeed if the former what liquid was being carried? Unfortunately no details of incidents on the section north of Newbury have been located – there probably were some!

The last reported accident on the DNS was also arguably the most devastating. This took place on Saturday 23 March 1963 at Hackley - sometimes referred to as Hockley Hole cutting, between Highclere and Burghclere. On this day an early morning mixed freight to Eastleigh had been terminated at Didcot because it only consisted of a small number of wagons. Control decided to attach these

The Eastleigh District Inspector Fred Capon (left), on what was reported to be the occasion of the retirement of the Worthy Down signalman - whose name was unfortunately not reported. Unfortunately the date was not reported either although we can be very general and say 'sometime between 1957 and 1964'. (After 1957 a number of levers where made 'spare' and painted white in consequence of the up siding being taken out of use.) The hand-generator and token machine are also visible. Notice on the concrete lintel the word 'leak', indicative of the problems the wartime ARP boxes suffered from in later years. South of Newbury it was practice for the signal lamps only to be lit between 1 September and 31 March, although lamps were lit during darkness on Saturdays throughout the year - this was because of the late evening Saturday services.

2nd. Special Excursion 2nd.
"The NORTH HAMPSHIRE DOWNSMAN"
(C.M.3631) 22nd. MAY 1960
London Bridge or Victoria to
EASTLEIGH
Via Reading General & Litchfield (Hants)
and back
(S. FOR CONDITION... E OVER

0045 0045

On Sunday 22 May 1960 the 'Railway Enthusiasts Club' of Farnborough organised and ran the 'North Hampshire Downsman' tour over the DNS. Starting at London Bridge, the route was via Streatham and Wimbledon to Reading, over the connection to the WR and thence via Newbury and the DNS to Eastleigh. A 9.30 a.m. departure from London had the train turn on to DNS metals at Enborne Junction at 11 48 a.m. There were two-minute photographic stops at Highclere, Burghclere and Litchfield with tickets also being issued to any passengers who might wish to alight at those stations. Eastleigh was due to be reached at 12.53 p.m. the train continuing into the loco yard. Here the party would dismount, having until 6.20 p.m. to satisfy their locomotive interests. The return leg followed the same route, again pausing to collect any passengers at the same three stations - whether anyone did avail themselves other than for photographic purposes is not reported. The engine was unusual for the line, being an SECR E1 No 30169, which took the train in both directions. Arrival time this time back at Victoria, was 9.44 p.m. The eight coach load, which included a restaurant, was a fair test for the engine over the gradients of the DNS but there is no reason to believe it was not up to the task.

Opposite top - At Highclere on the outward leg: **opposite bottom** - southbound and just north of Litchfield.

This page top - the return working 'turning right at Shawford Junction: **this page bottom** - a short break at Highclere. (Note the positioning of the headcode discs has altered for the outward and return workings.) (See also illustration p107).

Another view of the 'East Midlander' tour of 9 May 1964. This was an ambitious event starting at Nottingham running south to Didcot, thence over the DNS non-stop to Eastleigh returning north via Swindon. Motive power for the DNS leg was No 34038 'Lynton'. The train is seen passing the shell of Highclere signal box, the latter out of use for the previous nine years. This was around the same time a similar engine was used for the diverted northbound 'Pines Express' working over the DNS. (See view pages 218/219.)

The privately sponsored 'Wintonian' railtour of sometime in 1963, believed to have been run from Southampton to Winchester in connection with the centenary of an educational establishment. Period dress was clearly the order of the day - including for the locomotive, T9 No 120, resplendent in LSWR colours. This was the same engine that had hauled the last down passenger train three years earlier. Since that time it had only had occasional use, having been selected for preservation. Three years of lack of maintenance to the station are also starting to show, whilst the passenger footbridge and station canopy have been removed.

*Two final examples of railtours. **Top** we see a tour which started at Winchester Chesil on 9 March 1963, hauled by B4 No 30096 and appropriately called the 'B4 Dock Tank'. The train ran to the Southampton Ocean Terminal and returned this time to Winchester City station via Eastleigh Works. It is seen here running alongside a deserted Winchester by-pass. (It is believed there was one other tour involving a B4 running as far as Winchester Chesil around this time although details are not confirmed.)*

__Bottom__ - The LCGB 'Anton & Test Valley' working of 6 September 1964. No 82029 having shunted its train to the down platform runs round ready to depart to Romsey, Andover, Ludgershall and return to Eastleigh. At least two other special workings traversed the DNS in whole or part in the 1960s. On 30 April 1961 'The Solent Limited' ran north between Winchester and Newbury with No 30117. Thee years later on 14 March 1964 came the 'Hampshire Hogg' involving No 41329 and believed to have traversed the complete route north through to Didcot.

wagons to the next down through working which comprised a number of empty tank cars. All was well when the train left Didcot behind a D65xx locomotive (Class 33) and the train progressed normally until reaching the above location. At 9.23am driver and guard reported a marked snatch, the latter (the guard, Bernie Briggs – a former signalman at Shawford Junction and who later retired as Station Master Eastleigh) was thrown from one end of his van to the other. The engine was quickly brought to a standstill and the driver walked back expecting to find a broken coupling with his train parted. What he found instead was a mountain of debris, wagons at all angles and underneath the remains of open wagons reduced to matchwood.

Whilst the crew were conferring on their course of action, some farm workers appeared atop the cutting carrying sheep hurdles and pronounced they would use these as makeshift stretchers, "to fetch away the dead". Fortunately there were no injuries, although both driver and guard admitted they were fearful for each other as neither could see each other through the mountain of debris. The railway was now completely blocked, although it would

only remain so for two days.

Recovery involved cranes from both Eastleigh and initially Reading, although later the Old Oak Common crane would replace the Reading equipment. As the accident had occurred in a cutting, it was necessary to lift the derailed vehicles high into the air to clear the cutting sides before they could be swung around and, where possible, be replaced on the track. They were then towed away to either Burghclere or Woodhay to be cleared off the site.

Men would then replace sleepers and rails, so allowing the cranes to proceed further. The local fire brigade was also on stand-by at the scene due to the presence of the empty tank cars. Subsequent records from Eastleigh indicate 12 petrol cars and 4 other wagons were derailed. The Eastleigh gang was involved for 15 hours and 50 minutes, again under the guidance of S C Townroe. From the north end the Western Region crane had been propelled to site from Woodhay by an unidentified 4-6-0 –possibly even a 'Castle', a type normally prohibited from the section south of Newbury*. The cause of the accident was never fully established, although a number of theories were put forward

22 May 1964. The 'Pines Express' behind No 34105 'Swanage' calls at Winchester Chesil, diverted away from its normal route via Basingstoke. Along with those travelling on the 'East Midlander' special of 9 May 1964 (see previous page), these were probably the last fare paying passengers to travel the length of the DNS line. It was also possibly the only public 'named' train, albeit no headboard is being carried, to traverse the DNS.

Minor derailment, just south of the station, Friday 8 August 1958. One set of wheels from the tender of the engine has become derailed and the Eastleigh breakdown crane is in attendance. (The engine had been due to arrive at Winchester with empty stock from the Western Region at 3 05 pm. It was scheduled to leave with its train northbound at 4.05 pm to form the 4.30 pm special from Worthy Down to Paddington.) The question is how was the locomotive turned? Was it due to work tender first all the way back OR was the turntable still in use at Bar End? Rerailing was complete by 6.00 pm - reported as 2½ hours after the incident - and by which time another engine had taken over the duty. There is no mention of delays to other services.

including poor trackwork, a defective wagon or excess speed. (*Eric Best recalls one lunchtime in 1947 when returning home from school at lunchtime he had witnessed a 'Castle' and 28xx at Bar End for the purpose of testing the newly installed replacement turntable.)

1963 was destined to be the final full year of operation for the railway as shortly afterwards the remaining through-traffic began to be transferred away to the alternative route via Basingstoke and Reading.

Enter 1964 and Sutton Scotney goods yard finally succumbed from 3 February 1964, not with a little irony as the station had been awarded a prize in the best kept yard competition for the previous year. In collecting the award from the management of the Southern Region at a special presentation, Ernie Penny representing Sutton Scotney was asked what he would use the cash prize for - the usual answer being to purchase additional flowers etc. On this occasion though, a hushed silence fell onto the assembled gathering at Bournemouth, for the reply given was along the lines of, "...I don't really know, 'cause you're closing our station next week."

Everywhere else the overgrown sidings at the various wayside stations were secured out of use. Engineers attended Highclere on 2 March 1964 and Woodhay, Burghclere and Whitchurch on 8 June 1964. In practice this meant point rodding was disconnected with clips and padlocks attached to the siding points thus rendering them inoperable from the respective signal box or ground frame. The former goods siding at Kings Worthy was also recovered on 13 April 1964.

This was the time of the final special workings, both enthusiast and operational, the signal boxes remaining open often for long hours without trains. One of the very occasional 'box-to-box' specials involved a 28xx on a Didcot to Eastleigh special freight seen passing Winchester Chesil around 8.00am one weekday morning. Then one Saturday in early May 1964 a derailment at Reading West caused a sudden change of route for the northbound 'Pines Express' already diverted from its former Somerset & Dorset haunts and now normally routed via Winchester City, Basingstoke and Reading.

Now came an example of enterprise with the control office at Southampton diverting the train via the DNS, waiting passengers at Winchester City ferried by bus to Winchester Chesil and Newbury. At 'Chesil, many of the platform edge coping stones had already been removed (reportedly to the garden of one of the inspectors from Eastleigh!), and instead planks were laid to allow passengers to enter their carriages across the partly demolished platform. Those who travelled north through Newbury and on to Didcot that day had the melancholy distinction of being the last fare-paying passengers ever to travel the complete route of the complete route. At Didcot the train, hauled by No 34105 'Swanage' regained its intended route to Oxford and the north.

Even at this late date in history, here was proof the DNS afforded a useful diversionary route. But such luxuries were not a requirement of British Railways and strict instructions were issued that, in the event of a similar occasion arising in future, passengers should be offered a refund on their tickets rather than a train be re-routed over this line.

Behind the scenes political pressure was being exercised on the railways at both a national and a local level. Nationally we can now reveal the situation as existed in the 1960s from a now retired very senior manager who, when commencing his railway career in the 1960s had it abundantly outlined to him that the way to get on was by enforcing closures and with it economy. One Paddington man in the 1960s known to have taken these words to extremes. To be fair it was not all the fault of railway management. In order to bring in modernisation savings had to be made, there can be no doubt investment was needed, whether it was spent in the correct form is another question, but hindsight is of course wonderful. Suffice to say the DNS was another example of an economy that had to be made – after all, all the regions maintained 'Redundant Assets' sections well into the 1980s!

Opposite, continued- One other undated incident at Winchester is known of when the driver of a 22xx on a down service from Didcot reported a knocking noise from his engine. A fitter was summoned and the engine moved to Bar end. When a crane arrived to lift the front, the crank-axle fell into two pieces.

This page - Further views of (top) the puzzling steam/ diesel 'service'. Below a diesel is seen having entered the tunnel and is using what was originally intended as the engine release crossover to return to the down platform.

Locally Hampshire County Council were putting pressure on the railway over the way it criss-crossed the ever busier A34 trunk road to the Midlands. The council's Roads & Bridges Committee had reported Tothill bridge carrying the road over the railway just north of Highclere station was unsafe and had imposed an emergency 7-ton weight limit and a diversion taking A34 traffic through Penwood and along the A343 in both directions. No sooner had this been set up than it was promptly ignored by several hauliers who preferred to take the road west of Tothill through the nearby village and cross the railway immediately north of Highclere station. Not used to prolonged and heavy traffic, it was not long before this bridge too began to show signs of strain.

The council estimated repairs to the Tothill bridge would cost £84,000 against £67,000 to infill the cutting should the railway be closed. There was also another issue facing the council, that of the three Litchfield bridges. This was where the A34 passed under the railway each with a double bend all having become notorious as accident black-spots. With the councils north of Newbury making similar noises over the A4 and the humped arch carrying the A417 across the railway immediately south of Upton & Blewbury, the end was inevitable.

Whilst a case might have been made for retaining the route as a line for freight and diversions, the road lobby was too vociferous and gave the railway the excuse they needed. A joint decision by the Western and Southern Regions was that through-traffic would cease with effect from 10 August 1964 at which time freight facilities would also be withdrawn from stations between Didcot and Newbury. (Full closure had been intended for a few weeks

Interlude - Redundant Assets

Top - *Upton and Blewbury towards Didcot.*

Middle - *Hampstead Norris up home signal on 22 April 1962, the station is just around the corner. The bridge carries the B4009 over the railway and is still present today although now filled in underneath with the trackbed part of a footpath. The station site at Hampstead Norris has been a development of private houses for some years whilst the village is also referred to as Hampstead Norreys.*

R F Roberts

Bottom - *Hermitage looking south towards Newbury. The presence of the long line of carriage stock in the refuge siding is not explained.*

Top - No 6304 arriving at Woodhay. On Saturday evenings staff living near the railway south of Newbury would place their orders for 'faggots and peas' to be collected from a shop near to Winchester station: later Ken's chip shop. These would be collected and distributed in pudding basins on the last up train. Most of time it worked well, unless (and as did happen) the wrong order was given to the wrong family….

Bottom - Winter 1959/60 No 75006 arriving at Litchfield. The lack of footprints in the snow is indicative of the amount of trade.

Opposite top - Unusual motive power in Larksbarrow cutting, probably standing in for a failed tender engine. A derailment of five wagons in the cutting sometime in the late 1950s necessitated a 25 mph speed limit being in force here for some time. (See page 165.)

Mike Esau

Opposite bottom - Some business at least at Sutton Scotney. At nearby Kings Worthy one driver would deliberately allow his train to run on towards the end of platform whenever there were young ladies on the platform.....

This page - Leaving Worthy Down and commencing the climb through Christmas Hill cutting (since filled to the top with rubbish) on the way to Sutton Scotney. The engine was No 76011.

P J Cupper

Opposite page - The Winchester Junction to Worthy Down spur. Top is the curve down through the cutting to join the formation of the existing route and then running parallel to Worthy Down itself. The signal post once displayed both a stop and distant arm. For some years it was possible to see lines of either coaches or wagons stored awaiting works attention or in the case of the former, re-entry into service for the summer season. Unfortunately the attention of the vandals meant they were of little use later and stored stock was instead concentrated at Micheldever. (Some semi-official vandalism also took place with signalman up and down the line acquiring cushions from the coaches to make their own work environment more comfortable.)

This page, top - There will be no more need for tickets to be issued at Worthy Down. Post 1960 there was also at least one theft of the copper cable from the telegraph poles in the area.

This page, middle - And the warning of catch points to drivers of down trains approaching Whitchurch has warned its last engine crew.

This page bottom - Near Hampstead Norris, a probably WW2 replacement has served its purpose.

Opposite top - Winchester as it should be remembered, not as a road, multi-storey car-park or nuclear shelter. In the view top left, the gates leading to the platform at the tunnel end may be seen, the wire screen an attempt to deter those without tickets from making their entry or escape. The design of the station was as per contemporary GWR practice of the period and was also to be seen at Ross-on-Wye - although now demolished. However, in the 1980s the Severn Valley Railway at Kidderminster built their new station based on this type of design whilst Milestone's museum at Basingstoke has a full size replica of part of the main building.

Brian Connell

Opposite bottom - No 2240 departs south in March 1960. The presence of the Southern 'Mogul' in the background is not explained.

Above - No 3211 arriving with a Newbury - Didcot train. Although tablet and token set down / pick up posts were provided, in practice these were rarely used with most signalmen preferring to effect a hand exchange. In 1962 the main crossover between the down platform and single line (outside the signal box) was renewed. Additionally, much of the point rodding in the area was changed from round to channel section .

Opposite top - On 27 August 1953, No 76006 comes off the viaduct by Shawford Junction with the 2.56 p.n. Oxford to Southampton service. A few months earlier this would have been the province of a WR 22xx based at Winchester. The whole of the line between Shawford and Enborne was eventually sold by BR to the various councils, Winchester Council nowadays being responsible for the viaduct. After an abortive plan to blow-up the viaduct as a military training exercise it has established its place in history as an early example of a concrete structure although faced with brick. In addition to now serving as a cycle-way it also provides a valuable screen keeping the view of the M3 motorway from the water meadows. The signal on the viaduct has recently been replaced.

Opposite bottom - 'Off the timetable and on to the calendar' - next stop Winchester Chesil.

This page top - Fireman's view from a BR standard waiting for the southbound train to clear and the Shawford Junction signalman to reverse the road ready to join the DNS. The train on the right has come off the DNS and been routed around the back of Shawford station (where until 1966 there was no platform). On more than one occasion a train that should have stopped at Shawford was routed this way.

This page, middle - Busy times at Shawford Junction with down trains on both the main line and down relief. Post 1966 a facing connection was provided for down Bournemouth line trains at this point so that they might take the line on the left. It is still called Shawford Junction but without the significance of before. The M3 motorway also crosses the railway at this exact point and the overbridge in the distance is no more.

This page, bottom - Shawford Junction and renewal of the double connection to and from the DNS is under way,
R Blencowe

Three wonderfully evocative views by Henry Meyer of DNS trains near Shawford.

Opposite top - *The crew of No 2240 have passed Shawford station and will already be slowing for the junction.*

Opposite bottom - *No 3212 on the down main line ready for a stop at Shawford station.*

This page - *No 2202 also on the down main and just crossing the bridge underneath passes the Winchester by-pass.*

Two further views by Henry Meyer. Above - again near Shawford and right on the last leg of the run past Mount Pleasant goods yard and the shores of the River Itchen before reaching Northam and Southampton Terminus. Whilst DNS trains are seen here on the Southern main line it may be mentioned that on at least one occasion on the DNS when Kings Worthy signal box was operational, the wrong token was carried over to Worthy Down - fortunately without incident. This was possibly not a unique affair but could indeed have had disastrous consequences. Whilst rail traffic no longer uses any part of the DNS there were in the early 1980s serious plans to relay a stub siding from Winchester Junction to Worthy Down in connection with oil being drilled nearby, the plan being to remove the product by rail. It is believed nothing further was made of the proposal partly due to anticipated difficulties in moving an electrical sub-station located almost on the site of the junction and also the need for a facing connection into the main line at this point.

Above - *Might and majesty, No 92206 at Winchester in the early 1960s. It has been suggested there were occasions when a 9F would be temporarily stabled in the loading dock opposite the signal box with 'Chesil being used as the changeover point of motive power on northbound oil trains. This in itself raises a number of questions, firstly why effect the changeover at Winchester and also could a 9F legitimately run over the sharp reverse curve into the loading dock - seen behind? On similar lines is the story that No 92220 'Evening Star' once failed at Winchester and spent some time in the dock waiting repair. (More likely is the story of an ex LMS 4F that failed at Whitchurch on a sound-bound goods and was placed in the goods yard there.) The headcode on the 9F is that for 'light engine'.) The coal wagon may well be supplies for the signalman. In 1964 the signalman here recalls having a visit from officialdom whereby he was informed that when the Bournemouth line resignalling took place, Winchester Chesil was to become a fringe to Eastleigh panel!*

Rod Hoyle

Opposite top - *In the last days of working, a Class 4MT 2-64T runs back towards Bar End and Shawford . The engine will have come up to the signal box for the tablet to Shawford Junction and will now return to Bar End - using the tablet to unlock the ground-frame and access the yard if necessary, The rational for the up home signal being deliberately placed part way down the post is apparent.*

Rod Hoyle

Opposite bottom - *An almost deserted goods yard at Winchester. The main running line is in seemingly good condition and was visited by a weedkilling train on two occasions annually. Sidings were attended to by the local gangs, who would spray weed-killer received in 50 gallon drums. Fifty years earlier the area would have been bustling with 675 wagons dealt with over the four days of the Royal Counties Agricultural Show....*

A travel stained BR Standard Class 4 tank edges carefully what is somewhat worn track. Surprisingly the line from Shawford Junction as far as Winchester Chesil was passed as suitable for 'Merchant Navy' to work over - not that one ever did! Time for the 6.15 p.m. fast goods to Reading.......

earlier but was postponed until August whilst final staff consultation took place.) There would be no further reprieve.

Many of the staff who remained until the end were also senior in years and service, younger staff having seen the writing on the wall and transferred away whilst they had the chance. Others moved to new roles, often totally different from ones they had occupied before. This was especially so for signalmen, multiple aspect signalling meant signalling vacancies were far fewer than before and men who had once been skilled in their own field were now storemen or even reduced to pushing a broom on a platform. Ironically, and seen by some as a deliberate act by management to prove the line as uneconomic, signals boxes were still manned 24 hours a day, although the chance of any special train at night was almost non-existent. Even so one enterprising man at Whitchurch, fed up with having to remain at work with nothing to do, slowly brought the parts into the box to make a bed. It was finally complete - but he never had the chance to use it as before his turn came around for the next session of night shift the line closed.

The weekly traffic notices now proclaimed as follows, 'Didcot East to Newbury East' and 'Enborne Junction to Shawford Junction' – "Line closed, delete all entries." Even so the last remnants of the DNS did still survive as an operational railway. At both Didcot East and Newbury East short sections remained as shunting spurs, while there was still a twice-weekly freight working from Eastleigh to Winchester Chesil, the yard at Bar End still busy with traffic. In the main this was operated by a member of the Standard 80xxx tank series although on occasion a 76xxx tender engine would also deputise. Rather than operate as a long siding, tablet working remained in use from Shawford Junction to Winchester Chesil and would remain so until goods were finally withdrawn on 4 April 1966. Three former iron mink vans remained at Bar End deemed as unfit to travel and carried 'Not to Go' labels, they were subsequently cut up on site. One final irony was when the signalman at 'Chesil saw some official looking men taking measurements and notes at the station who then disappeared into the tunnel. When they reappeared some time later they were challenged only to exclaim, 'Oh we are

Top - *Inside the Goods Shed at Bar End, or a time used by a car scrap merchant but also still surviving today. (It is NOT the former engine shed as has been reported!) Post 1966 the office was originally left replete with is original leather bound ledgers and record books of wagons dealt with, regretfully they did not remain for long, all it is thought destroyed.*

Bottom - *Inside-key rail alongside the loading dock in the yard and on sleepers that have seen better days, small wonder the engine seen on p205 was being cautious.*

just making plans for when you become a fringe to Eastleigh Panel' – clearly the various departments of the railway did not communicate, for whilst Eastleigh Panel was in the planning stage and would indeed 'go live' at the end of 1966 spelling the end for Shawford Junction signal box, the end at Winchester Chesil was scheduled for some months earlier.

On the now closed railway south of Newbury some of the older and semi-retired staff would spend their last working days as caretakers, although unfortunately this did not stop the vandals. Worthy Down was one of the locations badly affected, so much so that years before BR had already ceased to store coaches on the former spur because of these attacks.

Any reusable equipment was also quickly salvaged from the stations. Passenger tickets had been removed years earlier but now it was the safe and, within the signal boxes south of Newbury, the token equipment and occupation control instruments. The former were taken to store at Eastleigh intended for possible re-use in connection with the planned singling of the main line west of Salisbury. In the end they were not used as tokenless block was installed.

Meanwhile the cutting at Tothill under the A34 was infilled with almost indecent haste, it is said, without even removing the rails from underneath. A long section of trackwork was also removed from Kings Worthy to Worthy Down, thus rendering the section from Highclere southwards isolated. Enborne Junction meanwhile was 'secured out of use' on 2 August 1965 and ceased to be a block post from 29 January 1967.

Final demolition between Shawford Junction and Enborne commenced in the autumn of 1966, the trackbed and all the station sites between Kings Worthy and Woodhay sold to Hampshire County Council in 1968 for £21,245 which included, 'a quantity of usable ballast.' South of Newbury much of modern day dual carriageway A34 now follows the railway or has been returned to farmland. Kings Worthy and Woodhay stations are almost completely obliterated from the map, but despite earlier protestations, the Litchfield bridges were not finally demolished until 1974.

Several of the unique DNS station cottages remain, initially as secured tenancy to railway staff and later converted to desirable private residences. Other structures, bridges, signal boxes and huts also still exist, while elsewhere the earthworks bear silent witness to the overgrown trackbed.

North of Newbury, Western Region records reported that the final Station Master at Compton, Mr. D J D Rees, had been 'withdrawn' from 29 June 1964. The same record also reveals a useful inventory of station equipment remaining after closure later recovered from various locations.

At Upton & Blewbury this was reported as: GWR First Aid Box, two chairs with padded seats - bad condition, GPO telephone, one wooden table - poor condition, one wooden rack, one telephone (omnibus circuit). All were located within the Booking Office. Within the Parcels Office were a Pooley weighing machine, a cupboard - fair condition and a table in poor condition. The Booking Hall contained a wooden stool and a fire appliance. On the platform was a single two wheeled barrow, another weighing machine and a ladder.

LITCHFIELD GROUND FRAME
(between Burghclere and Whitchurch Town)

To be carried out on Monday, 10th February, commencing at 8.0 am

The 3-lever ground frame situated on the right hand side (in the Down direction) of the Burghclere—Whitchurch Town section of Single line, will be removed.

The facing points (in the Down direction) and the facing points (in the Up direction) leading to the siding, situated adjacent to and controlled from the ground frame, together with the siding and trap points therein, will be put out of use, the points being clipped and padlocked in the normal position.

(P/EW 6, S.W.D. 1964)   (1)   (LM—SW/R/SA/402)

HIGHCLERE GROUND FRAME
(between Woodhay and Burghclere)

To be carried out on Monday, 2nd March, commencing at 10.0 am

The points in the Woodhay—Burghclere single line (trailing for down movements) leading from the siding, situated adjacent to and controlled from the ground frame, together with the siding and trap points therein, will be put out of use, the points being clipped and padlocked im the normal position.

(P/EW 9, S.W.D. 1964)   (1)   (LM—SW/R/SA/467)

KINGSWORTHY GROUND FRAMES 'A' AND 'B'
(Between Worthy Down Junction and Winchester Chesil)

To be carried out on Monday, 13th April, commencing at 8.0 am

The 2-lever ground frames 'A' and 'B' which are situated on the right hand side (in the Down Direction) of the Worthy Down Jn.—Winchester Chesil single line, which are at present out of use, will be removed.

The connections adjacent to and formerly controlled from each of these ground frames, leading from the Siding, which are at present clipped and padlocked in the normal position, will be abolished.

(P/EW 14, S.W.D. 1964)   (1)   (LM—SW/R/SA/438)

WHITCHURCH TOWN

To be carried out on Monday, 8th June, commencing at 10.0 am

The trailing crossover between Down and Up Main lines and the slip connection leading from Up Main to Down Siding 127 yards and 93 yards Burghclere side of signal box respectively, will each be put out of use, the points being clipped and padlocked in the normal position.

The trailing points in the Down Main line leading from Down Siding 77 yards Sutton Scotney side of signal box, together with the Down Siding and trap points therein, will be put out of use, the points being clipped and padlocked in the normal position.

(P/EW 21, S.W.D. 1964)   (1)   (LM—SW/R/SA/504)

WOODHAY

To be carried out on Monday, 8th June commencing at 10.0 am.

The points in the Woodhay—Burghclere single line (trailing for Down movements) leading from Up Siding 142 yards Burghclere side of signal box, and the trailing points in the Up Main line leading from Up Siding 45 yards Enborne Jn. side of signal box, together with the Up Siding and trap points therein, will be put out of use, the points being clipped and padlocked in the normal position.

(P/EW 21, S.W.D. 1964)   (1)   (LM—SW/R/SA/469)

This page and opposite - Extracts from the regular special traffic notices advising of the cessation of facilities at the various stations.

This page, bottom left - A new use for the goods yard at Sutton Scotney.

Bottom right - The former enginemen's cabin at Winchester now derelict - it had been in use for just over ten years - see p115.

Opposite bottom - The nameboard for Highclere, like the station itself, was now redundant in every sense of the word. (At one time there were plans for a relief road along the trackbed at Highclere which would have resulted in the demolition of the station house.)

240

BURGHCLERE

To be carried out on Monday, 8th June, commencing at 10.0 am.

The trailing points in the Down Main line leading from Up Siding and the trailing points in the Up Main line leading from Up Siding, 37 yards and 163 yards Woodhay side of signal box respectively, together with the Up Siding and trap points therein, will be put out of use, the points being clipped and padlocked in the normal position.

(P/EW 21 S.W.D. 1964) (1) (LM—SW/R/SA/511)

WINNALL SIDINGS NORTH AND SOUTH GROUND FRAMES

(Between Worthy Down Jn. and Winchester Chesil)

To be carried out on Sunday, 5th April, commencing at 6.30 am.

The 2-lever South Ground Frame situated on the right hand side (in the Down direction) of the Worthy Down Jn.—Winchester Chesil Single line, at the Winchester Chesil end of Winnall Sidings, will be removed.

The points in the single line (facing for Up movements) leading to Winnall Sidings, situated adjacent to and controlled from the above mentioned Ground Frame, together with the trap points in the Siding, will be abolished.

The 2-lever North Ground Frame situated on the right hand side (in the Down direction) of the Worthy Down Jn.—Winchester Chesil single line at the Worthy Down Jn. end of Winnall Sidings, will in future be known as 'Winnall Sidings Ground Frame'.

The points in the single line (facing for Down movements) leading to Winnall Sidings, situated adjacent to and controlled from the above mentioned Ground Frame, will be moved approximately 4 yards nearer Worthy Down Jn.

(See Section 'D' of this Notice for addition and alterations to Western Section Appendix concerning the working of Winnall Sidings).

(P/EW 13, S.W.D. 1964) (1) (LM—SW/R/SA/5/57)

The atmospheric railway. Four wagons and a brake van make up the load departing from Bar End for Eastleigh. In the same way a clerk and then a signalman had been sent from Winchester City as required, so it was practice at the end to send a goods checker from Eastleigh to deal with any paperwork on the twice-weekly goods.

Rod Hoyle

WINCHESTER SHED TURNS c1950

Early - Book on 5.15 a.m. Prepare loco, work 7.05 a.m. passenger as far as Sutton Scotney, return with down goods to Winchester. Shunt yard, trip work to Winnal Gas Works, prepare later up goods and finish.

Middle - Book on 7.50 a.m. Work 8.16 a.m. passenger as far as Woodhay, return on down stopping goods from Reading. Shunt yard at Bar End, prepare vehicles for 6.15 up fast goods. Turn loco thence to shed.

Late - Book on 12.15 p.m. Work 12.25 up stopping goods as far as Woodhay. Return with down passenger to Winchester. Prepare loco and work 6.15 p.m. fast goods as far as Woodhay, return with down passenger, arrive 8.15 p.m., turn, dispose of loco and finish.

The other stations revealed similar items including (at Compton) six fire buckets from the Gentlemen's toilet and two waste paper bins from the Booking Office.

A safe was also recovered from each station which was returned to Swindon stores, the keys being sent under separate cover. Possibly the most interesting reference is that appertaining to the railway clocks. All were of GWR origin as follows:

Upton & Blewbury - No.2502 from the Waiting Room, and No. 407 from the Signal Box.

Compton - No. 4524 from the office, No. 1367 from the outside wall and No. 4195 from the signal box.

Hampstead Norris - No. 3412 from the waiting room and No. 404 from the Signal Box.

Hermitage - No. 730 from the office, No. 3800 from the Signal Box, and No. 2899 from an unspecified location at the station.

Because formal closure took place from 10 August 1964, there should have been no rolling stock remaining but on 21 August 1964 it was reported that a number of wagons were still present at Hampstead Norris, while the signal boxes had yet to be classified as officially closed. The wagons were still present on 7 September but recovered shortly after.

This of course was at a time when the overall railway closure programme was gathering momentum and as such there appeared little urgency to dispose of the remaining assets. Some minor sales did occur at Compton, with the parcels office and contents, weighbridge hut, downside passenger shelter, shed next to the signal box, two desks and one chair, plus a building next to the parcels office known as the milk hut sold to Mr. Rees for the sum of £6 15s. The occupier of Hermitage station arranged a similar, though smaller sale around the same time. On 13 October 1964 arrangements were made for the sale of the station name boards from Compton and Churn to a private collector for £1 10s. The former coal hopper from Upton & Blewbury was also sold privately in November 1965.

North of Newbury the railway was now rusting and unused while behind the scenes at Paddington we may only speculate on a surviving memorandum of 30 December 1965, which reported that the Divisional Manager had previously asked for the cost of the removal of just one set of rails to leave a single line in situ. Indeed it appeared as if the Western Region was unduly sensitive to the final removal of all facilities as the following comment added, "...leaving the remainder suitable for use should the Ministerial decision be to reinstate passenger traffic." Was this really a possibility? We may only speculate but it is interesting to note that at this time the A4 and A417 bridges remained intact – they would not be for much longer. The memo requested an unnamed recipient investigate, ".. as to which track can be removed so as to secure largest credit."

What was almost the final nail appears in a note from Paddington dated 31 January 1966. Here it was revealed that, allowing for the cost of removal, a credit of £29,100 could be achieved. "This includes removal of the 'top' only of the bridge which carries the railway over the

Winchester. What Station Master?

A4 at 0m 40½ ch near Newbury, which the Minister had agreed to allow. Should instructions be subsequently given for passenger services to be restored, it would be necessary to reinstate the bridge before operating the single line."

Matters then rested for a few weeks, although within the file there is a brief reference to two private individuals who had expressed an interest in taking over the railway for an unspecified purpose. Not surprisingly nothing further is heard of this. More serious was an application in March 1966 by Messrs. Wright Excavation Co. to use the railway northwards up to a point 20ch. from Newbury for unloading spent ballast from railway wagons which would then be gravitated back to Newbury. This likewise proceeded no further although on this occasion it was because the applicants were unable to obtain local planning permission.

Finally on 6 March 1966 Paddington gave written consent to the recovery of the remaining single line of rails. This would be carried out by railway staff at a cost of £14,600 offset against assets worth £43,700. Work then proceeded quickly, the file also showing the Police were called to arrest a man at Hampstead Norris on 26 July 1966 who had been caught 'dismantling the waiting room'. He attempted to protest stating that he had permission to do this, his subsequent fate is not reported.

Even so, it appears Paddington may have been unduly hasty in their instruction to dismantle the rest of the route, for it was not until 22 September 1966 that the Minister of Transport gave formal permission for removal. What probably happened was the proverbial 'nod and a wink', the formal notice appearing later. Matters may also have been hastened by a deputation sent to the Minister from Wallingford District Council with particular reference to the A417 bridge at Upton where the intention was now both to widen and level the road.

Final demolition of the northern section was by both BR and Messrs Eagre Ltd. A site meeting between the parties took place on 27 November 1966 at which the conditions for the removal and demolition were clearly outlined. These included at Upton & Blewbury recovery of the signal box name boards, concrete lamp standards, crane and demolition of the signal box. At Compton, the nameboards, footbridge, crane and signal box would be removed. At Hampstead Norris, the goods shed, station buildings, nameboards, crane and signal box, at Hermitage, the yard crane, signal box and shelter. Also to be recovered were all signals, telegraph poles and permanent way huts,

also the concrete slab platform at Hampstead Norris. The word 'recovered' may not perhaps be taken in its literal sense. The term is certainly used in the official report and so consequently is reproduced here. Whilst certain of the items above may well have been recovered for possible further use, it is hard to imagine how a brick signal box, as at Hampstead Norris, could be so treated! The paperwork concluded that the contractor was responsible for leaving the site tidy but having seen the results soon afterwards, I would personally doubt that this particular requirement was complied with.

Following a further meeting at Didcot, work commenced from there on 12 January 1967. Some 60 common user wagons were made available and placed in blocks of six at intervals of 220 yards. These were shunted as required using either D63xx or D70xx diesels up until the end of May 1967.

As with the line south of Newbury, various bridges were quickly removed while in other places the track-bed has been reclaimed as farm land. Except at Hampstead Norris, now known as Hampstead Norreys, the station cottages have again been given over to private accommodation whilst elsewhere industry or housing occupies much of the railway's course.

Rod Hoyle

245

Above - *A prelude to demolition at Winchester. In early 1966 and the loading dock siding was recovered, the associated ground disc signal dumped on top of the platform. By this time the track stopped abruptly at the end of the loop beyond the tunnel. From here to Worthy Down there was nothing, the route already cleared in preparation for what would become the 'Kings Worthy link' joining the A34 from Three Maids Hill into the Winchester by-pass at Winnall.*

This page - At Compton all is still, the rust coated rails tell their own story. A playground perhaps, but look carefully and there appear to be some coal wagons still resident in the yard. The Western Region will not them go to waste - they were removed soon afterwards. Closure of the Didcot to Newbury section had been planned by the WR to take effect from 20 August 1964, but in the event it was brought forward 10 days to coincide with the arrangements of the Southern Region.

Opposite page, bottom - Upton and Blewbury, with grass instead of passengers. The wooden shelter on the up side has already disappeared. The views were taken from the A417 bridge which crossed the railway immediately south of the station. It was this bridge which was regarded as a priority for removal in connection with road improvements. 2 June 1966. RCTS

Last knockings at Compton, the signal box is switched-out of circuit and the line is clear for......the demolition train.

By the time the down line was lifted the down side shelter had vanished in similar fashion to that at Upton & Blewbury, (The wooden shelter at Woodhay was purchased for £1, probably as firewood. No doubt a similar price was paid here.)

Above - Compton Crossing looking north in May 1967. No longer was it a requirement that the crossing keeper be 'always in residence' and expected to arrive to open the gates for the railway and road whenever required. (One might pause for a moment to consider how this arrangement worked during the peak of WW2 traffic, although then there probably would have been limited road transport.) The two crossing keepers cottages on the DNS, both on the northern section, at Compton and Fishers Lane, matched the style of the stations.

Middle - Hampstead Norris, 2 June 1966. Possibly the station yard was still in use as a coal dump - judging by the amount scattered over the dock siding. At this stage and even after nearly two years of closure, the railway remains basically intact with little if no sign of vandalism to the operational equipment.
RCTS

Bottom - Part 1 of the demolition, the coal dump is still present but much else has gone.

Top and middle right -
Hermitage, perhaps
waiting for a resurgence
that never came.
Compared with the several
of the locations south of
Newbury, notably Sutton
Scotney, Worthy Down and
at Winchester, the lack of
apparent damage is
remarkable. RCTS
***Middle left** - Remains of*
the cold store (with later
additions) shortly before
demolition. By now the
rails had been salvaged
from the loading platform
although their position can
still be identified.

***Left** - The A4 overbridge at*
Newbury. The height above
road level is not confirmed
but from memory it was
under 15 feet. This alone
was another reason for the
council wishing to see it
removed. Today not only is
the bridge gone but there is
absolutely no trace of the
embankments on either
side.

This page (3) - Demolition trains, top: believed to be near Hermitage, centre at Compton Crossing, and bottom: at Fishers Lane Crossing. In the bottom view the signal has been deliberately lowered by hand, operation of the railway at this stage was under the 'long siding' principal. (Possibly it may also have already been severed by the removal of the A4 bridge at Newbury.) John Coles

Inset below - A few bridges between Hermitage and Hampstead Norris are still maintained by what is now Network Rail not having been sold off by BR. These may be identified by a small white painted area and the words 'NDL' followed by a bridge reference number, the latter based on the original number of bridges on the line.

Top and middle - *Meanwhile south of Newbury the junction was 'secured out of use' on 2 August 1965. Enborne Junction signal box closed on 29 January 1967 and was demolished before the line to Winchester had been lifted. The DNS was still in place - but it would never see another train.*

Bottom - *Burghclere, the trackbed now used by tractors. For some time after closure Bill Hiscock, one of the last two signalman at the station,was still resident in the building. (The other signalman was Jack Green who resided in the first of the lime workers cottages.) Not necessarily related to Burghclere but folklore has it that on one occasion a bored signalman decided to borrow one of the permanent-way trolleys to go for a ride. Unfortunately he chose the one occasion when a 'box to box' special working of a light engine was suddenly added as a special working…. .This may well have been the same man who on another occasion borrowed a trolley with the avowed intention of raiding the traps previously set for rabbits by the local gang… .*

Amyas Crump

Top and middle - *Dear Litchfield: where the porter in charge would invariably have to find his own amusement such was the sparcity of traffic. Long vacant, the house quickly fell into disrepair but was later rescued and lovingly restored. The influence of the Southern in the form of the paint on the bargeboards, window sills and gutters will be noted. All the brick station buildings south of Newbury lost their canopies at the time of demolition, recovered so that the metal columns might be recycled into whatever was the current fashion end of the time. The signal box had been empty for some years, and by now was showing signs of neglect. Unlike the station building it would be demolished with the widening of the A34, the road passing within a few yards of the scrub on the left.*

Amyas Crump

Bottom - *And so under the South Western main line at Whitchurch. Note the small arch on the left was provided merely to maintain an access route and never had anything to do with the proposed Whitchurch loop(s). The influence of the Southern is again apparent in the concrete p/way huts, shaped as such so that they might be transported by rail to the required site and then placed in position by crane. We may be sure they are post 1950. Beyond the bridge and slightly further on is Whitchurch Town station.*

This page - Harry Hiller's home at Whitchurch also the signal box he so lovingly looked over for so many years. Even after demolition there are few broken windows. In connection with road improvements in the area a large door was later cut in one end and the area formerly used as the locking room found a temporary home as a motor vehicle garage. Two ARP signal boxes out of the nine provided on the DNS remain, Highclere and Burghclere, the former put to a new use and the latter an empty shell.

Bob Winkworth

Opposite - Sutton Scotney has seen better days. The worst is not quite over, where a 9F and Bulleid 'Pacific' once ran, a road lorry (or should it be a ballast lorry?) stands. The road bridge over the A30 at Sutton Scotney was removed at the same time as the lines were lifted, not this time for road improvements but for its scrap metal value.

This page, top - Following railway use the station building and yard at Sutton Scotney were taken over for use by a civil engineering contractor. As their work expanded so to did the buildings on site so much so that eventually the station building was demolished to be replaced by a 1970s 'eyesore'. Operations ceased many years later and the site, including the 1970s office and the shell of the signal box were cleared, but the goods shed remained standing. There was an attempt to have the latter listed, indeed it is the only survivor of its type south of Newbury and certainly dates from 1885. (Of larger construction than the other goods sheds provided north of Whitchurch, the directors of the DNS were perceptive that goods at Sutton Scotney would dominate the line north of Winchester in later years). In 2013 the site is fenced off and moribund awaiting redevelopment.   *Amyas Crump*

This page middle and bottom - Worthy Down almost but not quite trackless. Beyond the bridge in the middle view was where the track suddenly ended after1965 - until full demolition took place.

Opposite top - Rod Hoyle alongside a derelict but still basically intact signal box at Worthy Down. The token set down and pick-up posts for up trains were later rescued for use by the Great Western Society at Didcot. Years earlier military exercises would be held at Worthy Down with a machine gun mounted on the roof of the signal box - the camp CO supervising events from inside the signal box. *Rod Hoyle*

Opposite bottom - Winchester tunnel, north end. Subsequent to closure this end was sealed and used for a time as a rifle range. Nearer the station the tunnel has had various non-railway uses, from the storage of new cars and arena seating to a nuclear shelter for the local council. It is now re-opened on certain days for guided tours. The tunnel is recorded as having 13 recesses on either side.

Opposite - From Ebdon Road bridge looking back towards the tunnel. Local folklore has it that at times a ghost train is heard here - a tale no doubt populated from earlier times when a young girl had been killed by one of the navvies at the time of construction. The sudden ending of the sleepers will be noted. It was from here through Kings Worthy to Worthy Down that the track was lifted, possibly by BR themselves in advance of the main demolition contract.

Above - Winchester during its brief tenure as a warehouse. At this end of the building was a motor-factor although the majority was given over to Messrs Courts, furnishers who had a shop in the High Street. 1960s behaviour has resulted in the need for wire netting at the windows. The remaining piece of platform was all that had been left to assist passengers when the diverted 'Pines Express' used the railway in 1964.

Bob Winkworth

Above - Demolition in Winchester tunnel during the autumn of 1966. The contractors had their initial base at Bar End where a caravan acted as a mobile office. A visit to Winchester around this time found the bolts securing the track to the sleepers removed and the rails themselves like a winding snake devoid of any support. This view appeared in the Hampshire Chronicle with the headline, 'Demolishing the railway from Southampton and Winchester to Cheltenham'. Not quite accurate of course although sadly the former MSWJ route to Cheltenham was suffering a similar fate around the same time.

Opposite top - Waiting the end, already the vandals have smashed almost every pane of glass in the signal box and certainly in the signal lenses.

Opposite bottom - The sad scene inside Winchester signal box. Almost everything that could be broken has been. BR removed the hand generator and the token instruments, the rest was either looted or destroyed. When the time came for the contractors to salvage the metal of the lever frame, they simply passed a chain through the windows, attached it to the levers and pulled using a bulldozer. The whole structure collapsed around it. Winchester signal box was no more.

Above - Lampman's view of the station in 1966, taken from the top of the bracket signal.   Bob Winkworth

Next two pages - The lasts months, weeks and days. The platform edge stones were removed by a BR lorry - it was said for use of a manager in his rockery

Top - No more trains to Newbury.

Middle and bottom - A new use for the goods shed at Bar End. Prior to the removal of the track, the now redundant large ganger's trolleys were worked to Winchester and removed by road lorry for use elsewhere.

Top - The approach to Bar End from Shawford. Some concrete sleepers remain, they were later recovered as indeed was the ballast.

Right - Between Winchester and Shawford some bridges still remain and have found a further lease of life as part of the national 'Sustrans' cycle network. Ironically, and despite the end of Bar End for goods on 4 April 1966, it was another seven weeks before the connections at Shawford Junction were put out of use.

Top - *'A rose amidst the thorns?' T9 No 30120 on one of the occasions it worked through to Didcot from Southampton not long before closure south of Winchester.*
The Kellaway collection

Centre *- Ready to return to the Southern. Sister engine No 30285 at Didcot in 1957 prior to setting off for Newbury and Winchester..*
Colour Rail 340003

Bottom - *All is at peace at Hampstead Norris. Although as both starting signals are showing 'off' it is likely the signal box is switched out of circuit and possibly no trains are imminent. Hampstead Norris was the only location between Didcot and Newbury where a new signal box had been required in 1942/43, the original structure had been removed with ground frames provided in the early 1920s. The top of the original timber box was then repositioned on the platform as a goods store - and was still serving this purpose 40 years later in the early 1960s.*

Above - *Driver's eye view of, left, the approach to Churn, and right, Upton and Blewbury from the front of a single unit diesel car.*

Centre - *No 7324 southbound between Compton and Hampstead Norris with empty oil tank cars for Fawley, 23 July 1964. The train is just passing the unique (for the DNS) double distant signal, the down distant for Hampstead Norris and up distant signal for Compton.*

Amyas Crump

Bottom - *An unidentified 9F on a similar working. The location is believed to north of Newbury.*

Amyas Crump

Contrasts in light. **Above** - *No 3210 has arrived in the up main platform at Newbury and appears ready to leave. Compared with the down side, the lack of passengers will be noted.*

Right - *On 6 February 1960, the late afternoon sun illuminated No 7327 as it leaves Woodhay for Enborne and Newbury. The station building may just be seen in the background.* Amyas Crump

Page 262 top - *The ubiquitous T9 leaves George Behrend's Highclere for Woodhay and Newbury. (George's recollections of Highclere in the 1920s published in his 'Gone With Regret' volume are well worth a read.)* David Smith

Page 262 bottom - *A few months later and the only traffic now dealt with at Highclere is local freight and that will not last much longer.*

Page 263 - *With an almost deserted A34 alongside, No 76062 coasts downhill towards Litchfield on an auspicious, 5 March 1960.* T B Owen / Colour Rail 390241

"26 July 1956. I noted that the 4.20 to Didcot left with 2251 class 0-6-0 No 2252 on 3C nearly full with about 90 passengers. I was waiting for the 2.56 Oxford - Southampton Terminus, there were about 24 on the platform 6 minutes after it was due, which was at 4.18, and its departure was scheduled at 4.32. T9 30117 arrived on 3C(W.R.) 7¼ late, and we departed ¼ late ¼ full with about 18 2nds + 1 1ˢᵗ – 93T/95. After Emborne Jct., passed in 2m. 56s., I have only the public times until leaving Winchester. We called at all stations and, until Winchester, the most that joined were 6 at Whitchurch Town, and the most to alight were 7 at Burghclere. Litchfield to Whitchurch took exactly 6m. with a maximum of 60. We arrived 2½ early at Winchester Chesil where about 16 joined and about 5 alighted. Because of the single line, we had to await the arrival of the last up train of the day, the 4.56 Southampton Terminus – Newbury, due at 5.30, which did not put in an appearance until 5.49! 0-6-0 No 2240 had 3C nearly full and about 80 alighted! We got away 1m. later, 10 late, but suffered 2 signal stops before we could access the main line at Shawford Jct. and reached the station 12½ late where just 1 joined. There were further signal checks before Eastleigh, reached 13½ late, where about 30 joined. A generous allowance here saw us 7½ late away, then 4m. 25s. to Swaythling where some alighted, several did at St. Denys and a final signal check made us 5 late terminating where about 10 alighted." - Anon

Above - *Whitchurch, 5 March 1960 - time for a quick photograph before departure north.*   *David Smith*
Below - *Whitchurch, 21 February 1960. The damaged tender from No 76026 pulled into the goods shed siding by sister engine No 76065.*   *Trevor Owen / Colour Rail 390242*

Views at Worthy Down. **Top -** *No 76061 at the north end of the loop heading south with a through freight for Eastleigh. It was common practice to join trains at Didcot if this was feasible. Notice the GWR 2-bolt track fishplates and mixed wooden and metal keys. Track circuiting wires are also apparent.*

Bottom - *No 2240 makes a spirited getaway south from Worthy Down. Apart from service personnel there were rarely any civilian passengers here - safe for a few railway photographers! The advertising posters on the end of the signal box will be noted.* Both the Kellaway collection

Opposite top - *No 2246 arriving at Worthy Down. GWR colours are present on the door of the signal box indicating no repaint had taken place since at least 1950.*
The Kellaway collection

Opposite bottom - *No 31067 on the down (outward) leg of its journey. Assuming the service was running to time, it would have been seen here at 12.35 p.m. Apart from the return working due to pass at 6.41 p.m., no other trains were scheduled on the DNS for this day. (Sunday 22 May 1960.)*

*This page, Kings Worthy early 1960. Although undated, meteorological reports for mid February 1960 indicate this as having been the time of the month when snow was present. In the **top view** we see the remaining station platform and line looking north. The down side platform has been demolished although the running-in board remains. In the distance the 'dog-leg' in the track may be identified. **Bottom view** - No doubt taken on the same day, No 3210 arrives from Newbury. Notwithstanding its external appearance, the engine would appear to be in reasonable mechanical condition as there is no evidence of any external leaks of steam which would certainly have been visible on a cold day. Both, the Kellaway collection.*

Opposite - Having taken the ride to Winchester, we see the signalman with the single line tablet from Worthy Down in his hand. (The loop and pouch for the Shawford Junction tablet were physically smaller.) Possibly the signalman has deliberately walked to collect this item as No 3210 will be waiting awhile for an up train which will itself need the same token to proceed. The Kellaway collection.

This page - Despite the ending of passenger services, Doug Hannah captured this picture postcard view of the station in 1962.

Opposite top - Winchester Chesil seemingly with more passengers than normal. As will be gathered this was the last day, Saturday 5 March 1960, No 2240 hardly a good exponent for cleanliness at Didcot shed as it sets off south.

Trevor Owen / Colour Rail 390240

Opposite bottom - 2-car DEMU unit No 1104 at an otherwise deserted station in the summer of 1960/61. Would a diesel service have made a difference? According to Harry Hiller who certainly advocated such a working it might, but in reality it would only have put off the inevitable for a short time. The lack of patronage shown is enough to indicate there was simply not enough traffic even at Winchester.

Amyas Crump

This page - Perhaps appropriately described, as a station which sleeps. As undated image but which is useful to show how the influence of the Southern Region was slow yet creeping. The green painted tops of the lamp posts and the barge boards of the former station master's house similarly treated. The footbridge, and buildings on both sides remained stubbornly 'Western', defiant to the very end.

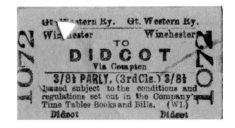

Tickets on this and page 281 courtesy David Littlefair.

Opposite page - Disturbing the peace, No 76061 rattles through the station southbound, watched by a solitary passenger - or train-spotter perhaps.

Tony Woodforth collection

Above - A slightly earlier view taken from a departing train. The name 'Chesil' has yet to be added to the running-in board on the up platform whilst the shabby paintwork of the footbridge appeared to alter little over the years. The coaches may well be Great Western design and built 'toplights' from the period up to the 1920s.

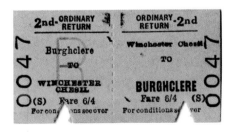

*Moving south and probably all taken on the same day as the view of No 76061 seen earlier. We have (**opposite top**) No 76061 having gained the single line and heading south towards Shawford Junction and Eastleigh.*

***Opposite bottom** - This time it is No 6302 arriving with a local passenger working.*

***Above -** The ubiquitous No 2240 also on the single line with passengers for Eastleigh and Southampton. Again the presence of the Southern 'Mogul' will be noticed in the background. In the gardens of the houses on the right hand side were boundary markers, cast and dated 'GWR 1885'.*   *All, Tony Woodforth collection.*

Winchester, Tuesday 3 February 1925.

"Some consternation was caused at Winchester Station on Tuesday morning by an explosion of gas which took place in the ladies waiting room on the up platform. In the process of cleaning out the waiting rooms, a smell of escaping gas was detected in the ladies waiting room and the Station Master, Mr Sexton, was duly informed. Obtaining a ladder, he with the assistance of two members of staff, went to ascertain where the leak occurred. Mr Sexton, by standing on the table, was able to demonstrate to his own satisfaction that the escape did not arise from the burner. Porter Stacey, ascending the ladder to get at the top of the gas pendant, noticed that the smell was more pronounced nearer the ceiling, and when striking a match to closely inspect an upper joint in the pendent, an explosion immediately occurred. For a moment the ceiling of the waiting room presented the appearance of a sheet of flame. Fortunately the window of the room had already been opened and as the members of staff entered they had also left the door open: otherwise the results might have been more serious. Porter Stacey hurriedly descended the ladder, and was assisted out on to the platform, where it was found his hair was singed and his face and hands slightly blistered. Happily his sight was not affected. He was removed to the Royal Hampshire County Hospital and detained for treatment, but expects to be out in the course of a day or so. The Water and Gas Company were notified of the occurrence, and their repairing staff were soon on the scene. It was then discovered that the joint of the pipe had rusted out, thus providing an outlet for the gas, and the same must, apparently have been escaping for several hours."

(Reported in the 'Hampshire Chronicle for Saturday 7 February 1925.)

*Contrasts at Winchester and Bar End. **Opposite top** - It is 1962/63 and the footbridge has gone along with the platform canopy together with the waiting room and gentlemen's toilet on the down platform. Also missing are the canopy supports, the whole taken away for scrap or in the case of the timer component, waiting to be burnt as firewood. Trains though are still running even if, according to the signals at the end of the platform, nothing is expected at the present time.*

***Opposite bottom** - Winchester was not an easy place to photograph. In winter when the leaves were gone from the trees there was perhaps more light but then it would lack the brightness of the summer months. Recorded at the same time as the image above, the tunnel mouth was an oft photographed feature of the station, the gloom within accentuated by the curve near its mid point. George Behrend would romanticise how years earlier when the loop ended within the tunnel, how passengers might find themselves waiting in the gloom for the home signal (within the actual tunnel) to be lowered whilst, as he put it, 'smoke and steam would wander round'. Look carefully and there is the influence of the Southern even here - the finials at the top of the signals having lost their red-painted ball and replaced with overall white - Southern practice for painting The sighting panels appear recently painted whilst in-between the sleepers of the down main line the ramp covers the mechanism for a facing point lock allowing passenger trains to depart north from the down platform.*

***Above** - And the difference is the sunshine! Bar End goods shed, easily the largest on the whole of the DNS and representative of the traffic both anticipated and actually handled. On the end nearest the camera was the office and secure store, hence the barred windows. A green notice board appears on the brickwork displaying opening times and contact details. Already a few windows are broken whilst the canopies above the three loading / unloading points also show their age.*

David Littlefair

Nothing for ages and then feverish activity. The scene (opposite top) on the days the train did not run and where a film of rust has quickly covered the rails. The hut is 'Winchester Ground Frame' and contained just the levers for the crossover and lock for the connection on to the single line and also the access and lock to the Simmons and Gifford siding. In the other views the goods has arrived from Eastleigh and the wagons are being marshalled into their required positions. The engine will be seen to be a Class 4 tank, but tender engines were also known to have been used on occasions.

David Littlefair

Bar End circa 1964/65. The image tells its own story. Lunchtime perhaps, or just a diminishing need for the railway? The goods shed sports the remnants of the GWR 'dark and light stone' colour scheme whilst the buffer stop shows evidence of a few 'rough shunts'. In the background is the concrete loading ramp added in WW2, whilst on the right where infill and rubbish already accumulates, is the position of the former turntable. The engine shed too has gone, but there is life still - albeit only just. Two of the three 'iron minks' that would be abandoned to the contractors may be seen in their usual position just peeping out of the goods shed.

David Littlefair

The public footbridge across the yard throat at Bar End leading to Domun Road. Here was the ideal place to stand and just watch the trains - without the risk of being told to 'Gerrr off 'aught of it!'

David Littlefair

With its train almost complete the engine pulls the wagons on to the headshunt ready for one final shunt and then a propelling motion to the station ready to collect the tablet for the journey back to Shawford Junction. In the view opposite top, the engine is seen on the headshunt where the passenger train was running when it was derailed on 28 August 1942.

Opposite page - *Approaching Bar end from Shawford Junction. (Perhaps not quite at the speed the blurred hedgerow might imply.)*
The distant signal was a Great Western item and appears to still retain its yellow painted ball to the finial. At least once a week a porter from Winchester would replenish the oil and trim the wick in the lamp - the same as he would for all the other 20+ signals in the area.

This page - *The 'Dock Tank' special of 9 May 1963 - see p 217 - at three points along its journey south from Winchester. Top, the engine has just passed over Garnier Road bridge and is about to start running parallel to the Winchester by-pass: as at Whitchurch, the set of SR concrete permanent way huts will be noted. In the centre the little train has progressed further and is probably travelling at a heady 15-20 mph. Bottom it is seen on the viaduct close to Shawford Junction.*

Prior to the permitted opening of any passenger carrying railway, an inspection of the facilities was carried out by an Officer of the Board of Trade. This inspection covered items such as the condition of the permanent-way, number and type of bridges, plus in the case of under-bridges their deflection, signalling including locking, and passenger facilities at stations. Only if a railway satisfied all these requirements was it permitted to operate and carry passengers. (Goods lines were not included, neither was the safety of the men operating goods and passenger lines considered.) The DNS passed these necessary inspections and opened to Newbury in 1882 and thence to Winchester in 1885. A further inspection was carried out in 1891 at the time of the extension to Shawford Junction. Subsequent inspections were made when new works encroached upon an existing passenger carrying line, i.e., the provision of a siding at Burghclere, the new stations at Churn, Kings Worthy, Worthy Down and Pinewood Halt, and later on, the new works of WW2.

In addition to the above, the GWR as the principal operating company of the DNS carried out their own inspection(s) of the new works, often arriving at some strange requests. These inspections took place between early 1885 and the summer of 1886 involving the GWR, DNS company and on at least one occasion a representative of the contractors. These records have survived at the National Archive under the reference 'RAIL 1057/783 - DNS Historical file'. On initial perusal the handwritten papers might appear almost repetitive, but on closer scrutiny they afford a fascinating insight into the condition of the railway at varying times and more importantly indicate the apparent shoddy state not only in which it opened but which it persisted for some months.

It is also clear that items which appeared to be perhaps in order at the time of one visit and indeed might well have satisfied the Board of Trade, were deemed unsatisfactory to the GWR on the occasion of another inspection. Was this then simply the views of individual GWR men?

Reference is also made to further reports, letters, or plans / drawings. None of these are in the above file and it is likely they have not survived.

The first report, (below) albeit undated and unsigned, is most likely prior to May 1885, as it would appear unlikely Board of Trade sanction as to opening could have been secured with the amount of work referred to left undone. From the style of writing it appears the actual compiler was also someone associated with the DNS themselves.

It is unfortunate that no earlier reports have been discovered for the Didcot to Newbury section but there is every reason to believe Paddington had been equally pedantic - unless of course it was only when the DNS had actually succeeded in reaching Winchester and were thus within striking distance of Southampton and the potential risk of antagonism with the LSWR, that the GWR decided to act. Paddington were always keen to allow the DNS to survive, seeing them fail might well allow a competitor to venture north, but if the DNS were too successful then this in turn might well mean the controlling influence of the GWR were lessened.

Didcot, Newbury & Southampton Railway – Southern Section. List of incomplete works.			
Great Western Co. requirements	Didcot Co. remarks	Great Western Co. further remarks	Didcot Co. further remarks
Junction Signal Cabin (Enborne)			
The down distant signal cannot be seen, the post should be lengthened to enable the semaphore to be seen over the GWR bridge. Hedge inside the Company's fence should be cut down opposite the junction to obtain a clear view of the points from the Box. The following fittings are required here and also at the other cabins along the line;- Notice Board (50" x 50") for pasting notices upon. Brass clock dial. A lock -up with desk top. A shelf along one end of cabin under cabin floor. A skirting board to keep out wind and dirt. A shelf (3.0 x 2.0) covered with zinc to keep lamps on. Petroleum signal lamps, and a petroleum swing lamp for cabin. Caution plate on outside of cabin door, "No unauthorised person is allowed in this cabin." Name of cabin outside thus;- 'Enborne Junction signal cabin', "Woodhay signal cabin", etc.*(Note - Cast nameplates were not in fact ordered until some years late –see p315, does this imply wooden names may have been provided beforehand?)*			

Woodhay Station

In Lamp, Porters and Store Room as follows; a shelf covered with zinc on wall opposite door. A shelf whole width of building. Lock up cupboard with desk top under end window. In General Waiting Room, a stove. A seat along back of apartment. In Booking Office, a counter across under booking window, a cash drawer under, and three cupboards the centre one being for safe. A shelf by side of window at the back of office for block instruments with cupboard under for batteries (4.6 x 1.6 x 4.6 high.) A stove. A shelf width of room for books (out of use). In Ladies Room, a stove. A fixed seat two sides of room. Lamps. 1 in waiting room, 1 in ladies room, 1 in porters room, 2 in office, 1 in urinals. These should be bracketed lamps, I understand the GWR could supply. Urinals, the door to be screened off. Outside Building, a clock 10" dial. Coal and dust bin outside goods store. Platforms, lamps should average 50' apart one being at each ramp, and the opposite entrance or by wicket. One should also be put at entrance gate from road. A name board at arrival end of each platform: these should be blue on white enamel if possible. Station Masters House. A closet. Outside place for coal and wood in a bricked in yard. Water supply both to Station and House. Woodhay Signals, a repeater will be required for the up distant signal and perhaps also for the down distant, the latter not being up yet and we could not be sure.

Highclere Signals

An electrical repeater will be required for the down distant signal which cannot be seen on account of the deep cutting being on a curve. Highclere Station, in Waiting Room, a bracket lamp over fireplace. In Office, a counter 3.6 x 2.6 x 3.8 high, between this and corner of fireplace a shelf same height but 12" wide only. Under counter, a lock up drawer for cash and remainder of space a cupboard for stores. On opposite wall a book rack 3' x 2' divided up with partitions. The bottom of the rack is to be continued full width of room for block instruments, with cupboard under for batteries. Above top of booking window for full width of room, a shelf 12" wide. A bracketed lamp at side of ticket window and another in opposite corner of room to light instruments. In Porters Room, a shelf covered with zinc for lamps. A lock -up cupboard with a desk top. A bracket lamp. In House Yard, at back of door into road, a coal and wood bin with cover. Outside House Yard, a coal and dust bin for station use, the latter with lid. Outside, a lamp on corner of building by porch and another by corner of goods store to light entrance into yard.

Burghclere Signals

An electrical repeater required for the down distant signal. Burghclere Station, outside lamps and other requirements same as at Highclere.

Litchfield Signals

Repeaters to both distant signals are required. Litchfield Station, requirements as at Highclere.

Whitchurch Signals

Trees are in the way of the up distant signal. Whitchurch Station. In Booking Office, a counter same as at Highclere, shelf right hand side of window with cupboard under for batteries. A book rack on wall opposite ticket window the top continued on full width for books (out of use). In Waiting Room, a seat round 3 parts of it, and other requirements same as Highclere. Gas Lamps, each road approach should have 3 lamps along it. 1 lamp should be provided at the corner of the building to light wicket and in Goods Shed. 1 gas bracket in office, 2 gas brackets on platform. In Goods Shed, a lock up place at south end for the checking porters use with an entrance from the yard through the existing arch opening and from the office onto the platform by a door. An office to keep weighing machine in by weighbridge, about 6.0 x 6.0 with desk in it.

Sutton Scotney Station			
In Booking Office, as at Whitchurch, the counter being modified thus. Outside, a lamp at entrance from public road to station approach. A lamp corner of station building by porch. Carriage shoot.			
Winchester			
Booking Office, fill up .... Well.(?) Remove present ticket shelf and substitute a counter as shown on the general plan. Drawers to be fitted under counter for the whole length, the centre one being fitted up with tills etc for cash. Under the cash drawer, a lock up cupboard and also one on each side, remainder of space between cupboards and walls to be divided up into 3" spaces as book racks. Blind rollers and racks required. 1st & 2nd Class waiting room, fill up .... well. Porters Room, fill up .... well, provide cooking oven to fire place. Twelve lockers, the tops to be made as seats and fastened with padlocks. A cupboard to be fixed over the lockers on one side of the fireplace, high enough to allow men to sit upright on locker. A hanging cupboard to be placed between fireplace and window looking on to platform, size about 7' 0" x 1' 6" deep one side being fitted with shelves, the other provided with hooks or nails for hanging coats up. Lamp Room, foot warmer tank to heat 150 warmers exactly like one at Newbury Station. A lamp shelf 2' 0" wide covered with zinc to be fixed along wall between tank and door, this should have small drains along it with well at the centre and under it a zinc lined drawer to catch the waste oil. Under lamp shelf two cupboards for stores one each side of oil drawer. Above lamp shelf along wall a strong shelf having strong hooks along edge of it to hang lamps on. On opposite wall to that on which lamp shelf is fixed, a lamp-rack the size of which Mr. Gibbs will send. Urinals, screen outside door. Name boards on the platform side as follows; 'Parcels Office & Cloak Room', '3rd class Ladies Room', 'Booking Office & 3rd class waiting room', also over door on Road side, 'Booking Office' only but rather larger. '1st & 2nd class waiting room', ' 1st & 2nd class ladies room'. On the Booking Office door, 'Private', on enamel plate or simply painted. 'Porters' & 'Lamps' also painted on their respective doors. 'Gentlemen' painted on a flat board pointing towards the platform. Name board 'Winchester' on arrival end of platform. In Store Room. A rough cupboard along the sides with shelf above. A stout batten in opposite wall with strong hooks to hang up ropes to. In Parcels & Cloak Room, a counter (2' 6" wide) along side opposite entrance with drawers and cupboards and round door on entrance counter. Having a flap opening 3' 6" wide to enable a luggage truck to be wheeled through. On the side of the fireplace nearest platform, a left luggage crib, on the other side of the fireplace thus shelves without partition. A book rack opposite fireplace divided up into 3" spaces by partitions, the rack to be 3' 0" long x 2' 6" high x 2' 0" deep the bottom being 4' 0" above floor. To have .... well filled up flush with floor. 3rd Class Ladies Room., fixed seats all round with backs and elbows. Booking Hall and 3rd Class waiting room, seats half round, thus. Ticket barrier with a 9" top for depositing luggage upon. The lights required are as follows, 4 suspended lamps under verandah. 1 post lamp at end of platform by tunnel, 3 post lamps along remainder of platform. On the Road side, 1 on corner of building by exit, 1 over Booking Office door, 1 opposite the Booking Office door by path crossing. 1 at foot of approach, Cheesehill Street, 1 at bend of approach. The lights in building are correct as already arranged. A paved footway along front of building across opposite Booking Office and down side of approach. Goods Shed Office, counter as arranged on plan, the entrance counter having a lifting flap. Under the desk counter lock-up drawer all round, one fitted with tills as a cash drawer. Four lock up cupboards under the drawers and 2 sets of book racks about 3' x 2' each. In Shed, in place of the screen shown on drawing a 14' x 10' covered in office fitted up like that for Whitchurch Goods Shed for checking clerk. Lighting, two brackets in office, 2 suspended lamps over platform one bracket in checking office. 1 lamp at each outside corner of building nearest the line - 7 in all."			

Second report - **"Newbury & Winchester Line. Supplementary list of requirements still unsettled. 15 August 1885.**			
Enborne Junction			
The rain water pipes from roof of cabin empty themselves onto the foundation, a tub is required so that the water may be caught and utilised for the cabin.	*(DNS response by H.O. Baldry - all of which in this report are dated 24 August 1885) - Has been done.*		
Woodhay			
The surface of Passenger platforms being of old pickled timber; ladies have complained of damage to their dresses in hot weather from tar adhering. The platforms are very rough, and some fine top ballast is required.	*Station Master informs us that the lady whose dress was damaged in the manner described crossed by the footboards provided for the porters instead of by the platform incline. The stones have been picked off and there is no fault to be found with them. (?).*		
Highclere			
The road to the yard crane is not finished, and round timber cannot be loaded	*Road was widened to 18 feet as required by the GWR officials when they settled these matters with us. After making our inspection with Station Master cannot see what the difficulty is in loading round timber.*		
Burghclere			
Platforms still very rough and fine top ballast required.	*Platforms are in good order and Station Master makes no complaint.*		
Whitchurch			
There is not sufficient width of goods shed line for a passenger carriage to clear without striking wall of goods shed. A carriage was damaged there a short time since. Line should be slewed.	*The road through goods shed is not quite in centre of the space between platforms and door jamb at each end requires to be slewed 4" at one end and 2" at the other, which I have given instructions to be done. The openings at the end are 10' wide which is very nearly the width of some guards vans. The centre of rail at the point where the communication cord rollers struck is 2' 2½" from the brickwork.*		
Sutton Scotney			
The yard crane has been fixed too near the cattle pens and a wagon cannot be passed. Nearly half the siding is therefore lost to use. The jib of the platform crane does not plumb the centre of a wagon and when reversed it strikes the outside of the goods shed.	*The crane was fixed in accordance with plan supplied from London: copy of which is attached. A road could not be formed for the purposes required between siding and the fence, a portion of the earthwork has already been shifted to form the occupation approach for Mr. Canning and the remainder could be finished at a very small expense. The cranes for goods shed were ordered of same pattern and size and as this shed is smaller than Whitchurch or Winchester the crane will not swing completely round and the remedy is to shorten the jib.*		

Winchester			
The yard crane will not plumb the centre of a wagon.	*This has been done.*		
Goods yard gates not yet provided and consequently people get onto the line.	*Instructions were given to provide these gates at the time the line was opened and I understand they have been ordered.*		
Direction boards at entrance to passenger and goods stations not yet provided.	*Do not understand what this remark refers to.*		
Carriage shoots not safe for loading vans.	*An extra runner was wanted and has been provided.*		
Large open space in front of signal cabin on up platform requires to be boarded over.	*Contractors have long had instructions to cover this in and it is now in hand. "*		

Note: A copy of the report was also passed to Mr. Grierson at Paddington on 26 August 1885.

"Newbury and Southampton Railway 'Southern Section'. Uncompleted Requirements 23 January 1886.

Woodhay			
Flooring of platforms of old pickled timber should be removed. It is unusual to use creosoted timber for platforms and the Didcot Company must be held responsible in the event of any further complaints or claims	*Not in original requirements. I wrote fully to Mr Beasley on the 20 October 1885 that I could not understand how ladies using the platforms legitimately could soil their dresses. I think the Didcot Company might take the responsibility in case of future complaints.*	If the Didcot Company will take the responsibility that will be sufficient.	*Yes*
Water still bad	*Not in original requirements. Would not a filter be sufficient?*	Water not even fit for washing purposes. No filter would purify it.	*Water supply to be taken from the river as now arranged.*
Cattle pens finished but gates not properly hung	*The Contractors should attend.*		

Burghclere			
Road in goods yard still very rough.	*There appears to be much difference of opinion as to the roughness complained of.*	Not so rough but requires attention	*Is receiving attention.*
Rough blocks projecting from side of chalk cutting should be taken off. In some cases the projections have crumbled and should be cleared away.	*Will the mileage of this cutting be given as we cannot discover any place where rough blocks are dangerous to the public?*	The first cutting after passing Burghclere towards Winchester. Frost has brought them down.	
Accommodation has not been provided for wharfage purposes and ground should be levelled and formed.	*Several hundred yards are available for wharfage purposes; where should the required additional be placed, and what traffic is expected?*	This space is not available until levelled and covered with a coating of chalk.	*Present siding to be moved parallel with main line and ground levelled to the extent of 50 feet from home signal and end of cattle pen.*
Lock up desk in signal box should be fixed to floor.	*The contractors should strictly do this, but it appears rather absurd for them to be required to send a carpenter 20 miles to drive a few nails or put in a few screws. As a rule these have been removed to the Booking Office where the instruments are now.*	Not done	*Done.*

Whitchurch

Goods platform and outside lamps not fixed.	*I cannot understand this as lamps have been returned as fixed, and unless extra lamps are required I should think this must be an error.*	No lamps fixed, lights but no lamps. No outside lamp or light.	*Where are outside lamps to go and who supplies the Great Western with the lantern for outside of Goods Store.*
Water tank has been provided, but the Gas Engine and pumping apparatus which the Didcot Co. were to supply has not been provided, and there is no water. An estimate of the cost of providing the apparatus has been sent to Mr Bingham. The Loco. Supt. In pressing the matter.	*Mr Grierson wrote to me with reference to this and I saw Sir John Fowler upon the matter. He said that he would reply to it but I presume it escaped his memory. His opinion was that the existing pumps were quite sufficient for providing the supplementary and occasional supply required and that a Gas Engine, as suggested by Mr Armstrong to me when the line was inspected, was all that was necessary. No mention of pumps was made in the original list of requirements of the G W Co. but if they insist upon it their offer to do the work for £250 should be accepted. It may be mentioned that a temporary supply has been provided since the line has been opened, but I understand that it has never been made use of.*		

Sutton Scotney

Yard crane fixed too near the cattle pens and a wagon cannot be passed, nearly half the siding is therefore lost for use. It is considered that if the ramp of the cattle pens is reversed, and a corner cut off to enable traffic to get between the pen and the crane the proposed road might not be necessary.	*Not in original requirements. The contractors promised me that they would do the required work.*	In hand, nearly complete.	*This has been done.*
Jib of platform crane does not plumb the centre of a wagon and when reversed strikes the outside wall of goods shed, jib should be shortened.	*Not in original requirements. The contractors promised me that they would do the required work.*	Not done	*This has been remedied.*
Gravel on platforms loose and rough.	*This will be done.*	Still very loose.	*Now in good order.*
Carriage shoots have not been slewed towards the approach roads, the approach is too steep.	*If this is absolutely necessary it must be done, but as the end of the shoot is 40 feet from the building I can see no difficulty in loading of vehicles, if the approach is too steep it should be remedied.*	Not done. It is absolutely necessary that it should be done before vehicles are loaded.	*Mr Voss's decision as to mode of carrying out this alteration will be complied with. We await his report.*

Winchester

Paving of cattle pens to be made with ridges.	*Not in original requirements. The paving was originally formed with ridges, these were complained of and the pens re-laid.*	Should be made with ridges. At present paved with bricks laid flat.	*Must the work be done over again? What decision has Mr Voss come to as to the necessity of further alterations?*
Pickled timbers in roof of Enginemen's House and W.C. very objectionable.	*Not in original requirements. I understand that no further complaints have been made, but if there is, the timber shall be replaced.*	There has been no further complaint, but probably there will be when the weather gets bad.	*In this worth pressing further?*
The roof of the Engine Shed is not quite finished at one end and neither is it whitewashed and the water pipes are still uncovered.	*Not in original requirements, but the pipes, where necessary have been protected from frost.*	Not done.	*We believe this has all been set right.*

"Great Western Railway. Southern Division Engineers Office, Reading. 12 June 1886."
Didcot, Newbury & Southampton Railway, South Section...... . Report on the state of works to be carried out by the Contractor, - replies by T.H. Falkiner and unless otherwise stated these are dated 24 June 1886.

Enborne Junction

The Signal Cabin has not been stopped and painted nor roof made water tight.	*Saxby & Farmer have sent a foreman down who is supposed to be attending to the signal requirements agreed with Inspector King. We have written them that if the matters are not quickly completed we will do the work and charge them with the cost. 5 July 1886 - Saxby & Farmer have promised to do this but it is not satisfactory, our men will sort it out as soon as they have finished Woodhay Station where they are now at work.*		
From 0¾ to l½ mp. The side ditches have not been cleaned out.	*Now done to the satisfaction of Great Western Inspector. .*		

Woodhay

Station not stopped or painted	*This will be done by the end of next week. Shortly afterwards - They are at work on this it has taken longer than expected.*		
Water still bad	*The well and pump house now moved to the river side as arranged with Mr. Vass, we believe the Station Master is now satisfied.*		
Not sufficient soil sent for Station Masters garden.	*30 trucks of soil have been dispatched as arranged with Mr. Vass.*		

Highclere

Gravel in goods yard to be levelled.	*Done.*		
Fence not erected to Station Master's garden.	*Done.*		
Water to house is in a dangerous position being placed in the 6 foot way. Pipe should be laid to back yard and proper cistern built.	*This will be done by end of next month.* Shortly afterwards - *There is not room for a cistern in this yard. Mr. Dunston (?) Mr. Vass' assistant asked to leave the matter for a few days as they have not made up their minds how the pump should be arranged to best advantage.*		
No water supply for drinking purposes. Water has to be fetched from a farm ¼ mile away.	*We will send a filter, the water is 130 feet deep in chalk.* Shortly afterwards - *A filter has been sent addressed to the Station Master from ....*		
Coal wharf not completed, but is in a forward state.	*Coal wharf completed.*		
Pipe drain to be extended and old chalk culvert taken out.	*Done to satisfaction of GW Inspector.*		
Buffer stops to be erected.	*Buffer stop erected.*		
$8\frac{1}{2}$ to $8^3/4$ mp. Brick arch bridge under line. Requirements not attended to.	*Done*		

Litchfield

Platform wall requirements not attended to.	*Done*		

Whitchurch

Front door of house will not open properly, fanlight useless.	*There is nothing wrong except that the door does not open completely back. We do not know how to remedy it, it opens width of doorway which we think is sufficient. We do not know what is meant by fanlight useless.* Shortly afterwards - *Mr. Dunston wants the door moved and the panels made of glass to give more light inside the house. We will have this done.*		
Goods platform and outside lamps not fixed.	*Goods Platform lamps are being made at the Great Western Works.*		

Sutton Scotney

Battery cupboard (height) not attended to.	*Foot stool is being made and will be fixed by Saturday.*		
South end of house not weather tiled.	*Tiling done.*		
Station Master's garden not fenced off.	*Done.*		
Carriage dock alterations, plan sent herewith.	*Waiting for plan to be approved by Sir John Fowler.* Shortly afterwards - *plan received from Sir John Fowler on 3rd inst. work will be put in hand without delay.*		
Water Lane Bridge.	*We understand that the £250 paid to the Great Western Company covered this.*		
23 to 23 ¼ mp. Fence not erected as asked for.	*Will be done next week.*		
24¾ to 25 mp. Fence not erected as asked for.	*Done.*		

Winchester

Fences between Station and Goods Yard not attended to.	*Will be done next week, materials on the ground. All the fencing is now in order except the ballast pit at Enborne and Goods Yard Winchester. We will start the former at once, the latter when we receive necessary instructions.*		
Lamps not yet fixed in Goods Shed.	*Lamps being made at Great Western Railway works. Glass not repaired in same. We object to repairing the glass which was broken willfully by one of the Great Western Railways servants,*		
Goods roads require more metalling or drainage.	*A question of maintenance, taken over by Great Western.*		
No knobs, knocker or bell provided to outer door of Station Masters House.	*A knocker has been put on, a knob will be attached*		
Coal bunker not fixed for goods department.	*Will be done next week.*		
Pickled timber not removed from enginemen's house or WC.	*Does not require removal,*		
Roof of engine shed not yet finished neither is it whitewashed. Water pipes still uncovered.	*We do not know what is unfinished nor how they want the waste pipes covered. They run along the wall a few inches above the floor inside the engine shed. We have written to ask the Locomotive Department what they want done. Roof will be whitewashed next week.*		
Signal Cabin window fastenings not fixed. Stoves still dangerous in signal cabins. Locking requirements, little has been done.	*Saxby and Farmer have promised to attend........... and will be in place in a few days. The rods and cranks which have got out of place at Woodhay by the subsidence of the bank will be set right without delay.*		
The fences in many places are still insecure and have not been properly attended to.	*They will be all set right by the end of month.*		
Station Masters Houses and Station Offices have not been papered and ceilings whitened.	*We have obtained tenders for this work and will submit patterns of paper and specifications to Mr. Gibbs.*		
Signed: Henry Vass. 12 June 1886."			

In the course of compiling this work I was privileged to be passed the DNS notes collected by long term friend David Littlefair. Amongst these was an 18-page draft for a lecture prepared by the late T B Sands. Whether this was ever presented and if so to whom is not known, although we know Sands was for many years a member of the now defunct Railway Club. A scholarly dissertation, it gives a considerable insight into the workings of the DNS between 1900 and 1922. As such it will certainly be of interest to readers. Rather than 'cut and paste' items within the other sections of this book, it is reproduced in its entirety. T B Sands lived at Burbage and was responsible for the first published work on the DNS produced by Oakwood Press in 1971.

Nobody would claim that the Didcot, Newbury & Southampton Rly was a very glamorous line. Among the small independent railway companies it had little to catch the eye, such as the blue engines and coaching stock of the Somerset & Dorset Rly, or the red which the Midland & South Western Junction Rly flaunted so brazenly in the heart of Great Western territory at Swindon. Yet in spirit and in character the DNS was just as independent, and in its constitution even more so. For the DNS always retained a large and very vocal body of shareholders with whom the ultimate control of the company rested.

Compare that with the Somerset & Dorset Rly. That company had leased its undertaking jointly to the London & South Western Rly and the Midland Rly, on terms which gave S&D shareholders the right to exchange their shares for cash, or for Midland Rly 3% Debenture Stock. Most of them seem to have grasped this opportunity with both hands, because well before the end of last century the bulk of S&D stock had been exchanged, leaving only a dwindling handful of shareholders. The S&D board was appointed entirely by the two owning companies.

On the MSWJR, a few big debenture holders and creditors had effective control, among them the Midland Rly which had lent the company nearly £250,000. It had spent 13 years in the hands of a Receiver, and although it was put on its feet again by the genius of Sam Fay, the holders of the preference and ordinary shares remained always a downtrodden minority.

The DNS was at times extremely hard up, but it never went bankrupt. Moreover, about three quarters of the total capital raised by the company had been subscribed by ordinary and preference shareholders, who retained control so long as the relatively small number of debenture holders got their interest - which by and large they did. They were very critical of anything that might allow the working companies, the GWR and the LSWR, to increase their grip by stealth, and were always on their guard against infiltrators. I recall the case of a man who was in the habit of getting up at half-yearly meetings to advocate the sale of the DNS to the GWR, until somebody took the trouble to look into his antecedents and discovered that he was an employee of the GWR. So when he next made a nuisance of himself, this fact was brought to light and he was shot down in flames!

Another source of this robust, independent spirit came, I think, from the character of the people who founded the DNS and imposed their stamp upon it from 1879 onwards. Take, for example, the first Chairman, Colonel Sir Robert Loyd-Lindsay, V.C. a very forceful character. He was a national figure, a most distinguished soldier, a founder of the Volunteer Movement that grew into the Territorial Army; he was also very wealthy. He could (and did) demand interviews with Sir Daniel Gooch, Chairman of the GWR, and he was not the sort of person that Sir Daniel would have dared refuse, let alone keep waiting in a corridor at Paddington station before being admitted to the presence. Some of Sir Robert's colleagues on the DNS board of those days were hardly less distinguished.

So in 1883 one of the biggest guns in the railway world in the person of James Staats Forbes had to be brought into action to stop this group of high-powered men from pushing their railway right into the heart of Southampton. Had they succeeded they would certainly have wrecked the prospective peace agreement that was then being negotiated between the GWR and LSWR, and which was felt to be of vital importance to both companies.

It is worth mentioning that those two companies had a lot of shareholders in common - influential people who could see no point in wasteful competition, and regarded a line like the DNS as a trouble-maker. They wanted to maintain the status quo, and maximise profits. Forbes was a very skilful operator. He was able to manipulate the board and to a large extent carry it with him, while the shareholders were split into warring factions. In one way or another he was able to impose his will upon the company for over ten years.

He faded into the background in 1894 and the shareholders then came together again, reasserting themselves in an effort to make their railway pay. In April 1894 a Traffic Committee composed of Southampton business men was appointed with full responsibility for the commercial management of the DNS.

The position at that time was that the two working companies, the GWR and the LSWR, were required to work and maintain their respective portions of the railway for such traffic as was presented to them, but were under no obligation to go out and look for traffic. Still less were they required to use the railway as a route for through traffic despite the saving in distance of six miles that it provided as between Southampton and Didcot compared with the Basingstoke and Reading route. However, if traders could be found who were prepared to consign traffic via the DNS, then the working companies would be hard put to refuse it.

The problem was that it was nobody's job to canvass for through traffic, nor if it were found were there any through rates at which it could be charged.

So the first thing that the Traffic Committee did was to appoint a Traffic Agent in Southampton. This was Mr. W.H.H.M. Gipps, who came from the London & North Western Rly and combined his job on the DNS with that of General Manager of the Lambourn Valley Rly. His title was soon changed to that of 'Traffic Manager' of the DNS. Office accommodation was leased at 11, Oxford Street, Southampton with the name of the company "Didcot, Newbury & Southampton Rly" prominently displayed outside. And there Gipps established himself complete with telephone, a stock of headed notepaper, and a junior clerk - very junior, I should think, as his starting salary was only 8/- per week!

Gipps opened his campaign by preparing and submitting to the Railway and Canal Commission an application for an order (and I quote), "...allowing through rates for merchandise traffic and the apportionment of such through rates as proposed by the applicants and objected to by the forwarding companies, or either of them." (The applicants, of course, were the DNS, and the objectors the GWR and LSWR.) Also for an order, "enjoining the forwarding companies, and each of them to afford all reasonable facilities for the through traffic of the applicants, and to desist from giving an undue and unreasonable preference and advantage to their own traffic, so that no obstruction may be offered to the public desirous of using the railway of the applicants as part of a continuous line of communication."

The DNS won its case, despite the opposition of the two big companies. Moreover it was confirmed on appeal, including the grant of through rates for merchandise traffic' "...from and to the Great Western stations at Reading and Paddington, to and from the South Western stations at Southampton and Southampton Docks."

Strictly speaking, this part of the order referred only to merchandise traffic, but that did not stop the Traffic Committee from persuading the GWR to put on a through passenger service between Southampton and Paddington starting on 1 July, 1897.

The up train left Southampton at 9.9am and was due at Paddington at 11.45am.; the return service was Paddington 5.45pm due Southampton at 8.20pm. I doubt whether these trains carried many through passengers - in fact the GWR was always complaining that they did not pay - but the up train at anyrate was very handy for getting valuable parcels and perishable traffic up to London fairly early in the day.

Then at the end of the century the advent of a newcomer caused a flurry of excitement. The London Extension of the Great Central Rly was opened in 1899, and while this line-was under construction the DNS Traffic Committee had considered a suggestion that it might be possible to build a connecting railway about 24 miles long from Didcot via Thame to Quainton Road. It was clearly rather a pipe dream - far too ambitious for either the DNS or

the Great Central to contemplate seriously. Instead, the Great Central, by agreement with the GWR, and with Great Western money, built the Woodford - Banbury link, 8¼ miles long, opened in 1900.

The Great Central, as a newcomer, was not tied by old traffic agreements to any particular route for its Southampton traffic. It could use the DNS route, which was in any case the shortest. So in 1901, a through passenger service was put on as an experiment between Leicester and Southampton. The DNS Traffic Committee on its part appointed an Inspector, "...to specially canvass for through passenger traffic to the Great Central Rly, for which that Company had proposed to pay half the expense, viz 30/- per week and commission."(to quote the actual minute). The man appointed was Mr. J. Donohoe, the DNS 'outdoor man' from the Southampton office. The through passenger service appears to have been a success, for on 1 July, 1903 it blossomed out into a restaurant car train between Southampton and York (later extended to Newcastle-on-Tyne) with stock provided by the Great Central.

Gipps died in 1903, and the DNS board then took a further step in strengthening the alliance with the Great Central by appointing a Great Central man to replace him. This was Alfred Murton Price, who left his job as District Superintendent at Leicester and took over the DNS office in Southampton in August 1903. He had then a staff of three, namely, Inspector Donohoe and a junior clerk, plus a senior clerk, Charles Bain, who had been appointed in 1898, and who remained with the company until it was absorbed by the Great Western in 1923.

Price provides most of this early information for it was his habit to submit monthly reports to the Traffic Committee through the DNS head office in London, and by great good fortune many of these have survived. Neither are they soulless documents, quite the contrary, for they contain all sorts of vivid and *far-ranging* comment which adds up to an almost day-to-day picture of events on the DNS as seen through the eyes of its Traffic Manager.

They are also revealing of Price himself, and to me at any rate suggest a rather engaging personality. Indeed, I will introduce him to you by reading in full a tribute that he paid to Frederic Goodenough, a member of the Traffic Committee who had recently died. Price included this with his report dated 14 December, 1916.

"If I may be pardoned perhaps for adding to my report a few words in appreciation of the services Mr.Goodenough rendered to the Company. Meeting him as I did almost every week in the Corn Exchanges at Newbury and Winchester, and often at Reading, I knew well the keen interest he took in the affairs of the Company, and how in his own quiet way he worked for the good of the Company.

Mr.Goodenough was a trader in a large way of business himself and in the days before the War he had a considerable traffic through Southampton.

All this traffic, wherever it was possible to do so, he sent over our Railway, and if he had any doubt as to whether traffic could or could not be conveyed by our Railway, he invariably advised me and left the routeing in my hands.

Many have been the disputes I have had with the London & South Western Rly as to Rates and Routes from information I have obtained in this way, and in most of them I have been able to establish the Company's position.
But in addition to his own traffic he was in a position to ascertain, and did ascertain, the movement of other traffic, and the information he gave me from time to time was of the greatest assistance in my efforts to increase the traffic over the line.

I have spoken only of Mr.Goodenough as I knew him, but I have been told of, and have records of the valuable evidence he gave in the Company's 'Rates and Routes' case before the Railway Commission in 1895, and also of the good work he did in connection with the 'Southampton & Winchester Great Western Junction Railway Bill' before Parliament in 1901.

By his death the Traffic Committee have, I think, lost a valuable member, and I know that I have lost a good friend".

This, I think, gives some idea of the nature of Price's job, how he set about it, his disputes with the working companies, while it reveals also his obviously very friendly relationship with his employers.
Much of his comment was intended to explain variations in traffic receipts as between one period and another. For the great bulk of the originating traffic on the DNS was farm produce, subject to seasonal variations, and at the mercy of the weather. Here is a typical reference in a report for February, 1910.

"The effects of the bad harvest last year are still noticeable in the weight of agricultural produce, hay, straw etc. put on rail, especially at stations on the Newbury Section.As an instance, I may mention Upton Station where, during the month of February, little or no straw traffic was put on rail, whereas under ordinary circumstances a considerable traffic is done at that time of year. There was also a decrease of 25 tons in the quantity of apples sent from Upton to London as compared with 1909".

Under the heading of farm produce comes milk, with the attendant problem of getting it fresh to the consumer. Farmers at Hampstead Norris complained of delays in getting milk to London, so, Price went off to investigate (October, 1912:

"I have made full enquiry into the matter at Newbury, and have also seen the Great Western Company at Paddington. The milk is now getting to London at 11am, but the farmers consider that it should arrive at 10am.I have satisfied myself that under existing circumstances it is impossible to get the milk away regularly from Newbury by the 8.40am train, and that there is not much cause for complaint of the 11am arrival.

Mr.W.A. Mount has interested himself in the matter on behalf of Mr. Wasey and Mr. de Vitre, I have seen Mr. Mount and explained the circumstances to him, and have also seen Mr. Wasey and Mr. de Vitre."
W.A. Mount was a director of the DNS, owner of the large Wasing Estate east of Newbury. Mr. Wasey and Mr. de

Vitre were presumably two of his tenant farmers. Price had frequent battles with the GWR about poor services, especially for goods traffic. Here he is in November, 1912 complaining about the working of goods trains: "I have had much correspondence and many interviews with the Great Western Company's officials at Paddington and at Reading....The Great Western Company state that much of the delay to the down trains has been caused by fog and by congestion of traffic, particularly at Reading. I am, of course, well aware of the difficulties caused by fog but the continuous bad working of the trains cannot be put down altogether to this cause. I have also pointed out that some of the congestion now experienced at Reading may be removed by making more use of our Railway for Through Traffic and so avoiding Reading altogether".

The Great Western then proceeded to pass the buck." With regard to the working of up trains" Price continued, "the Great Western state that late arrivals of trains from the London & South Western line cause late departures from Winchester, and further delays after leaving Winchester through the trains getting out of course".

Price's comment about congestion at Reading, and the possibility of relieving it by using the DNS as a through route touched a very sore spot - the cause of much ill-feeling between the two companies. For, if it suited them, the GWR was not above using the DNS as a kind of pawn in disputes with the LSWR. Witness a reference to the traffic in January 1909, when, according to Price, the Southampton Docks traffic, "...was worked over this Company's line for eleven days instead of via Basingstoke in consequence of some dispute between the Great Western and London & South Western Companies".

This limited and brief diversion of traffic from the Basingstoke route seems to have yielded about £500 additional revenue to the DNS, so it is not surprising that the shareholders felt aggrieved when the GWR declined to make a proper use of their line. In diplomatic terms I would say that relations between the two companies were correct, but never cordial.

Twelve months later, in November 1913, Price once more complained of bad timekeeping: "The working of trains, both passenger and goods trains, has of late been far from satisfactory, and I have devoted a good deal of my time to this matter during the past month in travelling with the various trains, the only means I have of ascertaining the actual working.

On 31 October I addressed a strong letter of protest to the Great Western Company on the subject, pointing out that working such as had been experienced of late could under no circumstances be considered a proper fulfilment of their obligations under the Working Agreement.

Since then there has been a decided improvement, and the Great Western Company inform me that they have put on additional men to cope with the work, and so ensure more punctual working".

The Working Agreement referred to by Price required the GWR to work, staff, and maintain about 42 miles of the DNS between Didcot and Winchester, charging for their services 60% of the gross traffic receipts applicable to that section. The LSWR was likewise responsible for just over two miles from Winchester to Shawford Jct. For this they received a lump sum of £750 per annum, plus 50% of the gross receipts in excess of that figure arising from traffic using that bit of line.

The Great Western does not seem to have been over-generous with staff and did not take kindly to criticism of the arrangements made at Winchester Sheep Fair on 23 October, 1912, when 41 wagons of sheep were conveyed to places north of Winchester, but only two for London & South Western stations south of Winchester.

"We might", says Price "have done better this year with traffic for the London & South Western line if better arrangements had been made at Winchester for dealing with the traffic, and I have got rather into trouble with the Great Western Company for suggesting that there were not sufficient men on duty at Winchester for loading up the traffic, or at any rate that the best use was not made of the men available during the busiest part of the morning.

The Fair is held at Bar End, which is just outside our yard at Winchester, and all the traffic for the London & South Western line has to pass the entrance to our yard to get to the London & South Western station.

Owing to the delay in loading up the sheep etc. during the earlier part of the morning, our yard and pens were blocked up with stock, and drovers preferred to walk their stock on to the London & South Western station rather than wait about in the road until they could get into our yard."

What a fascinating glimpse of life in Winchester a century ago - hundreds of sheep milling around, and being driven through the town from one station to the other in the middle of the morning!

Sheep both as creatures and also as traffic were also quite unpredictable. At Overton Sheep Fair on 18 July, 1916 "We loaded up 27 wagons of sheep at our Whitchurch Station, compared with 17 last year".

That was quite good. But, alas, at Alresford Sheep Fair held about 10 days later (27 July, 1916) it was a different story: ""We usually get a fair amount of traffic at our King's Worthy station from this Fair, but on this occasion we got none, although we had made all arrangements and had 20 cattle wagons at the station.

Owing to the intense heat and dusty roads, the sheep could not be walked the six miles to King's Worthy station".

It was the same the following day at Weyhill Sheep Fair, "In ordinary times we get about 10 wagons to load at our Whitchurch station, but last year, owing to heavy military movements from Salisbury Plain, we dealt with the bulk of the traffic from Weyhill at our Whitchurch station, loading up 55 wagons of sheep on the two days following the Fair. This year the intense heat prevented any sheep being walked the ten miles. Inspector Donohoe attended both Fairs".

Other livestock included horses, about 7,000 per annum, mostly at stations north of Newbury, but some at stations serving the Highclere Estate, from Lord Carnarvon's famous stud.

Fruit was important - and very perishable, especially strawberries. Price secured for the line a share of the Hampshire crop, and claimed that he could offer growers a better service than they would get at London & South Western stations. In a single day (19 June 1922) 12,000 baskets were despatched, "…from our Winchester station to London, the Midlands, the North of England, and Scotland. I have already mentioned (he claimed) that strawberries which left Winchester between 3pm and 4pm in the afternoon were in Edinburgh at 4am the next morning".

Quite a lot of fruit from South Africa passed over the line, described by Price as "Cape Fruit Traffic". In a report dated 5 February, 1912 under this heading, he says, "This traffic has commenced again, and we have had several consignments to the Continent via Grimsby".

He then gives the number of consignments forwarded at weekly intervals up to 3 February, when 209 packages were despatched, but on that date "the Cape Boat arrived late, and a large quantity of fruit could not be loaded in time for despatch by our 9-8am train". Now this was the through passenger train from Southampton to Paddington, and if Grimsby fruit was carried on this train, how did it reach its destination?

Perhaps it was transferred at Reading on to the Great Central's through train from Deal via Sheffield to Manchester. In that way, it could have reached Grimsby in time to catch the Great Central's night sailing to Hamburg.

In the opposite direction, there is reference to fish traffic from Grimsby via the DN S to Southampton, but no details are given.

The new potato traffic from St. Malo, mainly for the London market, was an enterprise started in 1901, and continued until the outbreak of war in 1914. The DNS chartered vessels and charged the traffic at through rates per ton from St. Malo to destinations in this country. The proceeds were credited to a separate account called the 'St. Malo Fund' free from the prying eyes of the working companies who, of course, got their agreed proportion for the railborne part of the journey, but did not share in the profits of the enterprise as a whole.

I will read an extract from Price's report on the 1912 season to give some idea of what was involved:-
"I finished up the St. Malo Potato Season on Saturday, July 6 when the boats were redelivered to the owners:-
S/s Puffin on Friday evening July 5
S/s Ophir on Saturday evening July 6.
Since the commencement of the season on May 20 we have made 40 voyages, 20 with each boat, and have brought over 4,930 tons, an average of 124 tons per voyage". (He then gives the results for the previous three years, and goes on): "I cannot say that the season has been altogether a satisfactory one. I commenced running the boats on 20 May, somewhat earlier than usual, on strong recommendations to me from merchants in London and also in St Malo that the crop was exceptionally early, and that heavy shipments would be made at once.

The result of the working during May was, however, somewhat disappointing, our average cargoes being only about 70 tons. Then again in June, when heavy cargoes were coming over, we had the strike of Transport Workers in Southampton. From June 11 to June 20 we were unable to coal the boats in Southampton and had to do the coaling at St. Malo. Although there was no great difficulty in getting labour for discharging the cargoes in Southampton during the continuance of the strike, we had some difficulty in protecting the men who were at work from the interference of the Strikers 'Pickets, who did their utmost to prevent the men from working.

This somewhat delayed the work, and we had a hard push to get the boats discharged and back again to St. Malo for the following day's sailing".

Now everybody must have worked very hard, not least the crews of the little ships on charter to the DNS, and it is typical of the company that it appreciated their efforts.

The Traffic Committee minutes of the 29June, 1904 contain this entry: "The Traffic Manager reported that it was usual to allow the captains of the boats a gratuity at the end of the season, and asked that an allowance be made this year. RESOLVED - that an allowance of £15 for each boat be made for the gratuities to the captains etc."

In 1904 £15 was quite a lot of money - quite enough to enable "the captains etc." to have a pretty good night out in Southampton, if that were the intention, as I suspect it was!

Tuning now to passenger traffic, it was the job of the working companies - of the Great Western in particular - to advertise services, including excursions etc., but the DNS Traffic Committee through its Traffic Manager was always on the lookout for improvements. Thus Price reports that "commencing 1st October, (1912) our 7.44am train from Newbury to Southampton was altered to leave at 7.32am, and to arrive at Southampton at 9.20am instead of 9.41am as formerly. The train now gives a connection at Eastleigh with the 9.12am Eastleigh to Portsmouth due to arrive Portsmouth at 10.6am, and thereby meets complaints which I have received from time to time of the want of an early morning service to Portsmouth from stations on our line. The train also gives now a connection to the Bournemouth line by the 9.17am from Eastleigh due to arrive Bournemouth at 11.0am".

Price gave most attention to special traffic of all kinds, and to through traffic. He always reported on the race specials from Southampton to Newbury. These seem to have carried an average of about 200 passengers per train and went through to the Racecourse station. Starting with the Autumn Meeting of the 23 and 24 September, 1910 they were worked throughout by London & South Western engines and crews - not always with complete success. For on Friday, 27 September, 1912 (to quote Price), "…the engine of the Special Train failed when near Litchfield. A goods engine was standing at Burghclere at the time, which was utilised to work the train forward to Newbury. The train arrived at Race Course Station about 30 minutes late".

The cause of the failure is not stated, but with 260 passengers on board the South Western engine may have run out of steam on the 1 in 106 gradient up to Litchfield. Whatever the cause, I fancy there would have been some red faces at Eastleigh or Southampton when it became known that a Great Western goods engine had come to the rescue!

1912 was a rather unlucky year for the race trains; bad weather ruined the January meeting. Heavy rain on the 17 of the month caused a very small attendance, and the special carried only 50 passengers. "On Thursday, 18 January" says Price, "a heavy fall of snow necessitated the abandonment of racing. Our train left Southampton before the official notice of the abandonment of the fixture was received. The train was, however, turned back at Shawford, and the fares were refunded to the passengers who had taken tickets".

The DNS staff met ships on arrival at Southampton, on the lookout for passengers wishing to travel north. "From the S/S 'Dongola' which arrived on January 17 (1912) we had 21 passengers for stations in the Midlands and the North of England. Prom the S/S 'Somali' which arrived on January 21 we got 12 passengers for Tynemouth and North Shields".

These were in fact troopships - a fairly regular source of through passenger traffic. More exotic was a Norwegian Ship's Crew: "On 30 October (1912), we secured a ship's crew Southampton to Grimsby on their way to Norway. For this crew, who had with them a large quantity of personal effects, I was able to arrange a Through Coach Southampton to Grimsby".

I wonder how Price got hold of his through coach. Not, I fancy, from the GWR or LSWR, neither of whom would have relished the idea of one of their coaches going off into the wilds of Humberside, not knowing when or in what condition it would return.

It is more than likely that Price wired his former colleagues on the Great Central for one to be sent down from Woodford or Leicester. One knows from other entries that he had a sort of 'hot line' to senior Great Central officers, perhaps even to the General Manager. For the matter of that, he could bring influence to bear in a number of places, and was quite capable of a bit of 'arm twisting' if needs be: "During the past week" (this was in March, 1913)"we have had a large Furniture Removal from Preshaw House near Winchester to Thame. The removal consisted of 8 Furniture Vans and 6 Box Wagons. Through outside influence with Messrs Maple & Co. of London (who did the work) I was able to arrange this, after the Great Western Company had failed".

But he was not always successful. On the 3 March, 1913,the 1st Battn. The Wiltshire Regiment was due to disembark at Southampton, so Price at once tried to secure this traffic for the DNS. "On February 25 I ascertained that the Regt. would go from Southampton to Devizes, instead of to Tidworth as had previously been announced.

I at once wrote to the War Office asking that the "route" to Devizes might be issued by this Company's line via Newbury, pointing out that during the present Trooping Season my Company had not been favoured with the movement of any large number of Troops. "Mr. Vokes" (he was Secretary of the D.N. & S. at the Head Office in London) "was good enough also to write to Sir Edward Ward on the subject, who replied expressing regret that arrangements had already been made for the transit of the Regt., and promising to bear the matter in mind. "The Regiment travelled to Devizes via Andover and Wolfhall Junction, but was brought back from Devizes to Tidworth the same afternoon"!

This brings me to the subject of military traffic in peacetime an important but unreliable source of revenue, as is shown in Traffic Report for July, 1910, to take but one example.

Here Price explains that "...the principal cause of the large decrease in Through Passenger Traffic has been the entire absence of Military Traffic over the line in July this year compared with July last year, when a large muster of Territorial Troops was held in the New Forest, Lyndhurst, and Beaulieu Road district.

To this we carried 1,000 men of the Berkshire Regiment and the Oxford Light Infantry, the latter over the whole length of the line, and the former between Newbury and Shawford Junction".

Then in his end-of-year report he says, "1910 as a whole was a disappointing year. There was less Military Traffic, as the Summer Manoeuvres were held on the western side of Salisbury Plain and there were very few troops in Churn Camp. Winchester College Cadet Corps went to Highclere in November, 1909, but not in 1910".

Sands then adds a personal note, "This reminds me that my own first journey over the line south of Newbury was in an OTC special train from Marlborough to Winchester in the summer of 1923. I was lucky enough to get a corner seat on the outward journey, when we had a couple of GW Dean 0-6-0s from Newbury to Winchester."

Churn Camp, up in the Berkshire Downs, is worthy of special mention, as it was almost entirely dependent upon the railway for access. One or two rough farm tracks passed within reach, and it was possible to take vehicles over the open down in dry weather, but it was a long way from any. metalled road.

All postal telegrams to and from the Camp were dealt with at Churn station, and the DNS received commission on every telegram. This amounted to quite a useful sum. Commenting on the results for the second half of 1909, Price mentions an increase of £27-14-6 in Commissions from Telegrams "attributable to the large military camp at Churn".

It was a tented camp, normally open from early May to mid-September, and served mainly as a training place for Territorial units. It could hold upwards of 2,000 men, plus the army transport of the period, horses, mules etc., all requiring fuel and fodder. So Churn Camp was capable of generating a lot of traffic. Incidentally, a first-class row broke out in 1906 between the DNS and the working companies when it was discovered that Government traffic from Southampton to Churn, under some pretext or other, was being conveyed via Basingstoke

and Reading, although legally it was 'local' to the DNS.

Churn station[1] was staffed only whilst the camp was open, and consisted of a single platform plus a siding controlled from a ground frame. It was not a Block post.

The outbreak of the first World War on 4 August, 1914 found the camp full of troops, and they seem to have been left there whilst Regular Army formations were assembling within easy reach of Southampton before being shipped overseas. Then towards the end of the month there was a clearout, followed immediately by a fresh intake on 30 and 31 August when, according to Price, "19 special trains with troops, mostly cavalry, were worked into Churn Camp".

A Sunday passenger service was put on for their benefit, starting as one train each way on 6 September, increased to two on the 13 September, and to four on the 20 September. This Sunday service continued until the camp was closed on 19 October (a month later than usual) when the troops were moved into billets in Wantage and neighbourhood.

The camp reopened on 7 May, 1915 when the South Midland Brigade assembled there, 2,000 strong with a large number of horses, before moving away on 23 June in 12 trains to King's Lynn.

Price's wartime reports are of absorbing interest, as Southampton was the main port of embarkation for large bodies of troops, and the DNS was very much involved. From the 6 to the 22 August, 1914 activity was intense, and again early in September. Price mentions the 8 September as one of the heaviest days, when 116 trains were worked into Southampton, during 24 hours, followed by 92 trains on the 9 September. Most of these came down the LSWR main line, but during the earlier phase in August, the DNS was extensively used, and it was the practice to load up troop trains at Winchester (DNS) and also in Bar End goods yard in preference to the LSWR.

In the middle of August there was an 'invasion' scare. "On the 14 and 15 August", says Price," the passenger service between Winchester and Newbury was entirely suspended. On these dates 16 trains with troops were loaded up at Winchester, Cheesehill, and despatched to the East Coast".

Then reinforcements started to roll in, including 950 recruits from the Manchester area, who arrived at Winchester (DNS) early in September. And on 10 October, two specials from Fishguard were worked over the line from Didcot with troops bound for Hursley Park, where the 8th Division was assembling. All these men needed proper accommodation for the winter months, and on 7 November, 1914, Price reported that "a new Military Camp is now being formed at Avington Park about 2¼ miles from our Winchester Station".

This camp, with others at Morn Hill and Winnall Down north east of Winchester, developed into a large military complex, and some quite elaborate plans were drawn up to serve it by rail. These were whittled down to a modest branch from the DNS leading into the camps from the north end of Winchester tunnel, but even this was not ready until nearly the end of the war. Price says that the connection to the DNS was put in on 20 October, 1918.

Throughout the war there was a very heavy two-way traffic up and down the line. Army units assembled at various centres nearby, dispersed on embarkation leave, and the men then rejoined their units before moving down to troop ships at Southampton.

As to goods traffic - it was overwhelming. "On one day", says Price, "we had 250 wagons standing in our yard at Winchester, and about another 100 standing at Newbury and Didcot waiting to come down".

Of course, the railway just did not have the capacity for traffic on that scale. It was still single-track throughout, and some of the crossing loops were unduly short; Highclere loop could take no more than 19 wagons plus engine and van. So normal services suffered very badly. Passenger trains were often cancelled without notice, and the service was cut right down.

In February, 1915, the last Didcot line train out of Southampton departed at 11-45am; all the afternoon trains were taken off.

Price complained bitterly in the course of some heated correspondence with Charles Aldington, General Manager of the GWR, who pleaded "the abnormal times", and lack of rolling stock. Price admitted all this, but added, "I feel, however, that it does not pass the wit of your Company and the London & South Western Company to make some arrangement whereby it will be possible for us to have one train in the late afternoon from Southampton".

For the DNS staff at Southampton, the outbreak of war meant virtually the end of their normal commercial activities. The Junior Clerk, E J Burley, joined the Army, was drafted to the 5th Battalion, The Hampshire Regiment, and was later sent out to India. It was typical of the DNS board that they at once decided to make up his Army pay of 7/- per week to the 25/- per week that he was getting from the Company. It was equally typical of Price to mention Burley from time to time in his reports, and express concern about his health in India.

These wartime reports reveal some very mixed feelings. Frustration and dismay, that the DNS could no longer give a normal service to the growing band of regular customers that Price and others had so patiently built up, were mingled with the satisfaction of seeing the railway properly used for the first time in its history.

When the war was over, Government control of the railway system continued while the grouping of the independent companies was discussed. Inevitably, under the Railways Act, 1921 it was the fate of the DNS to be absorbed by the GWR.

Under the terms of the Absorption Scheme and in accordance with the Act, the Great Western Company was required to compensate or provide for the Didcot Company's staff. But in addition the directors of the DNS on 14 December, 1922 placed the following minute on record; "The Board deferred to the long service of the Secretary (Mr. J G Vokes), 42 years, the Traffic Manager, nearly 20 years, and the two Clerks, and it was moved by Mr.Sidney Herbert, seconded by Sir William A. Mount, Bart, and unanimously RESOLVED; That the sum of £800 be voted and paid to Mr. Alfred M Price, Traffic Manager to the Company, £600 to Mr James G Vokes, Secretary to the Company, and the sums of £100 to Mr Bain and Mr Dineen as gratities and special compensation allowance for loss of office from this Company on its absorption by the Great Western Company" (Mr. Dineen was Clerk in the London office).

One feels that they had richly deserved it, Price in particular and also his Chief Clerk, Charles Bain, who had been at the Southampton office since 1898, and was often left in charge. For it had been an uphill fight in which every item counted - every additional passenger, every basket of strawberries, every gasping sheep being driven along some hot and dusty road.

But quite a lot had been gained. In the 20 years from 1894 to 1913 inclusive traffic receipts on the DNS more than doubled, and were still rising when war broke out in 1914.

The exploits of Sam Fay in rescuing the MSWJ from bankruptcy are well known, largely because they formed the prelude to a dazzling career in the railway service. The achievement of Alfred Murton Price and his efforts over a period of 20 years to increase the traffic on the Didcot, Newbury & Southampton Rly were less spectacular perhaps, but no less rewarding to his company. Moreover there have survived these fascinating, personal reports on his activities, which I feel deserve to be better known."

1 . It may be of passing interest that Churn features in a fictional book of railway detective stories by (Canon) V L Whitechurch , under the title, 'Thrilling stories of the Railway', originally published in 1912. The book was reissued as 'Stories of the Railway' in 1977. The facilities at Churn are described well, even if the plot is perhaps somewhat far-fetched.

Meeting at Newbury on 14 January 1943 re DN & S line. Thirteen persons present, representing Traffic, Engineering, Signal and Chief Mechanical Engineers departments.

"The proposal to bring the Didcot and Newbury doubling into use (except for temporary single line between Upton and Compton) was discussed and accepted. Temporary hand-worked catch points will be required at both Upton and Compton on the second line upon which the contractors will be working. No plant will be in use. Mr. Cunningham [Engineering Department] will inform the Divisional Engineer when the lines will be ready for inspection. Ilsley Signals will be brought into use when the double line is opened. The doubling between Newbury East Junction and Hermitage was brought into use on the 10th instant. It was agreed that a fortnights notice shall be given of the opening date. In the meanwhile the signal department will submit the usual particulars for the printed notice.

Newbury and Winchester line.

The jobs in hand on this section are too numerous to permit of the reinstatement of the passenger service but this will be borne in mind and a proposal submitted as early as possible. The outstanding works are;

Enborne to Woodhay - Opening of the double line, contractors still working on adjustments etc.

Litchfield - Work in hand, but no dates can be quoted.

Whitchurch -Work progressing and the Up facing points will be laid in next Sunday. The Down loop will be temporarily out of use and the south end of the yard will be closed for two days. A variation in the type of catchpoint at the Winchester end will involve an alteration in the position of the picking up post and an alternative site will be selected.

Lodge Bridge - Work in hand.

Worthy Down. - Work in hand. The divisional engineer is arranging for the contractor to work with plant on a chalk face in the cutting for 3-4 weeks. This work will foul the single line but can be fitted in with other work and save line occupation later. Attention was called to the proposed semaphore arms leading from the two up single lines (GW and SR) to the sidings, and ground discs were suggested. The distance from the signals to the catch points is 130 yards and the detection at three pairs of points is necessary. The signal department stated this could not be satisfactorily achieved with ground discs.

Wagons under load. - Special attention was called to the number of ballast wagons under load, viz. 148 at Didcot, 168 at Newbury Racecourse, 50 at Hermitage and 60 at Yarnton........

Runaway Catchpoints. - The diagrams have been approved by local officers. The engineer asks for early approval to enable the work to be put in hand. Agreed catchpoint boards be fixed at signals where such exist in advance of catchpoints in station loops.

Water columns. - Whitchurch. The local water supply should be connected up at once and the Loco Department will press for this.

Level Crossings. - Fishers Lane completed except that a 2' extension of the cattle grid on the up side is necessary and the fence has to be made good.

Compton. - Work still in hand.

Picking up and setting down posts. - Proposals have been agreed but Whitchurch (down) requires reconsideration.

Air raid shelters for signal boxes. - Inspector Mealings [Traffic Department] will chalk out positions for the shelters in the signal boxes any adjustments of fittings etc. will be carried out by the contractor. ....

Next meeting 21 February 10.30 a.m. Newbury.'

It would appear these progress meetings were held weekly with a further report reproduced below and believed to date from 4 February - *or perhaps even a combination of reports..*

'Didcot to Newbury. - Work has been delayed by the recent bad weather and the programme has been amended as set out below for openings for goods trains. Didcot to Upton and Hermitage to Hampstead Norris: 14 February, Hampstead Norris to Compton: 28 March, (token Instruments will be installed in Hampstead Norris Box for use between Feb. 14 and 28. Compton to Upton - date in March.

Newbury to Winchester

Agreed that subject to the effects of any bad spell of weather the Bank of England trains can be restored as from Monday 15 February.

Worthy Down station is incomplete, the Winchester to Worthy Down train is not to be reintroduced at present. The signal department work at Worthy Down Box will not be completed but the token instruments will be installed and semaphore signals will be erected but not connected up until March 1 when it is to be hoped that the signalling work will be completed. The traffic department will provide a Groundsman to work the points as required for train running and to assist the signal department. As from midnight on Sunday 14 February, absolute block (token) working will be reintroduced between Whitchurch and Winchester and any Engineers or Contractors occupations will be arranged between trains.

Enborne Junction to Woodhay. - Work still not completed but will be ready for the divisional engineers inspection next week and the doubling will be opened on February 15.

Litchfield. - New crossing loop will be opened on February 28.

the Divisional Engineer will inspect the work in the meantime.

Whitchurch. - Permanent way work is complete and the new box and signalling will be brought into use on February 21.

Worthy Down. - The position of the two up distants has not yet been agreed.

Wagons on hand. - Attention was called to the 116 on hand at Didcot. These are required at the northern end of the Didcot to Newbury line and the number will be reduced shortly.

Ballast, Contractors trains etc. - The future daily requirements are estimated to be; Didcot and Newbury section - 3 trains. Newbury and Winchester - 1 train. The present number varies from 4 to 7, the military train crews will be reduced accordingly.

Services for contractors staff. - Two trips will be saved if a bus is provided commencing at once to convey 18 men connecting with the 7.10 a.m. Oxford in the morning and the 6.45 p.m. Didcot in the evening. Messrs McAlpine wish to run their train (contractors engine, coach and brake) into Newbury station, returning to pick up men at their depot at Shaw at 7.30 a.m. on the following morning. A pilotman will be required on each trip and the locomotive department will arrange this.'

Due to labour shortages on the railway, most of the rebuilding work at this time was carried out by the contractors McAlpine using a variety of available labour. In certain areas GWR staff acted as supervisors and with the following brief account appearing in the *GREAT WESTERN ECHO* for Spring 1991, penned by D.H. Constable.

".....Six months before I finished my Pupilage, Mr. Page called me in and said that he wanted me to assist Jack Milton, the Chief Inspector, in the doubling of the Didcot-Newbury line and extension of crossing loops from Newbury to Winchester, ready for the invasion of Europe. Through this I was exempted from army service. We had a very tight schedule to work to, I won't detail the construction of the line, this has already been covered in various books, suffice to say I personally marked out and unloaded from special trains every signal from Didcot to Winchester and walked the line throughout at least three times. In the middle of this job I was made responsible for the construction of a new box, Bulls Lock at Newbury Racecourse.... . Half way through the work Jack Milton retired and Jack Howes took over as Chief Inspector. Jack Howes more or less let me get on with the job on my own, it was a great experience for one so young, not yet 21. I could write pages about the boxes on the Winchester-Didcot line and the LPTB staff on loan to do the work, the WBS Co. staff and the American Negroes who erected the new telegraph route from Didcot to Winchester in record time.

One last story against myself. Each crossing loop from Winchester to Newbury had a different War Office Account plus others for Bulls Lock and Didcot-Newbury. At the end of the job Mr. A.W. Woodbridge, who eventually took over from Mr. F.H.D. Page, gave me the accounts to settle up, as I had pinched Peter to pay Paul it was poetic justice! I especially remember allocating the sub-contractors account for painting signals! I forgot to add that while I was on this job I was paid £150 per year so for the last six months of my pupilage I paid the GWR and they paid me."

Former Didcot Fireman, Harold Gasson in his series of reminiscence books also refers to duty on the works trains over the line and that three trains were often working simultaneously on engineering tasks between Didcot and Winchester at any one time. Often this would involve a bus ride from Didcot in one or even both directions, little actual movement of the train being made.

Appendix - Examples of Train Services

	Passenger services Didcot to Newbury (Saturday only services in brackets)	Passenger Services Newbury to Winchester (Saturday only services in brackets)	Mixed services	Goods North of Newbury	Goods South of Newbury
October 1889	4	4	1	4	2
July/Sept 1894	5	5	1	Not given	Not given
Jan/Apr 1902	5	8 (1)	1	Not given	Not given
July 1923	5	6 (1)	1	7	2
Jun-Sept 1937	8 (1)	7		3	3
Winter 1955/56	6 (1)	6		Not given	Not given
Summer 1957	6 (1)	6		Not given	Not given
Winter 1957/8	6 (1)	6		Not given	Not given
Sept 1960 - June 1961	5 (1)			Not given	Not given

Appendix - Electric Token Configuration as originally installed c1919

Section	Configuration Type.	Token Machine No.	Section	Configuration Type.	Token Machine No.
Didcot East Junction - Upton & Blewbury	A	20	Enborne Junction - Woodhay	A	71
Upton & Blewbury - Didcot East Junction	A	78	Woodhay - Enborne Junction	A	73
Upton & Blewbury - Compton	B	86	Woodhay - Highclere	B	10
Compton - Upton & Blewbury	B	420	Highclere - Woodhay	B	85
Compton - Hermitage	C	105	Highclere - Burghclere	C	38
Hermitage - Compton	C	81	Burghclere - Highclere	C	225
Hermitage - Newbury East Junction	D	84	Burghclere - Litchfield	D	153
Newbury East Junction - Hermitage	D	66	Litchfield - Burghclere	D	23
			Litchfield - Whitchurch	A	56
			Whitchurch - Litchfield	A	349
			Whitchurch - Sutton Scotney	B	35
			Sutton Scotney - Whitchurch	B	2
			Sutton Scotney - Kings Worthy	C	157
			Kings Worthy - Sutton Scotney	C	53
			Kings Worthy - Winchester	D	263
			Winchester - Kings Worthy	D	215

Note: Electric Token working replaced the Electric Train Staff c1919. Authorisation was given for the work on 4 July 1918 at an estimated costs of £600. No date is given for it being brought into use although this likely have been shortly afterwards.

Details of any temporary installations provided in WW2 are not known.

Notes:

1. Up to 1942/43, token machines were located within the respective booking offices and therefore under the direct supervision of the Station Master. Consequent upon the rebuilding in WW2, replacement token machines were installed in the resited signal boxes although it is likely most configurations remained unaltered with the actual tokens moved by the signal department from the old to the new equipment. The instruments between Didcot and Newbury were of course removed at this time. The recovered instruments were returned to the signal stores at Reading and may well have been used elsewhere. Instrument No 85 (Highclere - Woodhay) was discovered in the signal stores at Shrewsbury in the late 1980s. It was subsequently saved by a private collector in the New Forest.

2. The removal of the crossing loop and closure of the signal box at Litchfield in 1936 would have altered the token section to read 'Whitchurch to Burghclere'. Whether the configuration was now 'D' or 'A' is not reported.

Appendix - Signal Boxes and Ground Frames

	Opened	Closed	Number of Levers	Cast nameplate and wording	Plate ordered from Reading Signal Works(1)	Notes
Upton & Blewbury	12-4-1882	10-8-1964	25	Upton Signal Box	3 –5-1894	25 levers from 2/1943
				Upton & Blewbury Signal Box	16-5-1911	
Churn	Not given		7	Churn Signal Box	12-7-1894	A GF rather than a SB
Compton	12-4-1882	10-8-1964	20	Compton Signal Box	3-5-1894	20 levers from 3/1920
Ground Frame	12-4-1882	April 1943		Compton Ground Frame	31-5-1894	
	12-4-1882	10-8-1964		Compton Crossing	Mar / Apr 1896	
				Compton Crossing Ground Frame	28-2-1898	
Hampstead Norris	12-4-1882	c1920	13	Hampstead Norris Signal Box	3-5-1894	
	18-4-1943	10-8-1964	23			
Ground Frame	c1920	18-4-1943		Hampstead Norris North Ground Frame	c1920	
Ground Frame	c1920	18-4-1943		Hampstead Norris South Ground Frame	c1920	
Brain's Siding (Pinewood Brickworks) Ground Frame	c1908	10-8-1964		Brains Siding Ground Frame	12-5-1908	
Hermitage	1-6-1891	10-8-1964	16 29	Hermitage Signal Box	3-5-1894	A GF would have been required prior to 1891. 29 levers from 1942
Ground Frame	12-4-1882	10-8-1964		Fishers Lane Crossing	Mar / Apr 1896	
Greenham Junction Newbury East Junction	c1882 6/1906	c1886 c1909 20-3-1978	24 84	Newbury East Junction Signal Box (2)	28-8-1908	
Enborne Junction	C1885 1907	1907 29-1-1967	21	Enborne Junction Signal Box	30-5-1894 and 7-10-1907	39 levers from 1942
Woodhay	4-5-1885 9-10-1942	9-10-1942 19-8-1964	16 23	Woodhay Signal Box	30-5-1894	
Ground Frame				Ground Frame	30-5-1894	(for Woodhay)
Highclere	4-5-1885 28-10-1942	28-10-942 6-2-1955	16 21	Highclere Signal Box	30-5-1894	
Ground Frame	6-2-1955	10-2-1964	2			

Burghclere	4-5-1885	13-11-1942	17	Burghclere	30-5-1894	
	13-11-1942	10-8-1964	28	Signal box		
Litchfield	4-5-1885	5-7-1936	16	Litchfield	30-5-1894	
	3-3-1943	23-1-1955	22	Signal Box		
Ground Frame	5-7-1936	3-3-1943				
	23-1-1955	10-2-1964	3			
Whitchurch	4-5-1885	3-3-1943	16	Whitchurch	30-5-1894	
	3-3-1943	10-8-1964	27	Signal Box		
Ground Frame	4-5-1885	3-3-1943	8	Whitchurch Ground Frame	30-5-1894	
Lodge Bridge	28-3-1943	7-3-1950	15			
Sutton Scotney	4-5-1885	6-11-1942	16	Sutton Scotney	30-5-1894	
	5-11-1942	10-8-1964	25	Signal Box		
Ground Frame	4-5-1885	4/1926		Sutton Scotney Ground Frame	30-5-1894	
Worthy Down	14-2-1943	10-8-1964	30	Worthy Down Jct.		
Ground Frame	c9-1917	14-2-1943		Worthy Down North Ground Frame	20-12-1917	
Ground Frame	c9-1917	14-2-1943		Worthy Down South Ground Frame	20-12-1917	
Kings Worthy	1909	21-12-1942	16	Kings Worthy	3 July 1908	
	21-12-1942	30-1-1955	28	Signal box		
Ground Frame	1909	21-12-1942		Ground Frame	3 July 1908	The reference states "For Kings Worthy"
Ground Frame 'A'	30-1-1955	13-4-1964	2			
Ground Frame 'B'	30-1-1955	13-4-1964	2			
Ground Frame		4-4-1966	2	Winnall Siding North Ground Frame	14-9-1904	Renamed Winnall Ground Frame from 5-4-1964
Ground Frame		5-4-1964	2	Winnall Siding South Ground Frame	14-9-1904	
Junction for Winnall Camp	1918	1920		Camp Siding Ground Frame	11-4-1919	
Winchester	4-5-1885	1922	17	Winchester	30-5-1894	16 levers plus 6 slides for route setting.
	1922	4-4-1966	16 later 27	Signal Box		Conventional 27 lever frame from 6/1933
Winchester Ground Frame	1891	4-4-1966		Winchester Ground Frame	15-3-1892	Located at Bar End

1. Signal Box nameplates: No reference has been found for Worthy Down signal box, although a cast plate in standard GWR style 'Worthy Down Jct.' was certainly fitted - see illustration p257. Records post 1939 are not necessarily complete hence there is no reference to Lodge Bridge. Stamped aluminium type nameplates 'Whitchurch Town' and 'Winchester Chesil' were fitted as replacements post 1950.

Prior to the inauguration of the GWR Country Lorry Service, the railway had only been responsible for goods whilst in their care or in rail transit. Movement of goods to the railway station or yard accomplished either by the consignor or an independent carrier. (These independent carriers were sometimes contracted by the railway for the delivery and collection of goods within a set radius.)

This type of arrangement lasted a number of years although it should be mentioned that certain of he larger employed an Outside Porter whose job it was to make local deliveries by hand-cart. As far as is known Winchester was the only DNS station to engage such a person: in 1904 this was Mr George Dean, of 14 Cheesehill Street (sic) Winchester.

Away from Winchester station, one of the local coal merchants at Bar End, A E Early also operated a parcels and delivery service. They combined this with furniture removals using horse-drawn vans. Soon after the turn of the century, Messrs White & Co who had offices at Silver Hill and also Station Hill (the later leading to the LSWR station) took over the cartage. White's also used horse drawn drays with stables for eight beasts at station hill approximately one mile from Bar End. In later years , the drays were supplemented by two Foden steam-wagons and a one-ton Ford van. Messrs White's were also engaged on similar work for the LSWR at Winchester.

Goods arriving at Winchester were various and would arrive by the 7.15 a.m. goods from Didcot. This

service would often run late which caused problems for the railway staff and drivers by having less time to unload and sort their wares – much sorting was undertaken in the goods shed – before having to leave and deliver to the shops in time for opening. Railway staff would simply unload the goods wagons, it was up to each White's driver to assess how he loaded his dray.

Each week there would be eight to ten trucks of beer arriving from Burton on Trent destined for the Winchester Brewery in Hyde Street. This load was treated as a priority whilst the weight demanded the use of one of the steam lorries. To clear the load the horse drawn drays would assist, although each was limited to a one ton load due to the hump in Bar End Road leading to the railway overbridge.

An additional vehicle working from Bar End was a Huntley & Palmers van: Huntley & Palmer had a large biscuit factory at Reading. The biscuits themselves were transported by railway wagon but unloaded at Bar End and delivered by the company van.

At the other stations on the DNS south of Didcot, similar local arrangements applied. Examples are at Sutton Scotney where Messrs Wheelers coal merchant, had a delivery contract whilst at Whitchurch it was a Mr Arthur Flint. At Burghclere various local persons were used including two carriers from nearby Kingsclere, Messrs Tom Chalk and George Pryer. Mr Chalk ran a coal merchants from the railway yard at Burghclere and in the process acted as carrier. (Litchfield appears to have used the services of the local lad-porter.) At Winchester Whites maintained their contract until 1931 when the GWR took over.

Meanwhile the GWR set up their 'Country Lorry Service' in the 1920s, with road vehicles based at Didcot (1928), Newbury and Kings Worthy (July 1928). From the outset the lorries would work anywhere in the area being able cover a wider range than their horse drawn predecessors. Neither was their work, initially at least, entirely railway orientated, for it was possible to hire a vehicle and driver for general haulage. It would appear there was some overlapping of the sphere of operation of each vehicle whilst the drivers were instructed to take the goods that had been collected to the nearest suitable station for transshipment to rail and which might not necessarily be their own home location.

In general the system worked well although there was for a time confusion with goods consigned to a location where there was a similarity or duplication of name. So far as the DNS were concerned this invariably happened at Litchfield (Lichfield–Staffordshire) and Whitchurch (several of this latter name existing on the GWR system). Locally difficulties would also arise where the railway station was not in the immediate vicinity of the village of the same name, Woodhay, Highclere and Burghclere.

The first road lorry (perhaps the term 'road motor'

GWR Delivery lorry outside the front of Winchester Chesil.

Recorded at a country fair some years ago was this restored Thorneycroft road-motor. The colour scheme may be doubtful for GWR days but even so it does provide for an delightful example of earlier days.

might be better used) at Kings Worthy was an AEC, later replaced by a Daimler having solid tyres and finally a Scammel and trailer. The choice of Kings Worthy rather than Winchester might appear strange but this was to effect a saving for if a vehicle was based in what was then classified as area overseen by a Rural District Council, then a saving of 4/- weekly was possible on the wage for the driver compared with a City Council area. The fact the vehicle after it left Kings Worthy invariably spent most of its time around Winchester was irrelevant.

Just three men are believed to have been involved with the Kings Worthy lorry. From 7/1929 to 7/1930: W Rolfe. Mr Rolfe had transferred from Compton where he had been employed as a Porter, after leaving Kings Worthy he went to Maidenhead. He was replaced by J F Bates who remained in post until June 1930. It is believed Mr Bates may have been employed beforehand at Newbury, although it is known he came to work each day by motor-cycle. He left following an accident on the way to work. The final driver was Fred D Cooper who was at Kings Worthy from July 1931 and remained with the railway after the vehicle was transferred to Winchester in 1935. Fred had previously been employed at Morris Cowley which is where he first became acquainted with motor vehicles. He recounted he was 4/- a week worse off by taking up the Kings Worthy post. (Two other men were also employed as drivers at Bar End and which may be taken to probably refer to the post of 'relief driver' or if the fleet were subsequently increased on a temporary (seasonal?) basis. These were, in May 1935: J Lawson who transferred from High Wycombe, and then in October 1940: W J Ewins, who moved to Winchester from Paddington.)

At Kings Worthy, the lorry was parked overnight on the slope leading from the yard to the road with the practice to 'bump-start' it in the morning. If this failed recourse had to be made to the starting handle and if this was unsuccessful a fitter would have to be summonsed, the nearest GWR man being at Theale.

Petrol was kept in a locker in the yard, the driver being the only man with the key whilst he also had to account for its use. Fred recalls he was sometimes engaged by Framer Bragg from nearby Headbourne Worthy who would entrust the lorry with odd jobs, such as transporting hurdles to Newbury. (It was considered more convenient to take the load the whole way by road rather than transshipping twice at the local station and again at Newbury. In this way the future fortunes of the railway as a carrier for goods could already be seen.)

Other jobs undertaken were collecting sacks of corn from fields destined for the flour mill at Andover, after which the vehicle would definitely require a wash. There were even times when it was necessary to leave the lorry at Newbury, Fred having to return home by train and repeat the rail journey in the morning.

The Daimler especially is recalled with affection as it was fitted with a windscreen. Even so there were disadvantages as the headlights were only of paraffin and had a habit of going out on the longer journeys. The Daimler was also the first time the words 'Country Lorry service' appeared on the side, previous to this it was just the letters 'GWR' as indicating ownership.

With the vehicle transferred to Winchester it was the practice to provide some limited protection from the elements by parking overnight under one of the goods shed loading canopies. Fred recalled a long distant trip when some sheep destined for the Midlands were taken as far as Banbury by road and here transferred to another lorry which had come down from Birmingham.

Shortly after Fred's transfer to Winchester the first Scammel arrived, several trailers being provided. At the time there were now three horse-drawn vans used for local work, one retained specifically for parcels and the other two for general and shop goods. The horse drawn vans were withdrawn after the outbreak of war with the former stables converted for other uses after 1940. (Horses were apparently used for wagon shunting at Bar End until this time. Elsewhere it was not uncommon for the local coal merchant to use his own horse to move his wagon to a more convenient location and possibly assist the station staff on occasions with a wagon they too might need re-positioning. It should be mentioned that at Upton & Blewbury and probably at other stations as well, tethering rings were provided on the side of the good sheds.)

The Scammel was employed in the cartage of steel used for the Winchester by-pass, often grossly overloaded, with the metal scraping the road behind.

After 1950, the Southern Region withdrew the Bar End vehicle concentrating road services at Winchester City although much of the work still emanated from the former GWR yard. The SR lorry from Micheldever also took over dealing with the stations from Litchfield south, whilst a strange quirk was that the WR lorry from Newbury was still responsible for the stations as far south as Burghclere. Eventually the Andover based lorry took over south of Newbury, as indeed has been spoken of earlier when referring to the delivery of drinking water to Woodhay.

Appendix - Operating Instructions from the 1931 GWR Sectional Appendix

UPTON AND BLEWBURY.

When vehicles are detached from Down Trains the Points must always be set for the Siding while a vehicle is standing on the running line.

No shunting operations must be performed at Compton end of Station until "Train out of Section" has been received for previous Train.

After the passing of the last Train, the Didcot East End Signalman must withdraw a token which will be used for shunting operations on the Branch Line during the time Upton Box is closed. The token to be replaced in the pillar when Upton Signal Box is opened.

CHURN -GROUND FRAME.

1. The Frame controlling the Siding Points is locked by a key on the Upton and Compton Electric Token.

2. The person in charge of the Station will be held responsible for seeing the whole of the work performed at the Siding is properly carried out and that the Staff is handed back to the Engineman after the necessary work has been done, the Points properly set, and the Ground Frame locked.

3. The Head Guard of any Train requiring to call at the Siding must satisfy himself that the work is complete and that the Token has been handed back to the Driver, before giving the "Right Away" Signal.

COMPTON LEVEL CROSSING.

The Gates at this Crossing may be closed across the Railway between Trains.

The Gatekeeper will be responsible for keeping a good look out, and immediately the bell rings and the Disc shows that a Train is approaching from either direction, the Gates must be closed across the roadway, and the Signals lowered for the Train to pass.

Before the Gates are closed across the Railway, the Gatekeeper must be sure that the Signals are standing at Danger.

HAMPSTEAD NORRIS - GROUND FRAME.

1. The Frame controlling the Station Points is locked by a key on the Compton and Hermitage Electric Token.

2. The Officer in charge of the Station will be held responsible for seeing the whole of the work performed at the Station is properly carried out, and that the Token is handed back to the Engineman after the necessary work has been done, the Points properly set, and the Ground Frame locked.

3. The Head Guard of any Train requiring to call at the Station must satisfy himself that the work is complete and that the Token has been handed back to the Driver before giving the "Right Away" Signal.

BRAIN'S SIDING BETWEEN HERMITAGE AND HAMPSTEAD NORRIS.

1. This Siding is connected with the Didcot and Newbury Line by a facing junction for Trains coming from the direction of Newbury and is situated on the East side of the line about 1 mile from Hermitage Station.

2. The Points are worked from a two-lever Ground Frame, which is locked by the Annett's key attached to the Hermitage and Compton Electric Token.

3. The Siding, which runs alongside the Single Line, is divided by the connection from the Didcot and Newbury Line into the Sand Pit Siding on the North and the Brick Kiln Siding on the South. A gate is placed across each of these Sidings and one key is kept by the Foreman of the Works and the other must be kept in the Ground Frame. The gates must always be locked across the rails when the Siding is in use

4. The Guard in charge of the Train must obtain the Token from the Driver and unlock the Ground Frame and the Lever Frame and work the Points as required, and also unlock the Siding gates. He will also be held responsible for leaving everything in order, locking the Siding gates and returning the Token to the Driver.

5. The Siding is on a gradient of 1 in 106 falling towards Hampstead Norris, and Guards must use every care to avoid vehicles running away, and before the engine is detached they must pin down a sufficient number of wagon brakes to firmly secure the Train.

6. The work at the Siding will be done by the Trains shewn in No. 3 Working Book.

7. Trains from Newbury will pick up and put off traffic in the Brick Kiln Siding, and Trains from Didcot will pick up and put off traffic in the Sand Pit Siding. Compton and Newbury must advise Hermitage when the Trains have wagons for the Siding.

FISHER'S LANE -LEVEL CROSSING.

The Gates at this Crossing may be closed across the Railway between Trains.

The Gatekeeper will be responsible for keeping a good look out and immediately the bell rings and the Disc shows that a Train is approaching from either direction, the Gates must be closed across the roadway and the Signals lowered for the Train to pass.

Before the Gates are closed across the Railway, the Gatekeeper must be sure that the Signals are standing at Danger.

WOODHAY STATION - GROUND FRAME.

The Points leading from the Main Line to the Down Sidings at the South end of Woodhay Station Yard are worked from the Ground Frame. They are Facing Points to Up Trains, and are worked from the Ground Frame; they are also bolted from the Station Signal Box by Lever 7.

The man working the Ground Frame must, when it is necessary to work these Points, see that the bolt is taken off in the Signal Box, and must then take the lock off the Facing Points in the Ground Frame. After using the Points, and when the work is finished, the Points must be set right for the Main Line, the bar-lock put on, as also the bolt in the Signal Box.

HIGHCLERE.

When vehicles are detached from Up Trains, the Points must whenever possible be set for the Siding during the time the vehicle is standing on the running Line.

WHITCHURCH STATION - GROUND FRAME.

The Up Loop Line Facing Points at the South End of Whitchurch Station Yard are worked and bar-locked from the Ground Frame, and when set for Up Trains are bolted with Lever No. 11 in Signal Box. The Points leading to the Down Siding from Main Line at South End of Yard are worked from the Ground Frame and are locked with Levers Nos. 9 and 12 in Signal Box.

The man working the Ground Frame must, when it is necessary to work these Points, see that the bolt is taken off in the Signal Box, and must then take the lock off the Facing Points in the Ground Frame. After using the Points, and when the work is finished, he must lock them, and see that the bolt is put on again from the Signal Box.

KING'S WORTHY STATION - GROUND FRAME.

The Locking Frame controlling the Up Siding Points is locked by a key on the Sutton Scotney and King's Worthy Electric Token.

The Officer in charge of the Station will be responsible for seeing the whole of the Shunting is properly carried out, and that the Token is handed to the Driver after the necessary work has been done, the Points properly set and the Ground Frame locked.

The Head Guard of Trains required to do work at the Up Siding must satisfy himself the work is complete, and the Token handed back to the Driver before giving the "Right Away" Signal.

SIDINGS AT WORTHY DOWN BETWEEN KING'S WORTHY AND SUTTON SCOTNEY.

The two facing points on the Single Line are worked from two Ground Frames situated on the Down Side of the Line at the North End and South End of the Sidings; the Ground Frames will be locked by a key on the King's Worthy-Sutton Scotney Electric Token.

WORKING ON 1 IN 106 GRADIENT.

The Single Line at the Siding is on a gradient of 1 in 106 falling towards and extending through King's Worthy Station, and whenever possible the whole of any Train having work to do at the Sidings must be shunted into the Sidings. When this is not possible, sufficient wagon brakes must be put down to prevent wagons running away. The scotches provided at the Siding must also be used, and before any division of the Train or vehicles takes place the buffers must be compressed.

The District Inspector must see that a good supply of scotches is always available at the Sidings.

CATCH POINT AT KING'S WORTHY.

A Catch Point controlled from the Signal Box is provided at the North End of the Up Loop Line at King's Worthy Station.

Whenever a Goods Train is doing work at the Sidings at Worthy Down, the Points at the North End of the Up Loop Line must be set for that Line in order to form a "trap" in the event of a runaway from the Sidings.

GUARD TO BE RESPONSIBLE FOR THE WORKING AT THE SIDINGS.

The Guard of any Train calling at the Sidings will be held responsible for the whole of the work performed at the Sidings, and for seeing that all wagons are left clear of the running lines.

The Guard or Porter must see that the Points are properly closed before leaving the Sidings.

WINCHESTER.

WINNALL SIDING GROUND FRAMES.

A Siding for the Winchester Water and Gas Company's traffic has been laid in on the Down Side of the Line, between King's Worthy and Winchester, about one mile from Winchester Station.

There are Up and Down connections from the Single Line to the Siding, the Points of which are worked from Ground Frames.

The Ground Frame working the Up connection is called the Winnall Siding Ground Frame North.

The Ground Frame working the Down connection is called the Winnall Siding Ground Frame South

The Ground Frames are locked with Annett's Key, which forms part of the King's Worthy and Winchester Electric Token.

A Ground Disc is fixed on the Throw-off Point at each end of the Siding.

Traffic to and from the Siding will usually be worked by Pilot trips as arranged by the Winchester Station Master. The Head Guard of any other Train requiring to stop at the Siding to do work will be held responsible for the whole of the work performed at the Siding, for closing of the Points, and for leaving the Siding in order in every respect.

The Pilot trips will be worked by the Winchester Porter Shunter.

When the Train is ready to start the Signalman at Winchester must send to King's Worthy a telephone message, explaining what is to be done. He must then send the proper "Is Line Clear ?" Signal and with-draw a Token, which must be given to the Driver, and the Driver must be verbally warned that on the return journey he is to regard the Line as clear to the Home Signal only. When the Train leaves, the "Train entering Section" Signal must be sent in the usual way, and until the Train has returned no shunting must be allowed outside the Home Signal.

On arrival at the Siding the Porter Shunter will take the Token from the Driver, and unlock the Ground Frame Box and the Ground Frame Levers; when he has finished the work he must set the Points in their normal position, lock them with Annett's Key, withdraw the key from the lever lock, close and lock the Box door, and then hand the Token to the Driver to proceed back to Winchester; the Driver on arrival at that Station must hand the Token to the Signalman on duty. When the Train has returned to Winchester complete, the Token must be replaced in the instrument, and after this has been done the Signalman there must advise the Signalman at King's Worthy by telephone that the Tram has returned, and then send the Canceling Signal.

Instructions for Working Goods Trains.
Before allowing a Goods Train or Light Engine to enter the Goods Yard, the Signalman must obtain the permission of the Yard Shunter on the telephone and ascertain whether the road in the Yard is clear for the Train to run into.
The Shunter must confer with the Signalman on the telephone when a Train or Engine is ready to leave the Yard, and ascertain whether the Train may be allowed to draw up to the Yard Home Signal.

EXCHANGING ENGINES OF UP TRAINS.
An Electric Bell is fixed on the Down Home Signal Post affording communication with the Signal Box,

CODE OF SIGNALS. To set Points for Down Line   1 ring.
To set Points for Up Line ..   ..   ..   3 rings.

The only person authorised to use these Bell Signals is the man in charge of the shunting.
The Engines of Up Trains must be changed at the North end of the Station, and the following instructions must be observed :—
On arrival of an Up Tram for the S.R. Company's Line, the Engine must be detached from the Train and sent over the Points in the Tunnel, and the Engine must always carry a lighted tail lamp showing red. A Shunter with a lighted hand lamp must, in all cases, accompany it, and he must see that it goes well out of the way, leaving plenty of room for the Great Western Engine to go over the Points to back on to the Train at the Up Platform.
As soon as the S.R. Company's Engine has gone quite clear ahead of the Points, the Shunter must give one ring on the bell for the Signalman to set the Points from the Down Line to the Tunnel.
The Signalman, as soon as he receives the ONE RING, must set his Points and lower the Shunt Signal for the Great Western Engine to go out over the Points.
As soon as the G.W. Engine is over the Points, the Shunter must ring three on the bell for the Signalman to set Points for Up Line ; the Signalman will then turn them to let the Engine back to the Train on the Up Line, and as soon as it gets back clear of the Down Line the Shunter must ring one on the bell, and the Signalman must set the Points for the Down Line for the S.R. Engine to come back on that Line, and as soon as he sees that the Engine is clear, he may set the road right for the Up Train to leave.
The Station Master, or person in charge, must not give right for the Train to start away until he sees the S.R. Engine has shunted clear on the Down Road and the Shunter is back on the Platform.
When there are vehicles attached to the Great Western

Engine the Shunter must, after seeing that the vehicles are over the Points, ring three on the bell for Signalman to set Points for Up Line, and when they are set right to come back on Up Line, he must give the Great Western Driver a green light to come back, and then walk on towards the standing Tram, and keep in sight of the Driver, so that he can give him a signal in proper time to stop; the Shunter must then return to the Tunnel, ring one on the bell for Signalman to set points for Down Line, and when the S.R. Engine comes out clear of the Up Line the Shunter must return and connect the vehicles to the Train.

INSTRUCTIONS FOR WORKING ENGINES BETWEEN STATION AND ENGINE SHED AND YARD.
Bell communication is provided between the Signal Box and Engine Shed at Winchester.
No Engine must be brought out of the shed lines without first communicating with the Signalman on the bell and receiving his acknowledgment.
Bell Codes to be used :—
1.   Loco. Shed to Signal Box Engine ready to come out   .. 3 rings.
2.   Signal Box to Loco. Shed if Engine may proceed 3 rings.
3.   If Signalman unable to give permission   .. .. 6 rings.

This signal is to be acknowledged by the Driver of the Engine by returning 6 rings, and when the line is clear the Driver must again ask permission by giving the 3 rings as prescribed above.

SHUNTING AT SOUTH END OF YARD.
A Klaxon Horn is fixed on Telegraph Pole near Ground Frame for use of Shunters.

CODE OF SIGNALS. Go Ahead	1
Set Back .	2
Stop ..	3
Ease Coupling .	4

WORKING GOODS SIDING.
A Goods Siding is situated at Winchester on the Up Side of the Winchester and Shawford Junction Extension Line, and the points are worked from a Ground Frame which is locked by the Electric Tablet.
The Shunting operations will be done at specified times under the supervision of the Winchester Station Foreman.

S.R. AND G.W. EXCHANGE.
The Exchange Point is at the Scissors Crossing.
The S.R. Engine takes the S.R. Trains to and from the Goods Yard and assists with the shunting.
The Great Western Traffic Staff at Winchester obtain and register all exchange numbers for the Railway Clearing House, alternate months with the S.R. Company, who take the numbers at Eastleigh and Bishopstoke Station.

On 4 April 1966 the final nail in the coffin that was the dream of an independent through route from the Midlands to the South was nailed home. It had taken less than a century, 84 years to be exact, for that dream to be born, come to fruition and finally wither away. Now almost half a century later may be the time to examine more closely whether that 1966 decision was indeed correct.

To do so we must first of all discard all notions of romanticism, steam trains and the like and instead ask the one fundamental question, 'Could (and should) the DNS have survived?"

In reality the answer is simple, based on the pure economics of the 1960s, a resounding 'no'. But when seen against a modern day background the answer is less than objective.

Consider first of all the railway itself. Conceived as a part of a grandiose plan for a shortening of the route between the Midlands and the South coast did a mere reduction of seven miles in route distance, compared with the journey via Reading and Basingstoke, really make any difference? Here we have to say probably not. The 1870s (when a line along a similar route was first proposed) was also not a good time for such a railway. The principal locations of business and commerce were already interconnected, what was left were the 'fill-in areas', the 'lower divisions' the places where cost and / or returns were unlikely to equal let alone provide for a return upon investment.

We should also not discount what might well be described as the 'snobbery' factor in all of this. The titled and landed gentry of the period were not adverse to a degree of one-upmanship with their cohorts. "Lord 'so and so' has a railway through his land and in consequence a station, why then should not I?" For this *do-not* infer any deliberate reference to any particular individual ever associated with the DNS, for it also did not have to be physical advantage, to be involved at senior level as a director might well also be enough. Shareholdings might well be purchased in numerous other established and reasonably performing railways, but the chance to be a 'big cog in a small wheel' should not be discounted. Directors also often had engines named after them or their seats…… . (It did not apply here, but there were also cases where a landowner wished the convenience of a railway through an area where there was no commercial need but which presence might tempt a railway company nearer a goal that was indeed attractive. An example would be Squire William Nicholson of Basing Park near Privett in Hampshire. Nicholson courted both the GWR and LBSCR to build a line across his land with the tempter that they might thus reach into territory previously denied to them. The GWR might thus have been within striking distance of Portsmouth, whilst the LBSCR could have spread further west.

Fearful of the consequences, the LSWR for is part then promoted its own line, not necessarily anywhere near the route of the aforementioned speculators, but confident in the knowledge that Parliament would never sanction a competing line in the same area. The result was the Meon Valley 'white-elephant'. Opened in 1903, the LSWR and its successors The SR and BR(S) had half a century to mull over their rash decision before it finally succumbed in 1955. Like the DNS, the question may well be ask how it ever managed to last so long. Closures were not just a product of the days of Dr Beeching.

To return to the nineteenth century, the DNS board were men who, despite their wealth and social standing, were naïve when it came to the practicalities of running a railway. Their route is proposed, surveyed, and indeed subsequently built, but why should anyone want to put traffic upon it? Why should the GWR and LSWR loose revenue themselves by consigning goods which might just as easily have remained on their own metals AND equally importantly, covered the distance between Southampton and Didcot faster by not swinging off at Winchester Junction.

So we now look at the route itself. Didcot to Micheldever as originally proposed, and Didcot to Southampton as was the second plan. The Micheldever scheme was probably the stronger of the two, but only if there had been a flyover at Newbury as indeed originally proposed. This could well have substantially reduced the time for traffic to reach Southampton and this saving in time, which the GWR (and in the reverse direction the LSWR) could well have sold to their customers, might well have achieved financial benefit.

Unfortunately once junctions at Newbury became involved and likewise the Shawford Junction debacle, there was every opportunity for delay, as indeed was the case at Shawford Junction. Here we may quote T B Sands, "The presence of a light engine on the South Western was quiet sufficient to delay a DNS train by upwards of one hour." (No doubt with the sanction of the LSWR itself.) It may well be the GWR adopted similar tactics at Newbury.

Later the GWR were perhaps equally subtle but just as hard in their approach. The rebuilding of Newbury station in the early years of the 20th Century and at the almost total cost to the DNS was an example of the stranglehold the large company had on its neighbour. The DNS had no option to comply, without access to Newbury they could not run a service, the criticism that DNS trains were causing congestion was farcical, it was the GWR who wished to rebuild Newbury for their own ends – as part of their new main-line to the west - the DNS were the unfortunate scapegoats left to pick up the bill.

We may also refer as to why the GWR were never prepared to fund the DNS in its expansion plans. Here the answer is simple, to have done so would have created the

Rural Hampshire, an exactly the type of countryside served by the DNS throughout its length from Didcot to Winchester. The location is Litchfield, where road and railway run parallel and where either side of the station were sharp bends as the road crossed under the railway. The railway exhibits but a single track, the road a single carriageway. On the railway there are no trains, instead an empty station and the shell of a signal box. No wagons appear in the yard. The road has a lorry and one car following, both slowly heading south. Northbound there are one or two sporadic cars. Could the politicians really see a several hundred-fold expansion for road traffic into the future or was this simply an excuse to close the line? 'Accident black-spots', the Litchfield bridges was another reason mentioned and the need to make meaningful road improvements: but a road is not dangerous - it is the people that use it who make it so and road improvement is an easier option than driver education. Both road and rail COULD have existed in harmony, even a rebuilt A34, but that was not in the grand plan of the 1960s. At that time almost everything rail was old fashioned and road was the way forward. (Fifty years later the impracticalities of re-opening the former Great Central main line has fuelled the debate over 'HS2'.)

A - A34 and location of the middle of the Litchfield bridges under the railway.
B - Litchfield station, goods shed and signal box shell.

potential for hostility in whatever area the GWR and LSWR came into contact: Plymouth, Exeter, Yeovil, Salisbury and Basingstoke are the obvious examples, there would have been no winners, but the passengers would have been the losers.

At this point the railway historian may well enquire how it was the GWR managed to maintain supposed cordial relations with the independent Lambourn Valley Railway at Newbury against the antipathy that appeared to be exerted towards the DNS? The answer is simple, the LVR like the DNS had been promoted mainly by the wealthy of the district. The involvement of such worthy's sufficient to attract investment from lesser mortals and who thus followed the example of the great and the good. For their part the Lambourn was no threat to the GWR, indeed a little extra traffic might well be generated from it, the DNS on the other hand was intent on taking traffic away.

But unlike the LVR, the DNS never rose to the position of owning and operating its own locomotives and stock. There is no record that such was ever discussed by the Board but it is interesting to sit back and ponder for a moment on what might have been. As such, in the eyes of the enthusiast alone the DNS could never match the charisma of its north-south neighbours, the Somerset & Dorset, and Midland & South Western Junction.

But aesthetically the DNS could certainly hold its own. The quaint and picturesque charm of its station cottages unique to the line, the barren yet rolling landscape of the Berkshire Downs and then further south in Hampshire the crossing of the chalk ridge south of Burghclere could hardly fail to impress the passenger. Scenery though was hardly sufficient on its own to generate traffic and indeed there is no record excursions were ever run to capitalise on the views of Beacon Hill south of Newbury and also the highest point in Hampshire. (By comparison the LVR did venture into the tourist realm very early on with combined rail / road excursions to Lambourn and on to the land of King Alfred near Wantage.)

This desire by the GWR not to create unnecessary antipathy will also explain why Paddington were unwilling to contribute towards a Burghclere – Aldermaston route, and so create a potential competitor to the South Western for traffic from Winchester, and possibly Southampton to the Capital. The reader should not see this in any way as implying the GWR were in any way subservient to the LSWR, nor indeed the other way around. Instead by this period in history there appears to have existed a tacit recognition that specific areas were the province of one or the other and that competing lines would not be proposed in what was identified as 'belonging to the other'. The various other minor expansions off the DNS were non-starters from the outset, likewise the thoughts of reaching Portsmouth or Bournemouth were examples of direct incursion into territory that was already spoken for. Had of course the DNS operated its own line rather than relying on the GWR/LSWR matters might well have been different, but then the company would have faced the wrath of the LSWR in particular and a costly war of attrition would only have seen one winner. Undoubtedly the

best means of breaking the strangle hold of the GWR would have been expansion to Quainton Road and a link with the GCR. Once this opportunity passed the fate of the DNS was forever sealed.

We should not forget that whilst this "gentleman's agreement" existed between the GWR and LSWR any opportunity indicating a lack of control by the other would still be grasped. It was for this reason that the GWR never allowed the DNS to reach a state of total financial destitution. Had that occurred and bankruptcy resulted the LSWR might well have seized their chance. In this way the MSWJ had become a thorn in the side of the GWR: an independent concern having good relations with the LSWR but passing right through the very heart of the GWR at Swindon.

So, having set the political scene, let us turn to practicalities and the way the DNS handled its traffic. A one word answer may suffice here – slowly. A single line north of Newbury (until 1943) and similarly for the majority of its length south of Newbury, also a single line, did little to permit of fast running. Any advantage over distance was lost by the technology of the day necessitating slowings to 15 mph for the exchange of the single line staff / token. Neither were the gradients in its favour either, at 1 in 106, this was twice as steep as anything likely to be encountered via Basingstoke and Reading. A single line with passing loops, even after having been 'modernised' in WW2 (we may indeed use the word), was still a restricted railway.

Most important of all was that the DNS served no-one of consequence along its route. North or south of Newbury there was no major centres of industry or population. Instead were just rural communities and although grateful no doubt for the opportunity to reach markets previously denied or difficult, it would been primarily the respective landowners who would benefit by seeing the produce from their own tenant farmers similarly turned into greater profit than might be achieved locally.

The time the DNS came into its own was during national turmoil. World Wars fought overseas require supply lines, and to this end the DNS and also the MSWJ, made a vital contribution. Clearly the mobility needed in WW1 was insufficient to require any obvious costly upgrade – was anything ever considered at this stage? But certainly during WW2 the DNS was a main artery, an essential component in a machine whose sole aim was to assist in the destruction of Axis tyranny.

To this end it was again a case of 'needs must', but with a return to peace, what then, what use for a railway now heavily over-equipped, more costly to maintain and operate, and yet whose local traffic was diminishing almost on a daily basis. Small wonder so many questioned how long it might and indeed did survive.

Retrenchment and economy in the 1950s was an obvious and logical step, but did it go far enough? In reality singling north of Didcot in post-war days might have reduced operating costs but the eventual outcome would not have been any different.

We only need to look at the image of the railway near Litchfield, where rail and A34 run in parallel, to see the road was not in the early 1960s at that time overburdened. Road transport had not yet begun to dominate. True the advancement of the motor car (and lorry) was accelerating, but we may even question whether the mind-set of the railway were awake to the threat, personally I think not. To be fair whilst towns were already being choked by traffic this was in part due to their own legacy of design and piecemeal built over countless previous generations. Roads had been designed for the traffic of the period, horses and carts, we cannot blame our forefathers for failing to recognise how things might change.

The loss of passenger services on the DNS was a foregone conclusion, for as mentioned more strange is indeed how it hung on for so long. The situation was certainly not helped by the railway being operated since 1950 by two masters, Paddington and Waterloo. Through promotion was missing, future planning discussed by memo rather than face to face.

With through freight now the only justification for the railway it becomes an obvious question for the operators as to whether this traffic could be accommodated elsewhere. The Winchester to Basingstoke and Basingstoke – Reading – Didcot route was always busy but in the near future were plans for multiple-aspect signalling and with it the associated promise of greater line capacity and associated savings. The timetable planners will have looked at the situation as existed in 1964 and come up with the obvious solution, the DNS was surplus to requirements, it had to go, what traffic as existed at the time could be accommodated into spare paths on other routes. Remember also this was a time when investment in railways was limited. The railways desperately needed to modernise, to re-equip themselves and reinvent for a new era – the 1960s and beyond. Quaint branch lines and 'just in case' routes had no place in the modern railway. To be given money to invest it was essential to show savings elsewhere. Senior railway managers were being judged on their performance by how many savings they could make – and this included closing lines. Paddington in particular had seemed to take delight in wielding its own axe long before a certain Doctor brought his own.

But away from Paddington and Waterloo there was one group that was indeed planning for the future and it must be said being both reactive and in many ways also pro-active to the future. These were the councils at both County and as was then Rural level. For their part they were responding to pressure from the motor car to smooth out and reduce delays, railways had often got in the way, with a closed railway there might well be the opportunity to upgrade a road or

The abandoned connection between the Southern Railway at Winchester Junction and the DNS at Worthy Down. More than a decade after the last train ran and with no more need for coach / wagon storage, nature is slowly starting to reclaim what was once hers. Might this, the final piece of 'new' railway to have been added to the mileage of the DNS also have been its saviour?

The Kellaway collection

indeed plan for major investment in later years.

No doubt aided and abetted by the Ministry of Transport, it is interesting to note how Hampshire County Council singularly failed to raise any serious objection to the withdrawal of passenger trains south of Newbury. Also how quick they were to replace the bridge at Tothill. No doubt somewhere there was grand plan even then for a major upgrade to the A34, the DNS was when it was open, in the way. There must have been contrivance between railway and road to remove one for the benefit of the other.

In 2014 we may well look back and state, "but what if" and "was there an alternative?" Certainly there were different options, different planned routes, a Newbury by-pass east of the town an obvious example, but with no railway it made perfectly logical sense to (part) use what already existed.

The trouble is that now in 2014 the DNS *would* be useful, but in 1964 that need was not there nor could it have been foreseen. Could any of us alive who are able to remember 1964 have accurately predicted life half a century later?

The question is often asked, "Why did they not simply leave it alone, why rip it up at all?" Why not do as they do in France (and I am told North America): when a railway is considered redundant it must be left moribund for 10 years or so in case the situation changes?

The facts are simple. For a start the south of England is not generously given to land, re-use for a different purpose was logical. Even if it had been intact in 1974/1984/1994/2004 etc., with the volume of traffic then running on an upgraded A34, how do the railways tempt both passengers and goods away from the road and on to the train? The jury is still out as to whether today's resurgence in rail travel is in consequence of improved services or road congestion meaning taking the car is no longer a considered option. (Some with memories of times not all that long past will recall how the A34 was upgraded in stages, firstly as a new single carriageway and then as a dual carriageway throughout its length. What may come as surprise though is that when plans for the M4 were first exhibited they showed a bridge over the railway line north of Hermitage.... .)

And as the decades have passed so freight traffic from and to Southampton has increased – we may conveniently leave the passenger out of this for the present. In 1991 there were something like 24 container trains daily in each direction to and from the docks at Southampton. Twenty years later that figure was close to doubling. The railway between Southampton and Basingstoke and on to Reading is now very close to total capacity even with modern signalling and reversible working. Add to this the almost 50% increase in the number of passenger trains and the need for an alternative, albeit longer route between Southampton and Basingstoke via the Laverstoke loop at Salisbury becomes understandable. All that traffic could have gone by the DNS, but not an historic DNS, a modern railway, possibly a 90% freight only line, single but with passing loops and remote signalling. The 10% could be a peak hour only commuter service from Winchester to Newbury and also possible re-routing of certain cross-country services. Ironically it is faster today to travel from Southampton to Didcot via Basingstoke and Reading than it was direct via Newbury years ago. Southampton to Newbury today is a different matter.

So is this an advocacy for 'turning right' at Shawford Junction – certainly not. But instead why not turn left at Winchester Junction through Worthy Down, Sutton Scotney, Whitchurch and on to the north? Where the A34 takes the trackbed simply run parallel to it, the same north of Newbury, follow the existing main road, modern traction can cope with steeper gradients than were considered appropriate in the past   A rebuilt DNS on the same route,

The northernmost of the three Litchfield road bridges on the original A34, one of the reasons the HCC wished the railway be closed in order to improve the roadway.

no, a new north-south link yes. (A connection at or near Enborne to provide a commuter service to Newbury would be required.) So would this be attractive to passengers and goods? The answer is to make it so although whether this would be though pricing in favour of or even against the road is one for the politicians. For people to use public transport it *must* be attractive and accessible. It must also be competitively priced with each passenger able to feel they have at their disposal an area of 'personal space', this compared with so many of today's trains where the term 'cattle class' is not inappropriate.

Will it happen? Not in my lifetime and probably not anyone else's either. The alternative is to increase capacity on the existing route, or for freight most of which is destined for the Midlands, by the upgrade of other existing lines, that from Salisbury and Westbury is the obvious example. All are likely to be more attractive to both the political and financial purse. Widening the main line to four tracks from Basingstoke all the way to Southampton would be the perfect solution but the cost would be considerable, not just in financial terms either (too many 'safe seats' at risk..... .).

A case to rebuild the MSWJ could also be made, but again not a task that could be easily undertaken. Are we able today to look forward and accurately forecast the needs for our transport infrastructure 50 years hence, a simple 'No'. It really was the same situation that was faced by those in power 50 years ago. What has happened in the 1960s and indeed in subsequent years, is that the physical traces of this particular railway were slowly dismantled. But what cannot be done is to destroy history. Hence within these pages at least there still is a railway from Didcot through Newbury to Winchester.

Acknowledgements

The idea for this volume has been in my mind for over 30 years. I had always felt the latter years of the railway needed full coverage, not least as this is the period those alive today will more likely remember. That is no way to decry the previously published histories of earlier times, for that story needs to be told in order to arrive at a cohesive record of more recent times.

Thus the idea was conceived, but as time passed so new information arrived, and which in turn led to more digging and in turn more records began to surface which had simply not been available previously.

Now in no way do I criticise the works of the past. I have been privileged to have been involved with a few and like others in other areas, I have felt it was my duty to put on record what I have been able to assimilate in half a century of collecting material on 'my favourite bit of railway'.

Of course that now led to the dilemma, do I include the extra material on the early years or ignore it to concentrate solely on the present? In the end the answer was simple, let us do it properly, hence the 300+ pages and illustrations contained herein. Neither do I ask anyone else to risk their money, my publishing business, my risk. I do

not seek a profit - but to cover costs would be nice!

So firstly I must thank my friend of 40+ years David Littlefair. David's family commitments, career and subsequent calling to the Ministry precluded him from compiling his own book(s) on the DNS. I have no doubt they would have been superb. Even so he remains as enthusiastic today as he was when we first met. Much of what has been included within these pages is from his own archives, I sincerely hope I have done it justice.

I must also record my grateful thanks to ALL who have assisted. I know I will have omitted some names, my fault entirely. So in alphabetical order only: Neville Bridger, Paul Chanceller at Colour Rail, John Coles, Amyas Crump, Graham Hawkins, Les Hiller and the Hiller family, Bill Hiscock, the Kellaway family, Ron Plumb, Ian Shawyer, Roger Simmonds (whose own love of the DNS is at least as equal as my own), Ted Talmage, Tim Timpson, Chris Turner, Dave Waldren, Chris Webb and Rodney Youngman. Others are mentioned in the text or in the photographic credits. Ladies and Gentlemen, it has been a pleasure and a privilege to have worked with you all.

Others books associated with the DNS line (in print and

Coloured memories of black and white times.

Further Reading

otherwise) which may be interest are:

The Didcot, Newbury & Southampton Railway - published by Wild Swan

Didcot, Newbury & Southampton Railway Supplement - published by Wild Swan

The Didcot, Newbury & Southampton Railway - published by Oakwood Press

The Didcot, Newbury & Southampton Railway - published by Ian Allan

The Railways of Winchester - Published by Platform 5

Burghclere Signalman - KRB Publications

Winchester (Great Western) - KRB Publications

Sutton Scotney - Life at a Country Station - Kestrel Railway Books.

Didcot Engineman published by Wild Swan.

Firing Days / Signalling Days - Published Oxford Publishing Co.

Signalman's Reflections - Published Silver Link

Gone With Regret - published Jersey Artists

Great Western Echo, Spring 1991 - Published Great Western Society

Readers may also interested to know that a full size replica of part of the station building from Winchester together with a superb 4mm scale layout of the station is on display at the Milestones Museum at Basingstoke.

The model makes involved are: Jeremy English, Paul Garnsworthy, Mike Jolly, Paul Markasie and Peter Squibb.

The last train has indeed now gone!

The Kellaway collection

GREAT WESTERN RAILWAY.

OPENING OF NEW STATION

AT

KING'S WORTHY

On MONDAY, FEB. 1st, 1909,

A New Station will be Opened at King's Worthy, situated on the Newbury and Winchester Line, between Sutton Scotney and Winchester, for Passenger and Parcels Traffic.

THE FOLLOWING TRAINS WILL CALL AT KING'S WORTHY—

DOWN TRAINS.		UP TRAINS.	
From Newbury.	**King's Worthy at**	**From Winchester.**	**King's Worthy at**
7 45 a.m.	8 47 a.m.	7 32 a.m.	7 36 a.m.
8 59 ,,	9 59 ,,	11 4 ,,	11 8 ,,
11 42 ,,	12 42 p.m.	12 21 p.m.	12 25 p.m.
1 55 p.m.	2 46 ,,	2 54 ,,	2 58 ,,
4 15 ,,	5 16 ,,	4 55 ,,	4 59 ,,
7 0 ,,	7 51 ,,	8 53 ,, } Saturdays only }	8 57 ,,
8 47 ,,	9 37 ,,		
10 5 ,, } Saturdays only }	11 2 ,,		

The Goods Station at King's Worthy will be Opened Shortly.

For Full Particulars of Fares, Parcels Rates, etc., apply to Mr. W. A. HART, Divisional Superintendent, Paddington Station, or to Mr. J. MORRIS, Superintendent of the Line, Paddington Station, W.

Paddington, January, 1909.   **JAMES C. INGLIS**, General Manager.

(6,000).   WYMAN & SONS, Ltd., Printers, Fetter Lane, London, and Reading.—6103a.